KIDS
in
DANGER

KIDS IN DANGER

◆

ROSS CAMPBELL

with Carole Sanderson Streeter

A DIVISION OF SCRIPTURE PRESS PUBLICATIONS INC.
USA CANADA ENGLAND

Unless otherwise indicated, all Scripture references are from the *Holy Bible, New International Version*®. Copyright © 1973, 1978, 1984 by International Bible Society. Used by permission of Zondervan Publishing House. All rights reserved; other references are from the *New English Bible* (NEB), © the Delegates of the Oxford University Press and the Syndics of the Cambridge University Press, 1961, 1970; the *Authorized (King James) Version* (KJV); *The New Testament in the Language of the People* (WMS) by Charles B. Williams. © 1966 by Edith S. Williams. Used by permission of Moody Press, Moody Bible Institute of Chicago; *The Holy Bible in the Language of Today* (BECK), © 1976 by Mrs. William F. Beck. Published by Holman Bible Publishers. Used by permission; *The Message* (TM). Copyright © 1993. Used by permission of NavPress Publishing House.

Editor: Barbara Williams

Design: Paul Higdon

ISBN: 1-56476-471-0

1 2 3 4 5 6 7 8 9 10 Printing/Year 99 98 97 96 95

CONTENTS

Introduction

Dear Parents,

I know you are deeply concerned about the future of your children. So am I. And I know that you are wondering why it has become so difficult for families in our society to feel optimistic about the future. This book deals with one answer to those perplexing questions.

At the root of most problems in our society we find mishandled anger. Why is this? Because the appropriate ways of handling anger must be learned. They do not come naturally. And the mature management of anger must be taught in the home. Tragically, this is seldom done today.

Anger is a little understood emotion—why we feel it, how we express it, and how we can change the way we deal with frustration. Unless we parents know what anger is and how to handle it in appropriate ways, we will not be able to teach our children what to do when they feel angry. Yes, *when,* for we all get angry every day.

In this book, we will be looking at some important definitions of anger, as well as at our own expressions of it. We will also talk about the various stages of our children's lives and the expressions of anger appropriate to each.

The challenge for all of us is to come to the point where we do not sin in our anger. That's a tall order, but one in which God will help us.

Ross Campbell, M.D.
Signal Mountain, Tennessee
1995

ONE

Your Child and Anger

It may surprise you that the primary lifetime threat to your child is his or her own anger. If it is not handled well, it will damage or destroy your child. The mishandling of anger is related to every present and potential problem your child may have — from poor grades to damaged relationships to possible suicide. It is imperative that you do all you can to safeguard your child now and in the future.

Violence is eating away at families and at society. We parents are the only ones who are empowered to teach our children how to handle their anger. And yet, in most homes this is not happening, and the majority of children are being taught how to handle anger in an inappropriate and immature manner. The reason for this is that most parents have been taught wrong ways of dealing with their own anger, and they pass along misguided ideas to their children.

Because children are basically powerless, they seek ways to control their world. As they grow older, they want to feel and appear autonomous. This desire for areas of control and the levels of independence is not bad in itself, but it needs to be exercised in appropriate ways for each age-level and station in life.

You want your children to learn respect for others and also for authority. This means that they must know how to handle conflict—not just over a toy now, but over contracts and relationships and sensitive issues later on. Because poor control of anger is a national epidemic, the only hope for your children is proper parenting. The way anger is managed in your home is the example they will probably follow. They will not see many demonstrations of good anger management in society or on television.

You also want your children to become people of integrity. This word is defined as "soundness, incorruptibility, completeness, honesty, unity." It means that a person is whole, all of one piece, acting with the same character qualities in one situation as in another.

The goal of this book is to help you raise your children to be people of integrity. The following definition of integrity is one that you should teach to your children as soon as they are old enough to understand it, and then teach it again and again as they grow older and the definition has larger meanings for their lives.

> A Person of Integrity Will Always . . .
> - *tell the truth*
> - *keep his or her promises*
> - *take responsibility for personal behavior.*

Poor management of anger and anti-authority attitudes are the enemies of integrity. The person who is rebelling against authority is tempted to lie, to break promises, and then to excuse bad behavior.

As this book was in process, the scandals of the young royals in England seemed to be at a peak. In a book written about Prince Charles, he was quoted as saying that he had taken his wedding vows with less than full intention to keep them. Following the release of the book, a member of the Anglican clergy appeared on television to question whether Charles should ever become King of England, since he had taken sacred vows dishonestly and possibly would do so again.

While your children will not take royal vows, the promises and commitments they make are just as important, and the way they conduct their lives will have impact not only on their peers, but also on succeeding generations.

WHY ARE PEOPLE SO ANGRY?

Why are children so angry? Why do they become angry adults? The most prevalent cause of anger in children is the feeling in their hearts that they are not loved enough. Children instinctively know that they need love, and they also know that it is their parents' responsibility to give them that feeling of love.

While most of them could not explain it very clearly, children know they cannot live happily or develop normally without the security of unconditional love. Yet, few of them feel genuinely loved and cared for by their parents.

Since children instinctively understand that parents are responsible to provide this gift of love, their natural response when it is withheld is anger. Of course, there are other causes of anger or rage in a child, but these are usually specific events such as disappointments, conflicts, abuse, fears, losses, and so on.

In the majority of homes, even in the best of homes,

the children do not *feel* loved. Many parents find this hard to understand, since they truly do love their children. How do we explain these opposing perceptions?

The reason is that few parents know how to transmit their heartfelt love to the heart of the child. Most parents are *verbally oriented* and they believe that telling a child, "I love you," communicates their love. While the verbal expression of love is important, it is far from sufficient.

Children are *behaviorally oriented,* which means that they must be loved on their terms. We will be talking about this more in future chapters, and you can find the subject dealt with at greater length in my books, *How to Really Love Your Child* and *How to Really Love Your Teenager.*

For now, let me say that when the child does not feel loved, he cannot grow to be his best, and as a result, he will feel continuing anger at his parents. This anger interferes with the child's basic development and later with adult behavior.

Perhaps an example will help you to see the difference between verbal and behavioral orientation. When my younger son, Dale, was five years old and I was out of town, I could call home and say to my wife, "I just wanted to tell you that I love you." That would make her the happiest gal in Tennessee.

But if I got Dale on the phone and said, "I just wanted to tell you that I love you," he would likely respond, "Sure, Daddy, but why did you call?"

The verbal expression of love was meaningful to Pat, but it didn't have very deep significance for Dale. Being a child, he was behaviorally oriented. To convey the message of love from my heart to his meant doing something behavioral when I returned home.

ANGER AND POWERLESSNESS

In his book *Make Anger Your Ally,* Neil Clark Warren offers some definitions and causes of anger that we need to look at and then apply to children:

> The capacity to become angry is an impressive gift which comes as part of our biological inheritance.
>
> Anger is a physical state of readiness. When we are angry, we are prepared to act. . . .
>
> The whole purpose of anger is to give us the wherewithal for managing our environment — particularly those parts which cause us to feel hurt, frustrated, or fearful. If we do that poorly, we will regularly experience a sense of inadequacy and helplessness.[1]

As you read this, did you apply it to yourself? If so, you will want to read it again, thinking about your children, and also about those children whose experiences cause them to regularly feel hurt, frustrated, and fearful.

Think too about children in good homes where certain events and emotions are well beyond their capacity to understand or interpret correctly.

Dr. Warren makes another observation that is worth our consideration in this regard — that the most important factor in handling anger is to get our self-concept into shape. "When it comes to taking charge of your life, literally nothing is as important as a solidly constructed self-system." The main reason for this is that "when your self-concept is well put together and you have a plentiful supply of self-esteem, you have ample energy to run your life."[2] Also, fewer things will make you feel angry.

Like all of us, children become angry when they perceive a situation or person as frustrating, threatening, or hurtful.

But, unlike adults, children do not have the power to make radical changes in their lives. They have a weak power base, little autonomy, and only occasional independence.

And, unlike most adults, children do not have a self-system in place. They live with parents or other adults who are there to help them in the formation of a self-system and self-concept. Yes, many children do possess a remarkably well-formed self-concept for their age. What they lack is the knowledge and experience to interpret the world in relation to themselves.

The formation of children is within the care of their parents. To deliberately threaten, hurt, or frustrate these children is something like putting on your hiking boots and then walking through the beautiful flower garden your neighbor has spent months cultivating, destroying the blossoms as you go. But deliberately causing harm to children is far more serious than this, because we are dealing with human souls, with God-given potential, with eternal consequences.

You may want to think about the dynamics in your home, and possible ways you might be causing or allowing hurt or frustration to your children, even unintentionally.

Put yourself in the place of each child and ask how you might react to specific situations and attitudes.

EXPRESSIONS OF ANGER

When we are faced with a threatening situation, why do we express anger? We do so to "manage those internal and external sources of hurt, frustration, and threat" and keep "inner pain to an absolute minimum."[3]

Children and adults don't express anger all that differently. Yes, adults use a larger vocabulary and have a wider variety of resources to draw from, including physical strength, but it is uncanny to watch an angry adult through squinted eyes and to imagine that you are seeing an eight-year-old. There often isn't that much difference.

When adults express anger, they do it from a power base. When children express anger, they do it from a dependent state, as well as from their immature understandings. They are clever at using all the leverage they can manage, but it still isn't enough to effect the changes they want.

When you feel angry, you usually—but not always—know what is wrong and what you wish would change. When a child is angry, he or she sometimes knows what is the matter, but probably not as often as you do. For this reason, you need to ask, "What is bothering this child? What does he want? Is it possible? Is it reasonable? Did someone else cause the distress or frustration?"

What the child wants often is neither reasonable nor possible. He may just wish he were older or bigger, or had more power or space or money. He may be responding to growth cycles or hormones. He may have been treated unfairly by people none of you can control. He may wish he had some of the advantages his friends enjoy.

If, however, you know what caused the hurt or frustration, and if—God forbid—you are the one who did it, make tracks to correct the situation. Growing up is hard enough as it is, without people we love making it more difficult.

———————

SIX ANGRY CHILDREN

Teaching a child how to handle anger is the most difficult part of parenting. Because it is sometimes hard to recognize demonstrations of anger in our children, I want us to look at six children, ranging in age from four to sixteen, to see how they are showing their anger.

♦ Four-year-old Janie was potty-trained when she was eighteen months old. For the past six months, however, she has been soiling her pants. Her parents have talked to their doctor and have tried everything they can think of. There is no physical problem, and yet Janie continues this behavior.

♦ Eight-year-old John continually picks on his younger brother and sister, often hurting them. His parents don't know how to stop this behavior, and they worry about John.

♦ Nine-year-old Joey gave his parents no unusual problems until the middle of the school year, when his teacher sent home a note saying that Joey had not been turning in his homework. His grades were going down, and this became a matter of concern for both teacher and parents.

♦ Thirteen-year-old Debbie has always been vivacious and outgoing. Now she is withdrawing from her parents and is very difficult to talk to. She acts sullen and spends much time in her room alone. Her parents don't know if this is part of early adolescence or if they should be concerned.

♦ Fifteen-year-old Jessica was always a delight to her parents and teachers, as well as to her friends. You can imagine how shocked her parents were when they found marijuana paraphernalia in her room. When they took her to the doctor, they also discovered that she was pregnant.

♦ Sixteen-year-old Ken did well in school until last year when his grades began to fall. Now there is danger of his failing the semester. Ken is a bright boy with no learning disabilities, and is capable of doing fine work in school. He still has a good attitude and wants to do well, so that he can be accepted at a competitive university.

What is happening in the lives of all these children? As I counseled with them and their parents, I discovered that each one was acting out anger, either consciously or unconsciously. None of these children was being trained to handle anger properly, because the parents didn't understand how important this is.

I am not blaming the parents as I say this, because most parents believe that anger is always bad and should be "disciplined out of the child." As a result, the parents respond in confusing ways when a child becomes angry.

That parents are confused about anger is not surprising, since many professionals are also. Anger is very difficult to understand. After studying it for twenty-five years, I still am not sure about some aspects of it.

However, I do know how crucial it is for parents to train their children how to properly express their anger. One caution—you can never do this with a how-to manual.

SIX CHILDREN IN NEED

It is time to return to our six children and try to determine what each one was saying through the expressions of anger.

♦ Janie was indeed expressing anger as she soiled her pants. Because this is generally not recognized as a sign of anger, it is usually treated by physical means alone, and the anger which is causing the behavior is left to grow and cause even worse problems for the child later on. This is a classic example of passive-aggressive behavior, a subconscious expression of anger. We will talk about this in chapter 6.

♦ John's belligerence and violence toward his brother and sister was creating chaos for the entire family. This type of situation is difficult to correct, because the behaviors become entrenched in all the family members and get worse. Until John's aggression was identified as an outworking of anger, no progress could be made.

Aggression is one of the common immature expressions of anger. Passive aggression was also adding to this situation, making it even worse.

♦ Joey's "forgetting" to turn in his work is a classic sign of anger which often begins around age nine or ten. It is another example of subconsciously motivated passive aggression.

♦ Debbie's radical change in behavior was an indication of teenage depression. But it was the anger component of the depression that was so destructive and so out of proportion to the other factors in Debbie's case. If nothing had been done for her, she would have faced a bleak future.

Teenage depression is a special and often dangerous source of anger that needs to be understood by parents. As we will see later, passive-aggressive behavior is to some extent normal in the early adolescent child. But in Debbie's case, it had been maximized to dangerous proportion by her depression.

If you would like to receive a pamphlet about teenage depression, you can write to me in care of Victor Books.

♦ Jessica's situation is all too common today. Her drug use and her pregnancy were signs of desperation. We can wonder why her deep needs came out in such heartbreaking ways.

Jessica's poor means of handling her anger began years ago and her parents suspected that something was wrong. And yet, her many strengths and winning ways convinced them that she was all right. Her parents did the best they could do, but their best was complicated by the fact that they had never learned to manage their own anger well. And, of course, they didn't know that one of their most critical responsibilities as parents was to train their children to manage anger.

♦ Ken's falling grades were due to teenage depression and the resulting passive-aggressive behavior which usually accompanies depression. As you read on, you will better understand how the various immature ways of handling anger cause so many childhood and adolescent problems. It is particularly crucial that you understand passive-aggressive behavior, since it can intensify existing difficulties.

LOOKING AHEAD

As you think toward your children's future, you may have never considered what their anger will do. It is always easier to worry about what someone else's anger might do.

As I said at the beginning of this chapter, the primary lifetime threat to your child is his or her own anger. It can harm your child in every way, and is related to all other problems he or she may have.

With the devastating situations in our world, it is essential that we as parents do all we can to safeguard the future of our dear children.

Since few parents manage their own anger well, most children are not being taught how to handle their anger. As a result, our society is falling victim to this growing destruction.

If you want your children to be able to express anger in mature ways, you will need to make sure you know how to do this also. In chapter 8, we will be discussing the self-knowledge that parents need in order to be able to train their children.

I am a fortunate father. When my children were young, I did not know how to train them in handling anger. But I learned these vital lessons early enough so that my wife and I could train them when they were small. Our goal was to have them reach a significant level of maturity by the time they were seventeen, so that we and they could feel confident of their passage into the adult world.

Carey, David, and Dale are now adults who are managing their anger well, sometimes better than I do. As I observe them, one of my greatest joys in life is to see them functioning as morally and ethically strong people.

I am also profoundly thankful that my children are free of the typical emotional scars and pain that so many children carry into adult life. I refer especially to that sense of deprivation, that nagging sense that something vital is missing from their lives. It is this which prevents many adults from being and doing all that they would like to be and do. This feeling of deprivation comes not only from a lack of unconditional love, but also from the mishandling of anger.

Two of the greatest gifts you can give your children are to love them unconditionally and to teach them to manage their anger in ever more mature ways.

T W O

Society and Anger

I am astounded at the change in perception of children in our country over the past several decades. Until recently, children were accepted as innocent, endearing, and lovable by almost everyone. But over time, this has changed.

Today, growing numbers of people consider children to be annoyances, hindrances, and often undesirable. Even worse, some are depicting children as creatures with evil intent.

So much anger today is expressed against children, either in outright violence or in passive ways, that it is easy to wonder how many people in America really like children. Consider what is happening:

♦ Children's needs are generally given low priority. Even hardened criminals receive better services than many of our children. It is not that public officials are unaware of the needs of children. They even push state lotteries to finance education. But after millions of dollars have been collected, the funds for schools often don't increase.

♦ Many schools have become places of chaos instead of orderly refuges where children can learn. The Centers for Disease Control in Atlanta have listed school violence as a public-health concern in the United States.

♦ The media has moved in deliberate war against teenagers and children, sending degenerate "entertainment" into our homes.

♦ Advertisers exploit the weaknesses and desires of the young.

♦ Crime is rampant, and often its victims are children. The weapon of choice may be hands, guns, knives, or cars. Some people are so twisted that they mourn the death of murderers more than they mourn the victims.

♦ We have become a nation of victims, with millions of people blaming others for their own antisocial behavior.

Children grow up so fast. Today, they hardly have time to catch their breath before they are launched into an aggressive and permissive adult world.

No longer are they seen as the meaning of our lives, our hope for the future, our heart-warmers, the ones who keep us going. As society concentrates more and more on adult desires, children are the losers.

We parents who care deeply about our children have been pushed into a cruel place in society. We love our children, and want what is best for them. Yet, beyond our own efforts, we often feel helpless in a world that is so alien to our Judeo-Christian values. It is easy to be angry at the powers that be, at the named and unnamed forces in society that make this world an unfriendly and difficult place for families.

As a recent article in *Reader's Digest* said, "The bar-

barians are not at the gates. They are inside. The question of the hour—and of the next century—is whether all this can be turned around."[1]

If anyone is to make a difference in society for children, it will have to be parents—those of us who care, who band together to say, "Enough is enough!"

WHERE DO CHILDREN FIND LOVE?

Children receive love and personal identity from three sources. It is in these places that they find out who they are and how they are to think about life.

♦ Home and family. This includes the extended family, those who also love our children and make room for them in their homes and hearts.

♦ Community. This reaches to school, neighborhoods, work, clubs, sports, and social pursuits.

♦ Church. This is where they learn of God's love for them and discover their identity as part of the people of God. In church children should also feel a part of the supportive fellowship that is to characterize the body of Christ.

The sad fact today is that many children are growing up with only two, or one, or even none of these sources of love and identity functioning for them.

The adults in these children's lives may have never experienced adequate love when they were young, or perhaps they are too busy with their own schedules, and the children are left to fend for themselves. Some of them fend with every material benefit, but they still can't manufacture unconditional love and a satisfying sense of identity.

REBELLION AGAINST AUTHORITY

Because so many people are starved for love, they are angry and they show their anger in rebellion. Where does this anti-authority attitude come from?

Anti-authority attitudes are formed in childhood. They are an expression of subconscious anger that comes from children not being taught to express their anger in appropriate ways and, ultimately, from not feeling sufficiently loved. This subconscious anger has contributed to the decline of authority in our public life.

By *authority* I mean the legal and moral forces that enable us to live in an orderly society, with a reasonable chance for security and safety. For many people today, this chance does not exist, and fear is epidemic among Americans, fear for themselves and for their children.

A primary cause for this fear is the rebellion of others against valid authority. Where does such rebellion come from?

At the risk of sounding simplistic, I want to suggest a simple answer.

♦ Rebellion against authority comes from anger.

♦ Anger comes from not feeling adequately loved.

♦ A lack of love in the lives of children comes from adults who don't know how to show love — or don't care to.

Many years ago, Robert Nisbet wrote *The Decline of Authority,* a book that stimulated much discussion. At that time the problem seemed more academic than actual. But more than he ever predicted has come to being.

Dr. Benjamin Spock, famed baby doctor, describes himself as "in despair" over the condition of our society today. In his book *A Better World for Our Children*, he says that he is deeply saddened by the "brutal state of our neighborhoods where our children now dodge bullets instead of playing dodge ball," and where children must deal with divorce and violence in their daily lives. Dr. Spock believes that the deterioration in America has been caused by a fundamental loss of values.[2]

But this loss of values is a demonstration of the anti-authority attitude so prevalent in society today. When a child does not learn to handle anger appropriately, this misguided anger will manifest itself in childhood and later in adult life against parents, laws, and all types of values, including the spiritual.

We just need to pick up a newspaper or watch the news to be convinced of the anti-authority attitudes so rampant in the world. Or, look at MTV, if you can stand it, or the many ads that are on the edge of rebellion.

Morality in this country has reached an all-time low in the last twenty-five years. In this short span, we have heard educators tell teens that their bodies are their own, and that they can do with them what they want, including any kind of sexual activity or abortion.

The language and actions common in "family entertainment" used to be prohibited on stage and screen.

And crime? Well, just look at the cases that were in the news during the months this book was in preparation.

♦ The O.J. Simpson murder trial

- ◆ The Menendez brothers' murder trial

- ◆ Chicago children who killed children

- ◆ The Smith toddlers drowned by their mother

These are the sensational cases. But every day the local news is filled with the same kinds of rebellions by people who never learned how to handle their anger.

Rebellion against authority also affects the church as people want a more individualized expression of their "faith" that may or may not express the historic doctrines of the Christian church. This is evident from the numbers of people who say they believe in God and in Jesus, but who do not have a vital relationship with Jesus Christ as their Lord and Savior. It is also evident in church fights that end up in hostility or in church splits.

TAKING RESPONSIBILITY

Integrity is in short supply in society, and nowhere is this more evident than on the political scene which has become a picture of unkept pledges and disregard of the public. Basic trustworthiness, where a person's word "is as good as gold" seems to be a thing of the past among public persons.

But it isn't only the politicians who are at fault. When did you last hear someone take full responsibility for his or her actions? Taking responsibility means facing the fact that we may be wrong, in opinion or behavior. It means constantly evaluating our behavior and being willing to correct it when we need to. If we fail to do this, we end up blaming others.

I just read of a classic case of blame. A dentist who had molested some of his female patients lost his license. His response was to sue his insurance company for disability pay to the tune of a million dollars. How did he justify this? He claimed that his behavior resulted from "mental illness."

We need a return to the quality of integrity expressed by General Eisenhower during World War II. Before the invasion, he prepared a press release, in case the invasion failed. It said, in part, "If any blame or fault attaches to the attempt, it is mine alone."

SIGNS OF HOPE

Not all public demonstrations of anger are violent or inappropriate. Just think of MADD, Mothers Against Drunk Driving, which was started by mothers who lost children to drunk drivers. Of course, they were angry, but they chose to channel their anger into a crusade against public toleration of those who drive while intoxicated.

A spinoff of MADD is SADD, Students Against Drunk Driving, an organization that meets in many schools, to educate and also harness young energies against this plague that affects so many teenagers.

Most of us remember Martin Luther King's peaceful marches against discrimination. The fact that they were non-violent made them all the more powerful.

In 1982, Deborah Larbalestrier, an older woman living in Los Angeles became a household name on the West Coast because of her courageous use of her anger. Living in a crime-ridden section of the city, she felt helpless to stop what was happening all around her. But then, one day she saw two boys trying to steal her neighbor's car. They knew she was watching and the whole scene outraged her. As the story was reported in the *Los Angeles Times*:

> I went out there with a stick and I told them, "How dare you insult me that way, robbing this car right in my face as if I didn't exist?"
>
> The teenagers ran off, but Larbalestrier wanted to make sure they didn't return. So she called a meeting on her block and told them, "We've become prisoners in our own homes. . . . We have to take our neighborhood back."
>
> Then Larbalestrier went to the Los Angeles Police Department's Wilshire Division to organize a Neighborhood Watch club for her street.[3]

At the time the article was written, the neighborhood had been crime-free for eighteen months.

CHILDREN AND HOPE FOR SOCIETY

Every society reflects what its children know. Yesterday's children are today's adults, and the children in your home will soon be grown. There is hope for our society if enough people learn how to use their anger appropriately and constructively. Anger does not have to lead to violence. It does not need to get out of control. Anger is a gift we can learn to use in beneficial ways.

There is hope for society if parents will become more intentional about teaching their children how to manage anger. For many parents, this will first mean learning to understand and manage their own anger in better ways.

It will also include teaching children to respect authority, even when they don't agree with what is happening.

Children need to learn from example and from history that there are more acceptable ways to disagree than violent behavior.

If you feel that your children are doing well in their expressions of anger, you can't avoid the fact that many others are not. At least one third of adolescents are subjected to abusive relationships. Children are committing unprecedented cruelty and violence. Teenagers are 7 percent of the population and commit 17 percent of violent crimes.

Above all, you do not want your children to become part of those statistics, or to become victims of others who have not learned to control their anger. You want them to grow into adults of unquestioned integrity.

If your family is doing well, you may want to reach out to children and families who are in need of help. For there is hope only as we work together. The problem is too big for any one of us; but all of us together *can* make a difference.

THREE

Your Home and Anger

Wouldn't it be wonderful if all the anger in society could be left outside the doors of our homes? If what happened inside our homes was in contrast to what all the members of the family faced every day at work, school, and in the community?

As wonderful as that would be, it won't happen, because we are carriers. Rather like carriers of disease, we carry anger and frustration with us. We bring stress and tension and tiredness home with us, and then we each play off the tensions and angers of others in the house.

If we are sensitive enough to realize what is happening and to change course, we can go a long way toward altering the script. But if we don't do this, chaos can result. And children are the victims — in two ways. First, they have to live with the unmanaged anger of adults. And second, they don't learn how to deal with their own anger.

You know of the Centers for Disease Control in Atlanta. Maybe we need Centers for Anger Control, and not just in one place. Every home could be such a center, where anger is diagnosed and then managed to the benefit of all. If this is what you want for your home, you can make it happen.

THE ATMOSPHERE OF YOUR HOME

One of the most powerful influences on a child's self-esteem and self-concept is the atmosphere of the home. When I enter a home, I can quickly tell whether a child will thrive there. Each home has its own atmosphere, and some qualities of this are fairly neutral, like colors and styles, while other qualities tend to be more positive or negative.

The atmosphere in one home may be warm, relaxed, calm, friendly, accepting, and upbeat. People feel comfortable in such a home, and a child living there can grow to be her best. She can relax in the support and encouragement that the parents provide, and can use her energies to develop in every part of her life.

However, few children are blessed with such a setting. Instead, they live in homes that are tense, judgmental, pessimistic, and rejecting. When children live in this type of environment, they have to use most of their energy trying to cope with the lack of love and support. Because it is more difficult for them to develop normally, they probably will feel angry at their parents. Also, they will likely not learn to handle their own anger in a mature way.

As parents, you need to remember that you control the atmosphere in which your children grow. They are powerless and have to depend on you to provide what they need.

I know that you want to feel good about the kind of job you are doing as parents. You are making a major investment of love and care and money and time in your family and you want this investment to turn out well, not just for you but for your children. You care deeply about them and want them to have happy and successful lives.

When children are small, it is so easy to feel hopeful

about them. They are innocent and manageable and dependent. But as they grow older, many parents feel discouraged and disappointed about what is happening in their families. One of the key causes for this is unmanaged anger.

Without an understanding of childhood anger and how they can deal with it, parents are likely to feel like failures, in spite of all the things they know they are doing right. Many children have an anti-parent attitude because they don't feel loved, and they can express this attitude in horrifying ways. Consider the stories of Ann and Todd.

ANN

A smartly dressed couple entered my office. I saw in my appointment book that they were Jim and Mary Perkins. The notation beneath their names said that their fifteen-year-old daughter, Ann, was pregnant.

As they sat down, I realized that Mary looked familiar. "We've met somewhere, haven't we?" I asked.

She managed a tight smile. "I've shown you a table several times at the Sailmaker Restaurant."

"You're the hostess at lunchtime. I was there last Tuesday."

I turned to Jim, and asked about his work. "I'm an accountant," he replied.

"That figures," I punned, trying to lighten the air.

We spent a few minutes more on small talk and discovered that we had mutual friends at their church.

With a glance at my appointment book, I turned to Mary and said, "You came to talk about Ann. Tell me about her."

Tears welled up in Mary's eyes. "Dr. Campbell, she's only fifteen, just a year out of middle school. The youngest of our four. And she's pregnant! What are we going to do?"

The words were gushing out as she kept dabbing her eyes. "We did everything we knew to be good parents to Ann. We've both worked for years to give her and the others the good things in life. We took them all to Sunday School and church. We gave Ann piano lessons and sent her to music camp for several years. She is so talented and beautiful. How are we ever going to handle this?" And Mary's voice trailed off in sobs.

Jim twisted in his chair and then began. "I just don't know where we went wrong. Why did she get herself into this mess? Why has she become so defiant? She's against everything Mary and I try to do for her."

As I talked with Mary and Jim, I realized that they truly loved Ann, but too often communicated that love by giving her things and advantages. They honestly felt that this would make up for not spending time with her.

When I met with Ann, my suspicions were confirmed. She did not feel that her parents loved her or that she was important to them.

Defiantly she said, "I don't know why I got pregnant. I just did. I could have prevented it — I know how. Maybe I wanted to be somebody too, like my mother. If I became a mother, then I would be important. *Someone* would love *me*."

For several weeks, I met with the Perkins family. At first, Ann was reserved and expressed few feelings, but I could see that she was angry and frustrated. After several sessions, she began to open up.

"Remember the night of the mother-daughter banquet, Mom? You couldn't be there because you had to go with Daddy to that accountants' seminar. I was the only one there without a mother!"

"But Ann," Mary interrupted, "we talked about that and I bought you a lovely dress for the banquet. I thought you didn't mind that I went with Daddy."

"Well, I did mind! You guys never seem to be around when I need you. My friends' parents always drive us to games and stuff; you never offer to drive. I'm always bumming rides with someone else."

"Now wait a minute, Ann," her father jumped in. "You're talking like we never do anything for you. I happen to know that you are quite an accomplished pianist. Who took you to all those lessons? And who paid for them?"

"Big deal, Daddy! Anyway, how would you know whether I can play the piano? The last time you attended one of my recitals was when I was ten!"

During outbursts like these, Jim would often leave the room. But over the next weeks, he and Mary began to understand Ann's feelings. They realized that the things they had given her could not begin to replace the personal attention she needed from them. They had left Ann with an empty emotional tank.

As we continued to talk, Jim and Mary worked hard to gain insights into Ann's problems and to find ways to share in her life. As Ann heard her parents express their love and concern for her, and as she experienced it daily at home, she began to communicate with them in a more positive way.

It was a slow and painful process, but Ann and her parents began to really get acquainted with each other. A key to their success was their desire to have a loving family. As Ann felt her parents' love, her anger began to subside. Their love, and the feelings of self-worth that Ann experienced, went a long way toward sustaining her in the difficult months that followed.

TODD

Mark Johnson sat across from me, impatiently tapping his well-manicured fingers on the arm of the chair. His appearance suggested affluence. His wife, Brenda, whose attire was equally perfect, was also impatient.

The Johnsons were active in a large church, and all indications gave them the mark of being a successful couple in more ways than financial. Their daughter, Amy, was six and their son, Todd, was eleven. I wasn't sure why they were in my office.

Brenda began, "Dr. Campbell, we need to talk with you about Todd. Six months ago, he seemed to change from a normal boy into a quiet stranger who is angry all the time. He constantly finds excuses to stay away from us. Goodness knows, we have little enough time to spend with each other. Mark's law practice is growing, and my children's shop keeps me there many evenings."

"Yes, Dr. Campbell," Mark agreed, "and you'd think the kids would appreciate all that we can do for them because we work such long hours. Amy hasn't given us any trouble, but Todd is a different story. A few nights ago, some of his older friends brought him home drunk. What in the world would make an eleven-year-old kid who has everything do such a thing?"

"We're shocked beyond words," added Brenda. "And to make matters worse, Todd has disrupted the entire household with this silly stunt. Mark had to reschedule his clients, and I am taking time away from the store for this appointment. Don't get me wrong—we want to help Todd, but we don't understand why this has happened. As Mark said, we've given him everything, and this is the way he thanks us!"

As Mark paced my office floor, he asked, "What in the world is wrong with our boy? Or, could it be us? I can settle legal matters for the most important people in this city, but I can't make my own son happy."

What indeed would make an eleven-year-old use alcohol? For as we talked further, it came out that Todd had been drinking regularly but had been able to conceal it from his parents until now.

Todd was not alone in this behavior. Studies show that an increasing number of young teens and preteens are using alcohol and drugs. Many of them are from Christian families.

In Todd's case, as in so many others, the answer was in the deterioration of family life. His parents were too busy to make special time for him. As a result, he and Amy were receiving little nurture from the very people who were supposed to be giving it. This lack of time and nurture resulted in Todd having a very empty emotional tank. He did not feel loved. This made him angry and also put him in a position of vulnerability to peer pressure, to gain attention and acceptance.

MAKING TIME FOR FAMILY LIFE

Mark and Brenda Johnson are prime examples of parents who look perfect, but who put something else in place of family. In this instance, it was career. As a result, they had two lovely but unhappy children. Yes, we discovered that six-year-old Amy was also angry at her parents.

Both the Johnsons and the Perkins thought their children should just know that they were loved. But children don't "just know." They can't. All they know is how they feel, and both Ann and Todd felt unloved. Their feelings were based on the amount of time and emotional energy their parents invested in them.

Many parents today live with far too much stress and they just don't have the resiliency to deal calmly with normal childhood behaviors. I realize that it takes a lot out of parents to keep family and career and other obligations in good shape, especially when both of them are working. Many parents don't have the energy or perseverance or desire to do all that is required. Therefore, when something slips, it is almost always the quality of family life.

I want to say a word here about single-parent families, since some people believe that parents alone just can't do an adequate job of parenting. I have seen countless single parents give loving nurture and discipline to their children.

The key to a successful family is not whether it has two parents, but whether the parental focus is in the right place. A single parent can raise a child well and guide him through the "terrible teens" into responsible Christian adulthood, just as two parents can.

QUALITY TIME OR TIME?

We often hear about *quality time*. What really matters is TIME. Spending time with your family — getting to know your children, telling them that you love them, and letting them know they are important to you — these are the important things.

Commitment to the Christian family is based on the notion that we love one another, that we care about the emotional, physical, psychological, and spiritual needs of all family members.

If we love each other, we will want to be together for more than covering the necessities. We will want to enjoy the others in the family. It doesn't really matter what we do, just so long as we are having a loving and happy time together. As parents, we want our children to know that they are more important than the many influences that tend to separate parents and children.

The loving times shared by a family add to the strength of the individuals and also of the family as a unit. We make memories together as we spend leisure time in play or rest or travel or reading or whatever we like to do.

Think of your own happy memories from childhood. Are they more about presents and privileges or about gifts of love or time? What gives you warmer memories — the gifts you received or the feelings of closeness with your parents?

As I counseled with both the Johnsons and Perkins, they discovered that they were able to find time for family. The very fact that they could make time for the counseling sessions told them that. By carving out periods of time to enjoy one another, they were going a long way toward preventing further problems in the future.

It takes time to correct established patterns and form new ones, but these families are determined to make life better in the future.

FAMILY COMMUNICATION

In your communication with your children, you want to be personal to them. Family life should not look and sound like communication in any organization you are a part of. As parents we should be reaching in love for the personhood of our children.

Aaron, who took part in a survey of 1,055 teenagers said, "Even when my parents are here, it's like they're not, because they don't have any time." Although Aaron eats dinner with his parents, he said, "We never talk about anything. Maybe school. A lot of times they're paranoid about my friends. They always get on my case when I come home."[1]

One type of family communication which has received a lot of attention in recent years, particularly in certain religious circles, is the chain-of-command approach. If you have been in a military or business or family organization where this kind of communication is strictly followed, you know how depersonalizing it can be. For some reason, many religious leaders have advocated a chain-of-command approach to family life. What this actually means is that the father is the only really responsible person in the home. Anyone down the chain is responsible to do only what he or she is told, and this includes the wife and mother!

I realize that not everyone carries it to such an extreme, but I also know the devastating results in many families who have adopted this philosophy.

I think the approach began to strengthen in the 1960s, when people were alarmed at increased permissiveness and at the rebellious demonstrations against the Vietnam War. Certain "experts" were trained in behavior modification which is based on experimentation with rats. Failing to understand normal adolescent behavior and counterculture dynamics, these "experts" blamed parental permissiveness for most of the nation's problems. A subtle but fundamental change in parenting and parent-child relationships began to take place.

The change was from a cooperative and mutually supportive bond to a hierarchical chain-of-command based on discipline. In the first type, both the child and the parents assumed responsibility for the child's behavior. In the second, the parents assumed more responsibility for the child's behavior and the child less.

We are now trying to cope with a generation of children who refuse to take responsibility for their behavior and also refuse to learn how to do so.

Such miscommunication results in distrust, resentment, and lack of close-knit affection. This becomes a vicious cycle, for the more problems our young people experience, the more emphasis is placed on "discipline." The stricter the "discipline" without love and support, the angrier are the youth. As they have more problems with anger, the more anti-authority they become, and this translates into being antiparent, antimorality, anti-other people, antichurch, antilaw, and so on. We now have more than one generation of such people.

Some educators have suggested an answer to the inner needs of these children — to try to make them "feel good" through self-esteem techniques. Therefore, a child may receive special commendation for behaving in a pleasant and cooperative manner, something that should be expected, not rewarded.

In 1993, we were transfixed by a horrifying display of youthful rebellion, as the Menendez brothers were on trial for murdering their parents. Writing in *National Review*, Stuart Goldman suggests that the Menendez murders and the trial are an example of the self-esteem philosophy gone awry:

> In the cosmology of the self-help movement all human failure stems from our lack of ability to love ourselves; the worst thing a person can have is a bad case of low self-esteem. . . . In a world where morality is dictated by therapists rather than God, where evil is discounted as a myth, where feeling good is the end-all and be-all, they can be comforted by the thought that murdering an "abusive" parent is not only permissible — it is healthy.[2]

In later chapters we will talk more about specific communication with angry children. For now, though, I want to stress the importance of personal and loving interaction with your children. It is in this way that you will be able to teach them respect for other people and for themselves, and also help them to increasingly take responsibility for their behavior.

Such responsibility includes relationships with siblings in your family. If you treat each child with respect and firm love, and give proper guidance, you should be able to minimize conflict between brothers and sisters. In the Bible, God's children are told to love one another. Surely, the children in a family should do as much.

THE IMPORTANCE OF EXTENDED FAMILY

Because of time and career pressures, most parents feel the need of some relief and help with their children. I would like to suggest that grandparents and other extended family members consider taking a more active role in the lives of their young relatives.

Many grandparents today opt out of active participation with their grandchildren. While they may think that they are gaining independence and freedom, in the long run, they are losing years of loving interaction that can never be replaced.

Many nuclear families live with constant stress because they are far from relatives and have little or no support from close friends. I believe they need to ask themselves if this is really how they want to live. Their constant tension, and at times fear, is communicating all the wrong messages to the children.

I realize that solutions to this are not easy. Family members the same age as the parents probably have their own share of stresses. And some grandparents just don't want to be involved very much with their grandchildren. They seem to be saying, "I raised my family. Now you raise yours."

However, there may be some answers. If family members do want to be closer, someone may decide to make a geographical move to foster more involvement in extended family.

If this is impossible, the next best thing is to find some friends who can feel like family, and with whom you can build a small community of trust and mutual helpfulness. These may be people in your neighborhood or church, people close enough to you that they can know you and your children well and offer the kinds of support that family members would give, if they were just down the road, as aunts and uncles and grandparents used to be in another generation.

Making such arrangements for extended family, either actual relatives or close friends, will take some planning and may involve major changes. But after you decide what you most want for your family, and who can best contribute the gifts of time and love to your children, the sacrifices may be well worth the cost.

Trying to stretch yourselves beyond your resources will inevitably take a toll on you and your family. One result will probably be increased impatience and anger with your children.

Because children have no defense against parental anger, their hurt and frustration goes down deep inside and festers. To have one or more adults nearby who can love and care for your child will give you relief, and will also soothe your child's feelings, especially if you succumb to the pressures and express anger that you later regret.

AN ATMOSPHERE OF LOVE

Early in this chapter, we talked about the atmosphere of the home and the impact it has on the growing child. This familiar poem by Doris Law Nolte expresses so well the influence that the home environment has on a child.

Children Learn What They Live

If a child lives with criticism,
he learns to condemn.
If a child lives with hostility
he learns to fight.
If a child lives with ridicule,
he learns to be shy.
If a child lives with shame,
he learns to feel guilty.

If a child lives with tolerance,
he learns to be patient.
If a child lives with encouragement,
he learns confidence.
If a child lives with praise,
he learns to appreciate.
If a child lives with fairness,
he learns justice.
If a child lives with security,
he learns to have faith.
If a child lives with approval,
he learns to like himself.
If a child lives with acceptance and friendship,
he learns to find love in the world.

FOUR

Your Child's Need for Unconditional Love

Although they don't say it in so many words, the question our children are asking us all the time is, "Do you love me?" If we only *say*, "We love you," they are not going to receive the answer they need. The reason for this is that growing children are more *behaviorally oriented*, while adults are more *verbally oriented*. This means that we respond to words much more than children do. They need demonstrations of our love to really believe that we care.

Even in their unacceptable behaviors, including acting out their anger, children are asking, "Do you love me? Do you love me enough not to give up on me?" Because they are immature, children express anger immaturely, with ventilation and aggression. Therefore, this is what we must work with as we guide them into more mature expressions of anger. This means accepting their ways of expressing anger, not as desirable but as normal, if we hope to lead them away from these childish ways.

When our children are very young, we don't have a problem accepting other behaviors appropriate to each age. But many parents do have difficulty dealing with anger. And then in their feelings of frustration, they often fail to give unconditional love and acceptance to their children at the very time they most need it. In fact, the parents may anger them even more, because they treat them harshly.

When my children were younger, I had to frequently remind myself of several facts that should be obvious:

♦ Because they are children, they will act like children.

♦ Much childish behavior is unpleasant.

♦ If I do my part as a parent and love them despite their childish behavior, they will be able to give up their childish ways.

♦ If I love them only when they please me and convey my love only at these times (conditional love), they will not feel genuinely loved. This will make them feel insecure, and will prevent them from moving on to more self-control. Therefore, their behavior and development is my responsibility as much as theirs.

♦ If I love them unconditionally, they will feel good about themselves and be comfortable with themselves. They will then learn to control their anxiety and also their behavior.

♦ If I love them only when they meet my requirements or expectations, they will feel incompetent. They will believe it is useless to do their best, because it will never be enough. They will be plagued by insecurity, anxiety, and low self-esteem. Therefore, their total growth is as much my responsibility as theirs.[1]

CHILDREN NEED UNCONDITIONAL LOVE

Children are like mirrors. They reflect love much more than they initiate it. If love is given to them, they return it. If none is given, they have little or none to offer.

As your children are reaching for wholeness and for the completeness of character and experience you want them to have, they find their way by seeing reflections. They come to know themselves by looking in the mirror of your love. Some mirrors give a clear and full reflection, while others are cracked or marred.

When parental love is unconditional and constant, children can look into the mirror of that love and see themselves as they are today and also as they want to be in the future.

When parental love is conditional and inconstant, children become confused and are unable to move confidently toward the completeness they seek. Their self-concept suffers as they question who they are from day to day.

It was the Apostle Paul who wrote that we see imperfectly, as in a mirror that offers us dim reflections. But one day we will have full sight and knowledge and will see God face to face. Now we know in part, but then we will fully understand ourselves, even as we have been fully understood.

> One of the characteristics of the child is that he knows and understands things partially. Part of growing up into mature love is to reach a fuller, face-to-face understanding. Our pictures and our feelings about ourselves come largely from the pictures and the feelings we see reflected in our family members — what we watch in their expressions, hear from the tone in their voices, and see from their actions. These reflections tell us not only who we are, but also what we are going to become. As the reflections gradually become part of us, we take on the shape of the person we see in the family looking glass.[2]

In *Healing for Damaged Emotions*, David Seamands writes of the mirrors in amusement parks that twist our features into caricatures of ourselves. In a similar way, conditional love in the family twists a child's developing self-concept into something it was never intended to be.

> Someone has said, "Your childhood is the time of life when God desires to build the rooms of the temple in which He wants to live when you are an adult." What a beautiful thought! Parents have the great privilege, *and* heavy responsibility, of giving the basic design to the temple — the child's self-image.
>
> If he is convinced he is of low worth, a child will place little value on what he says or does. . . . If this kind of low self-esteem has been programmed into a person, it is difficult, and in some cases almost impossible, for that person to feel beloved of God, accepted by Him, and of worth to Him in His kingdom and service.[3]

Although they could not explain it clearly, children know their need of full acceptance and unconditional love. Without these, they cannot grow and develop properly.

When children cannot become what they know deep inside they should be, when they cannot be themselves, when life is a series of trick mirrors, they become angry.

As adults, we know how long it has taken some of us to feel that we can at last really be ourselves. And we know the anger we have felt at those who should have accepted and loved us without placing conditions on that love. Yet, many parents who have known the pain of not being able to develop with confidence are now withholding unconditional love from their children. In so doing, they are asking for their children's anger.

When your relationship with your children is based on conditional love, you will find it impossible to really understand your children or to give them proper guidance. You will also find parenting to be a very confusing enterprise.

But when your relationship with them is built on unconditional love, you can be confident in your parenting. With your love as a guiding light, you will be able to meet your children's needs.

PARENTS WHO PROVOKE THEIR CHILDREN

I'm sure you know the commandment God gave to Moses about honoring one's parents. Two thousand years later, the Apostle Paul emphasized this command as he wrote to the Christians at Ephesus:

> Children, obey your parents in the Lord, for this is right. "Honor your father and mother"—which is the first commandment with a promise—"that it may go well with you and that you may enjoy long life on the earth" (Eph. 6:1-2).

But do you know what the next verse says? While we don't hear it as often, it is crucially important. I'd like you to read it in several versions of the Bible.

> Fathers, again, must not goad your children to resentment, but give them the instruction, and the correction, which belong to a Christian upbringing (NEB).

> Fathers, provoke not your children to wrath: but bring them up in the nurture and admonition of the Lord (KJV).

> You parents, too, must stop exasperating your children, but continue to bring them up with the sort of education and counsel the Lord approves (WMS).

> And you fathers, don't make your children angry, but raise them by letting the Lord train and correct them (BECK).

Fathers, don't exasperate your children by coming down hard on them. Take them by the hand and lead them in the way of the Master (TM).

It sounds as if Paul had visited in lots of homes in Ephesus, and maybe even when the parents weren't expecting him to show up. He knew what was happening in all too many families — parents were failing in patience and in training of their children. They were forgetting their long-range goal of raising mature young Christians who could in a few years be responsible men and women.

Paul was offering a balance. The responsibility for raising good children was not on the children but on the parents. Yes, the children were to obey, but the parents were responsible for their training as well as for the atmosphere of the home.

If Paul visited your home, would he say, "Don't provoke? Don't goad? Don't exasperate? Don't make them angry? Don't come down too hard on them?" A lot of provoking goes on in homes that profess to be Christian.

♦ A three-year-old girl picked a flower and brought it to her mother. Because the flower was from the neighbor's yard, the mother slapped the child and ignored the gift of love.

♦ In a snack shop, a father yelled at his young son when he saw some ice cream falling from the boy's cone onto his shirt.

♦ A mother asked her daughter, "Why can't you play the piano better, like your sister does?"

♦ A father hollered from a window to his son, "Get your friends out of our yard. They are ruining the grass!"

♦ A mother and her three-year-old son were in a mall. When the child started to wander away, the mother grabbed him and jerked him roughly, yelling, "You stay right here where I put you!"

♦ A father was kind to his son one day, but screamed at him the next, "Get your bike out of the driveway!" His mixed messages confused the boy.

If Paul were to visit your home, he wouldn't suggest ignoring bad behavior or being too lenient. But he would urge you to be constant in training your children, not only religiously but in every part of their lives.

FOCUSED TRAINING

If you have read my first book, *How to Really Love Your Child,* you already know of my emphasis on *focus* in loving and training your children. This takes the form of eye contact, physical contact, and focused attention in both listening and responding to your children. Focused love is a way of impressing deeply how much you love them.

I want us to look at each of these, especially as they apply to dealing with an angry child. It is not that hard to focus on a child who is pleasant and agreeable. But when a child is angry and rebellious, focusing with love is far more difficult. And yet, that is the challenge we all must confront again and again, as a child is growing up.

EYE CONTACT

Eye contact is one of the most powerful ways of transmitting love to a child. With eye contact, you pleasantly look into the eyes of the child while the child is looking at you. Although this sounds simple, it is actually a complex and critical behavior which is seldom done. While most parents believe they are using loving eye contact, research shows that this is not the case.

Eye contact with a child can be as simple as looking into the eyes of an adorable baby who is smiling and cooing for you. But eye contact can also be amazingly difficult. When your thirteen-year-old is angry with you and is verbalizing that anger in a loud voice at a time when you are stressed out and feel you can't handle one more thing, you probably don't even want to think about giving him loving eye contact. And yet, it is critical for you to come through at this time, for your own sake as well as for your son's. It is in situations like this that you teach him how to manage his anger in a mature fashion.

Because this type of teaching is one of the toughest parts of parenting, you need to employ self-talk during a child's angry outbursts. This technique will help you maintain self-control when you are angry. You need to remind yourself that it is normal for your child to express his anger *verbally* to you, even if it is unpleasant, for only in this way will you be able to train him to control his anger. Self-talk will keep you focused on giving your son pleasant eye contact during this difficult but important time. Regardless of his actions, it is essential to maintain eye contact with him. If he glares at you, it will be tempting to glance away. However, to avoid eye contact will further increase his anger.

With a teenager, you may run into what I call the "grunt stage." This is a period of emotional withdrawal when all you can get out of the teenager verbally is a grunt. At such noncommunicative times, the child will usually avoid eye contact. Of course, this will hamper and even hinder your ability to continue giving loving eye contact.

It is crucial that you continue to fill your child's emotional tank. You dare not dump your anger on your child. Because you want to maintain communication with him over the long haul, you need to stay in a position of training your child to manage his anger.

PHYSICAL CONTACT

When your child refuses eye contact, you do have something else at your disposal—physical contact. And yet, research shows that few children receive sufficient physical contact to keep their emotional tanks full. When everyone is feeling pleasant, giving physical contact can be rewarding to both parent and child. In times of unpleasantness, it may save the day.

With teenagers who are in the grunt stage, physical contact may be the only means of genuinely relating to them. When they are angry, they are so engrossed in their own thoughts that they are less intent on what is happening around them. At such times, gentle, light, quick touches to the back of the shoulder or arm may keep the communication open. However, if they are still angry with you, eye contact alone may have to be enough, until they calm down.

FOCUSED ATTENTION

Focused attention means spending time with a child in such a way that she feels she is the most important person in the world to you. This is most often done alone with the child. Focused attention requires sacrifice from you — the sacrifice of time. When you give this, you will also be using eye contact and physical contact.

Giving focused attention can be a real challenge, particularly if your teenager has been moody and difficult to be around. You may want to take her somewhere to improve your communication with her. You may also want to make sure her emotional tank is full. Focused attention will help you discover why she is so moody or angry.

If your child is generally unresponsive, be patient. Her silence does not necessarily mean that she is hostile or disrespectful. Teenagers often need time to pull themselves together during and after periods of anger. When you are with your child, do not pressure her to talk or respond to you. Eventually she will open up and may even allow meaningful conversation and also a resolution of her anger.

An example of focused attention during a tense situation may explain better what I mean. When our son David was thirteen, one of his best friends, Joe, invited David to spend the night. Joe's parents had recently divorced and Joe and his mother were living close enough to us to be very valued neighbors.

However, on this particular occasion, we found out that Joe's mother, Katy, was having a boyfriend over for the night. As much as we liked Katy and Joe, we just couldn't allow David to stay there overnight.

David was furious with us and refused to calm down. He assumed that we were condemning Katy, and he went to bed that night in a furor. The next day he was still angry with us, but I decided to ask if he would like to go with me to his favorite restaurant for breakfast. As we waited for our food,

David finally told me how hurt he was by not being allowed to go to Joe's house. And then he asked me what I thought about Katy's behavior.

Now I could offer an opinion that would be heard, since he had asked for it. I told him that his mother and I loved Katy and Joe as much as he did, and that we were still sad about the divorce and Joe's father moving away. I also told him that what Katy did was her own business. However, as his father, I did not feel that I would be doing my job if I permitted him to spend the night under those circumstances. Eventually David came to understand our position.

YOUR CHILD'S EMOTIONAL TANK

I have mentioned keeping your child's emotional tank full. In the context of unconditional love, the purpose of eye contact, physical contact, and focused attention is to fill your child's emotional tank. Just as a car needs gas and oil to run properly, and a furnace needs fuel, and your body needs healthful foods to function as it should, so your child needs your unconditional love, demonstrated in many ways, to become what he or she wants to be, can be, should be.

If your child has to wonder from day to day, or even hour to hour, if your love is constant or conditional, and if there is any point in trying to please you, that child will be discouraged from trying and will feel unsure of his or her own worth.

David Seamands writes of a young man named Bob who grew up in a home where "Measure Up" was the motto. He learned early in life that his measuring up was the basis for his being loved and accepted by his parents. And so he tried. Bob's parents did as so many of us do at times:

So subtly we withhold our full affection and love until we see that our children are striving at their highest level. Instead of affirming them at the level where they are, we think we are helping them to "do a little bit better." So whatever they do—eating their food or using good manners or making grades or living the Christian life on their own age level—we give our children the promise of our approval and love if only they will do a little bit better. Love becomes something just around the corner, just a hope away. The present level of achievement is subtly downgraded and belittled. We think we are saying, "We love you and want you to do better." Too often it comes across to our children as, "We will love you when you measure up," or "We will love you and be pleased with you, if only you'll do a little bit better."[4]

"The degree to which you are loved unconditionally will *determine* your level of self-esteem."[5] The same is true for your child.

Unconditional love has two fundamental qualities: (1) It is given without regard for the objective value of the person or thing which is loved; (2) It is given without any strings or conditions attached. . . . That's the kind of love which can turn your life around and raise your self-esteem level to new heights. When you find love like that, you are set free to become the person you were meant to be in all your uniqueness. And when you experience yourself in the middle of that kind of freedom, you can't help feeling good about who you find yourself to be. . . . We want to be loved *for no good reason at all.*[6]

Dr. Warren suggests that you know you have found this kind of love when you are sure that nothing you could ever do would separate you from the love the other person has for you. Such a love frees you from what Carl Rogers calls " 'conditions of worth.' You no longer have to be anything in particular in order to be loved. You can begin the journey toward self-discovery with no preset destination. In each moment you can simply be authentically yourself."[7]

To become who they are demands that your children have a strong sense of self. A strong sense of self comes from the freedom of unconditional love. And persons with a vital self-concept, nurtured in unconditional love, have the best chance of dealing well with their anger.

It is in your home that your children are learning the most important meanings of life, not only from what you say, but often from what you leave unsaid. Not only from what you do, but from what you leave undone.

It is in your home that your children are learning how much they mean to you, to God, and to themselves. Please help your children to know that they mean all the world to you, by your actions as well as your words.

Commit yourself to keeping their emotional tanks full!

UNCONDITIONAL LOVE

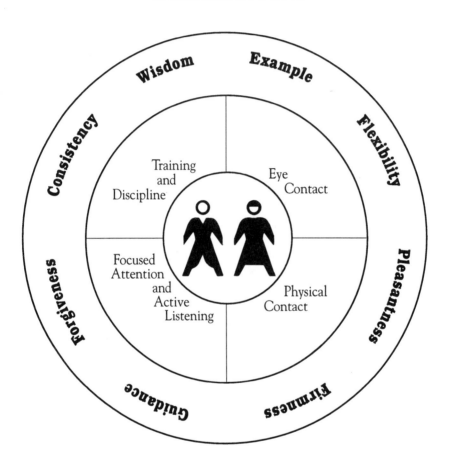

F I V E

What Is Anger?

Aggression, unconscious displays, and ventilation are three of the most common forms of handling anger for children. As we watch Jimmy, Danny, and Sue, we will see these in action.

♦ Jimmy was five years old. His teachers considered him outgoing, even-keeled, generally taking things as they come, and getting along well with other children. Yet, one day another boy accidentally pushed him down on the playground as he ran by. Jimmy reacted by attacking the boy with his fists; this left a cut over the boy's eye.

Jimmy's teachers and peers were shocked by his aggressive response. Later, his teacher learned that he was ill that day and had not been able to hold any food in his stomach. Jimmy was sorry for his behavior and apologized.

In Jimmy we see a child who normally handled his anger well. But under an adverse condition, falling ill, he allowed his anger to turn into aggression. The critical points to remember are that Jimmy was clearly conscious of his anger. He was also aware that it was wrong to hurt the other child. Even though he did not want to express his anger this way, on that day he was unable to control it.

♦ Danny, also five, was well regarded by his teachers and classmates. He had no difficulties in learning or in his relationships with other children. Yet, recently, Danny began soiling his pants with increasing frequency. Naturally, he suffered embarrassment from this humiliating pattern, but could not control it.

In Danny we see a child expressing anger unconsciously. He was unaware that he was angry and also that he was soiling himself, until it had happened. In this case, it would seem inappropriate to call his anger a feeling, since Danny didn't feel the anger. It was not evident in his behavior or his awareness, but its destructive outcome was.

♦ Six-year-old Sue is a verbal child who fluently expresses her feelings, and especially her anger. Her mother is proud of Sue's ability to verbalize. But the child has been using this ability to manipulate her mother and gain control.

As Sue expresses her anger in hostility, complaining, and arguing, her mother loses her temper and yells at Sue. Of course, this makes Sue's behavior even worse until finally her mother does one of two things. She either gives in, or she loses control and overreacts to Sue's behavior with even more intense anger which may include severe punishment.

After a short breather, the cycle begins all over again, with Sue ventilating verbally, and her mother believing that this makes Sue feel better, since her anger "should not be forced down inside of her."

Sue's mother is in a difficult position. She has fallen into the popular notion that a child should be allowed to express herself with total freedom. She fears that if Sue is forced to bury her feelings inside, her ego development will be thwarted. This "ventilation myth" is dealt with well in *The Cycle of Violence* by Suzanne R. Steinmetz.

CHILDREN ARE NATURALLY IMMATURE

Because Jimmy, Danny, and Sue are young children, they are going to handle their anger immaturely much of the time. This should be obvious, and yet, I find that many parents find it hard to accept childish forms of dealing with anger.

This lack of acceptance is a great problem for many parents. Even if they understand how to control their own anger — and few adults do — they still expect their children to handle theirs in a mature fashion. This is impossible. Most children express anger with ventilation and aggression. Unconscious expressions of anger involve suppression, and these, of course, need to be avoided.

What a dilemma! If it is unreasonable to expect our children to be mature, then it is also unreasonable to expect them to handle their anger in a mature fashion. Of course, we are not going to like their childish exhibitions of anger, but we must learn to accept them as they are, and this includes the way they express anger.

Our challenge as parents is to train our children to understand and control this anger, not all at once, but with a goal of arriving at mature expressions of anger by the time they are seventeen. This means that we will continually work at this task, dealing with our children on the age-level where they are.

Most parents have two problems with this process of training. First, they do not understand how adults should handle anger, since they generally do a poor job of this themselves. And second, they expect their children to handle anger in a mature way. When this doesn't happen, they react in a destructive manner when the child acts like a child.

There clearly is a different standard for children and adults in the handling of anger. We should have learned some things that our children don't know yet.

As we approach this difficult subject and try to find help for our homes, I want to tell you how we will proceed. In this chapter, we will be looking at what anger is, the values of anger, and some patterns of behavior common in families.

In chapters 6 and 7, we will consider the subconscious and conscious expressions of anger which are causing such havoc in increasing numbers of homes.

Because anger is a complex subject, it is not understood well, even by some of those who studied it and its results for years. What I hope to do in this book is to give you an overview that may motivate you to do further reading on your own.

In my book, *How to Really Love Your Teenager*, I included an Anger Ladder. It also appears at the end of this chapter because it shows most of the common ways of expressing anger. The number of rungs on the Ladder is unimportant. What matters is the progression upward from less acceptable forms of expressing anger to more acceptable. Healthier behaviors are printed in capital letters. At the top of the Ladder, most of the words are capped. At the bottom, none of them are. You will want to refer to the Anger Ladder as you read on.

REASONS FOR ANGER

Why do you get angry? A short answer is that you or someone you love is threatened. This threat can take many forms: physical danger, ridicule, irritation because someone has not done what he or she should have.

A threat to your selfhood or those dear to you causes anxiety. This is really a gift from God, because the combination of fear and anger at an impending threat causes you to act in readiness. Depending on the size of the threat, you may feel more fear at first, or more anger.

The threats may be to your physical well-being, your social standing, your family, your self-esteem, your economic security, your possessions, your inner peace of mind, your desires, your beliefs, or your relationships. Because these encompass most of your life, you could find yourself threatened at any point.

In a society where concerns over crime and the economy run high, and where the media reports fearful things all the time, it is natural that our self-preserving instincts also run high.

It is important that we learn to identify the sources of our anger and anxiety, so that we can better understand what is happening within us and also around us. In his book, *Coping with Your Anger: A Christian Guide*, Andrew D. Lester suggests a process to help us.

> When you are threatened, you have a natural, God-given response — you get anxious. One of the emotional parts of this anxiety is the anger that you feel. A helpful way to understand a particular experience of anger is to follow this process of evaluation. (1) I am angry, therefore I must be anxious. (2) If I am anxious, something has threatened me or something important to me. (3) What is this threat?
> . . . This process can also be used to understand the anger of other people. When other people (family, friends) are angry, that means they are threatened — anxious — angry. When the threats are recognized, you can

take responsibility for dealing with your anger (and perhaps the anger of others) more creatively and ethically.[1]

THE VALUES OF ANGER

When I am angry I can write, pray, and preach well, for then my whole temperament is quickened, my understanding sharpened, and all mundane vexations and temptations gone.   Martin Luther

It is important to distinguish between the God-given emotion or response of anger and the ways we express that anger. In this book we are referring to many expressions of anger that we consider unacceptable. But for now, I want us to consider some of the values of this gift God has bestowed on us.

In an earlier chapter, I mentioned about the importance of the self-concept. We all need enough emotional and mental space to express who we are and what we can do. We all need some degree of autonomy, appropriate to our age and responsibilities. We all need to know that we are loved by someone we value. When these are threatened, we may feel angry, and this is not necessarily bad.

Children are trying to discover who they are, at the same time they are also trying to learn all about the world they are living in. It would be surprising if they and we didn't get in each other's way sometimes.

We have names for some of the most trying periods in which our children want to express their individuality. We call them "the terrible twos," "puberty," and "adolescence." What is happening in these and other difficult times of our children's lives is the push toward independence and individuation. This push is generally accompanied by some anger, as children reach for more than we think is wise at the moment. What they are saying to us is, "Pay attention to me. I don't like what you are doing. Restore my pride. You're in my way. Danger. Give me justice."[2]

We will help ourselves and our children if we can remember that this striving for a greater sense of self is fully normal and necessary. When our children know that we understand their push for more space, freedom, and authority, they will more likely work with us than against us.

Anger has so many good uses, if we know how to direct it. Think of the scientific breakthroughs that have come from someone being angry with disease and death. Or the social advances such as child labor laws, because someone was angry at children being misused.

Anger mobilizes our reserves. But what we do with those reserves is up to us. We can employ them in positive or negative ways. But first, we need to know who we are, what we want, and what is being threatened. Then we can decide how to communicate to others what we feel, as individuals or as part of a group.

This reminds me of something that happened at our Center. Marilyn, one of our wonderful social workers, passed me in the hall and I couldn't help noticing the very satisfied smile on her face. I asked her what was going on.

She told me about Dot, a young mother of three, who had been physically abused by her husband for several months. Dot had sought counsel from a Christian "celebrity" who had continually advised her to be "submissive" to her husband, no matter how he treated her. Finally, Dot's friends could no longer stand seeing her so mercilessly abused, and they brought her to our Center.

As Marilyn talked with her, she discovered that Dot

was an extremely dependent person who simply could not take steps to protect herself. However, when Dot's husband threatened to harm one of their children, she at last responded with an anger she did not feel when she was threatened and abused herself. This anger was the motivation Dot needed to take action to protect herself and her children from harm.

This story illustrates one of the prime values of anger — as a life preserver. When we are threatened, most of us determine that we are going to survive. And the heightened awareness that we gain from this anger is actually a help in planning for our survival.

One aspect of that survival is the drive to find what we are fitted for. It is often the most creative among us who have the most difficulty finding their place, their niche for expressing who they are and what they can do. When they receive little help, or downright discouragement from those close to them, they will feel angry. But their very anger may be the impetus to continue the search.

CULTURALLY LEARNED ANGER

Anger responses are often learned behavior. A distinct culture may be a tribe or community in another country, or a religious or ethnic group in our own society. Each group has its own language or meanings, and those meanings affect behavior.

Men and women are often treated as cultural groups because they tend to express emotions in different ways. "Even among young adults, thought to be more liberated from traditional sex roles, 'Women are far more likely to suppress, repress and deny anger,' says psychologist Charles Spielberger of the University of South Florida, Tampa. 'They want interpersonal harmony much more than men do, and they inhibit their anger in order to keep peace.' "[3]

Another cultural setting is the family, where children learn about behavior. When extended families get together, they usually behave in similar ways. This is evidenced in speech patterns and in responses to events. When you are with your extended family, you will probably see some remarkable likenesses that are also being observed and learned by your children. If those patterns include many negative expressions of anger, you can be sure your children are absorbing those too, and learning that this is how "their people" express anger.

Meg Eastman calls these "dragons that inhabit families":

> Anger patterns — each family's personal Dragons — are familiar because you probably learned them from your own parents. You saw these patterns repeated at home so many times that you automatically fell into the same behavior as you grew up. Now you may be worrying that you have become a "dysfunctional" family, despite your best intentions. Many parents find themselves handing down these Dragons to their own children and wondering, *Why is everybody so mad all the time?*[4]

If, on the other hand, your children see anger moving into positive and socially acceptable channels, they will be learning this response.

If they watch you try to understand and forgive those who have done you wrong, they will know that forgiveness is an option, not to justify the wrong but to be one element in dealing with the wrong. They will learn that anger can be controlled and expressed positively rather than negatively.

Your family is a small cultural group. Listen to its language. Watch its behavior. Discover what your children are learning about love and life and anger as they live in this culture.

What you see will at times be amusing. But it can also be downright alarming when you discover that a child really isn't all that angry, but is acting in a highly disagreeable manner because he or she has learned that this is the way to respond in a given situation.

It is possible to change such behaviors within your own household, if you are determined to do so. But don't think it will be easy. And don't assume that your extended family will praise your resolve. When you change any aspect of the family culture, you may be suspected of disturbing the cohesiveness of the family.

If you are sure that you are moving in the right direction, don't be discouraged by family members. In the long run, you will be giving something very positive to your children and, ultimately, to the extended family.

POSITIVE

1. PLEASANT • SEEKING RESOLUTION • FOCUSING ANGER ON SOURCE • HOLDING TO PRIMARY COMPLAINT • THINKING LOGICALLY

2. PLEASANT • FOCUSING ANGER ON SOURCE • HOLDING TO PRIMARY COMPLAINT • THINKING LOGICALLY

POSITIVE AND NEGATIVE

3. FOCUSING ANGER ON SOURCE • HOLDING TO PRIMARY COMPLAINT • THINKING LOGICALLY • unpleasant, loud

4. HOLDING TO PRIMARY COMPLAINT • THINKING LOGICALLY • unpleasant, loud • displacing anger to other sources

5. FOCUSING ANGER ON SOURCE • HOLDING TO PRIMARY COMPLAINT • THINKING LOGICALLY • unpleasant, loud • verbal abuse

6. THINKING LOGICALLY • unpleasant, loud • displacing anger to other sources • expressing unrelated complaints

PRIMARILY NEGATIVE

7. unpleasant, loud • displacing anger to other sources • expressing unrelated complaints • emotionally destructive behavior

8. unpleasant, loud • displacing anger to other sources • expressing unrelated complaints • verbal abuse • emotionally destructive behavior

9. unpleasant, loud • cursing • displacing anger to other sources • expressing unrelated complaints • verbal abuse • emotionally destructive behavior

10. FOCUSING ANGER ON SOURCE • unpleasant, loud • cursing • displacing anger to other sources • throwing objects • emotionally destructive behavior

11. unpleasant, loud • cursing • displacing anger to other sources • throwing objects • emotionally destructive behavior

NEGATIVE

12. FOCUSING ANGER ON SOURCE • unpleasant, loud • cursing • destroying property • verbal abuse • emotionally destructive behavior

13. unpleasant, loud • cursing • displacing anger to other sources • destroying property • verbal abuse • emotionally destructive behavior

14. unpleasant, loud • cursing • displacing anger to other sources • destroying property • verbal abuse • physical abuse • emotionally destructive behavior

15. passive-aggressive behavior

SIX

Passive-Aggressive Behavior

In this chapter and the next, we will be talking about negative expressions of anger. I want to begin with the very worst one, passive aggression.

Because everyone is passive-aggressive to some extent, none of us can claim complete freedom from this plague. However, some people are more extreme in their passive aggression, and are, therefore, easier to identify as users, and perhaps victims, of this disastrous behavior.

WHAT IS PASSIVE AGGRESSION?

Just as the name of this behavior seems contradictory, so the behavior itself is often difficult to understand and recognize. We first need to look at some definitions of the two elements, so that we will know how they combine in a most disastrous expression of anger.

In their book, *Speaking the Truth in Love: How to Be an Assertive Christian*, Ruth N. Koch and Kenneth C. Haugk help us to define passive aggression:

The word *passive* means "not resisting" or "not acting." Originally, the word *passive* was derived from a Latin word meaning "to suffer," which is an accurate description of what often results from passive behavior.

> Passive behavior is behavior that moves against the self. Passive behavior says, "I'll give up anything to avoid displeasure and to gain approval." Passive performers frequently give up important parts of their own personalities to avoid disapproval or criticism, so others will like them. . . .

> *Aggressive* behavior is behavior that moves against others. Aggressive behavior says, "I have the right to patronize you, put you down, dominate, or humiliate you in order to get what I want." The aggressive person has few internal restraints and recognizes few external limits. . . . Aggression may be expressed physically, nonverbally, verbally, and in a particular kind of aggression called passive aggression.[1]

Did you notice that passive people move against themselves? And that aggressive people move against others? Now we need to see how these two are joined.

> *Passive aggression* is a subtle kind of aggression, an underhanded way of moving against another person or manipulating others to get one's own way. Individuals who use passive aggression are sometimes called "powerful passives" because they use undercover ways to get their own way, to get even, and to express what they are not willing to say in a straightforward manner.[2]

While passive-aggressive behavior is not that hard to define, it is difficult to identify. As parents, we need to remember that not all misbehavior is passive aggression. I want to give you three characteristics of this behavior to help you identify it in your child, or in yourself.

♦ Passive aggression is irrational and illogical. It is primarily subconscious, and the subconscious mind seldom makes sense in the outer world or depends on logical thought. The behavior is designed to be the opposite of what is expected of the person, the opposite of what he or she *ought* to do.

♦ The purpose of passive aggression is to upset the parents or other authority figures. No matter what the parents do to correct the behavior, it won't work. The more parents try to correct the situation, the more pressure they put on the child, the more determined the child is to upset them. The more the parents get upset, the more the children feel that they are succeeding. And they will try even harder to disturb the parents. The most common areas of conflict are grades and values.

We want our children to take responsibility for their own behavior, the very opposite of passive aggression. For this to happen, we need to wait until they are ready and able to do so. If we demand it before this time, they will fight us.

♦ Although the subconscious goal of passive aggression is to upset the authority figures, children ultimately hurt themselves the most by this behavior. Those who insist on getting poor grades will have to live with the results of this for the rest of their lives. Approximately one third of college freshmen flunk out every year. The vast majority of these kids are capable of making decent grades. They don't even know why they aren't making the grades of which they are capable.

Those who strike out into the more serious kinds of passive-aggressive behavior may destroy themselves with drugs, alcohol, disease and poverty, and even suicide, the ultimate passive-aggressive behavior.

ROOTS OF PASSIVE AGGRESSION

In chapter 5, we mentioned a few childish means of expressing anger. While adults should know that these are inappropriate means of dealing with anger, children do not. In their immaturity, children express their anger through ventilation and aggression. Most parents have low toleration for these means and react in ways that cause the children to handle anger in an even worse manner. When children are not trained in dealing with anger, they will not only continue to use conscious manifestations of anger but will also resort to subconscious means.

You have watched this scene: Judy is angry and sasses her mother. Her father hears her and responds in a hostile tone, "I never want to hear you talk to your mother like that again! Do you understand?"

Because she is not being taught how to deal with her anger, she learns not only that what she said is inappropriate, but also that future overt expression of anger is inadvisable, and so she begins to suppress it.

Like other young children, Judy is unable to cope with parental anger, because she has no defense against it. When her father dumps his anger on her, she is incapable of dealing with it in a mature fashion — which would keep the anger outside of her. And so, her father's anger goes right down inside of her. But it doesn't stay there.

Parental anger unloaded on the child goes down inside and comes out later in anti-authority attitudes. These attitudes are the seeds of passive aggression.

When the suppression goes on for years, and the attitudes against authority grow into adulthood, we have a full-blown passive-aggressive person who has learned well to oversuppress anger and then let it come out in ways that are nearly impossible for others to deal with.

Let's look at Marge and Jane, two young women whose parents failed to train them in appropriate expressions of anger, and who also made it clear that the two, as children, had better suppress their anger.

MARGE

Marge was a blonde, blue-eyed, attractive nineteen-year-old who was brought to me by her profoundly worried mother. As they entered my office, Marge and her mother were friendly. Both seemed eager to tell me why they were there.

Marge began by saying, "Mom and Dad are upset about my engagement to Duane. You need to know, Dr. Campbell, that Duane is black. I met him at college and I love him. He is really wonderful and I wish my parents would accept him."

Marge's mother, Ellen, replied defensively, "We don't think we are prejudiced, Dr. Campbell. We are just worried about our daughter, and also about what this marriage will mean to Duane. And we are very concerned about any children they may have."

I was deeply impressed by the sincerity of both mother and daughter, and my heart ached for them.

"Tell me about Duane," I asked.

Marge immediately said, "He's wonderful. He's smart, good-looking, sweet, kind, and he loves me."

"You're good at putting things in a nutshell," I kidded her, trying to lighten the increasingly heavy atmosphere.

"What Marge says is true, Dr. Campbell. Duane is a fine boy. But how can they face all the problems they will have in the future?"

"What does your father say about this, Marge?" I asked.

Marge's face sagged with confusion, sadness, and anger. "He is totally against the marriage and refuses to even talk about it. But I'm going to marry Duane, no matter what he says. I don't care how he feels about it." Two spots of rage reddened on Marge's young face.

A week later I saw Marge's father, Fred. He was a stern man who spoke harshly and only when he was asked a direct question. During our time together, most of what he said was negative—complaints about his wife and children and his job. It was clear that Fred was a distressed and unhappy man. He was extremely angry about Marge's relationship with Duane, and could find little good to say about either of them.

Three days later I met with Duane and saw that he was all that Marge and Ellen had said of him. He was a fine young man with a pleasant disposition. He was also bright, talented, articulate, and seemed to genuinely care for Marge.

Testing and subsequent interviews increasingly clarified the tremendous rage Marge felt toward her father. Also, we saw that she was handling her anger in passive-aggressive ways.

Over the next few weeks, Marge's academic performance deteriorated until she decided to drop out of college. Her relationship with Duane also weakened, due mainly to her changing behavior. She became increasingly passive-aggressive toward him, lying to him and then secretly dating other boys. It wasn't long before the marriage was called off.

I have known people who are in wonderful interracial and intercultural marriages. But, sadly, many romantic relationships of this type are a result of passive-aggressive behavior — an unconscious determination to upset one or more authority figures, usually the parents. When a romance is induced by such a desire, it will be destructive for the couple and also for any children they have.

Prolonged counseling was necessary before Marge could handle her anger appropriately. As she learned to express her anger in more healthy ways, she was able to gain control over passive-aggressive behavior.

JANE

Jane was one solemn-faced teenager as she entered my office. She was obviously depressed and seemed reluctant to talk, so we sat quietly for several minutes. Finally she was able to tell me how difficult it was for her to come to see me. She didn't know if she would be able to reveal her reason for being there.

After a good bit of small talk, Jane finally said that she was terribly confused about a homosexual encounter she "fell into" at college with another basketball player. She had not previously experienced anything like this, and she was deeply worried about it.

When I asked about her parents, Jane told me that her father was a successful businessman who was devoted to his wife. He was well thought of in his community and church. Jane's mother was also a fine person whom Jane loved and respected. However, both parents were very busy and spent little time with Jane. But she readily volunteered that it was "quality time." She also said that her father was easily agitated; when he became enraged with Jane, he "dumped" his anger on her.

Testing and further interviews with Jane showed that she was a deeply depressed young woman who harbored a great deal of anger. The two primary causes of her anger were her feeling of being unloved by her parents and her severe depression.

Jane had learned to process her anger in a passive-aggressive manner, and this was the source of her sexual response to her teammate. After she was treated for depression and could handle her anger in more direct and appropriate ways, she was able to better understand herself.

Jane was not a homosexual; rather, she was using passive-aggressive behavior to express her intense anger. I have seen several cases similar to this one.

ADULT PASSIVE AGGRESSION

Although Marge and Jane were beyond my target age of seventeen for the development of mature character, I was able to help them overcome their passive-aggressive behavior during an extended period of counseling.

However, when this behavior goes unchecked into adulthood, it is often also unrecognized for what it is, and can be the cause of unending frustration and pain for other people. Two areas in which it creates havoc are work and marriage.

♦ Employees with an anti-authority attitude will probably keep this hidden for the first year or two. The reason for this is that they have no cause for anger at their new employer, and so have not built up subconscious anger. Since working with and for other people has its aggravations, over time the passive aggressives will accumulate causes for anger, real or imagined, but will suppress the anger for as long as they can, usually no more than two years.

When they can suppress it no longer, it begins coming out in subconscious ways. These people are unaware that they are now determined to do the opposite of what they should be doing. The process begins with a gradual change of attitude that moves from pleasant and cooperative to difficult and annoying. Eventually they are so intolerable that they lose their jobs.

Of course, employers may also be passive aggressive, creating difficult work situations for those under them.

♦ Passive aggression can have a ruinous effect on personal relationships, and nowhere is this more evident than in marriage. At the beginning of the marriage, the person suppresses the anger, but eventually it begins to be expressed toward the spouse.

You may wonder how the passive-aggressive person is rebelling against authority within marriage. However, authority figures include not only those we are responsible to, but also those for whom we are responsible.

Marriage to a passive aggressive can resemble an ongoing nightmare with no escape, for the possibilities for upsetting the spouse are endless and reach into all areas of life. Common expressions of passive aggression in marriage are lying, physical and emotional rejection, generalized blame, mismanagement of money, and seething anger. Not exactly what people are looking for in a marriage commitment.

"NORMAL" PASSIVE AGGRESSION

There is only one time in a person's life when passive aggression could be considered "normal." That period is early adolescence, when children are thirteen to fifteen years old. The behavior stays within the range of normal as long as it does not hurt anyone and is not destructive.

It is very difficult to be a teenager today, because there are so many dangerous ways to express passive aggression. In more rural times, teens might put Farmer Brown's cow on top of the barn, or overturn a few outhouses. When I was young, we took a friend's VW beetle apart and reassembled it in his bedroom, while he was away on vacation. When my children were teens, I was grateful for pranks such as toilet-papering the yards of their friends. But today, teenagers have access to drugs, guns, alcohol, and more. The problem is compounded because so many teenagers are severely depressed.

The normal expressions of this behavior tend to start around ten or eleven years of age, when the child begins neglecting ordinary chores, dawdling, or generally upsetting the parents. When parents know that such behavior is normal, they can handle it in a healthy manner, even though it is irritating and probably will continue for a few years.

The more effectively the parents deal with the behavior, the less it will extend outside the home. If the parents are not effective, the behavior will generalize outside the home and cause embarrassing and potentially dangerous problems. Therefore, it is far better to keep most of the annoyance inside the home.

As much as you may dislike your child's messy room, you need to remember that this is far preferable to some of the other passive-aggressive expressions we have mentioned. You hope your child will curtail his angry behavior to messiness, dawdling, noise, and strange appearance at times.

It is essential to remember that when children are in the deepest stage of adolescence, they will go more for the jugular, determined to do the opposite of what the parents want. In Christian homes, this rebellion will involve the spiritual part of life, since the parents want their children to love God and faithfully attend church. In our home, we knew adolescence was upon us when on Sunday mornings we heard, "I don't want to go to church today." This, from a child who had previously been enthusiastic about church attendance.

If parents overreact or become angry, they can actually drive their children away from God permanently. We all know of Christian homes in which the grown children want little to do with the spiritual values of their parents. If you can remember that the rebellion is normal and is not against you or God or the church in a personal way, you will retain your cool on days when you could easily lose it.

Another area in which parents and young teens have conflict is about grades and academic achievement. Because the kids know that the parents are so concerned about the grades, they also know that this is a prime area in which to rebel. The chances for upsetting the parents are excellent. If parents can keep from making a huge issue over somewhat lower grades, they and their children will recover more quickly and with less unpleasantness.

You may remember that I gave you a definition of integrity in chapter 1. One element of that was to take responsibility for personal behavior. Passive aggression refuses to take responsibility and, instead, tries to place it somewhere else, on parents or the teachers. They should refuse to take it, and insist that the child retain his or her own responsibility.

A classic illustration of this happens when children are about in fifth grade. Children who have done well in school will begin to "forget" their homework. When they don't turn it in, the teacher informs the parents who then make sure that the assignment and books make it home. They think they have solved the problem, but they haven't; even though the homework is done, the kids "forget" to take it back to school. When the parents make sure it goes back, the children "forget" to turn it in, and leave it in their desks.

When my kids were in the fifth grade, I would go to the open houses and sit at some of the desks to see which children had stashed their homework there.

When my older son, David, was in eighth grade, his grades slid from A's and B's to C's. Fortunately, I knew something about normal passive-aggressive behavior at that time, and didn't react to the falling grades. He coasted through ninth grade and into tenth, when I began feeling concerned. During that year, he made friends with some older boys who were about to go off to good colleges, and David became aware that his grades were important.

When he finally talked with me about the matter of grades, I could respond with my concerns. I knew he would hear me now, because he also was interested. When he asked about grade point averages to get into good colleges, I was prepared with the catalog from the school his sister was attending. He had asked her what average he would need to go there also. When he compared the requirement with his own average at the time, he was shocked and said, "Looks like I am going to have to get to work." From that day on, his grades began to improve and he was accepted at the school of his choice. If my wife and I had ranted and raved about his grades for three years, my guess is that he would have been lucky to graduate from high school.

DEALING WITH "NORMAL" PASSIVE AGGRESSION

Because dealing with "normal" teenage passive-aggressive behavior can be so provoking, it is easy for parents to move into the position of being the provoker of their children. We do this in the ways we talk to them and look at them. While these may seem insignificant in an already provoking situation, we need to remind ourselves that children cannot handle our anger. They have no mechanism to prevent it from causing harmful effects inside of them.

When parents are angry, most of them speak in a lower than normal tone. They will probably also issue commands in this tone. When they say, "I want you to empty the garbage *now*," with a lower infliction at the end, the child may automatically become angry and begin to behave in a passive-aggressive manner. I often suggest that parents take a "Yogi Bear" approach when they are angry — ending sentences with an upward inflection. This comes across as cheery and endearing rather than intimidating.

Another way that parents provoke their children is by wording something as a command rather than as a request. When we refrain from angry behavior, our children are most grateful, especially when they know that we have a right to feel angry with them.

Parents can also provoke their children by the ways they look at them, especially in a tense situation. During such times, it is critical to maintain loving eye contact and not look away from the child. But eye contact alone is not enough, for some parents keep this but look at the child in an angry or frowning manner that expresses disapproval of the child himself. The child can interpret such a look as the same as yelling or screaming. On the other hand, when a child is angry, it is important not to smile or laugh in a way that can be interpreted as ridicule.

Because looks are so important, I suggest to parents that they get in front of a mirror to cultivate the neutral look. This is particularly important if you naturally smile or frown most of the time. Without knowing it, you could seem to be ridiculing or scorning your child.

Does it sound as if I am trying to prepare you for your child's angry moments? I am. Children have the most annoying, frustrating, and totally upsetting ways of expressing their anger. When you are suddenly in the middle of such a conflict, it is difficult enough to control your own anger, much less remember to think about how you are coming across to the child.

When you are faced with an angry child, you have two obligations — to accept the child as he is, including his childish display of anger, and to express your own anger in a mature fashion. I know this is difficult, but it is so important, when you think of your goal — that your child will continually be learning to handle anger in a more mature manner. His best lessons in this ongoing education are from your example.

When a child approaches you with anger, the normal reaction is to be angry in return. But this response will not resolve the anger. You need to remember that you are the adult, and that he is the child. You should accept him as a child, but you should not copy his behavior.

If you refuse to accept the child and his childish display of anger, you are forcing the anger to go somewhere else, and the only place it can go is inside. This is setting the child up for passive-aggressive behavior now and in the future.

ASCENDING THE ANGER LADDER

I'm sure you saw the Anger Ladder in chapter 5. As you work with your children in the coming years, you will always be seeking to help them climb from one rung to the next, away from the negative expressions of anger to the more positive. This is a long process that involves both training and example.

You'll notice that passive aggression is at the bottom of the Ladder. If you have thirty rungs or sixty, passive-aggressive expressions of anger will always be at the bottom. Because passive aggression is common to teenagers, every parent has to deal with this form of anger. The key thing is that you don't let your child stay there.

You need to remind yourself that your child can climb only one rung at a time. This fact is frustrating to parents who want the process to be over soon. What is even more frustrating is that parents have to wait until a child is ready to take the next step. This calls for patience and wisdom. But I can tell you that the results are well worth the wait. Pat and I have seen our three children move to mature expressions of anger, as we let them grow at their own pace.

When you watch your child express anger, you'll want to identify where he or she is on the Ladder. Then you will know the next step. My most unpleasant experience of a child speaking to me in a very inappropriate manner was with David when he was about thirteen. Thank goodness the phase didn't last long. His unpleasant verbalization of anger occurred only when a particular event upset him. When he was verbalizing his anger at me in ways that I didn't want to hear, I had to do some self-talk to determine where he was on the Anger Ladder. I would say to myself, "Attaboy, David, Attaboy. Let that anger out, because when it is all out, I've got you." Of course, I didn't say any of this to David.

The reason I wanted the anger to come out was that as long as the anger was inside of him, it controlled the house. But once the anger was outside, then he felt silly, and I could regain control. He had gotten all the anger out verbally and was asking himself, "Now what do I do?" It was then that I was in a great position to train David.

Another reason I was glad to see it come out was that the more anger that came out of his mouth, the less there would be to come out in lying, stealing, sex, drugs, and all the other passive-aggressive behaviors going on today.

Fellow parent, I know that this is not easy to grasp, and you may have serious questions at this point. Allowing a child to express his or her anger is not being permissive. We must remember that children of any age will naturally express anger in immature ways. We cannot train them to express their anger in mature ways simply by getting upset and forcing them to stop expressing their anger. If we do this, their anger will be oversuppressed, and passive-aggressive behavior will then result.

If we want to train our children to express anger in a mature fashion, we must allow them to express it verbally, even though that may be unpleasant. Why? The best way to express anger is *verbally and pleasantly*, but children can't learn to do this if they are not allowed to verbalize it at all. Therefore, wise parents will want their children to express anger verbally, first, to prevent them from oversuppressing it, and second, to lead the children up the rungs of the Anger Ladder.

All anger must come out either verbally or behaviorally. If we don't allow it to come out verbally, our children must oversuppress the anger, and passive-aggressive behavior will be the result.

When your child brings anger to you in a verbally unpleasant way, it does not necessarily mean that the child is being disrespectful. To determine whether this is so, ask yourself, "How is this child's attitude toward my authority most of the time?" Most children are respectful over 90 percent of the time.

If this is true of your child, and now he or she is bringing verbal anger to you about a particular situation, this is just what you want to happen. You know what to do—and you are not alone. You have "Yogi Bear," eye contact, the neutral look, and self-talk with you. When your child has gotten the angry feelings out, you are then in an excellent position to train your child. In chapter 9, we will talk more about specific ways to train your child. For now, just a reminder that your own behavior during a child's anger is most critical.

It may seem unfair that when a child comes to you in anger, you are supposed to feel thankful that the child is expressing the anger verbally and then control yourself. I know it is not easy, but as you behave this way, you force yourself to mature. You also are saving yourself and your children from some of life's worst problems later on.

You may be asking, "What about the child who verbalizes anger most of the time, even when he is not upset about a particular event?" Some children use ventilation of anger to manipulate their parents and get their own way. This is quite different from anger at a specific situation. Such ventilation, with a motivation to upset and hurt others, is inappropriate and must be corrected. But in doing so, the same parental parameters apply: We must be pleasant but firm.

What I encountered with David was not ventilation but normal teenage anger. However, I would not want to leave the impression that I felt no tension or anger myself. And I had to let that die down before I could work with David. There is no one right way to work with a child, and you may find better methods than I did. The main thing is to keep your objective in mind.

When your child brings his anger to you, he is also bringing himself to be trained. It is crucial not to begin training your child until both of you have calmed down and reestablished a good feeling between you. It is also crucial that you don't wait too long, or you will lose the effect of building on what happened. As soon as things are stable between you, sit down together and do three things.

♦ You want to let him know that you are not going to condemn him. Especially if a child is very responsive to authority, a 25 percenter (see chap. 11), he may feel guilty about what he has done. Unless I let him know that I am not going to condemn him, he may never do it again. But if he never does it again, I won't have the opportunity to help him climb the Anger Ladder. Part of training is letting him know that I accept him as a person and always want to know how he is feeling, whether happy or sad or angry. And so I say to David, "When you are angry, I want to know that you are."

♦ Next, you want to commend your child for the things he did right. And so with David, I said, "You did let me know that you were angry, and that is good. You didn't let your anger out on your little brother or the dog. You didn't throw anything or hit the wall. You simply told me that you were angry."

Do you see where I am going with this? Whatever he did that was right I mentioned. Any time a child brings verbal anger to you, he has done some right things and avoided some wrong ones.

♦ Next, you want to help your child take a step up on the Anger Ladder. This involves giving a request rather than a prohibition. Instead of saying, "Don't ever call me that name again!" you say, "From now on, Son, please don't call me that name. All right?" Now this doesn't guarantee that he will never again say what you have asked him not to. But it does ensure that when he is sufficiently mature, he will take that step. It may be the next day or several weeks or months down the road. This kind of training is a long and difficult process.

After you have gone through the process enough times, your child will begin to do some thinking without your reminder. The combination of your training plus your good example of handling anger in a mature way will help your child to do his or her own self-training after a while.

The most crucial element here, as in all areas of dealing with your children, is to give them unconditional love. When they know that they are loved in this way, when they truly feel loved all the time, they will be far more responsive to your training. And you will be much more likely to achieve your goal of maturity by age seventeen.

SEVEN

More Immature Expressions of Anger

Although passive aggression is the worst expression of anger, there are other forms which can cause tragic harm to both individuals and families.

As a person matures, the way he handles his anger should also mature. But the fact is that we see many adults who are dealing very badly with their anger, and then teaching these behaviors to their children, consciously or by example. In this chapter we will be looking at some destructive forms of anger.

AGGRESSION

The purpose of aggression is to cause harm to a person or object or group. It can be expressed verbally or physically. For example, a child may attack with weapons, words, hands, or feet. The use of aggression is almost always inappropriate and usually results in irreparable harm in relationships. Any apparent gain will eventually be overshadowed by destructive consequences.

These consequences are especially serious between parents and children. Aggressive behavior on the part of parents toward their children will most certainly result in rebellion against authority. Also, the parents are failing as role models when they teach their children to use aggression.

If you look back to the Anger Ladder, you will see that aggressive actions are toward the bottom of the scale, and are usually combined with other destructive behaviors.

Living as we do in an extremely aggressive society, we know that violence begets violence. Watching others commit aggressive acts, in person or on the screen, increases one's chances of behaving aggressively.

I was particularly impressed with the findings of Dr. Leonard D. Eron, psychology professor at Yale University, in his study of causes of aggression in children. As he observed them over two decades, he found two things to be true: Those children who watched more television used more aggression; and the more television they watched, the more likely they were to become aggressive adults who would commit crimes.

As the subjects of his study were approaching thirty years of age, Dr. Eron revisited them and discovered that his earlier findings were indeed true.[1]

Of course, the problem is complex and cannot be placed solely on the amount of television a child watches. I believe the most critical component in determining how a person will eventually express anger is the degree of anti-authority bias in his or her makeup. That is, the amount of passive aggression that underlies expressions of anger.

In chapter 6, we pointed out the difference between aggression and assertiveness. This needs to be emphasized again, because assertive behavior is usually healthy and appropriate. Assertiveness is the direct expression of feelings, including anger, but without the intent to hurt another.

When it is expressed constructively, assertiveness can go a long way toward achieving a person's goals.

Aggression, however, is intended to cause harm, through violence to a person, to property, or both. In *Taming the Dragon in Your Child,* Meg Eastman includes a chapter titled, "The Aggressive, Out-of-Control Child," in which she offers helpful suggestions. After detailing specific behaviors such as fighting, blaming, and power struggles, she says:

> The problems of aggressive, out-of-control children may have stemmed originally from stress, impulsiveness, over-activity, abuse, or lack of training in self-control. It is often easy to excuse and overlook aggression in young children. However, by school age, their anger patterns often reach disturbing levels.
>
> These children may relish the power and control their aggressive outbursts achieve. They may show no remorse or conscience and may not care about how their behavior affects others. In fact, they often look for another person to blame for the problem. Refusal to accept responsibility is characteristic. . . .

Typical situations that trigger the anger of an aggressive child include:

♦ Anything that threatens to lower his sense of status and control.

♦ Being exposed as a failure in class or on a sports team, within his family or peer group.

♦ Challenges to his power base — not being able to have his way, having to follow a class rule, or to complete an assignment that "bores" him.[2]

Meg Eastman believes that the aggressive child needs "limits, limits, and more limits!" She offers valuable guidelines for discipline. If you have this problem in your home, I hope you will read her book.

VENTILATION

Ventilation is a verbal expression of anger. It differs from verbal aggression in that its intent is not to bring harm to another person, but simply to get rid of one's anger. This type of behavior may range from loud, angry screaming to muttered expletives, from complaining and arguing to hysterical tirades.

Regardless of how it comes out, ventilation of anger is unpleasant to be around and is definitely a behavior we want our children to outgrow by the time they are seventeen.

However, as disagreeable and immature as ventilation is, it serves a purpose in childhood, because it presents us with something we need in order to train our children about anger. As long as they are expressing anger *verbally*, they probably are not expressing it *behaviorally*, as in aggression or passive aggression.

We parents need to remember that anger comes out in only two ways — verbally or behaviorally — and we have a good deal of control over which of these two ways our children use. Most children employ verbal expressions of anger. The more parents prevent this expression, by telling children, "Shut up!" or "Never talk that way again!" the more the anger will come out behaviorally.

If we parents truly understand that we have a choice in determining how our children express anger, we will be glad, relatively speaking, to have them use verbalizations rather than physical aggression or passive aggression.

NAGGING AND WITHHOLDING

Nagging is an immature expression of anger that is closely related to ventilation. Yet, it differs from ventilation in that it has a purpose other than merely getting rid of anger. We nag when we feel ineffective or powerless in controlling or influencing another person or a situation. It is most common in close relationships, like the family.

Nagging is an underhanded way of saying, "I just want to help you." We parents must remember that nagging is a subtle way of dumping our anger on a child. It is highly destructive and is a sure way to push the child toward anti-authority attitudes.

Withholding can be a legitimate means of disciplining a child, or it can be an expression of anger. As a form of discipline, a parent may temporarily withhold something the child wants. As long as it is not done to hurt the child or accompanied by continued parental anger, this can be an appropriate means of punishment.

However, an angry parent may withhold affection and nurture. This is particularly dangerous, because the child then learns how to use this treacherous behavior and will probably employ it passive-aggressively by withholding affection, obedience, achievement, cooperation, pleasantness, and more.

SILENCE AND WITHDRAWAL

Silence and withdrawal are inappropriate ways to handle anger. They can be especially harmful in a marital relationship, when they are used to conceal anger.

We may use silence and withdrawal to avoid admitting we are angry and also to avoid confronting the situation and the other person in a healthy way. These devices are closely related to withholding; however, in silence and withdrawal we shut ourselves off from the relationship. Most people who engage in these adverse behaviors are unaware of just what is happening.

Silence and withdrawal are very harmful to a child because they are the opposite of unconditional love. To withdraw from the parent/child relationship is the same as telling the child, "Sometimes I love you, sometimes I don't." This classic example of conditional love is one of the greatest sources of anger and rage from child to parent. Dear parents, we must not fall into this immature and harmful behavior, with our children or in our marriages. The results are disastrous!

Writing from painful personal experience, Andrew D. Lester tells how he and his wife learned to deal with their anger constructively, instead of retreating into silence.

> Instead of being so afraid of our anger, we began to take the risk of sharing it with each other as we did our other thoughts and feelings. We started taking responsibility for using anger constructively instead of allowing it to rob us of our happiness. We know now that anger has the potential for increasing intimacy in close relationships.[3]

DISPLACED ANGER

Displaced anger uses innocent people as targets. This most often occurs when we are angry at someone we cannot confront with our rage — an employer, professor, or superior.

Displaced anger is quite easily vented on children.

When a child's immaturities annoy the parent, instead of handling this anger in loving and instructive ways, the parent may dump hostility from other sources on the child.

It is crucial to remember that children cannot tolerate parental anger, because they have no defenses against it. Dumping any anger on them is injurious, but dumping excess rage from other sources can be truly destructive. When we parents learn to control ourselves, positive control of our children's development will naturally follow.

OVERSUPPRESSED ANGER VERSUS VENTILATION

There is much confusion today about the suppression of anger. One school of thought advocates that feelings should never be suppressed or bottled up. Followers of this school believe that feelings, and especially anger, should be ventilated. In the 1960s and 1970s we heard a good deal about ventilation, and Theodore Rubin's *The Anger Book* is still a popular advocate of this position.

There *is* truth in the belief that oversuppressing anger in the subconscious mind may result in various problems, such as psychiatric illness and passive-aggressive behavior. Suppression of anger is also related to certain types of physical illness. In their research on suppression, Howard Friedman and Stephanie Booth-Kersley observed that the following emotions have been implicated in physical illness: anger, depression, hostility, anxiety, and introversion. In their statistical analysis of the results of 101 studies, they determined these five diseases to have emotional components: heart disease, ulcers, headaches, arthritis, and asthma.[4]

However, to simply ventilate anger does not alleviate or prevent these problems. In fact, ventilation as a means of getting rid of anger cannot only cause the problems I have just mentioned, but may also increase rageful feelings. In all too many cases, it is like throwing gasoline on a fire.

Because the case for ventilation has been so publicized in psychological circles, I want to underscore it further. Advocates of this position believe that "getting it out of your system" is always beneficial. However, this view "tends to overlook the social context and the consequences of anger. If your expressed rage causes another person to shoot you, it won't matter that you die with very healthy arteries."[5]

Carol Tavris offers us three myths of expressed anger in *Anger: the Misunderstood Emotion.*

Myth #1: "Aggression is the instinctive catharsis for anger."

Myth #2: "Talking out anger gets rid of it—or at least makes you feel less angry."

Myth #3: "Tantrums and other childhood rages are healthy expressions of anger that forestall neurosis."[6]

I can include only a fragment of her answer to each of these and I urge you to read her excellent book. Her response to these three myths:

#1: "When you permit children to play aggressively, they don't become less aggressive, as the catharsis theory would predict; they become more aggressive. . . . Verbal aggression usually fails because it riles up the other person and makes him or her inclined to strike back."[7]

#2: "Talking out an emotion doesn't reduce it, *it rehearses it.* . . . Talking can freeze a hostile disposition. This is true for children, teenagers, and adults alike. . . . Children who were encouraged to express their anger toward the child who had frustrated them later liked that child less than the children who were *not permitted* to express their anger!"[8]

#3: " 'Expressing anger' is not the same as 'acting aggressively,' but many parents, eager not to block the former, encourage the latter. When you allow a child to scream, kick, hit, or smash objects, however, you are not reducing the child's anger. You are increasing his aggressiveness."[9]

SELF-ABUSE

Although the growing tendency in our society is to blame others for one's problems, there are still many people who put themselves down when things go wrong.

Some send negative messages to themselves. The more they do this, the more they take life too seriously and personally. A few people are real champions at this.

Most of those who turn their anger inside do not feel the anger. Rather, they feel "hurt." They find ways to blame themselves for any problem and are quite prone to guilt. This habit of putting themselves down may cause despair, depression, and feelings of helplessness and hopelessness. Because depression is a major source of anger, a destructive cycle can result from this type of self-abuse.

People who tend to handle anger by directing it to the self usually fall into this trap when they have lost control over something such as a close relationship, their business, or money matters. They believe the situation is unmanageable.

The answer as to why some people handle anger in this way is complex. Part of it is genetic — certain personality types are more prone to direct their anger inside. Also, it is common to inadvertently train our children to handle anger this way. If we criticize and blame them, they may respond by criticizing and blaming themselves and may also develop the habit of directing the anger inward. This is especially true of 25 percenters. The 75 percenters, in contrast, will respond by "identifying with the aggressor": they will mimic the parents by criticizing and blaming someone else. These children may develop habits of refusing to take responsibility for their own behavior and of blaming others. Both means of handling anger are destructive.

Self-abuse is aggravated by passive-aggressive attitudes. For example, as the depression deepens and causes anger, a desire for revenge can form and grow. Finally, even suicidal thoughts and attempts may result. Suicide is the ultimate passive-aggressive act: "You'll be sorry when I'm gone!"

It is important to remember that all of these immature expressions of anger can be employed by both children and adults. This means that we parents will want to identify those we are using and then correct them, so that we can train our children to handle their anger correctly.

There are, of course, other inappropriate and harmful ways to express anger. But most of them are related to those we have mentioned. When you learn how to deal with the most basic ones, you can apply your knowledge to other behaviors.

EIGHT

Parents, Cure Yourselves!

Whether we like it or not, we parents have the greatest influence on our children — for good or bad. And the factor which has the most influence on them is the way we manage our anger. It is a double whammy. Our management of anger becomes an example for them to follow, and it also affects them in several critical ways.

Inappropriate control of our anger hurts our children's self-esteem, sense of identity, ability to relate to others, perceptions of the world, stress management, and overall ability to function in society. Also, our mismanagement of anger causes our children to develop passive-aggressive, anti-authority, self-defeating attitudes, which, if not corrected by their late teen years, will become deep-seated factors in their basic character.

If we handle our own anger maturely, we give our children one of the greatest and most caring gifts there is. This gift is a potent life force that will assure that they grow to their own maturity without the afflictions so many adults struggle with today.

One of the most wonderful experiences in life is to see our children develop into warm, caring, conscientious, energetic, motivated, respected, and well-liked adults.

The reason parental management of anger is so important is that children are so sensitive toward their parents' anger. It is impossible for them to pass it off or to take it casually. Even one incident of mismanaged anger will cause extreme pain, just as mature handling of anger can intensify the love between parents and children.

Every day we parents face situations in which we have a choice as to how we will handle our own anger. If we behave in a mature way, we will strengthen the bonds between us and our children. We may not immediately sense the increased respect and appreciation in the hearts of our children, but over the years we will find parenting to be ever more satisfying and fulfilling. If, however, we dump anger on our children, we will weaken the bonds of affection.

Before you can effectively train your children in their management of anger, you first need to look at yourself. That is what this chapter is about. In fact, I recommend that you read this chapter and the next one before you go to sleep at night. After a couple of readings, you will be able to review them in a few minutes. As you read each evening, you can then pledge yourself to handle your anger well for the next twenty-four hours. Every day you do this is like putting money in the bank to insure a secure future for you and your children. But, every day you handle anger poorly is like losing money and jeopardizing the future for your family.

TWENTY QUESTIONS

Do you remember the old television game show "Twenty Questions"? I have twenty questions for you to answer. They aren't as entertaining as those on the TV show, and they will take time to answer thoughtfully, but I can promise you that the rewards will be much greater than from any game.

As you read and answer the questions, take a moment to reflect on those areas where you may not be doing as well as you would like. For instance, you may take responsibility for your behavior most of the time, but in certain circumstances you fall down. If that is so, you need to ask yourself why that happens.

1. Do you take responsibility for your behavior?
2. Do you keep your promises?
3. Do you feel generally positive about your character and level of maturity? Or, do you feel negative?
4. Are you usually optimistic? Or pessimistic?
5. Are you still struggling with attitudes and events from your childhood and teenage years?
6. Do you often feel anger you cannot resolve?
7. Do you like who you have become? Do you have a plan for continued growth?
8. Does the idea of getting to know yourself better sound like a good adventure or a dangerous threat?
9. Do you show respect and fairness to each member of your family?
10. Do you show respect and fairness to those whom you manage at work? At church or in the community?
11. Do you often complain about those who are over you at work? In the church or community?
12. Do you give an honest day's work for your pay?
13. Do you frequently complain about your spouse?
14. Do you recognize and cultivate the presence of God in your marriage and family life? In your personal life?

15. Do you have an ongoing plan for training your children in all areas of their lives, including the spiritual? Does this plan involve people in your extended family, church, and community?
16. Do you want your children to develop a character like yours?
17. When you face problems, do you generally ignore them or do you think and pray about how you can confront and re-solve them?
18. Are you open to new ideas and developments? Or, do you find change threatening?
19. Are there people from whom you should ask forgiveness?
20. Are there matters for which you should make restitution?

If you have difficulty with some of these questions, that is all right, as long as you admit it and are willing to work to become a more mature person. If problem areas came to mind, you may want to write them down and spend some time considering what you need to do to grow or change. Pray about these areas, perhaps with your spouse or a friend, and trust that God will be with you in your desire to become more like what He intends.

TAKING RESPONSIBILITY
FOR YOUR OWN ANGER

In chapters 6 and 7, we talked about how not to manage anger. Now we need to talk about how we should be managing it.

The first step is a willingness to be responsible for our anger. This is difficult, because it is so easy to blame someone or something else for "making me mad" and to hold them responsible for what the anger "made" us do. Unfortunately, most people use their anger as an excuse for whatever they want to justify—their actions or attitudes. In fact, most people consciously or unconsciously seek out reasons to get angry, so that they may then justify their own wrongdoing!

Over the years, I have known of employees who have been fairly treated by their employers, and yet have caused devastating harm to them. In each case, the employees used trivial and unrelated occurrences to justify their anger, and then used that anger to justify their irresponsible behavior.

To take responsibility for anger, we must first identify it. Many people do not even realize when they are angry. One reason for this is that they may feel jealous, frustrated, or hurt, and are not aware that the basis of those feelings is anger.

But even if these adults are not conscious of their anger, we can be sure that their children are. When parents refuse to deal with the anger, their children feel less respect for them. But when the parents identify their anger, then they are able to name it, to admit, "I am angry." Only then can they assume responsibility for it.

No one can take responsibility for your anger but *you*. When you blame someone else for it, you give that person the power to upset you. Your anger is *your* responsibility. And how you handle and express that anger is also *your* responsibility.

Blaming your child for your anger is inexcusable. It is also dangerous, because you will naturally blame the child for anger caused by totally unrelated situations. For example, you may have had an angry disagreement at work which you did not resolve but simply "forgot." You get home and your child's behavior upsets you. If you blame your child for your anger, you will probably also blame him for your earlier en-counter at work. This sets you up to dump accumulated anger on your child. Without doubt, the results will be tragic, especially if you continue to use your child as a dumping ground for your accumulated anger.

DEALING WITH YOUR ANGER

Since we all get angry every day, we need some means of coping with it, so that it doesn't get the best of us.

♦ Because you don't feel proud of yourself when your anger gets out of control, it is easy to want to "forget" what hap-pened. However, it is important to identify and also to remember your anger. You want to remember how you behaved, or you are later likely to displace your anger on someone else, or oversuppress it and then become passive-aggressive.

I recommend keeping a notebook of your progress in coping with anger. For instance, if your boss or someone else treats you unfairly and you feel deeply hurt (angry), you may not be in a position to confront or deal with the hurt. But you can log the incident in your notebook and later record how you resolved the problem.

Just how do you resolve it? Remember, the best way to handle anger is verbally, pleasantly, and directly with the person you are angry at. If possible, you want reconciliation and greater understanding between you.

If your problem is with a manager at work, and if it is appropriate to confront this person, you will want to do so in a calm and controlled manner. You will express your concern and then listen to the response. If the response is mature and you can together negotiate a solution, that's great.

However, if you confront and the response is immature, and no solution is forthcoming, don't despair. And don't ventilate. Seek out a friend or your spouse or a counselor with whom you can *share* your feelings, not ventilate. Remember, ventilation increases the anger. Yet, if you keep it all inside, you will oversuppress it. Sharing your feelings with a trusted person will help.

Some people find relief in writing their feelings. I have counseled some folks to write a letter to the person with whom they are angry. But don't be in a hurry to mail the letter. It is usually better to throw it out after you feel more calm.

◆ I would now like to suggest some ways of reducing your proneness to anger. The better your condition physically, spiritually, emotionally, the more effective you will be in handling anger.

It is obvious that the body needs a healthy and balanced diet. We hear so much about this that I hardly need to say more. However, one little-known study has shown that too little fat in the diet can cause anxiety and irritability in some people. Your body needs an adequate amount of fat to remain healthy. I see increasing evidence of the wrong kind of dieting in my practice with behaviorally disturbed people. It is generally recommended that the fat in our diets should be 30 percent of our total caloric intake.

This, of course, reminds us of the growing problem on the other end of the spectrum, in that many Americans are becoming increasingly overweight and out of shape.

Spiritual health is just as crucial for balance as good diet and physical fitness. I have discovered that far too often in my own experience. We all need to make regular times for prayer, confession, reading the Scriptures, fellowship with other Christians, and church attendance.

♦ A common cause of anger is depression. This is a vicious cycle, because depressed people have increased problems in controlling their anger. If you think depression may play a part in your feelings and behavior, you need to seek help.

Children are acutely sensitive to depression in a parent. Also, parental depression can cause enumerable problems in the parent-child relationship, as well as in the child's development. Depressed behavior by the parent may cause guilt in the child, especially in a 25 percenter. This makes it hard for a parent to set and enforce limits.

WHEN YOU DO GET ANGRY, THEN WHAT?

When you are with your child and something happens that results in your feeling angry, how should you handle it? If you can stay within these three words—FIRM BUT PLEASANT—you are doing fine.

Remember, children are very aware of any anger or irritations you are feeling, and they are fearful that you will dump on them. When you are angry, they know it, and they feel profoundly relieved and grateful when you remain pleasant.

But, you are human, and sometimes you will lose it and risk dumping on your child. What do you do then? What I do in such times is to use self-talk. I tell myself something like, "You're losing it, Campbell. Don't make a fool of yourself and say something you will have to apologize for later.

Cool it!" That usually works. I might also say to myself, "If you don't want your children to be passive-aggressive and develop into irresponsible adults, you had better behave yourself."

If self-talk doesn't calm me down, I try to get away immediately. One ploy which has never failed me is to say, "I've got to go to the bathroom. I'll be back." And I go right to the bathroom. My children never followed me in, although some friends have told me that their young children have.

When I am alone, I think about the situation—how and why I got so angry and how I can handle it to make it a positive learning experience for everyone, including me. It helps to think of a funny incident from the past that involves the child I am currently dealing with. Not only does this calm me down, but it brings up pleasant feelings toward the child. What I am really doing is giving myself a time-out, just as we do for young children. Later, I confer with my wife to get her perspective. This usually helps me to handle the next encounter better.

When you get angry at a child, and in the tension of the situation have said or done something you regret, you have a great opportunity to make good come out of bad. One wonderful thing you can do is to ask your child's forgiveness. This teaches your child to forgive—not only you but himself as well. Your example of receiving forgiveness shows your child how to do this. In our world of so many miserable people who cannot forgive others or themselves, what a valuable lesson you are giving your child!

There are few genuine pearls of wisdom, but here is one I learned many years ago from a wise professor: "True intimacy comes from resolved conflict." This is just as true in the parent/child relationship as it is in marriage. This priceless pearl has removed my fear of conflict and of anger in my family relationships. It could "almost" make me look forward to conflict, because true intimacy follows in its wake.

When a conflict arises in our home, I see it as an opportunity to draw us closer together. But in order to resolve a conflict, I must first be able to handle my anger. If I can express it verbally and pleasantly and resolve the conflict, I will see our relationships grow and flourish.

WHEN MOTHER IS THE TARGET OF A CHILD'S ANGER

Let's assume that you have done your best to provide a loving and relaxed home atmosphere for your growing children. You and your spouse are growing in your marriage relationship and moving toward greater levels of acceptance and forgiveness and mutual support.

Even in such a home, perhaps especially in such a home, one childhood behavior can cause great distress to mothers. Often a child will express more anger at one parent than the other, and the mother is usually the target. I have talked with many wonderful mothers who interpret this as negative, and consider themselves "bad" mothers. This can result in guilt and depression. And yet, in most homes the child's behavior is not only normal, but indicates that the mother is doing her job beautifully.

In the majority of cases, the mother is the only person in the world with whom the child feels so loved and secure that he feels safe in expressing negative feelings. He knows that no matter how he behaves or what he says, Mother will always love him and never reject him. That is a wonderful assurance that mothers need to understand. Of course, this doesn't mean that the mother should permit inappropriate expressions of anger and do nothing about them.

What it does mean is that the child's confidence in the mother's love sets the stage for training. As long as the child is bringing his anger to his mother *verbally,* she and the father are in the position for training this child to handle his anger correctly.

If the child were unable to express anger verbally to the parents, they would have no means to train him. You see, the child's anger must come out somewhere. We want it to come out verbally, and it usually does so to the mother. That it happens this way does not mean that she is doing anything wrong or that the father is a better parent.

In single-parent homes, especially when the mother is the custodial parent, even more of the anger will be directed at her. Not only is anger drawn to her for the same reasons given above, but also because a single mother is around the child more. This is an example of passive-aggressive behavior raising its ugly head, making an already difficult situation even worse. The child is angry at the divorce but is taking it out on the mother.

When a child, and especially a teenager, is around one parent more than the other, the child will express more anger at that parent. Because the noncustodial parent spends less time with the child and is therefore less involved with discipline and other conflict situations, he will receive much less anger. This will make it appear as if the child is better behaved with this parent, usually the father. It then can be misinterpreted that the noncustodial parent is a "better parent." This makes the mother's job even more difficult. I have often seen this phenomenon used against the custodial parent in court.

It is critical for a mother who has custody to understand what we have just discussed, to maintain her courage and hope, and to prevent feelings of guilt and discouragement. She should remember that while she may seem to have an unfair disadvantage—and in some ways she does—if she will handle her own anger and her child's anger well, in the long run she will win the deepest respect and love from the child. That's a promise!

NINE

Training Your Child

As our society continues to lose its spiritual and moral direction, conscientious parents cannot leave the ethical education of their children to other people. We cannot count on a consensus of values that we once took for granted, from schools, churches, and other institutions. In saying this, I am not suggesting that there are no positive influences. But I am saying that there is alarming confusion today about basic right and wrong, in all segments of our society. As columnist Ellen Goldman writes, "At some point between Lamaze and the PTA, it becomes clear that one of your main jobs as a parent is to counter the culture."[1] This means that we parents need to assume responsibility for the total education of our children.

One of our most important responsibilities as parents is to teach our children to *think rationally*. They need to be able to evaluate and judge for themselves by the time they reach adolescence, since they then have such strong outside influences pulling them in directions that often are not good for them.

I have seen far too many dear parents in agony when they discovered the moral state of their children. Their teens had been subtly taught by those around them to rationalize their behavior. They were able to justify destructive acts such as illegal drug use, drinking, and premarital sex.

At the base of these rationalizations were two factors — passive-aggressive anger and a lack of parental training. Some parents think their children are automatically going to be able to think clearly, just because they are gathering information in school. But being filled with facts does not make one wise.

Parents need to intentionally teach their children how to think in correct and rational ways, at the same time they are teaching them how to handle their anger. This is not easy, because there are increasing numbers of sociopaths in our society and our children may meet these people anywhere — even in church.

READING TOGETHER

One of the most pleasant and valuable ways of helping your children to learn to think clearly is to read together, starting in infancy.

You will want to select stories and songs and poems that are appropriate and enjoyable for the age-level of your children, for this should be a warm, bonding time together with your children. Many stories have strong ethical and moral lessons, such as *Pinocchio* and *Peter Rabbit*. And, of course, you will want to have a Bible story book that your children can understand.

In *Honey for a Child's Heart*, Gladys Hunt provides a guide to children's classics. To help parents distinguish between a good book and one lacking significant value, she writes, "A good book has a profound kind of morality — not a cheap, sentimental sort which thrives on shallow plots and superficial heroes, but the sort of force which inspires the reader's inner life and draws out all that is noble."[2]

I also recommend *Books That Build Character* by William Kilpatrick and Gregory and Suzanne M. Wolfe, because the authors provide an extensive list of books and stories, as well as a rationale for using literature in teaching moral values.[3]

A more recent addition is William Bennett's *The Book of Virtues*, a collection of stories and other selections chosen for enjoyable family reading and also as a basis for discussions together about values and morality.[4]

As you read with your child, be alert to her reactions. When the child responds to a story, ask what she is thinking; this will enable you to enter the discussion on her interest level. For example, if you are reading about a little girl who got lost, and your child expresses concern for the girl, you have a wonderful opportunity to say how good it is that she is caring and kind.

This means of teaching children is especially critical in helping them *handle blame and criticism* — both toward themselves and toward others. Inappropriate blaming is typical in children: "It's not fair. He started it!" Here is where anger can confuse a child's thinking. It is common for children and immature adults to believe that blaming another person is justified, simply because they feel angry. This is a critical opportunity for parents to help their children think rationally.

When a child is calm and able to understand, a parent can review the situation, carefully explaining all sides of the issue. They are then teaching the child to understand the other person's point of view. Storytime may be a good setting in which to do this. Parents need to remember that it takes years to be able to handle blame and criticism well. As a child matures in this area, he will assume more responsibility for his own behavior.

Another important kind of learning through reading is to widen a child's world so that he understands life from other points of view. This means that you have the rare opportunity to teach your child empathy and sympathy — two qualities that are rare today.

Empathy is seeing and entering into a situation from another's point of view. *Sympathy* is understanding the feelings of another. It does not imply agreement with the other person, nor does it mean that we necessarily feel as they do. In learning to understand another person's situation and feelings, a child can become more fair-minded, encouraging, comforting, and compassionate.

I was proud of my six-year-old granddaughter, Cami. In her school class was an unfortunate child who was disliked and rejected by most of the children. Cami seemed to understand this girl's pain and made a special effort to be a friend to the child.

You are your child's teacher in the realm of emotions, and as you read together, you will encounter stories about love, anger, kindness, sadness, guilt, pity, and more. You can naturally identify and talk about these, encouraging your child to express his feelings and to talk about what you are reading.

Don't overlook the importance and pleasure of making up your own stories for your children. I noticed that there were times when our children loved my stories and at other times preferred stories from a book. Be sensitive to their age needs and preferences.

TALKING TOGETHER

It is crucially important that you take the time to talk with your child about difficulties he may be having. This opportunity may come when you are reading together, but it is also likely to happen in moments when you least expect it. As you talk, you hope to discover how your child responds to problems. As you assess where he is, you will be able to help him face the real world of his age-level. You want to teach your child to respond to difficulties in optimistic ways and help him to become a hopeful person.

People who tend to pessimism respond internally in totally different ways than more optimistic people. Excellent research by Morton Seligman and others have shown that there are three important differences between the two types.

Pessimists tend to consider a problem or mishappening as *permanent* — as though the effects will last forever. Second, pessimists see a problem as *pervasive* — as though it will ruin their entire lives. And third, they tend to *blame themselves* for the problem, thus causing guilt and depression.

Optimists do the opposite. They tend to consider mishaps as *temporary* and are able to slough them off and not worry about them. Second, they see problems as *localized*, affecting only a part of their lives. Because they don't dwell on the problems, they can keep their minds on positive thoughts. Third, optimists tend to *blame others* for their problems.[5]

Of course, neither response is always the correct one, and we can't use this research as a fail-safe guide. But I have found it helpful in keeping my own thinking and emotional responses on track, as well as in teaching my children.

Imagine that your daughter goes out for a sport but

doesn't make the team. She comes home in a terrible mood, sulking and behaving irritably. You want her to express her anger verbally, right? Yes, and you can expect it to be unpleasant. You keep yourself calm by knowing what to expect from her and by giving her your example of maintaining control of your anger.

If you handle your daughter well when she expresses anger, she will later want to learn from you how to cope with this and other disappointments. If she is young enough to enjoy reading stories together, you could find one in which a main character suffered disappointment. This could be used to comfort her as well as teach her how to approach similar problems. Then you could talk together about her discouragement and possible approaches to the way she is feeling. What a priceless opportunity to guide your daughter to become strong in hope. Naturally, you want to incorporate your Christian belief in the discussion as well.

As children grow older, you will want to talk more about specific feelings involved in their responses. In the situation just mentioned, you could discuss hurt, pain, disappointment, anger, discouragement, hate, or any other feeling your daughter experienced. One reason for this is to help her verbalize her feelings instead of acting them out behaviorally. The next step is to move her from unpleasantness toward pleasantness.

You will also want to use such situations to help your child handle blame. She will probably want to criticize and blame herself, if she is what I call a 25 percenter. If she is more of a 75 percenter, she will tend to blame someone or something else. It is vital for her to learn whether blame is appropriate and where it should be directed. Far too much blaming is destructive in nature. In our example, your daughter needs to learn that no blame is indicated. Trying out for a team is a risk that takes courage and you are proud of her for doing it. Trying out is an accomplishment in itself.

Even if your daughter does not respond positively to your encouragement, let me assure you that it will have a tremendous effect on her for the rest of her life. She will never forget it and will always be grateful that you cared about her so much.

BEING AVAILABLE TO YOUR CHILDREN

As children enter adolescence, they still need your guidance as much as ever. You will want to make yourself available to them, and also structure times when the normal adolescent defenses are down. This can best be done when both parent and teenager are relaxed and nonpressured. Nonpressured time is time when neither parent nor child feels the need to say or do anything. Examples of such times are when you are waiting in line together, eating in a slow restaurant, riding in a car, or watching television. At such times, teenagers feel free to relax, be themselves, and share their feelings, hopes, and thoughts with a parent.

You need patience to take advantage of such moments. You also should remember that teenagers are not miniature adults. They are children in transition and have the same basic needs as younger children do.

Of course, the primary quality all children need is unconditional love. But they also need help in *identifying and labeling their feelings*. A primary reason for this is that children often show anger when they are actually experiencing other feelings such as rejection, stress, loneliness, inadequacy, or weakness. When they are feeling bad already, the last thing they need is to have a parent's anger dumped on them. Yet, the child's display of anger could confuse a parent into taking the wrong tack. So, the sooner the child learns to tell the difference between anger and other feelings, the sooner he can express himself in more exact and pleasing ways.

Another approach which may present itself at random moments is one I call *predicting*. Since there are basic problems which provoke anger in the various stages of development, you can prepare your child to handle these situations. For example, school children need to feel that they are part of their peer group. Because of this need, they are extremely sensitive to rejection or criticism, including teasing.

During times with the child, you can use the art of predicting, especially as it applies to social interaction. You can tell your child beforehand about some positive and negative events that will likely happen to him. There are several ways to do this.

My favorite is to make up a story that includes a typical childhood encounter, in which a child is ill-treated by his peers and then learns to cope with it. Of course, I emphasize the positive, because I want the child to look forward to social interchanges, not dread them.

It is often helpful to share your own experiences. While you may not have encountered exactly the same kinds of events, you have surely had similar feelings to what your child is now dealing with, and it is the feeling content of your own experience that will communicate with him.

These natural encounters of availability enable parents to maintain a positive home atmosphere, confident that their children will learn to handle the negative interactions of life. Wise parents provide a safe and warm haven in which they train their children to cope with the harsh realities they will face.

No matter what occurs in the lives of your children, you want them to behave as people of integrity, who tell the truth, keep their promises, and assume responsibility for their own behavior. To develop this way, they need to be prepared for life as it is and can be.

Temptations to behave with less than integrity are everywhere, and rationalizations for unethical and immoral behavior are on the rise. But parents, and grandparents, are in a wonderful position to shape the lives of loved children. As we take advantage of our times alone with them, we can share who we are and what we hope and pray for them. Training a child is a long process, but one we dare not give up on.

HANDLING MISBEHAVIOR

With any child, parents have to expect some episodes that can be labeled as bad behavior. It is helpful when they know how to deal with these in the most effective ways. And so, let's look at some of the most common.

◆ Whining. How do you respond to a child's whining? It can be so irritating that you may need to fight the urge to dump your anger on the child: "Stop that whining right now or you will be punished!"

If you do this, you have lost the battle. When you dump anger on your child, you are giving him more ammunition to use against you. Also, you are letting him know that he really upsets you. Later when he wants to manipulate you by further upsetting you, he will know that whining works. The more you dump anger on the child for whining, the more likely he is to whine.

Also, the more you cast anger on your child, the more you are forcing him to oversuppress his anger and to develop anti-authority and passive-aggressive attitudes and behaviors.

It is possible to dump anger on a child not only by yelling but also by whining back. A parent who does this is unloading hostility as well as providing a poor example of how to manage anger. And, of course, the parent is ridiculing and mimicking the child.

You have several choices in how you will respond to whining and you need to select the ones which work best for you. With most children, simply ignoring the whining will suffice. If this is ineffective, you can talk to the child in a calm, cool tone, "I can't hear you when you talk in that voice. Use your nice voice so I can understand what you want."

Generally, children will respond to this approach, but not always. If they continue to whine, make doubly sure that you remain calm. If you respond emotionally and simply give up, the whining wins.

My favorite approach at such a time is to distract the child by involving him in something fun. If the whining still continues, then I leave him alone in a safe place, and tell him that I will be glad to talk further when he can use his nice voice.

Some children do seem to be natural born whiners. If you have one of these in your home, it is life-saving for you to learn the approaches mentioned above. Their whining will lessen, but the process will be slow and arduous. In extreme cases, you may consider time-outs or positive reinforcement which we will consider later.

♦ Tantrums and Violent Outbursts. Preschool children are especially prone to use temper tantrums as a way of controlling their parents. Various primitive triggers such as tiredness, thirst, hunger, heat, cold, or pain cause the tantrums. At that age, children find it hard to soothe themselves, and they need parents to help them learn to calm themselves and gain control over their behavior.

Temper tantrums are difficult for parents to deal with, especially when they happen in public. The same guidelines given for whining apply here. It is essential that parents remain calm and try to ignore the tantrum. They may need something to occupy their minds, like doing a chore around the house, particularly one that makes a loud background noise.

Usually, ignoring the tantrum without seeming upset will suffice. If the tantrum continues beyond a reasonable time, you can give the child a limit in which to regain control. At the end of this time, you should consider a punishment such as time-out, loss of privilege, or extra chores.

The parent's calmness shows the child that the parent is in firm control and will not be influenced by the tantrum. Something that helps many parents to keep themselves calm is to hum, sing, or think about pleasant memories or happy plans for the future. The singing or humming may soothe the child.

In school-age children, other factors that trigger anger are rejection and criticism by peers, insecurity in their parents' love, or judgments that seem unfair.

Deep muscle relaxation is a technique that aids children in calming down when they are angry. You need to teach this when they and you are feeling relaxed and happy so that they can then apply the technique when they are feeling tense or out of control. You teach the child to tense and then relax each body part — left foot, left leg, right foot, right leg, etc. It often works well to have the child imagine a favorite comic character doing the exercise at the same time.

As my children grew older, I selected a certain sign or word to link to relaxation. I could then use that sign or word as a signal when I saw that they were becoming upset. This helped them prevent increased anger on many occasions. The sign I used was to place my right index finger next to my nose and then suddenly move it forward. The signal I used was, "Cool it," said in a soft tone. Incidentally, if I started to get upset or tense, I would tell myself, "I think I had better cool it."

COMMUNICATION

Thomas Gordon, author of *Parent Effectiveness Training,* has long advocated the use of "I" messages rather than "you" messages. As parents use "I" messages, they are training their children to express feelings, including anger, without developing the destructive habit of blaming.[6]

For example, a teenager has forgotten to leave his muddy boots outside and walks inside the house, dirtying the floor and carpets. If a parent says, "Now look what you've done!" the statement is going to provoke anger and tension. The parent could say, "I feel upset when mud is brought into the house." That statement may seem almost too calm, but because it is said in a calmer tone than the first one, and because it lays no direct blame, it will cause less tension. And the real payoff comes when the teenager begins to use "I" messages. "I" statements go a long ways in teaching children to take responsibility for their own behavior.

Silence is a vital part of communication, and it can take many forms in the family. One of the most important uses of silence is the time spent calming down after there has been tension or anger between family members. Meg Eastman comments on this, "When you and/or your child are highly charged, trying to discuss what's wrong might make you both feel angrier and more frustrated."

Ms. Eastman also points out another value of silence, during those times when children want to contest with parents about nonnegotiable rules. Although there is really no point in discussing things that are already settled, the hardest task for most parents is to just be quiet.[7]

SETTING LIMITS

In any home, some behavior problems are going to lead to a need for further limits and, at times, punishment. When a child is out of control, being defiant, or challenging parental authority, we must use appropriate means of control.

Parents have five ways to control a child. Two are positive, two are negative, and one is neutral. They are:

Positive: Requests and Gentle Physical Manipulation.

Negative: Commands and Punishment.

Neutral: Behavior Modification.

The effectiveness of any of these is going to depend on how well we are keeping our children's emotional tanks full.

We certainly should use *requests* whenever we can,

because they are positive and can calm anger. Requests are questions, "Would you do that for me?" Requests give strong, positive, nonverbal messages, such as, "I respect you as a person. I also respect the fact that you have feelings and opinions. I expect you to take responsibility for your behavior."

I wish requests always worked, but they don't. This means that sometimes we must use *commands*. Because a command is an imperative statement and carries a negative connotation, it may elicit anger. It seems to convey, "I don't care that you have feelings or opinions about this and I am not concerned about your taking responsibility for your own behavior. I simply expect you to do what I say. In fact, I am taking responsibility for your behavior."

Gentle physical manipulation is a positive way to control a child's behavior. This works especially well with young children, as when you lead a toddler away from a hot stove or toward a kind of play that will be more acceptable.

Punishment is the second negative form of behavior control. Unfortunately, when they see misbehavior, most parents assume that punishment should be used. They are caught by what I call the "punishment trap." Parents who use punishment as the primary way of disciplining a child or teenager will provoke great amounts of needless anger in the child. They will also force the child to oversuppress anger and develop passive-aggressive attitudes and behavior. This is especially dangerous if the parents are angry when they use punishment.

Yes, we must occasionally use punishment, but we need to use it wisely and carefully. And we can avoid many problems associated with punishment by planning ahead. I recommend sitting down with your spouse or a good friend and planning the appropriate punishment for an offense. You know how obsessed children are with being "fair." The punishment must fit the crime. A child knows when a parent is being too harsh or too lenient. When the time comes that a punishment is warranted, you will already have your response ready. This kind of planning will keep your own anger from irrationally influencing your behavior, and your child will be grateful.

TIME-OUT

Every parent should be familiar with time-out. This is simply to have the child stand or sit in a specified place for a certain length of time. It can be quite effective when a child's anger is out of control. The widely accepted length of time is one minute for every year of a child's age.

If your child is calm after that time, praise him. If he remains out of control, tell him that he can discontinue the time-out when he has regained his self-control. If your child is destructive to the room or objects in it, find a place you know is childproof, with only a few of the child's toys or books. Time-outs are usually the first punishment to use for anger or rageous behavior.

LOSS OF PRIVILEGE AND RESTRICTIONS

Every child has a favorite TV program or play activity. If a time-out doesn't work, the loss of a privilege may be an effective punishment. I have seen many children who simply could not tolerate the idea of missing a TV show and who respond to this much more than to a time-out.

Restrictions are more appropriate to older children and teenagers. But if they are used too often, they may backfire on you, especially if you forget what you said or later find that the restrictions you set are unenforceable. When this happens, you greatly undermine your control of the household and lessen your children's respect for you.

You'll want to use restrictions frugally, making sure the situation is important enough to justify the penalty. If used sparingly and wisely, restrictions are extremely effective in training children.

COMPENSATION AND CHORES

If a child has caused hurt or loss to another person, you certainly need to consider having him make compensation or restitution. This should, of course, be appropriate to the child's age and ability to repay or make a sacrifice. Also, an apology is in order. Compensation is sometimes difficult to assess, and you may need to consult others to determine a fair amount.

Doing extra chores can be an effective means of reinforcing the consequences of misbehavior. If you use this method, be sure the time and number and difficulty of chores are appropriate to the child and also to the offense.

BEHAVIOR MODIFICATION

Behavior modification has its place in childrearing. However, it is a mistake to use it as a primary way to relate to a child.

Behavior modification is a system that uses *positive reinforcement*—interjecting a positive commodity into a child's environment; *negative reinforcement*—withdrawing a positive commodity from a child's environment; and *punishment*—interjecting a negative commodity into a child's environment.

An example of positive reinforcement is to reward a child's good behavior by giving him a treat. A negative reinforcement is to withhold valued privileges, such as a television program, for inappropriate behavior. An example of punishment, sometimes called aversion technique, is to pinch the child on the trapezius for inappropriate behavior.

My objection to using behavior modification as the primary way of relating to a child is that many parents substitute this for emotional nurturance. When they overuse this technique, the child does not feel sufficiently loved.

Another problem with overusing behavior modification is that the child will develop a disturbed value system, as he learns to do what is expected of him for a reward. Over time, he will develop an attitude of "What's in it for me?"

Wise parents use behavior modification sparingly. Some of the discipline techniques already discussed, such as time-outs, fall into this category. Behavior modification tends to be formal and impersonal, and should generally be used for specific, recurring behavioral problems for which the child is neither sorry nor defiant.

A situation in which this works well is when siblings fight with each other. When our boys were five and nine, they frequently fought, and our requests to stop had effect for only a few hours. Punishments also had brief effect and were unpleasant for everyone. But what did work was a reward system, a chart with stars—one star for every minute of peace, gradually increasing the time intervals until the fighting stopped. We gave each boy an appropriate reward for a certain number of stars.

One word of warning about this technique — it takes time, consistency, real effort, and patience. Don't start it unless you are prepared to stay with it. Otherwise, it will fail.

In all aspects of relationship with your children, you want to emphasize the positive whenever possible. When you do this, you will be more effective in discipline when it is necessary, and also in total training of your children, including teaching them to handle anger.

The most powerful "positive reinforcers" are the everyday, natural, nonverbal ways you give approval, such as listening attentively to a child, giving smiles, hugs, and spending time with the child. These natural ways of motivating a child are not part of the behavior modification model, and they go much further in helping you achieve the kind of family life you desire.

TEN

Innate Responses to Authority

In the chapters you've already read, you have seen some references to 75 percenters and 25 percenters. Now I want to explain what that is.

In my psychiatric practice over the past twenty-five years, I have observed that most people tend to respond to authority in one of two ways. They lean toward being either pro-authority or anti-authority. It has seemed to me that the pro-group is about 25 percent of the population and the anti-group about 75 percent. And, of course, some people lean more strongly than others.

I believe the best way to understand this distribution is by the graph, Attitudes Toward Authority, which you will find at the end of this chapter. As you can see, the pro-authority 25 percenters and the anti-authority 75 percenters are each on their own bell curve. A 25 percenter can be mild, moderate, or extreme, just as a 75 percenter can be anywhere from mildly anti-authority to extremely anti-authority. Everyone has a basic attitude toward authority which is present at birth as a personality trait. This attitude toward authority can be somewhat modified by a child's upbringing and environment, but the basic trait remains dominant.

These groupings do not connect to the many personality types so much discussed in certain circles today. An extrovert could be either pro or anti, as could an introvert. In both groups we find all kinds of people. So, please do not try to connect my groupings to intuitive, sanguine, choleric, obsessive-compulsive, or whatever labels you use.

How a person responds to almost anything in life depends on one's attitude toward authority, and that attitude depends on this personality trait.

Every child is born with a unique personality that is congenital in nature. At conception, the parents supplied the genetic traits from which the personality developed. Because personality is given, it is not a matter of better or worse, but different. The more we can understand a child's basic nature, the better we can work to enhance and enrich what that child has brought into the world.

To help you better understand the two responses to authority, I want to tell you about each of them, look at a few children who are part of the groups, and then suggest ways that you can best deal with your own children.

TWENTY-FIVE PERCENTERS

Twenty-five percenters are born with a need to be under authority. They want approval and praise. They want someone to tell them what to do and to structure their time for them. You might think that this kind of child would be very easy to raise — you just tell her what to do and she does it. Then you add the praise.

If you think this sounds too simple, you're right.

Twenty-five percenters are as difficult to raise as 75 percenters, because they must be taught to think for themselves, to stand on their own two feet, and stop depending so much on others.

Twenty-five percenters are easily controlled by guilt since they are so prone to it. Most parents of children in this group control them in exactly this way without realizing it and then take great pride in the fact that they have such wonderfully disciplined children.

Julie is the oldest of five children. She is a quiet and obedient girl whose parents, Evelyn and Richard, are controlling her by subtle guilt.

When a friend invited Julie to a swimming party, she asked her mother who replied, "Oh, I'm sorry, Julie. I had planned to meet your father for dinner downtown. I was hoping you could watch your brothers and sisters for me. Oh, well, never mind. I'll do it another time."

Although Julie knew her mother rarely got out of the house, she really wanted to go to the swimming party. However, she would have felt terrible being the one to keep her mom from some needed time away. "Go ahead, Mom. My swimsuit is faded anyway. I'd rather wait until I get a new one before I go to a swimming party. You go on and meet Daddy for dinner."

It became easier for Evelyn to ask Julie to stay with the children, because Julie never complained. In fact, she was so convincing that her mother thought she actually enjoyed it. And she did, once in a while, but many times she would have liked to be with her friends. It was guilt that kept her home.

When 25 percenters are very young, they are so easy to manage. Their parents are often overheard telling other parents, "If you would just be more firm with your child, she would be like Julie." But there is really no way to compare the two types, and many children are damaged by parents who think that all children can be raised in the same manner.

When parents control their children with guilt, they are controlling them in the worst possible way. Twenty-five percenters are so eager to please that they are easily crushed. They take everything too personally and seriously. They are also afraid that they are going to hurt someone or do something wrong. Because they can be perfectionistic, they want to do everything exactly right. A little bit of criticism can smash their egos and make them feel so guilty that they cannot develop into their own persons.

Most parents of such children don't see this. They just enjoy having a nice child who always does exactly what he is told to do and never gives anyone a hard time. What these parents fail to realize is that their children are keeping all their feelings to themselves. As perfectionists, they are very self-critical. They don't expect everything to be perfect, but they expect everything to be much better than they can make it.

Twenty-five percenters have such high expectations that each day can be a disappointment. Even if every event in a day is good but one, they will see only that one. Therefore, they are prone to depression.

Brett is a sophomore in high school. On this particular day, he made an A on a math test, an A on an English quiz, and got a book report back with yet another A. What a great day! That afternoon, he hit a home run which scored the winning point for his team.

When he got home from school, he found a note from his mom saying she would be late. That was fine with

Brett, since he was on his way to the bowling alley. He went to his closet and reached for his red bowling shirt, but it wasn't there. He discovered it in the laundry basket, with dark stains on it.

Now Brett's day was ruined. His team was bowling in a tournament and he didn't have a shirt! Everything good about his day left him.

Brett's story illustrates the way a 25 percenter thinks. He can easily become depressed over an insignificant happening, and depression causes anger. Because he wants above all to please, he keeps that anger inside, causing even deeper depression. This in turn causes more anger, which the child directs inward toward himself.

This kind of child can suffer from years of guilt manipulation, when his parents are not aware of what is happening inside of him. He has not been taught to think for himself or to express his feelings verbally. As a consequence, he is on his way toward becoming a depressed and angry adult.

The natural need of all humans to be loved and to feel self-worth is multiplied in the 25 percenter. When his parents do not realize his low self-esteem and unintentionally leave him with an empty emotional tank, he goes outside his home for need satisfaction. By the time he is a teenager, he may be involved in destructive behavior.

SEVENTY-FIVE PERCENTERS

Pat and I have two sons. Dale is our 25 percenter who was born asking, "Dad, is there anything you and Mom would like me to do for you?"

David arrived in the world with an order that could

be heard by everyone in shouting distance, "Would you people please step out of the way? I have a life to live, and I would like to get on with it with as little interference as possible!"

David was one of those "I'd rather do it myself" kids, and there was never any doubt about how he was feeling. These children want to do their own thinking and make their own decisions. They can become angry when anyone tells them what to do. They want to learn things on their own.

On the surface, 75 percenters may seem much harder to raise, but this is not really so. Even though they are born with an anti-authority attitude, they take about the same amount of patience, love, and understanding as their more compliant siblings.

The drive to think for themselves gives the 75 percenters a natural talent for leadership. And I find it easier to keep this kind of child under control than to teach the 25 percenter how to think for himself. However, this child is likely to become angry when you are trying to train and discipline him.

When our David was nearly fourteen, he announced one Sunday morning, "I'm not going to church today."

"Oh, come on, David," I replied, "you know that you have a good time, once you're there."

He gave in and went with us, and didn't say any more about it for a few weeks. And then, out of the blue he announced, "I'm not going to church today. I told you before that I didn't want to go, and I'm not going."

This time I could see that it was useless to talk with him more—he was so determined that forcing him would have created an anti-church attitude that could have been difficult to reverse. I wanted to handle this without alienating David, so that we could keep him on the road to maturity.

"Do you like Sunday School?" I asked.

"Yeah, I don't mind Sunday School."

"OK, I'll tell you what we'll do. You go to Sunday School and then your mother or I will drive you home and stay here with you during church."

David agreed to this. Knowing that he was a 75 per-center, Pat and I wanted to prevent the anger toward spiritual things which can develop when these matters are forced. David was naturally anti-authority, and so we chose for the moment not to pressure him. We didn't feel that we were being permissive; rather, that we had a plan. David knew how we believed and was just testing us.

After this arrangement went on for four or five weeks, I could tell that it was getting old for David. And he knew that Pat and I were suffering because of it. We wanted to be in church together. Finally he said, "Oh, all right, I'll go to church for your sakes." And that was that.

Now, I can't promise this strategy will work for all 75 percenters. It depends a great deal on the kind of overall relationship you have with your child. The key to handling this type of child is to keep things positive and not become too authoritarian, particularly in relationship to spiritual matters. The statistics are a bit hazy on the number of children raised in the church who leave when they are grown. However, whatever the actual numbers, they aren't good, as we can all attest from cases we have observed in our own churches and communities.

PASSIVE AGGRESSION AND 25/75

In chapter 6, we talked about the one "normal" period of passive aggression we will encounter with our children, the early teen stage. Remember that passive-aggressive behavior goes for the jugular. In most homes, one of the top priorities is for the children to do well in school. Therefore, this is one of the main areas in which passive aggression shows itself. Whatever is most important to the parents is where it will crop up.

When 75 percenters begin to do poorly in school, it is well for the parents not to make a big deal out of it. The bigger the issue, the more the child is going to continue the behavior. After all, as long as the parents and teachers are taking responsibility for the grades, why should the teenager? Our older son, David, was an extreme 75 percenter whose grades dropped dramatically in eighth and ninth grade. But, as I related in an earlier chapter, he was able to right the situation himself when he realized he wouldn't make it into a competitive college unless he changed his ways.

Dale, our 25 percenter, never wavered in his approach to schoolwork. He wanted to please and continued to make excellent grades all through high school.

Thirteen- to fifteen-year-olds are unconsciously and sometimes consciously against almost everything. This is especially true of the 75 percenters who are angry most of the time. What we need to do is to keep the anger coming out of their mouths instead of allowing it to stay inside.

This is very difficult for parents, because their natural inclination is to quiet their teenagers, suppress their anger, and keep peace in the house. But sometimes I have to ask the parents I counsel, "Would you rather have a son yelling at you or a son overdosed on drugs? Would you rather have daughter harping and screaming or a pregnant daughter?"

Of course, the answer is "Neither," but this is seldom possible. How many times I have observed wonderful parents in agony when they have discovered that their well-behaved and polite teenager is pregnant, on drugs, or having some other devastating problem. Please remember that unpleasant verbalization of anger is only temporary if we do our jobs in training our children in managing their anger. Some of my most wonderful experiences were in seeing my children make progress in expressing their anger verbally and pleasantly.

I always tell parents to remove the pressure from their younger teens by allowing them to verbalize their anger, and then to respond to them in a mature way. This is *not* being overly permissive as long as we are handling our children's anger appropriately and leading them up the Anger Ladder. Suppressing anger is something like depressing an inflated balloon with a bulge in it. If you push the bulge in, it is going to come out somewhere else. If you try to keep your children from expressing anger, you can be sure it will pop out in another area of their lives.

In passive-aggressive behavior, a teenager gets rid of anger by upsetting his parents. So whatever upsets parents most is what the kid goes for. What would upset Christian parents the most? Rebellion against spirituality, of course. So, where is the kid's behavior going to be targeted? Against the church and devotional practices. But this is no guarantee that other family priorities will escape notice. Parents will probably have to deal with rebellion against their top two or three values.

DENISE AND BILL

Many families are likely to have both a 25 percenter and a 75 percenter, and this can present a challenge. The siblings may experience real tension in getting along with each other and the parents may tend to favor one over the other, in their lack of understanding of what motivates the children.

Tall and slender Denise was a nursing student who came to talk with me. For a while she sat fidgeting and wearing a depressed expression on her face, as she tried to decide what to say. Then she suddenly blurted out, "I'm anorexic, Dr. Campbell. I attended a lecture on anorexia and it made me realize that I am anorexic and bulemic."

Denise began to cry. "I don't want to tell my parents, because they don't think I've done much of anything right in my life as it is. Now they'll be sure to hate me."

I looked into her tear-filled brown eyes. "What are you doing that makes you think you are anorexic, Denise?"

"Well, I starve myself for as long as I can stand it. Then I eat everything in sight, take a laxative, and purge."

"How long have you been doing this?"

"About four months."

I was glad that Denise had recognized her problem early enough that she had not yet reached the point of physical damage. I felt there was a good chance of helping her through this. What we needed to discover was why she felt so negative about herself.

As I began to counsel Denise, her problem unfolded. Her older brother, Bill, was outgoing and aggressive. Denise was the quiet one. Seventy-five and 25.

"Ever since I can remember, Bill had Mom and Dad's attention about something. When he was seven, he developed a life-threatening illness. I stayed with my grandparents while he was in the hospital. I was very lonesome, but hated to bother Mom and Dad because they were upset about Bill.

"When he came home from the hospital, he had to stay in bed for a month. I did everything I could to make him happy. I was glad we were all home together, but Mom hardly noticed me. I don't remember feeling that she should notice me, but now I realize how much I missed her attention.

"When Bill and I were ten and eight, Mom and Dad built a new house and we lived through some very hectic months. I remember that Bill and I fought and then were punished by our father. On one of these occasions, Bill took off, but I went back in the house to finish a job Mom had asked me to do."

Denise told me that she almost always gave in — not just to her brother and parents, but to anyone who crossed her. However, when she entered high school, she began to change.

"I still tried to keep peace at home, but I was a real character at school. In my junior year, I dated a boy who didn't amount to anything. He was just plain trouble. When my folks found out I was seeing him, they lectured me for two weeks. I never went out with him again.

"I always felt guilty if I did something that displeased my parents, and thought I was probably the worst person in the world."

In her second year of college, Denise's grades went from respectable to failing, because she skipped so many classes. She kept her grades from her parents for a while, until her mother made a surprise visit to campus and Denise had to tell her the truth. Her parents moved her home and informed her that she would have to get a job and pay them back for the money she had wasted on education, or lack thereof.

"I held two or three different jobs, finally succeeding in paying back the money, but feeling worse and worse about myself. I had no particular direction, and never completed anything I started.

"All this time, Mom was directing my life. Since I didn't think she had done such a great job with her own life, I resented her interference in mine. But I couldn't afford to move and so had to put up with her interference. When I told her that I was going to finish my education, she seemed pleased and offered to loan me the money but I refused. I knew I would have to do something on my own soon, or I never would. So I borrowed the money and moved out of my parents' home and started back to school.

"I fell into the same trap of trying to settle everyone's arguments. I felt I was always there for other people, but they never seemed to be there for me. As time for graduation drew near, I panicked. I had never completed anything of importance and was afraid I wouldn't finish this either.

"I had always been slightly overweight, or so I thought, and so I started on a diet about the same time I panicked about graduation. When I discovered I could lose weight easily, I felt I was doing something right at last. But the weight loss became an obsession."

After several weeks of intensive counseling, Denise began to understand that she was a 25 percenter. She also came to realize that her parents had not interacted with her in ways that would meet her needs. They had always loved her, and didn't know that her quiet ways were deceiving. Because she didn't demand extra attention, she didn't get any. Her parents just assumed that her emotional tank was full, and they tended instead to the obvious demands of Bill, a classic 75 percenter.

Fortunately, Denise's story has a happy ending. She graduated third in her class and is now working in a large hospital. She and her parents have a real relationship at last, based on love and understanding. Her parents now realize that she needs attention from them, even if she is quiet.

Do you see how easy it was for Denise's parents to control her? She wanted approval and praise, and tried to be the perfect little girl. But this finally became more than she could handle. Her lack of emotional fulfillment resulted in anger and frustration which turned inward and then manifested itself as anorexia and bulimia.

And what about Denise's spirituality? As an adolescent, she attended church and made a profession of faith. She became the exemplary teenager — until her junior year of high school when she rejected her spiritual training, considering it "baby stuff." However, she continued to attend church because she wanted her parents' approval.

Denise did, however, continue to feel a deep need for God. She was gradually drawn to prayer and Bible reading on her own, but avoided church activities. Like most 25 percenters, she did not believe her thoughts and decisions were as important as those of more assertive persons. As she came to understand that her intelligence, thought processes, and decision-making were as effective and legitimate as those of other people, she gradually learned to depend on herself and her own opinions with confidence. She was then more secure in groups, including the church.

We need to be very careful that we provide the nurture our 25 percenters need, in spirit and emotion, body and mind. Because they, like Denise, are not demanding, and because their siblings may be like Bill, always demanding the attention of parents, it is easy to have a family life that is very out of balance. We want all of our children to grow into strong and healthy and responsible adults.

BACK TO OUR 75 PERCENTERS

Our 75 percenters differ from their more cautious siblings in another important way. They tend to be more global and general in their thinking, while the 25 percenters are more focused on specific detail. This means that the two types reach conclusions in different ways.

I am a 25 percenter and my older son, David, is a 75 percenter. He and I perceive situations in our own ways and have had to learn to appreciate the perspective of the other. Often I have come to the conclusion that he has the better way of handling problems than I do.

When David was twenty years old, he and I decided to go scuba diving in another country. On our arrival, we found that our baggage was missing. I didn't think too much about it until we realized that it was in plain sight in an airport official's office. When we brought this to the attention of the authorities, they initially denied that it was our luggage. When we insisted that it was indeed ours, they said they had no key for that office. David and I waited several hours while they "looked for" the key. As they continued to ignore our inquiries, my anger mushroomed until I was ready to explode. Complicating the whole thing for me was that their attitudes were all too reminiscent of some prejudicial ways I had been treated as a child.

David knows me pretty well, and he could see that I was about to verbally attack the officials and possibly get myself in trouble — or at least give them another excuse to hold our luggage. The training I had given David in handling anger came to fruition as he took over and said, "Dad, you are too upset. Sit down and I'll handle this." I gladly sat down and kept my mouth shut while David kept his cool, handled it beautifully, and got our luggage back.

As a 25 percenter, I focused too much on one detail—the way we were being treated—and I overreacted to that. David, on the other hand, saw the whole picture and could keep his perspective. We were in a foreign land where the customs differed from ours. He also maintained that this was simply an inconvenience and did not need to interfere with the wonderful trip we had planned.

In this case, the basic 75-percenter tendencies prevailed. But, in other situations, 25-percenter traits work out best. How fortunate for the person who has learned how and when to use his strengths and when to let other people take over.

Seventy-five percenters do not always feel high respect for 25 percenters. Because the latter are more sensitive, feel deeply, and are more easily hurt, the 75 percenters usually consider them as weak, fragile, and easily intimidated. However, they tend to be less sensitive and also less prone to empathy and understanding of another's view. It is easy for a 75 percenter to become calloused, uncaring, selfish—and even a sociopath.

As parents of this type of children, we must not only keep their emotional tanks full so that they understand love and care, but also teach them empathy and sympathy. And, of course, we need to train them to handle their anger in a mature fashion. A strong 75 percenter who is not well loved, who has never learned to understand and respect others, and who has become even more anti-authority with passive-aggressive behavior, will most likely develop a sociopathic personality.

Because these children are less sensitive and tend to blame other people, they may have difficulty in experiencing guilt. And a certain amount of guilt is necessary for the development of a normal conscience.

As parents we want to be sure that we don't weaken the guilt they may feel. The most effective way to wipe away guilt is through punishment. When a child feels genuinely guilty about misbehaving, punishment and especially corporal punishment will wipe it away as clean as a slate. This is one of the reasons that punishment must be used wisely and sparingly. Punishment should *never* be used when a child feels genuinely sorry for misbehavior. If it is, it will prevent the child from developing a normal conscience, and nothing is more prevalent today than lack of conscience. One main cause is overuse of punishment when there has been too little unconditional love. The result of this punishment trap is an increasing number of sociopaths.

But our 75 percenters are our natural leaders. We need for them to care about their fellow citizens with understanding and good conscience.

We parents are in a wonderful position to truly leave this world a better place than we found it. A well-equipped 75 percenter is a rare delight. That is, a caring, unselfish 75 percenter of good conscience who has developed into a leader motivated for the common good and not just his own glory. What a worthwhile goal for us as parents to help these children grow into true leaders.

ATTITUDES TOWARD AUTHORITY

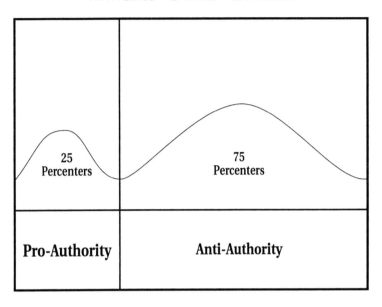

25
Percenters

75
Percenters

Pro-Authority

Anti-Authority

ELEVEN

Christians and Anger

As Christians, we experience the same kinds of stress and pain that non-Christians do. We share with them similar losses and privations, as well as some personal fears and memories we wish could be different.

As believers in Jesus Christ, we know that we are supposed to be different in some respects, and we hope that we are different in our responses and intentions. And sometimes, we are even tempted to believe that the "all things made new" is actually finished, inside and outside of us. But we frequently have to admit that we are very much still in process, and that the promise of completion isn't until the "Day of Jesus Christ."

Those of us who have been Christians for many years should be able to avoid many anger-producing behaviors. We have the words of Holy Scripture and support from the church, and we know in most situations how God wants us to behave.

However, within the Christian community, we find certain aspects of life and belief that actually intensify anger, and then lead people to suppress rather than deal with it.

In this chapter, we are going to look at the place where Christians come together — the church — and at two evils which directly threaten the well-being and ministry of both clergy and lay people as they seek to serve God—passive-aggressive anger and sociopathic attitudes and behaviors.

RESPONSES TO AUTHORITY

You'll remember that in chapter 10 we talked about 25 and 75 percenters and how they differ in their responses to authority. From my observation, I believe about three fourths of the population is innately anti-authority in orientation, although not necessarily in behavior. However, we don't find that kind of mix everywhere we go. An extreme example of imbalance is a prison, where we would find a higher percentage of anti-authority individuals.

Because 25 percenters are already such a minority, it seems unlikely that they would be a majority in very many places. However, this is just the situation we find far too often in a place where it ought not to be—the church.

Twenty-five percenters, as you will remember, are wonderful people. But they want and need to be under authority, and many of them have not learned sufficiently to think for themselves. While at first glance this need to be under authority might seem to be desirable, it does not work to the advantage of the local church or the kingdom of God. Nor does it reflect biblical teachings. Christ's words about being under authority are not just for those who have a need to be so, but for all people, including those who have had to learn through difficult experience that they too must be under authority.

Seventy-five percenters who have reached a significant level of Christian maturity are desperately needed by the church. We need them in the pews, for they bring a healthy—and biblical—skepticism to church with them. If they have learned how to deal with their own anti-authority attitudes and anger, and if they are reaching for Christian maturity, they are the very ones who can maintain a stable balance in the church in times of stress or disagreement. They are the ones who can prevent power-hungry people from taking control and advantage of the congregation. Mature 75 percenters can provide the sensible leadership so needed in our congregations.

We see these people using their talents in the business and professional world, as well as in government. So why are they so conspicuously absent from the church? And why are some Christians who regularly attend church not using their gifts in ministry?

There is no single answer to these questions. However, we do know that some people are repelled by the attitudes they hear expressed from certain church leaders, and we also know that certain groups of Christians are discouraged or prevented from using their real abilities. One such group that is excluded from meaningful service in many churches is women. While I don't wish to discuss ordination, I know that there are hundreds of creative ways women can serve God in and through the church, that do not require ordination or licensing. And yet, in far too many places, women have been relegated to the kitchen and the nursery. Of course, I believe that teaching young children is one of the most important responsibilities of the church, one that should be given only to the most qualified and Christlike members. But then, my opinion is not shared by most church leaders.

When a church does not have a natural balance of people and is lacking those who could offer gifted leadership, it is prone to more anger rather than less, because it becomes mired in situations that no one can solve and in feelings that are not resolved. Also, when people are not allowed to use their God-given abilities, they tend to feel resentful at the organization that talks about gifts and then prevents their use.

CONFUSION ABOUT ANGER

Even though we see multiple examples of anger in the Bible, and though there is no suggestion there that people will not get angry, many Christian people seem to interpret the Bible that way. And they do have reasons for this, verses such as Psalm 37:8 which says, "Refrain from anger and turn from wrath."

Most Christians I have known believe that anger is sinful. When they experience normal anger, two things happen. First, they think that they are displeasing God and so they feel guilty. This guilt lowers their self-esteem, causing them to feel unworthy. Many Christians are prone to some depression, because of specific personality traits. Over time, this depression can deepen and be the cause of more anger.

This increasing degree of anger results in the second consequence — the oversuppression of anger. As these people suppress more and more anger, their subconscious minds must find a way to deal with it and find an outlet. The most common outlet is passive-aggressive attitudes and behavior. As we have already seen, passive-aggressive behavior targets people in authority, who often have nothing to do with the actual cause of the anger.

So, here we are in church with people who have

denied their anger and then stuffed it until it has festered into passive-aggressive attitudes against authority. Who is the likely target when this subconscious anger begins to express itself? You're right—the pastor.

PASTORS AT RISK

The ministry has become one of the most stressful of all occupations. Because we live in such an anti-authority society, Christians also have picked up these attitudes and behaviors. One unique way of expressing them is the manner in which we relate to our pastors. They are highly visible authority figures and, as such, are natural targets for passive-aggressive manifestations of anger.

This problem does not diminish over time, because the longer passive-aggressive people know a pastor, the worse will be their attitude and behavior. In such a situation, no matter what the pastor does or doesn't do, he can't escape the increasing, underlying resentment, resistance, and attacks from those to whom he is trying to minister.

I have counseled with many ministers who have been crushed by this phenomenon. And parishioners who may have no part in the angry behaviors tend not to assume responsibility for this tragedy, but rationalize the behaviors of their angry co-members.

John Keaton was the pastor of a church my family and I attended years ago. He was a genuinely good person who had been at the church for seventeen years, and we had come to know him and his family intimately. He was a totally unselfish man, one of the most nonmaterialistic people I have ever met. He had pastored his flock through the ups and downs, joys and sorrows of all those years.

It still seems hard to believe that a prominent member of the congregation, Charles, tormented John for all those years. Charles was well known in the community because he was likable and had a winning way with people. Also, his opinion carried some weight in Christian circles.

I would have thought that Charles would be satisfied with his sphere of influence. And yet, almost daily he criticized John, calling him "liberal," claiming that he did not "preach the Word," and that we should "get rid of him." During all those years, John never retaliated.

Unfortunately, a family with similar opinions joined our church. The husband, Mike, was as vocal as Charles in his condemnation, but he went a step further. When he was elected to the church board, he took advantage of his office, talking to other board members about his discontent with John.

Finally, Mike made a proposal to church members with whom he felt he had influence, that the congregation dismiss John at the next business meeting. Of course, Mike didn't inform families who might be loyal to the pastor, as we were. Fortunately, enough of us who understood the situation were able to clarify the issue at the meeting and convince the thinking people of the church that such a move would destroy the church as well as end an outstanding ministry.

John weathered the crisis in a gracious manner and remained at the church for another three years before accepting a call to a church in a different city. I thank God that he was able to withstand the trials of passive-aggressive attitudes and to survive. He is still in the ministry today.

Thousands of clergy are not enduring as well as John did. In their book *Pastors at Risk,* H.B. London, Jr. and Neil B. Wiseman report the results of a 1991 Survey of Pastors done by the Fuller Institute of Church Growth. The statistics are sobering:

90 percent of pastors work more than 46 hours a week
80 percent believed that pastoral ministry affected their families negatively
33 percent said that being in ministry was an outright hazard to their family
75 percent reported a significant stress-related crisis at least once in their ministry
50 percent felt unable to meet the needs of the job
90 percent felt they were inadequately trained to cope with ministry demands
70 percent say they have a lower self-esteem now than when they started out
40 percent reported a serious conflict with a parishioner at least once a month
37 percent confessed having been involved in inappropriate sexual behavior with someone in the church
70 percent do not have someone they consider a close friend.[1]

The surveys indicated that 40 percent of the pastors had contemplated leaving the ministry in the previous three months. They felt caught in a swirl of an increasingly complex kind of work that places more emphasis on numbers and administration than on spiritual values.

Contemporary spiritual leaders are under a twofold assault—one within and one without.

On the inside of the church, many believers have succumbed to the snares of secularism. Pastors deal daily with diluted dedication, family disintegration, superficial commitments, and an accepted churchly consumerism no longer interested in sacrifice, suffering, or servanthood. Well-worn, friendly old words are still used, but the new meanings refer to a Jesus who provides comfortable happiness and makes no demand on conduct or money. Without our realizing it, the enemy has secularized the church without a shot being fired by anyone.

Outside the church, pastors face a new dark age where the masses have no Christian memory, success is king, and faith issues are far down the average person's priority list after the PTA meeting, latest video release, Little League game, or weekend diversion. The secular masses simply do not see the point. Even though they are sometimes magnanimous toward pastors, they really think ministers are wasting their lives for an absurd cause.[2]

One unique reason that pastors are touched by the anger of parishioners is that some members are extraordinarily "conscientious." Does that sound strange? We need to remember that personality traits may be positive in some situations and negative in others. Conscientiousness is usually positive. But, if it is misguided, it can be destructive.

Conscientiousness becomes misguided when it is contaminated with ambitiousness or anti-authority attitudes and behavior. When this happens a parishioner can misuse his desire to serve God by placing himself above the authority figure, the pastor, and undermining the ministries of the pastor and the church. Because this is increasingly common today, we need mature, clear-thinking Christians who can keep the basic ministries of the church free from the interference of "overly conscientious" (passive-aggressive) Christians.

Do you remember when the disciples James and John came to Jesus to ask for a special favor? When He inquired what they wanted Him to do, they replied:

"Let one of us sit at Your right and the other at Your left in Your glory."

"You don't know what you are asking," Jesus said. "Can you drink the cup I drink or be baptized with the baptism I am baptized with?"

"We can," they answered.

Jesus said to them, "You will drink the cup I drink and be baptized with the baptism I am baptized with, but to sit at My right or left is not for Me to grant. These places belong to those for whom they have been prepared."

When the ten heard about this, they became indignant with James and John. Jesus called them together and said, "You know that those who are regarded as rulers of the Gentiles lord it over them, and their high officials exercise authority over them. Not so with you. Instead, whoever wants to become great among you must be your servant, and whoever wants to be first must be slave of all. For even the Son of Man did not come to be served, but to serve, and to give His life as a ransom for many" (Mark 10:37-45).

Isn't that classic? James and John, the Sons of Thunder, or anger, were so "conscientious" that they wanted to be more "spiritual" than the other disciples. That is exactly what Charles and Mike did. In trying to be "conscientious Christians," they wanted to be more "spiritual" by placing themselves above the pastor.

Tragically, pastors who genuinely attempt to *minister* are the most susceptible to poor treatment from their parishioners. Why? Because it is easy to criticize and take advantage of pastors who are sensitive, caring, and unpretentious.

This is not the type we see on television or hear on the radio, and it takes little talent to compare our own pastors with the public preachers who have "magnetic" personalities. Also, we know our pastors and their families all too well—including their blemishes. As Christ said, "Only in his hometown . . . is a prophet without honor" (Mark 6:4).

SOCIOPATHS IN THE SHEEPFOLD

The unavoidable comparison between our pastors and public ministers does not mean that the more public ones are all striving for their own self-exaltation. But some are.

The mass-media religious phenomenon has undermined the church and provided platforms for people I call sociopaths because of their behavior. A sociopath has a natural ability to win the respect, love, and obedience of certain types of people, especially 25 percenters, who tend to avoid thinking for themselves. They are subconsciously looking for a strong and dynamic person to follow, to do their thinking, make their decisions, and to be their leader. Then they can please the leader, and win the praise and approval they crave.

Sociopaths are difficult to describe with precision. It is easier to point to extreme examples that we can all identify. But to do so might be more confusing, especially since I am not that concerned about the extreme sociopath. Many of us who study current happenings in the church are deeply concerned about the more subtle sociopaths. By subtle I mean that on the surface their sociopathic traits are difficult to recognize.

Sociopaths know what is right, but they don't really care. They lack conscience and experience little or no remorse, anxiety, or guilt. The more extreme the sociopathy, the more these persons will actually believe that the wrong they are doing is all right. This is particularly subtle when the underlying purposes of their behavior are wrong, but their behavior seems good *for a time,* before it eventually falls to truth.

The most dangerous sociopath is able not only to behave appropriately, but also to isolate his hearers from sources of information which disagree with what he says publicly. He makes sure that only his "teachings" are heard by Christians. He sets himself up as the "authority" and does not encourage his followers to think for themselves or to test knowledge to see if it is true. He assumes that anyone who disagrees with him must be wrong—even ungodly.

Distortion of truth is becoming increasingly widespread in the body of Christ today. Controlling the knowledge that Christians are exposed to enables the sociopath to mix truth and untruth as he sees fit. He can then manipulate trusting Christians to his own purposes.

Sociopaths strive for money, power, and sometimes sex, usually in that order. The most brilliant ones operate so that they never get caught doing anything wrong. The less brilliant may end up in jail or in disgrace.

Until mass media made religion so lucrative for the entrepreneur, few true sociopaths were drawn into the church or parachurch organizations. But now that a winsome, charming, and manipulative person is able to use the body of Christ for power and wealth, the domination of sociopathy is growing.

Sociopaths may look good on the outside, but their underlying purpose is to use people for their own ends. Among mental health professionals, the sardonic definition of a sociopath is someone whom everybody likes, who gets you to lend him $100, and then makes you feel grateful for the privilege. Does that remind you of anyone? Jesus asked some of those who followed Him:

> Why do you call Me, "Lord, Lord," and do not do what I say? I will show you what he is like who comes to Me and hears My words and puts them into practice. He is like a man building a house, who dug down deep and laid the foundation on rock. When a flood came, the torrent struck

that house but could not shake it, because it was well built. But the one who hears My words and does not put them into practice is like a man who built a house on the ground without a foundation. The moment the torrent struck that house, it collapsed and its destruction was complete (Luke 6:46-49).

I wonder if Jesus was talking about sociopaths. The most troubling aspect of typical sociopaths is that they cannot discern any wrong in what they are doing. They are totally convinced, usually through rationalization, that they are right. They are then able to convince many others that they have a corner on truth. There is certainly nothing wrong with contributing to the pool of knowledge and discerning what is biblically true and what is not. But when these people proclaim that they are the primary bearers of truth, they present a danger for those who follow them and also for the church. Ministries built on sociopathic motivations, especially the acquisition of power, are indeed houses without foundation. Why do they call Christ "Lord" when the foundation on which they build is their own elevation? Yet, some are so cunning, and some Christians so naive, that the leaders are back controlling people even after they have been exposed.

TELLING THE SHEPHERD
FROM THE HIRELING

How can we tell whether a pastor or leader of an organization is a sociopath or a true servant? Many times it is impossible to know for certain, and we should be very cautious in our following and in our condemning. It is usually impossible to understand a person's true character until we have known that person well for at least two years. And it is certain that we cannot know someone simply from a television or radio presentation, or a sermon or two from the pulpit.

Several biblical stories and passages offer us guidance in evaluating those who seek places of leadership. Consider the story of Absalom in the Old Testament as well as the question of James and John. Or, Paul's defense of his own ministry over against others of whom he said, "Such men are false apostles, deceitful workmen, masquerading as apostles of Christ. And no wonder, for Satan himself masquerades as an angel of light. It is not surprising, then, if his servants masquerade as servants of righteousness. Their end will be what their actions deserve" (2 Cor. 11:13-15).

In the Book of Proverbs, we read, "Do not exalt yourself in the king's presence, and do not claim a place among great men; it is better for him to say to you, 'Come up here,' than for him to humiliate you before a nobleman. . . . It is not . . . honorable to seek one's own honor" (25:6-7, 27).

And in Matthew we find the words of Jesus, "For whoever exalts himself will be humbled, and whoever humbles himself will be exalted" (23:12).

One thing is certain: we all need to be very careful of sociopathic persons. Because of poor parenting, as well as the rise in media possibilities, their numbers are increasing. Initially, they may come across as good folks, but as they gain an upper hand, they use people for their own exaltation.

While the tendency toward this evil is as old as mankind, and while we may meet it in any avenue of life, it has gained undue influence in the religious world, as spiritual authority has shifted away from the local congregation to organizations that come to us through the mass media. Many of these "popular" spokespersons are disseminating information that is false, but overlaid with some truth. It is very difficult to distinguish what part is truth and what part is falsehood, and even more difficult to question or confront the person who is speaking.

WHAT IS OUR CHALLENGE?

In a book about children and anger, this chapter might seem a digression from the main point. And yet, I don't think so, since you and your family probably attend a church that has experienced some of the problems we have mentioned, and also because you know the abuses of religion on the wider scale. God's greatest concern is about our character and that should be our concern also, our own character and that of our children, as well as the character of those who influence our families, especially in the church. A great part of character is integrity, and you'll remember that integrity includes telling the truth, keeping promises, and taking responsibility for personal behavior. This standard is for everyone, even "celebrities" and "experts."

We have discussed two destructive forces at work today, passive-aggressive anger which is undermining the ministries of so many local churches, and the sociopathic attitudes and behaviors which increasingly dominate the larger church scene. Both of these evils are the result of poor parenting: passive aggression from the failure to teach children to manage anger in a mature way, and sociopathy from the failure to provide children with adequate nurture and guidance.

To say this is not to condemn parents; they cannot

do the job of parenting alone. Parents need understanding about how to raise their children to be people of integrity who can become mature adults. Most parents don't have enough information and understanding about what their children need.

One reason that I included this difficult and risky chapter is to help parents recognize the dynamics of interaction that may be occurring in a place as important to them and their children as the church. As parents, we want to provide a positive and godly church experience for our children, one that will draw them closer to God and to the kind of life God wants them to live. We want them to become nurturing people who will want to serve more than be served.

WHAT ABOUT THE FUTURE?

Some pages back, we left our 75 percenters and now we want to go back to them, because we need them. Remember, they are indirectly anti-authority, which means that they do not need to be under authority to feel good about themselves. They don't need approval and praise from an authority figure.

These young people are the leaders of the future, and yet they face pitfalls as they are growing up. Those who are strongly influenced by our society, and who also fail to develop mature ways to manage their anger, will become passive aggressive. If they continue to resist authority, they will probably leave the church.

And yet, they *can* develop strong leadership abilities, and also be able to hold their own in conflicts. A clear-thinking 75 percenter of sound Christian character, who handles anger well and who is able to differentiate a genuinely caring ministry from a sociopathic one, is a rare bird indeed. We desperately need this type of person in the church today.

And for all our children, we hope and pray that they will become clear-minded thinkers who are able to make sound decisions and to handle their anger maturely. We want our children to be able to discern between legitimate, accountable, spiritual authority, and that bogus authority which seeks its own gratification without being accountable to anyone. Only then will the church be the haven of hope, rest, renewal, and worship, and have the spiritual influence Christ intends for it to have in society.

I pray that every child will have a church home that is a warm and positive place in which to thrive and grow in the knowledge of God.

TWELVE

Children with Special Problems

With a small percentage of children, nothing seems to work. Parents and teachers can do everything right and still end up with "problem children" on their hands. In recent decades, we have discovered much more about certain kinds of disabilities that can severely handicap children and cause chaos in the home and classroom. As we meet James, Matt, and Rick, you may be reminded of some children you know.

JAMES

James was a happy little boy. From the time he was born through his seventh year, he didn't seem to have any unusual problems. He walked when he was supposed to, and talked at the right time. He was easy to potty train. To all appearances, he was an average child.

What no one realized was that he was memorizing everything just to get through each school day. James' mother, Emily, is a very perceptive person who knew something was wrong, but she couldn't find anyone who could tell her what it was. Everybody just said, "Boys will be boys."

Toward the end of second grade, James became more difficult to manage. He often accused Emily of not really loving him, and he argued with her constantly. She never felt she was communicating with him in a comfortable, maternal way.

In third grade, James began having academic problems, as the subject matter grew more abstract. He was still trying to memorize everything, but he just couldn't any more, and his grades started to slip. In desperation, he put more and more energy into his lessons, since he really wanted to do well. And, for about a month, he did, until he became so exhausted with the high energy output that he couldn't keep it up any longer. Then his grades went down again and he panicked and also became depressed.

As James' concentration power waned, he had trouble remembering simple tasks. He also became a behavior problem at school and at home. He even started having little quirky body movements, but these were well enough hidden in an active child that no one recognized what they were. He told Emily that he wanted to let his hair grow longer. His reason for this was that he could flip his hair away from his eyes and conceal the nervous movements. Also, he started shuffling his feet, making clicking noises with his heels. As you might guess, James barely made it through the third grade.

As fourth grade began, he had even more trouble keeping up, and his behavior worsened — he was more defiant and harder to manage. When he started having temper tantrums, his parents brought him to see me.

After evaluating James, we realized that he was a depressed child with very low self-esteem. He unconsciously felt that no one cared about him. Also, he was filled with pent-up anger, especially toward authority figures. Passive aggression was exhibiting itself in misbehavior toward the primary authority in his life—his parents, and also toward his teachers.

We discovered three reasons why James was having such trouble in school. First, he had *perceptual problems.* The information coming into his mind was processed in a distorted fashion, and this made the material seem confusing to him. Second, he was *depressed*, and depression can intensify or create a learning problem because concentration is more difficult. Third, he was behaving *passively-aggressively*, getting back at authority by purposely, but unconsciously, making poor grades. However, he was not aware that this was his purpose.

By the time I saw him, James was doing poorly in every part of his life. His learning difficulties had developed into a total life problem. Also, his anti-authority attitude was out of hand. Even at his young age, he was against everything his parents stood for, including spirituality. He hated church and Sunday School, and was a constant disruption in his class.

We began treating James for depression and counseled his parents to deal with his anger by encouraging him to get it out from inside where it was destroying him. After taking these steps, we sought the academic help he needed.

After several months of therapy, James was much improved, and was able to be an affectionate child to his parents, receiving the love they so much wanted to give to him. Displays of affection were pleasant to him now, and he could really believe that his parents meant what they said and did, because he was beginning to develop a positive self-image.

We involved an educational therapist in James' treatment to deal with the passive-aggressive, anti-learning attitude that had grown inside of him. She first worked to create a personal relationship with James. Then, she built on this bond to develop a more positive attitude toward school. She also enrolled him in the special education programs he needed, and helped his teachers understand how to make James feel good about himself and about learning.

As his anger subsided and his depression lifted, James became less passive-aggressive and anti-authority. For the first time, he was receptive to spiritual teaching.

James is fortunate to have such a perceptive mother who wouldn't take a "Boys will be boys" answer to his problems. Both Emily and her husband have made a sincere effort to work with me and the educational therapist to give James a better chance in life. With patience and time, and by example in their home, they will be able to help him develop into a well-rounded adult who will want to follow their spiritual values.

CHILDREN WITH PERCEPTUAL HANDICAPS

In addition to coping with most of the same problems other children have, youngsters with perceptual handicaps must also deal with their own particular difficulties.

Because life is increasingly hard for them, they tend to be anti-authority in every way. As they grow older, they are prone to wrongdoing, even criminal acts. A recent study shows that adolescent males with diagnosed perceptual handicaps are more likely to be involved in juvenile delinquency. In fact, the odds of being judged delinquent are 220 percent greater for them than for their nonhandicapped peers!

Children with perceptual problems are usually depressed, and depression is the one thing we desperately want to avoid in all children and teenagers. The more depressed a child is, the more angry he becomes. Depression produces anger and angry children are much more likely to be passive-aggressive.

When we take an already depressed, passive-aggressive, handicapped child, and superimpose the "normal" depression and passive-aggressive behavior of adolescence, we have a kid who is profoundly depressed and profoundly passive-aggressive.

Long before we can teach values to this child, we have to help him through his anger and depression. We need to let him know that we love him unconditionally and are trying to understand his particular problem. Only then are we on the road to involving him in genuine relationships, including the ultimate relationship, with Jesus Christ.

ADD AND ADHD

In recent years, our educational system has become more adept at identifying children with perceptual problems. The terms Attention Deficit Disorder, ADD, and Attention Deficit Hyperactive Disorder, ADHD, have become well known and popularized. These conditions are highly complex, but many lay people have gained significant understanding about helping such children. As you read, you may wish to refer to the graph at the end of this chapter.

I want to consider ADD and ADHD together, since they have so many similarities. Children in both categories employ inappropriate and destructive ways of handling their anger. They also both involve two neurological problems—

perceptual difficulties and short attention span. ADHD adds the element of hyperactivity, but I am assuming that hyperactivity and short attention span are so closely related that we can discuss them together.

A child with a *short attention span* cannot focus or concentrate long enough to learn well. His attention shifts from one distraction to another and he appears to be restless, careless, and clumsy — hyperactive.

A child with ADHD has real problems focusing on the parent. This makes it difficult for the parent to maintain the child's attention long enough to transmit positive feelings of love. Also, the parent is forced to focus primarily on the child's problems and is repeatedly drawn into the trap of expressing negative feelings to the child.

The vicious cycle continues, the child harboring anger toward the parent because he feels unloved and unaccepted, and the parent in frustration dumping anger on the child. Also, the child is angry at himself for "failing." His growing depression increases the rage within him.

I dislike giving medications to children, but sometimes they are the wise and humane way to go. The medication Ritalin (Methylphenidate) is often appropriate for children with ADHD, so that the child's attention span can be brought to normal and the child can focus on the parents' love. I have seen countless children who for the first time were able to accept their parents' love after taking Ritalin. Of course, the most important factor in keeping the child's emotional tank full is the parents' unconditional love shown with eye contact, physical contact, and focused attention. But if the child has problems receiving that love because of a short attention span, Ritalin or other medications may help.

The other neurological factor in ADHD is *perceptual.*

In one or more of the five senses, and especially in sight and hearing, the child misperceives and misunderstands what she hears or sees. A common perceptual problem is *reversal* or seeing the mirror image of a letter or word. The child may see *was* instead of *saw,* or a *b* instead of a *d.* This condition can cause a reading difficulty called *dyslexia.*

A child with perceptual problems will also have a hard time in accurate reception of feelings from others, and will tend to receive feelings in a negative way. This is the reason a perceptually handicapped child will feel that her parents and other authority figures do not care about her. Of course, in most cases, they truly do, but the child doesn't feel it and so is angry and depressed.

Children with ADHD are extremely prone to childhood and adolescent *depression.* This is difficult to identify because it is not as apparent as in adults. It usually begins when the child is seven or eight years old and deepens to the point that it presents significant problems in the fourth grade.

Childhood depression causes decreased attention span which, of course, worsens the short attention span already present. Therefore, childhood depression decreases the child's ability to concentrate, to remember, and to think or reason clearly. It also causes great amounts of anger which can lead to passive-aggressive attitudes and behavior.

Adolescent depression is usually severe and is revealed in a variety of difficulties. Fortunately, medical people have made good progress in identifying and treating depression in both children and teenagers. Like many other doctors, I will prescribe two types of medication for such children — one to lengthen the attention span, as I mentioned earlier, and the other to control depression. I appreciate antidepressants because they are safe, nonaddictive, and work in a "natural" way. By natural, I mean that they not only make the child feel good, but also correct the biochemical imbalance caused by the depression—the concentration of three hormones, norepinephrine, dopamine, and serotonin. I have seen antidepressants bring children and teenagers out of depression when nothing else could help.

Unfortunately, many people think that a perceptually handicapped child is lazy or stubborn or just plain "dumb." They fail to understand that the child does not perceive or take information from his environment as the average child does. His understanding of the world is distorted.

Imagine the child's dilemma. He is angry because he cannot understand his schoolwork and because his parents nag him for not doing it. Therefore, he doesn't feel understood by his parents. Also, he doesn't get along well with his peers and so feels isolated. By the time he reaches adolescence, he suffers from severe behavioral and emotional disorders.

MATT

One afternoon some years ago, I attended my son Dale's baseball game. I recognized Matt, a member of the opposing team, since he and his parents had been to see me earlier that year. At thirteen, he was perceptually handicapped and the neighborhood nuisance.

I found a seat next to Larry, Matt's adult neighbor, just as Matt was coming up to bat.

"Hey, Larry," Matt called, "which side of the base is the right side? I think I bat righthanded. The kid who just batted is left-handed. Should I stand where he did?"

"No, Matt," Larry answered impatiently. "You should stand on the other side of the plate."

Larry turned to me, "Isn't that the dumbest thing? Matt doesn't know the right side from the left side of home plate."

"Maybe he has some learning problems," I offered.

"He sure does! If he wasn't so blamed ornery, he could learn something."

"No, really, Larry," I continued, "there are people who don't know left from right."

"That's impossible. There's nothing wrong with him that a little willow switch now and then wouldn't cure!"

Poor Matt! Besides the normal anxieties of competing, he has the added frustration of perceptual difficulties and a not very understanding neighbor. Fortunately, his parents and school have recognized his problems and are helping him.

It is critical that parents of children like Matt fill their kids' emotional tanks daily. Perceptually handicapped children have great difficulty understanding positive feelings for them. For this reason, they need extra helpings of love, physical contact, and focused attention from the important people in their lives.

To convey love, we use eye contact which involves visual perception; physical contact which is an overwhelmingly complex sense; and focused attention which requires seeing, hearing, and the possession of a certain degree of logic. If a perceptual problem exists in any of these areas, the child's understanding is distorted, thus creating great frustration for both the child and adult seeking to communicate with him.

It is not only the child who experiences great pain, for his parents run the whole gamut of emotions before they can come to grips with the fact that their child is suffering from perceptual problems. They may begin by denying that the problem exists. Then they take the child for second and third opinions. They also isolate themselves, thinking that no one understands them.

Next, they begin on a guilt trip, sure that they caused the problem. They question their childrearing: "Were we too strict? Were we too easygoing?" Then comes the anger: "We're surely not the guilty persons in this situation. We've done everything we can. It must be the doctor who doesn't know what he is talking about. And the school—they don't know how to educate properly!"

Finally, the parents start blaming each other. When the child sees this, he feels afraid and even more depressed. At this point, parents who really want to help their child will commit themselves to counseling. There they will find hope as well as specific information on how to deal with their child's problem. Once they have hope, they alleviate the child's depression and anger.

RICK

Rick, a handsome, dark-eyed, ten-year-old walked into my office well ahead of his mother, Joyce.

"I sure hope you can find out what is wrong, Dr. Campbell," he said, "because my mother worries a lot about me. Sometimes she even cries. I hate to see her do that. Maybe you can tell her something today that will make her feel better." What a great kid!

Joyce was a single parent. Her husband left a year ago, just about the time Rick's problem began to surface at school. She was a sincere mother who tried to do everything she could for Rick.

His teacher had told Joyce that there wasn't anything wrong with Rick except an excess of maternal attention! "You're trying too hard to compensate for the absence of his father, and you're spoiling him. He can read. He is just being stubborn to get all the attention he can," the teacher stated firmly.

And so, armed with this opinion, Joyce gave Rick less attention, but tutored him every night after school. Nothing worked. His behavior problems increased, and his grades dropped to failing. This was when Joyce brought him to me.

After we evaluated him, I called Rick and his mother into my office. I said, "Well, Rick, we'll just see what we can do to make your mother and you feel better."

I went over the tests with them, and showed them that Rick had a visual perceptual problem and a slight attention deficit. "But don't worry, you're a bright boy, Rick. And I doubt that you are too stubborn to try to read. I think you are all right and I'm going to try to help you."

Rick's eyes lit up. "Listen to that, Mom. I'm not dumb after all. You don't have to worry so much about me now."

Rick was feeling very responsible for his mother's unhappiness. After beginning treatment, Rick was able to get rid of some of the guilt which had caused him to feel even more depressed.

FAMOUS ADHD PEOPLE

When working with ADHD children, I love to tell them and their parents about well-known persons who had the problem. I emphasize my belief that ADHD and ADD are misnamed, that these children do not have a "disorder." They are normal children who were born about 150 years too late and so have to go to schools that offer a kind of learning that is hard for perceptually handicapped people.

When school attendance was not universally mandated, people with perceptual problems could learn in their own ways. I am something of a history buff, and several years ago I noticed that many of our outstanding forebears had perceptual problems. My favorite is Kit Carson. Being raised in New Mexico, I was fascinated with the way he excelled in almost every aspect of frontier life in the 1800s. Not only was he involved in most of the significant happenings in the Southwest, but he had a good heart and truly cared for Native Americans. He was well loved by the Spanish Americans and respected by the political leaders of his day.

Several people wrote biographies of Kit Carson, and finally he wrote his autobiography. I had trouble finding this last work because it was not highly regarded. When I finally did secure a copy, I began to realize that Carson had ADHD. When I visited the Kit Carson Museum in Taos, I was spellbound as I read his notes and letters and came to understand why his autobiography was one of his few failures. His penmanship and writing style were typical of many ADHD persons I have known.

One of my favorite contemporary persons is O.D. McKee who founded McKee Bakeries of Collegedale, Tennessee, the producer of Little Debbie Snack Cakes. What an inspiring story!

I love to tell children with ADHD and their parents that almost every person with ADHD has some special gift or talent. Sadly, these talents are not always allowed to blossom because of the problems we have already discussed. These families need to know that there is a special strength in these children. Their unique gifts will be discovered and allowed to grow only if the parents understand how to train the children to manage their anger appropriately. Only then can the defiant, anti-authority resistance of passive-aggressive behavior be prevented. It is almost always this type of anger that keeps the children from discovering and using their gifts — which are usually mechanical in nature, but can bloom in every area.

Finally, I love to tell these wonderful children and their parents that *everyone* has perceptual problems. No one is perceptually perfect. You know the result if ten people each tell you their version of an accident. Or you may remember that simple childhood whispering game, where one person tells the one next to him a message that is then passed along the line until the last person reveals what he or she heard.

The problems of most perceptually handicapped children can be minimized if they are caught early enough. James and Rick are fortunate because their parents discovered their problems in time. Catching the problem "in time" means before the child reaches adolescence.

When it remains untreated into adolescence, the child usually experiences much more than academic difficulty. He often has experimented with drugs, sex, stealing, running away, and may even have attempted suicide.

I have told the stories of James, Matt, and Rick so that you might better understand the dilemmas of perceptually handicapped children. Helping these learning-disabled children develop into wholeness takes time, patience, and understanding, but it is well worth the effort.

LINDA – A CHRONICALLY ILL CHILD

Perceptual deficits are not the only special problems that affect the behavior of children. Chronic physical ailments can also create emotional and behavioral controversy. We can become so involved in the daily needs of chronically ill children that we overlook their emotional needs.

As physically impaired children grow older, they become increasingly bitter about their disease or handicap. They also feel angry at their caring parents, because the parents have inadvertently replaced the natural giving of love with daily medical attention. These children can turn defiant, not only toward their parents but toward all authority.

Linda's mother described her as "a fussy baby from the very beginning. We tried everything we could think of, but we just couldn't seem to make her happy. When she was three, the pediatrician discovered a chronic heart defect. Since then, our life with her has been one trip after another to specialists."

"How is her physical health now?" I asked.

"It is stabilized," her father answered, "but her pregnancy certainly won't help her any."

"I see you have another child, a son," I noted, as I scanned their file. "How is his health?"

"Oh, it's perfect," Linda's mother answered. "We're so proud of Jeff. He's a fine athlete and an accomplished pianist."

"Has Linda ever developed any hobbies?"

"No," her father answered. "We've been so busy attending to her health problems that we never had the time to do much else with her. Don't get me wrong. It's not that we didn't want to. She has always been such a cranky kid that we never could talk her into doing anything other than going to school. And now, here she is pregnant. I guess it's too late."

"At least she is going to marry the father of the baby next week," his wife added. "Maybe that will make her happy. We have done all we know to do, Dr. Campbell, but we surely went wrong somewhere. She has been very depressed lately. I'm relieved that we talked her into coming to see you. I sure hope you can get through to her. She's in a sorry frame of mind to start a marriage."

"Why don't both of you wait outside, and let me talk with Linda," I suggested.

Curled up in a chair in the corner of the waiting room was Linda — seventeen years old and pregnant.

"Would you like to come in, Linda?" I asked, as I walked over to her.

"Why not? That's what they brought me here for." As she sat down in a chair in my office, she said with a frown, "I don't know what good my being here is going to do. You can't change things."

"You're right, Linda. I can't change things, but maybe in time I can help you to change the way you feel about things."

When Linda began to open up, my suspicions were confirmed. She was a classic example of the chronically ill child whose parents spent so much time caring for her physical needs that they forgot about her emotional needs.

" 'Jeff can do this — Jeff can do that!' That's all I ever heard. 'Let's go to Jeff's game, Linda. It'll do you good to get out of the house. Let's go to Jeff's piano recital, Linda. Maybe you'll decide to start taking piano lessons.' And you should see the grades Jeff makes — straight A's. I made C's and I think that is plenty good enough."

I've just begun counseling with Linda, but I feel that she can be helped with her depression. I know that her parents love her and didn't realize that they substituted medical attention for emotional attention. Linda's low grades and her pregnancy were both subconscious acts of defiance against this seeming indifference.

THREE PITFALLS

In my years of treating chronically ill and perceptually handicapped children, I have discovered that there are three principal pitfalls for parents. The first is the one illustrated by Linda's case — substituting medical attention for emotional fulfillment.

The second pitfall is a lack of behavioral control and firmness. These parents often feel such pity, and sometimes even blame and guilt, that they do not try to provide normal control for the child's behavior. This results in a manipulative child who uses illness to control the parents.

The third pitfall is failure to train these children to manage anger. Handicapped children are generally more difficult to teach because they tend toward anti-authority attitudes. Their parents are then caught between pity and guilt, on the one hand, and their own anger, on the other.

Everything we have discussed in this book certainly applies to these precious children. But their parents have little room for error. It is so easy for them to fall into the vicious cycle of rage and guilt. It is critical for these parents to understand the possible pitfalls as early as possible. The longer a difficult situation continues, the more difficult it will

be to correct, especially when it involves anti-authority attitudes.

Yet, as we have seen, success can come to the handicapped child if the problem is detected and help is obtained
in time. If you have a special problem child in your family, I
hope that you are finding appropriate professional help and
also that you are providing the unconditional love that will
keep your child's emotional tank full.

I have seen innumerable children with special problems who have done beautifully. For most of these dear ones,
their handicaps have become challenges which have helped
to mold their character in wonderful ways.

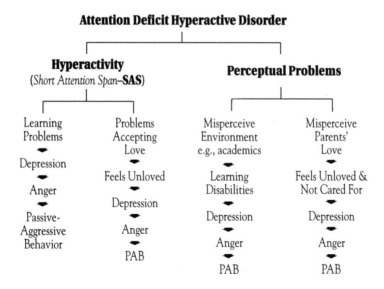

A Final Word to Parents

It is a difficult world you are preparing your children to enter. But now you have some key information that they and you need. When you teach your children how to manage anger, you're giving them a strong advantage for the future. It is something like giving them a compass so that they can avoid life's most devastating problems, stay on the positive side, and more ably reach for fulfillment.

As a last word of encouragement, I would like to share something with you that will help you put your parenting in perspective.

Some parents are so *overly conscientious* that they almost worry themselves to death. They tend to think that there is such a thing as being "the perfect parent." They're afraid that if they make even one mistake, their children will turn out terribly. This fear paralyzes them, making their parenting more difficult and less effective.

Other parents tend to be *authoritarian*, "captains of the ship." They issue commands and relate to their children as if they were military recruits. This type of parenting may seem to work well with some children, but in time they become progressively resentful and anti-authority in their attitudes.

Some of us vacillate between these two types of parenting. Yet, regardless of what type of parents we are, what matters most is to come to the place where we can relax and enjoy our children. Few parents do this naturally. One of the most wonderful happenings in my own parenting occurred when I learned to truly relax with my children and genuinely enjoy them — at any age.

Although parenting is a difficult and often perplexing responsibility, it can be understood as our means of meeting the needs of our children. Any conscientious parent can be taught how to do this, regardless of their personality. The main requirement is willingness and desire.

Since you are reading this book, you certainly qualify. As simple as this sounds, most parents have a deep fear of not being good enough, primarily because they don't know what is necessary to actually be good parents. And yet, if they are constantly uncertain, parenting will seem an overwhelming responsibility. Perhaps I can best illustrate this by telling you a story.

June, a forty-five-year-old mother of three, sought my advice about her elderly mother. June is conscientious and goodhearted. She had a close relationship with her mother until the last two years, when her mother became increasingly difficult. She criticized June for everything and became more and more demanding, complaining that June did not visit or call often enough. Eventually, June was spending so much time trying to care for her mother's needs that she was neglecting her own family. She had tried every tactic she could think of, including a frank discussion with her mother, but nothing had any effect on her mother's unreasonable demands.

I told June, "You are being a good daughter."

She replied, "How could I be when my mother is so disappointed in me all the time?"

I then asked her, "Have you considered what the requirements are for being a good daughter in your situation?"

June answered, "No, I've never thought about that."

I asked her to make a list of what she thought would make her a good daughter. She naturally assumed she would have a long list.

When June and I talked again, she said how amazed she was that she had only six items on her list—things like visiting her mother once a week and calling twice a week, sending gifts and cards for birthday and Christmas, etc. When June saw that she not only met the requirements but in many ways exceeded them, she felt better about herself, instead of confused and downhearted as she had before.

June's next challenge was to learn to be relaxed, upbeat, and pleasant, as well as firm with her mother, regardless of her mother's mood or attitude. June was able to do this because she *knew* she was being a good daughter.

I then asked June to make another list, but this time about her parenting. Of course, this role is much more complex than her role as a grown daughter, but the same rules apply. June determined the basic requirements of being a good parent and then made her list. She reviewed the list about once a week to keep it up to date for each child.

This had the same freeing experience with her children as with her mother. Now that she knew she was a good mother, she could be relaxed, upbeat, pleasant, and yet firm with her children. Best of all, June found herself enjoying each of them and appreciating their unique features more.

I urge you to follow June's example. You might use this book as a guide and make your own list. This will encourage you to reread this book as your children grow up. And be sure that you update your list as June did, to keep pace with your growing children.

God bless you!

Notes

Chapter One

1. Neil Clark Warren, *Making Anger Your Ally* (Colorado Springs: Focus on the Family Publishing, 1990), 77, 55.

2. Ibid., 121.

3. Ibid., 97.

Chapter Two

1. Thomas Sowell, "Who Says It's Hopeless?" *Reader's Digest*, June 1994, 180.

2. Benjamin Spock, *A Better World for Our Children* (Bethesda: National Press Books, 1994).

3. Neil Clark Warren, *Making Anger Your Ally* (Colorado Springs: Focus on the Family Publishing, 1990), 8.

Chapter Three
1. "Burdened Teens Feel Estranged from Adults," *The Chattanooga Times*, 14 July 1994.

2. Stuart Goldman, "Murder as Therapy," *National Review*, 45, 29 November 1993, 44–46.

Chapter Four
1. Adapted from *How to Really Love Your Child* (Wheaton, Ill.: Victor Books, 1977), chapter 3.

2. David Seamands, *Healing for Damaged Emotions* (Wheaton, Ill.: Victor Books, 1981), 61.

3. Ibid., 63–64.

4. David Seamands, *Putting Away Childish Things* (Wheaton, Ill.: Victor Books, 1982), 33.

5. Neil Clark Warren, *Making Anger Your Ally* (Colorado Springs: Focus on the Family Publishing, 1990), 123.

6. Ibid., 123–24.

7. Ibid., 125.

Chapter Five
1. Andrew D. Lester, *Coping with Anger: A Christian Guide* (Philadelphia: The Westminster Press, 1983), 34–35.

2. Carol Tavris, *Anger: The Misunderstood Emotion* (New York: Simon and Schuster, 1989), 47.

3. "The Traits of Wrath in Men and Women," *USA Today*, 11 August 1994.

4. Meg Eastman, *Taming the Dragon in Your Child* (New York: John Wiley and Sons, 1994), 4.

Chapter Six
1. Ruth N. Koch and Kenneth C. Haugk, *Speaking the Truth in Love: Now to Be an Assertive Christian* (St. Louis: Stephen Ministries, 1992), 16–17, 19.

2. Ibid., 22.

Chapter Seven
1. Leonard D. Eron, *Reason to Hope: A Psycho-Social Perspective on Violence and Youth* (Washington, D.C.: American Psychological Association), December 1994.

2. Meg Eastman, *Taming the Dragon in Your Child* (New York: John Wiley and Sons, 1994), 187–88.

3. Andrew D. Lester, *Coping with Your Anger* (Philadelphia: The Westminster Press, 1983), 59.

4. Howard S. Friedman and Stephanie Booth-Kersley, "The Disease-Prone Personality: A Meta-Analytic View of the Construct," *American Psychologist* 42, 1987, 539–55.

5. Carol Tavris, *Anger: The Misunderstood Emotion* (New York: Simon and Schuster, 1989), 129.

6. Ibid., 131–42.

7. Ibid., 137.

8. Ibid., 139–41.

9. Ibid., 146.

Chapter Nine
1. Ellen Goodman, "A Mom Fights Media Madness," *Family Circle,* 14 March 1995, 134.

2. Gladys Hunt, *Honey for a Child's Heart* (Grand Rapids: Zondervan Publishing House, 1989).

3. William Kilpatrick and Gregory and Suzanne M. Wolfe, *Books That Build Character: A Guide to Teaching Your Child Moral Values through Stories* (New York: Simon and Schuster, Inc., 1994).

4. William Bennett, *The Book of Virtues: A Treasury of Great Moral Stories* (New York: Simon and Schuster, Inc., 1993).

5. Martin E. Seligman, *Learned Optimism* (New York: Simon and Schuster, Inc., 1980).

6. Thomas Gordon, *Parent Effectiveness Training* (New York: David McKay, Inc., 1970).

7. Meg Eastman, *Taming the Dragon in Your Child* (New York: John Wiley and Sons, 1994).

Chapter Eleven
1. H.B. London, Jr. and Neil B. Wiseman, *Pastors at Risk* (Wheaton, Ill.: Victor, 1993), 22.

2. Ibid., 29.

Chapter Twelve
1. C.A. Oliphant, *Sweet Success* (Cleveland, Tenn.: Sundial Press, 1994).

Who Owns the Future?

Jaron Lanier

SIMON & SCHUSTER

New York   London   Toronto   Sydney   New Delhi

SIMON & SCHUSTER
1230 Avenue of the Americas
New York, NY 10020

First Simon & Schuster hardcover edition May 2013

SIMON & SCHUSTER and colophon are registered trademarks of Simon & Schuster, Inc.

For information about special discounts for bulk purchases,
please contact Simon & Schuster Special Sales at 1-866-506-1949
or business@simonandschuster.com.

The Simon & Schuster Speakers Bureau can bring authors to your live event.
For more information or to book an event, contact the Simon & Schuster Speakers Bureau
at 1-866-248-3049 or visit our website at www.simonspeakers.com.

DESIGNED BY ERICH HOBBING

Manufactured in the United States of America

1   3   5   7   9   10   8   6   4   2

Library of Congress Cataloging-in-Publication Data is available

ISBN 978-1-4516-5496-7
ISBN 978-1-4516-5499-8 (ebook)

*To everyone my daughter will know
as she grows up.
I hope she will be able to invent her place
in a world in which it's normal to find
success and fulfillment.*

Contents

Contents

PART FOUR

Markets, Energy Landscapes, and Narcissism

Contents

Contents

PART SIX

Democracy

PART SEVEN

Ted Nelson

Contents

Contents

Contents

Contents

Who Owns the Future?

Prelude

Hello, Hero

An odd thing about this book is that you, the reader, and I, the author, are the immediate protagonists. The very action of reading makes you the hero of the story I am telling. Maybe you bought, or stole, a physical copy, paid to read this on your tablet, or pirated a digital copy off a share site. Whatever the prequel, here you are, living precisely the circumstances described in this book.

If you paid to read this, thank you! This book is a result of living my life as I do, which I hope provides value to you. The hope of this book is that someday we'll all have more ways to grow wealth as a side effect of living our lives creatively and intelligently, with an eye to doing things of use to others.

If you paid to read, then there has been a one-way transaction in which you transferred money to someone else.

If you got it for free, there has been a no-way transaction, and any value traded will be off the books, recorded not in any ledger but rather in the informal value systems of reputation, karma, or other wispy forms of barter. That doesn't mean nothing has happened. Maybe you'll get some positive strokes over a social network because of what you say about the book. That sort of activity might benefit us both. But it's a kind of benefit that is unreliable and perishable.

The clamor for online attention only turns into money for a token minority of ordinary people, but there is another new, tiny class of people who always benefit. Those who keep the new ledgers, the giant computing services that model you, spy on you, and predict your actions, turn your life activities into the greatest fortunes in history. Those are concrete fortunes made of money.

This book promotes a third alternative, which is that digital networking ought to promote a two-way transaction, in which you benefit, concretely, with real money, as I do. I want digital networking to cause more value from people to be on the books, rather than less. When we make our world more efficient through the use of digital networks, that should make our economy grow, not shrink.

Here's a current example of the challenge we face. At the height of its power, the photography company Kodak employed more than 140,000 people and was worth $28 billion. They even invented the first digital camera. But today Kodak is bankrupt, and the new face of digital photography has become Instagram. When Instagram was sold to Facebook for a billion dollars in 2012, it employed only thirteen people.

Where did all those jobs disappear to? And what happened to the wealth that those middle-class jobs created? This book is built to answer questions like these, which will only become more common as digital networking hollows out every industry, from media to medicine to manufacturing.

Instagram isn't worth a billion dollars just because those thirteen employees are extraordinary. Instead, its value comes from the millions of users who contribute to the network without being paid for it. Networks need a great number of people to participate in them to generate significant value. But when they have them, only a small number of people get paid. That has the net effect of centralizing wealth and limiting overall economic growth.

Instead of enlarging our overall economy by creating more value that is on the books, the rise of digital networking is enriching a relative few while moving the value created by the many off the books.

By "digital networking" I mean not only the Internet and the Web, but also other networks operated by outfits like financial institutions and intelligence agencies. In all these cases, we see the phenomenon of power and money becoming concentrated around the people who operate the most central computers in a network, undervaluing everyone else. That is the pattern we have come to expect, but it is not the only way things can go.

Prelude

The alternative introduced in this book is not a utopian idea; it won't be hard to foresee its annoyances and messiness. However, I will argue that monetizing more of what's valuable from ordinary people, who turn out to be the uncompensated sources of the data that make networks valuable in the first place, will lead to a better future.

That will make power and clout more honestly distributed, and might even lead to a persistent middle class in an information economy, which would otherwise be an impossible goal.

Terms

It would be impossible to only use preexisting terminology to communicate the ideas in this book. The problem is not that there are no relevant, familiar terms, but that all the preexisting terms have baggage or common uses that are just enough askew from what I need to say that they bring more confusion than clarity. So unfamiliar terms and expressions will appear. An appendix contains a list of some of these terms, along with the pages on which they first appear. Think of it as the high-priority index.

PART ONE

First Round

CHAPTER 1

Motivation

The Problem in Brief

We're used to treating information as "free,"* but the price we pay for the illusion of "free" is only workable so long as most of the overall economy *isn't* about information. Today, we can still think of information as the intangible enabler of communications, media, and software. But as technology advances in this century, our present intuition about the nature of information will be remembered as narrow and shortsighted. We can think of information narrowly only because sectors like manufacturing, energy, health care, and transportation aren't yet particularly automated or 'net-centric.

But eventually most productivity probably *will* become software-mediated. Software could be the final industrial revolution. It might subsume all the revolutions to come. This could start to happen, for instance, once cars and trucks are driven by software instead of human drivers, 3D printers magically turn out what had once been manufactured goods, automated heavy equipment finds and mines natural resources, and robot nurses handle the material aspects of caring for the elderly. (These and other examples will be explored in detail later on.) Maybe digital technology won't advance enough in this century to dominate the economy, but it probably will.

Maybe technology will then make all the needs of life so inexpensive that it will be virtually free to live well, and no one will

---

*As exemplified by free consumer Internet services, or the way financial services firms can often gather and use data without having to pay for it.

worry about money, jobs, wealth disparities, or planning for old age. I strongly doubt that neat picture would unfold.

Instead, if we go on as we are, we will probably enter into a period of hyper-unemployment, and the attendant political and social chaos. The outcome of chaos is unpredictable, and we shouldn't rely on it to design our future.

The wise course is to consider in advance how we can live in the long term with a high degree of automation.

Put Up or Shut Up

For years I have presented complaints about the way digital technology interfaces with people. I love the technology and doubly love the people; it's the connection that's out of whack. Naturally, I am often asked, "What would you do instead?" If the question is framed on a personal level, such as "Should I quit Facebook?" the answer is easy. You have to decide for yourself. I am not trying to be anyone's guru.*

On the level of economics, though, I ought to provide an answer. People are not just pointlessly diluting themselves on cultural, intellectual, and spiritual levels by fawning over digital superhuman phenomena that don't necessarily exist. There is also a material cost.

People are gradually making themselves poorer than they need to be. We're setting up a situation where better technology in the long term just means more unemployment, or an eventual socialist backlash. Instead, we should seek a future where more people will do well, without losing liberty, even as technology gets much, much better.

Popular digital designs do not treat people as being "special enough." People are treated as small elements in a bigger information machine, when in fact people are the *only* sources or destinations of information, or indeed of any meaning to the machine at all. My goal is to portray an alternate future in which people are treated appropriately as being special.

*. . . though I'll make a suggestion at the end of the book.

How? Pay people for information gleaned from them if that information turns out to be valuable. If observation of you yields data that makes it easier for a robot to seem like a natural conversationalist, or for a political campaign to target voters with its message, then you ought to be owed money for the use of that valuable data. It wouldn't exist without you, after all. This is such a simple starting point that I find it credible, and I hope to persuade you about that as well.

The idea that mankind's information should be made free is idealistic, and understandably popular, but information wouldn't need to be free if no one were impoverished. As software and networks become more and more important, we can either be moving toward free information in the midst of insecurity for almost everyone, or toward paid information with a stronger middle class than ever before. The former might seem more ideal in the abstract, but the latter is the more realistic path to lasting democracy and dignity.

An amazing number of people offer an amazing amount of value over networks. But the lion's share of wealth now flows to those who aggregate and route those offerings, rather than those who provide the "raw materials." A new kind of middle class, and a more genuine, growing information economy, could come about if we could break out of the "free information" idea and into a universal micropayment system. We might even be able to strengthen individual liberty and self-determination even when the machines get very good.

This is a book about futuristic economics, but it's really about how we can remain human beings as our machines become so sophisticated that we can perceive them as autonomous. It is a work of nonnarrative science fiction, or what could be called speculative advocacy. I'll argue that the particular way we're reorganizing our world around digital networks is not sustainable, and that there is at least one alternative that is more likely to be sustainable.

Moore's Law Changes the Way People Are Valued

The primary influence on the way technologists have come to think about the future since the turn of the century is their direct experience of digital networks through consumer electronics. It only takes a few years, not a lifetime, for a young person to experience Moore's Law–like changes.

Moore's Law is Silicon Valley's guiding principle, like all ten commandments wrapped into one. The law states that chips get better at an accelerating rate. They don't just accumulate improvements, in the way that a pile of rocks gets higher when you add more rocks. Instead of being added, the improvements *multiply*. The technology seems to always get twice as good every two years or so. That means after forty years of improvements, microprocessors have become *millions* of times better. No one knows how long this can continue. We don't agree on exactly why Moore's Law or other similar patterns exist. Is it a human-driven, self-fulfilling prophecy or an intrinsic, inevitable quality of technology? Whatever is going on, the exhilaration of accelerating change leads to a religious emotion in some of the most influential tech circles. It provides a meaning and context.

Moore's Law means that more and more things can be done practically for free, if only it weren't for those people who want to be paid. People are the flies in Moore's Law's ointment. When machines get incredibly cheap to run, people seem correspondingly expensive. It used to be that printing presses were expensive, so paying newspaper reporters seemed like a natural expense to fill the pages. When the news became free, that anyone would want to be paid at all started to seem unreasonable. Moore's Law can make salaries—and social safety nets—seem like unjustifiable luxuries.

But our immediate experience of Moore's Law has been cheap treats. Yesterday's unattainably expensive camera becomes just one of today's throwaway features on a phone. As information technology becomes millions of times more powerful, any particular use of it becomes correspondingly cheaper. Thus, it has become commonplace to expect online services (not just news, but 21st century treats like search or social networking) to be given for free, or rather, in exchange for acquiescence to being spied on.

Essential but Worthless

As you read this, thousands of remote computers are refining secret models of who you are. What is so interesting about you that you're worth spying on?

The cloud is driven by statistics, and even in the worst individual cases of personal ignorance, dullness, idleness, or irrelevance, every person is constantly feeding data into the cloud these days. The value of such information could be treated as genuine, but it is not. Instead, the blindness of our standards of accounting to all that value is gradually breaking capitalism.

There is no long-term difference between an ordinary person and a skilled person in this scheme. For now, many kinds of skilled people do well in a software-mediated world, but if things don't change, those who own the top machines will gradually emerge as the only elite left standing. To explain why, consider how advancing technology could do to surgery what it has already done to recorded music.

Musical recording was a mechanical process until it wasn't, and became a network service. At one time, a factory stamped out musical discs and trucks delivered them to retail stores where salespeople sold them. While that system has not been entirely destroyed, it is certainly more common to simply receive music instantly over a network. There used to be a substantial middle-class population supported by the recording industry, but no more. The principal beneficiaries of the digital music business are the operators of network services that mostly give away the music in exchange for gathering data to improve those dossiers and software models of each person.

The same thing could happen to surgery. Nanorobots, holographic radiation, or just plain old robots using endoscopes might someday perform heart surgery. These gadgets would perform the economic role that MP3 players and smartphones took on in music delivery. Whatever the details, surgery would then be reconceived as an information service. The role of human surgeons in that case is not predetermined, however. They will remain *essential,* for the technology will rely on data that has to come from people, but it isn't decided yet if they'll be *valued* in terms that lead to wealth.

Nonspecialist doctors have already lost a degree of self-determination because they didn't seize the centers of the networks that have arisen to mediate medicine. Insurance and pharmaceutical concerns, hospital chains, and various other savvy network climbers were paying better attention. No one, not even a heart surgeon, should pretend to be indefinitely immune to this pattern.

There will always be humans, lots of them, who provide the data that makes the networked realization of any technology better and cheaper. This book will propose an alternative, sustainable system that will continue to honor and reward those humans, no matter how advanced technology becomes. If we continue on the present path, benefits will instead flow mostly to the tenders of the top computers that route data about surgery, essentially by spying on doctors and patients.

The Beach at the Edge of Moore's Law

A heavenly idea comes up a lot in what might be called Silicon Valley metaphysics. We anticipate immortality through mechanization. A common claim in utopian technology culture is that people—well, perhaps not everyone—will be uploaded into cloud computing servers* later in this century, perhaps in a decade or two, to become immortal in Virtual Reality. Or, if we are to remain physical, we will be surrounded by a world animated with robotic technology. We will float from joy to joy, even the poorest among us living like a sybaritic magician. We will not have to call forth what we wish from the world, for we will be so well modeled by statistics in the computing clouds that the dust will know what we want.

Picture this: It's sometime later in the 21st century, and you're at the beach. A neuro-interfaced seagull perches and seems to speak, telling you that you might want to know that nanobots are repairing

---

*A "server" is just a computer on a network that serves up responses to other computers. Generally home computers or portable devices aren't set up to acknowledge connections from arbitrary other computers, so they aren't servers. A "cloud" is a collection of servers that act in a coordinated way.

your heart valve at the moment (who knew you had a looming heart problem?) and the sponsor is the casino up the road, which paid for this avian message *and* the automatic cardiology through Google or whatever company is running that sort of switchboard decades hence.

If the wind starts to blow, swarms of leaves turn out to be subtle bioengineered robots that harness that very wind to propel themselves into an emergent shelter that surrounds you. Your wants and needs are automatically analyzed and a robotic masseuse forms out of the sand and delivers shiatsu as you contemplate the wind's whispers from your pop-up cocoon.

There are endless variations of this sort of tale of soon-to-appear high-tech abundance. Some of them are found in science fiction, but more often these visions come up in ordinary conversations. They are so ambient in Silicon Valley culture that they become part of the atmosphere of the place. Typically, you might hear a thought experiment about how cheap computing will be, how much more advanced materials science will become, and so on, and from there your interlocutor extrapolates that supernatural-seeming possibilities will reliably open up later in this century.

This is the thought schema of a thousand inspirational talks, and the motivation behind a great many startups, courses, and careers. The key terms associated with this sensibility are *accelerating change, abundance,* and *singularity*.

The Price of Heaven

My tale of a talking seagull strikes me as being kitschy and contrived, but any scenario in which humans imagine living without constraints feels like that.

But we needn't fear a loss of constraints. Utopians presume the advent of abundance not because it will be affordable, but because it will be free, provided we accept surveillance.

Starting back in the early 1980s, an initially tiny stratum of gifted technologists conceived new interpretations of concepts like privacy, liberty, and power. I was an early participant in the process and helped to formulate many of the ideas I am criticizing in this book.

What was once a tiny subculture has blossomed into the dominant interpretation of computation and software-mediated society.

One strain of what might be called "hacker culture" held that liberty means absolute privacy through the use of cryptography. I remember the thrill of using military-grade stealth just to argue about who should pay for a pizza at MIT in 1983 or so.

On the other hand, some of my friends from that era, who consumed that pizza, eventually became very rich building giant cross-referenced dossiers on masses of people, which were put to use by financiers, advertisers, insurers, or other concerns nurturing fantasies of operating the world by remote control.

It is typical of human nature to ignore hypocrisy. The greater a hypocrisy, the more invisible it typically becomes, but we technical folk are inclined to seek an airtight whole of ideas. Here is one such synthesis—of cryptography for techies and massive spying on others—which I continue to hear fairly often: Privacy for ordinary people can be forfeited in the near term because it will become moot anyway.

Surveillance by the technical few on the less technical many can be tolerated for now because of hopes for an endgame in which everything will become transparent to everyone. Network entrepreneurs and cyber-activists alike seem to imagine that today's elite network servers in positions of information supremacy will eventually become eternally benign, or just dissolve.

In the telling of digital utopias, when computing gets ultragood and ultracheap we won't have to worry about the reach of elite network players descended from today's derivatives funds, or Silicon Valley companies like Google or Facebook. In a future world of abundance, everyone will be motivated to be open and generous.

Bizarrely, the endgame utopias of even the most ardent high-tech libertarians always seem to take socialist turns. The joys of life will be too cheap to meter, we imagine. So abundance will go ambient.

This is what diverse cyber-enlightened business concerns and political groups all share in common, from Facebook to WikiLeaks. Eventually, they imagine, there will be no more secrets, no more barriers to access; all the world will be opened up as if the planet were transformed into a crystal ball. In the meantime, those true believers encrypt their servers even as they seek to gather the rest of the world's information and find the best way to leverage it.

It is all too easy to forget that "free" inevitably means that someone else will be deciding how you live.

The Problem Is Not the Technology,
but the Way We Think About the Technology

I will argue that up until about the turn of this century we didn't need to worry about technological advancement devaluing people, because new technologies always created new kinds of jobs even as old ones were destroyed. But the dominant principle of the new economy, the information economy, has lately been to conceal the value of information, of all things.

We've decided not to pay most people for performing the new roles that are valuable in relation to the latest technologies. Ordinary people "share," while elite network presences generate unprecedented fortunes.

Whether these elite new presences are consumer-facing services like Google, or more hidden operations like high-frequency-trading firms, is mostly a matter of semantics. In either case, the biggest and best-connected computers provide the settings in which information turns into money. Meanwhile, trinkets tossed into the crowd spread illusions and false hopes that the emerging information economy is benefiting the majority of those who provide the information that drives it.

If information age accounting were complete and honest, as much information as possible would be valued in economic terms. If, however, "raw" information, or information that hasn't yet been routed by those who run the most central computers, isn't valued, then a massive disenfranchisement will take place. As the information economy arises, the old specter of a thousand science fiction tales and Marxist nightmares will be brought back from the dead and empowered to apocalyptic proportions. Ordinary people will be unvalued by the new economy, while those closest to the top computers will become hypervaluable.

15

Making information free is survivable so long as only limited numbers of people are disenfranchised. As much as it pains me to say so, we can survive if we only destroy the middle classes of musicians, journalists, and photographers. What is not survivable is the additional destruction of the middle classes in transportation, manufacturing, energy, office work, education, and health care. And all that destruction will come surely enough if the dominant idea of an information economy isn't improved.

Digital technologists are setting down the new grooves of how people live, how we do business, how we do everything—and they're doing it according to the expectations of foolish utopian scenarios. We want free online experiences so badly that we are happy to not be paid for information that comes from us now or ever. That sensibility also implies that the more dominant information becomes in our economy, the less most of us will be worth.

Saving the Winners from Themselves

Is the present trend really a benefit for those who run the top servers that have come to organize the world? In the short term, of course, yes. The greatest fortunes in history have been created recently by using network technology as a way to concentrate information and therefore wealth and power.

However, in the long term, this way of using network technology is not even good for the richest and most powerful players, because their ultimate source of wealth can only be a growing economy. Pretending that data came from the heavens instead of from people can't help but eventually shrink the overall economy.

The more advanced technology becomes, the more all activity becomes mediated by information tools. Therefore, as our economy turns more fully into an information economy, it will only grow if more information is monetized, instead of less. That's not what we're doing.

Even the most successful players of the game are gradually undermining the core of their own wealth. Capitalism only works if there are enough successful people to be the customers. A market system can only be sustainable when the accounting is thorough enough to reflect where value comes from, which, I'll demonstrate, is another way of saying that an information age middle class must come into being.

Progress Is Compulsory

Two great trends are colliding, one in our favor, and the other against us. Balancing our heavenly expectations, there are also countervailing fears about such things as global climate change and the problem of finding food and drinking water for the human population when it peaks later in this century. Billions more people than have ever been sustained before will need water and food.

We bring the great problems of our times on ourselves, and yet we have little choice but to do so. The human condition is an evolving technological puzzle. Solving one problem creates new ones. This has always been true and is not a special quality of present times.

The ability to grow a larger population, through reduced infant mortality rates, sets up the conditions for a greater famine. People are cracking the inner codes of biology, creating amazing new chemistries, and amplifying our capabilities with digital networks just as we are also undermining our climate, and critical resources are starting to run out. And yet we are compelled to plunge forward, because history isn't reversible. Besides, we must be honest about how bad things were in lower-tech times.

New technological syntheses that will solve the great challenges of the day are less likely to come from garages than from collaborations by many people over giant computer networks. It is the politics and economics of these networks that will determine how new capabilities translate into new benefits for ordinary people.

Progress Is Never Free of Politics

Maybe the coolest technology could get very good and cheap, *while at the same time* crucial fundamentals for survival could become expensive. The calculi of digital utopias and man-made disasters don't contradict each other. They can coexist. This is the heading of the darkest and funniest science fiction, such as the work of Philip K. Dick.

Basics like water and food could soar in cost *even as* intensely sophisticated gadgets, like automated nanorobotic heart surgeons, float about as dust in the air in case they are needed, sponsored by advertisers.

Everything can't become free at once, because the real world is messy. Software and networks are messy. And the sprawling miracle of information-animated technology rests on limited resources.

The illusion that everything is getting so cheap that it is practically free sets up the political and economic conditions for cartels exploiting whatever isn't quite that way. When music is free, wireless bills get expensive, insanely so. You have to look at the whole system. No matter how petty a flaw might be in a utopia, that flaw is where the full fury of power seeking will be focused.

Back to the Beach

You sit at the edge of the ocean, wherever the coast will be after Miami is abandoned to the waves. You are thirsty. Random little clots of dust are full-on robotic interactive devices, since advertising companies long ago released plagues of smart dust upon the world. That means you can always speak and some machine will be listening. "I'm thirsty, I need water."

The seagull responds, "You are not rated as enough of a commercial prospect for any of our sponsors to pay for freshwater for you." You say, "But I have a penny." "Water costs two pennies." "There's an ocean three feet away. Just desalinate some water!" "Desalinization is licensed to water carriers. You need to subscribe. However, you can enjoy free access to any movie ever made, or pornography, or a simulation of a deceased family member for you to interact with as you die from dehydration. Your social networks will be automatically updated with the news of your death." And finally, "Don't you want to play that last penny at the casino that just repaired your heart? You might win big and be able to enjoy it."

CHAPTER 2

A Simple Idea

Just Blurt the Idea Out

Given both the momentum to screw up the human world and the capability to vastly improve it, how will people behave?

This book asserts that the choices we make in the architecture of our digital networks might tip the balance between the opposing waves of invention and calamity.

Digital technology changes the way power (or an avatar of power, such as money or political office) is gained, lost, distributed, and defended in human affairs. Lately, network-empowered finance has amplified corruption and illusion, and the Internet has destroyed more jobs than it has created.

So we begin with the simple question of how to design digital networks to deliver more help than harm in aligning human intention to meet great challenges. A starting point for an answer can be summarized: "Digital information is really just people in disguise."

A Simple Example

It's magic that you can upload a phrase in Spanish into the cloud services of companies like Google or Microsoft, and a workable, if imperfect, translation to English is returned. It's as if there's a polyglot artificial intelligence residing up there in the great cloud server farms.

But that is not how cloud services work. Instead, a multitude of examples of translations made by real human translators are gathered over the Internet. These are correlated with the example you send for translation. It will almost always turn out that multiple previous translations by real human translators had to contend with similar passages, so a collage of those previous translations will yield a usable result.

A giant act of statistics is made practically free because of Moore's Law, but at core the act of translation is based on the real work of people.

Alas, the human translators are anonymous and off the books. The act of cloud-based translation shrinks the economy by pretending the translators who provided the examples don't exist. With each so-called automatic translation, the humans who were the sources of the data are inched away from the world of compensation and employment.

At the end of the day, even the magic of machine translation is like Facebook, a way of taking free contributions from people and regurgitating them as bait for advertisers or others who hope to take advantage of being close to a top server.

In a world of digital dignity, each individual will be the commercial owner of any data that can be measured from that person's state or behavior. Treating information as a mask behind which real people are invariably hiding means that digital data will be treated as being consistently valuable, rather than inconsistently valuable.

In the event that something a person says or does contributes even minutely to a database that allows, say, a machine language translation algorithm, or a market prediction algorithm, to perform a task, then a nanopayment, proportional *both* to the degree of contribution *and* the resultant value, will be due to the person.

These nanopayments will add up, and lead to a new social contract in which people are motivated to contribute to an information economy in ever more substantial ways. This is an idea that takes capitalism more seriously than it has been taken before. A market economy should not just be about "businesses," but about everyone who contributes value.

I could just as well frame my argument in the language of barter and sharing. Leveraging cloud computing to make barter more efficient, comprehensive, and fair would ultimately lead to a similar design to what I am proposing. The usual Manichaean portrayal of the digital world is "new versus old." Crowdsourcing is "new," for instance, while salaries and pensions are "old." This book proposes pushing what is "new" all the way instead of part of the way. We need not shy away.

Big Talk, I Know . . .

Am I making a Swiftian modest proposal, or am I presenting a plan on the level? It's a little of both. I hope to widen the way people think about digital information and human progress. We need a palate cleansing, a broadening of horizons.

Maybe the approach described here to a humanistic information economy will be successfully adopted in the real world after some further refinement. Or maybe a new set of better ideas unrelated to and unforeseen by this book will have an easier time being heard because the deep freeze of convention will have been thawed a little by this exercise. It might merely serve as a check on the excesses of conventions that might otherwise become enshrined.

If this all sounds a little grandiose, understand that in the context of the community in which I function my presentation is practically self-deprecating. It is commonplace in Silicon Valley for very young people with a startup in a garage to announce that their goal is to change human culture globally and profoundly, within a few years, and that they aren't ready yet to worry about money, because acquiring a great fortune is a petty matter that will take care of itself. Furthermore, these bright little young bands succeed regularly. This is just Silicon Valley's version of normal.

Our idealisms and dreams often turn out to find fulfillment in events in the real world. Hopefully the ideas presented here work fractionally, and not just in the useless theater of ultimates. Even in the near term this framework of ideas offers an immediate way to understand how digital technology is changing economics and politics.

Need I add the obvious disclaimer? Even if the ideas turn out to be as good as they could possibly be, they won't be perfect. But if you believe that things can't really change, you might try wearing sunglasses as you read on.

Ancient Anticipation of the Singularity

ARISTOTLE FRETS

Aristotle directly addressed the role of people in a hypothetical high-tech world:

> If every instrument could accomplish its own work, obeying or anticipating the will of others, like the statues of Daedalus, or the tripods of Hephaestus, which, says the poet, of their own accord entered the assembly of the Gods; if, in like manner, the shuttle would weave and the plectrum touch the lyre without a hand to guide them, chief workmen would not want servants, nor masters slaves.[1]

At this ancient date, a number of possibilities were at least slightly visible to Aristotle's imagination. One was that the human condition was in part a function of what machines could not do. Another was that it was possible to imagine, at least hypothetically, that machines could do more. The synthesis was also conceived: Better machines could free and elevate people, even slaves.

If we could show Aristotle the technology of our times, I wonder what he would make of the problem of unemployment. Would he take Marx's position that better machines create an obligation (to be carried out by political bodies) to provide care and dignity to people who no longer need to work? Or would Aristotle say, "Kick the unneeded ones out of town. The polis is only for the people who own the machines, or do what machines still cannot do." Would he stand by idly as Athens was eventually depopulated?

I'd like to think the best of Aristotle, and assume he would realize that both choices are bogus; machine autonomy is nothing but theater. Information needn't be thought of as a freestanding thing, but rather as a human product. It is entirely legitimate to understand that people are still needed and valuable even when the loom can run without human muscle power. It is still running on human thought.

Aristotle was recalling Homer's account of the god Hephaestus's robotic servant creations. They were nerd's delights: golden, female, and servile. If it occurred to Aristotle that people might take it upon themselves to invent the robots to play music and operate looms, he didn't make that clear. So it reads as if people would wait around for the gods to gift some of us with automata so that we wouldn't have to pay others. That sounds so early 21st century to my ears. The artificial intelligence in the server gifts us with automation so we don't need to pay each other.

DO PEOPLE DESERVE TO BE PAID IF THEY AREN'T MISERABLE?

Aristotle is practically saying, "What a shame about enslaving people, but we need to do it so someone will play the music, since we need music. I mean somebody's got to endure the suffering to make the music happen. If we could only get by without music, then maybe we could free some of these pathetic slaves and be done with them."*

One of my passions is learning to play obscure and archaic musical instruments, and so I know through direct experience that playing the instruments available to ancient Greeks was a pain in the butt.† As hard as it is to imagine now, to the ancient Greeks, playing musical instruments was a misery to be forced on hired help or slaves.

These days music is more than a need to be met. Musicians who

---

*How prescient that Aristotle chose musical instruments and looms as his examples for machines that might one day operate automatically! These two types of machines did indeed turn out to be central to the prehistory of computation. The Jacquard programmable loom helped inspire calculating engines, while music theory and notation helped further the concept of abstract computation, as when Mozart wrote algorithmic, nondeterministic music incorporating dice throws. Both developments occurred around the turn of the 19th century.

†Getting strings to stay in tune on a lyre is not just difficult, but painful. You have to keep on twisting them and nudging them. Sometimes your fingers bleed. It's constant misery. The reeds on an aulos were probably a great annoyance as well, always too wet or too dry, too closed or too open. You futz with such reeds until they break, then you make new ones, and most of the time those don't work.

seek to make a living are goaded by the preferences of the marketplace into becoming symbols of a culture or a counterculture. The countercultural ones become a little wounded, vulnerable, wild, dangerous, or strange. Music is no longer a nutrient to be supplied, but something more mystical, a forge of meaning and identity: the realization of flow in life.

Multitudes of people want nothing more than to be able to play music for a living. We know this because we see their attempts online. There's a constant retweeting of the lie that there's a substantial new class of musicians succeeding financially through Internet publicity. Such people do exist, but only in token numbers.

However, a remarkable number of people do get attention and build followings for their music online. This book imagines that people like that might someday make a living at what they do. Improving the designs of information networks could result in the improvement of life for everyone as machines get better and better.

THE PLOT

Aristotle seems to want to escape the burden of accommodating lesser people. His quote about self-operating lutes and looms could be interpreted as a daydream that better technology will free us to some degree from having to deal with one another.

It's not as if everyone wanted to be closer to all of humanity when cities first formed. Athens was a necessity first, and a luxury second. No one wants to accommodate the diversity of strangers. People deal with each other politically because the material advantages are compelling. We find relative safety and sustenance in numbers. Agriculture and armies happened to work better as those enterprises got bigger, and cities built walls.

But in Aristotle's words you get a taste of what a nuisance it can be to accommodate others. Something was lost with the advent of the polis, and we still dream of getting it back.

The reward for a Roman general, upon retiring after years of combat, was a plot of land he could farm for himself. To be left alone, to be able to live off the land with the illusion of no polis to bug you, that was the dream. The American West offered that dream again, and still loathes giving it up. Justice Louis Brandeis famously defined privacy as the "right to be left alone."

In every case, however, abundance without politics was an illusion that could only be sustained in temporary bubbles, supported by armies. The ghosts of the losers haunt every acre of easy abundance. The greatest beneficiaries of civilization use all their power to create a temporary illusion of freedom from politics. The rich live behind gates, not just to protect themselves, but to pretend to not need anyone else, if only for a moment. In Aristotle's quote, we find the earliest glimmer of the hope that technological advancement could replace territorial conquest as a way of implementing an insulating bubble around a person.

People naturally seek the benefits of society, meaning the accommodation of strangers, while avoiding direct vulnerabilities to specific others as much as possible. This is a clichéd criticism of the online culture of the moment. People have thousands of "friends" and yet stare at a little screen when in the proximity of other people. As it was in Athens, so it is online.

PART TWO

The Cybernetic Tempest

CHAPTER 3

Money as Seen Through One Computer Scientist's Eyes

Money, God, and the Old Technology of Forgetting

Even if you think God is no more than a human invention, you must admit that another profoundly ancient idea we humans have invented has ensnared us even more. I am referring, of course, to money.

Money might have begun as a mnemonic counter for assets you couldn't keep under direct observation, like wandering sheep. A stone per sheep, so the shepherd would be confident all had been reunited after a day at pasture. In other words, artifacts took on information storage duties.*

Ancient people in Sumer and elsewhere made markings to keep track of trades and debts. A record of debt requires more complexity than a simple count of sheep. Individuals and intent must be joined to mere numbers, so some form of marking is required.

It used to be a huge bother to carve or paint records. That kind of hassle could not be sustained for just any information. Information storage was reserved for only a few special topics, such as laws and stories of kings and divinity. And yet debt made the cut.

Ancient money was information storage that represented events in the past. To the ears of many a financier, at this early stage

---

*This is a use beyond symbolic meaning, because the information that is stored can vary with increasing independence from any sense of flavorful symbolism. Three shells means the same thing as three stones. In other words, some embryonic prototype of nerdiness must have appeared.

"money" had not been born yet, only accounting. That kind of money can be called "past-oriented money."

The accounting, past-oriented, concept of money is concrete, which makes it cognitively natural. It is easier to think about a concrete number of sheep than about something abstract like statistics predicting the prospects of bundled derivatives.*

Modern future-oriented concepts of money only make sense in a universe that is pregnant with possibility. In the ancient world, when money and numbers were born as one, no one seems to have expected the world to embark on a project of inexorable improvement. Ancient cosmologies are often cyclic, or else the world was expected to slam into a wall, an Armageddon or Ragnarok. If all that will ever be known is already known, then information systems need only consider the past and the present.

Money has changed as the technology of representing it has changed. You probably like having modern money around, but it has a benefit you may not appreciate enough: You don't need to know where it comes from.

Money forgets. Unlike the earliest ancient clay markings, mass-produced money, created first as coins—and much later on a printing press—no longer remembered the story of its individual conception. If we were to know the history of each dollar, the world would be torn apart by war to an even greater degree than it already is, because people are even more clannish than greedy. Money allows blood enemies to collaborate; when money changes hands we forget for at least a moment the history of conflict and the potential for revenge.

Money forgets, but "god" remembers. God† knows how you earned that dollar and keeps a different set of books—moral books—based on that memory. If not god, then karma or Santa Claus.

Some conceptions of god seem to date back to the same era of

---

*Anthropologist David Graeber, in his book *Debt: The First 5,000 Years* (Brooklyn, NY: Chelsea House, 2010), proposes that debt is as old as civilization. However, simple debts are still representations of past events, rather than anticipations of future growth in value; the latter is what we call "finance."

†Here I am addressing only a moral aspect of divinity, not the whole of divinity.

The Information Technology of Optimism

Economics is still a young field, often unable to definitively falsify theories or achieve consensus on basic tenets. Much of this book concerns wealth creation, for instance, and yet a consensus on where wealth comes from remains elusive.[1]

I make no claim to be an economist. As a computer scientist, however, I consider how information systems evolve, and that can provide a window on economics that might be of use. Any information technology, from the most ancient money to the latest cloud computing, is based fundamentally on design judgments about what to remember and what to forget. Money is simply another information system. The essential questions about money, therefore, are what they always have been with information systems. What is remembered? What is forgotten?

When professional economics is unsettled, popular ideas about wealth creation can veer toward paranoia when it comes to we~~~~ creation. Widespread wealth creation is hard to s~~~~
~~~~th," h~~~~ ~~~~ometi~~~~

antiquity as money. You can think of some aspects of god
today, as being similar to the sum of the karmic memories
coins were fated to forget. God as a moral authority is almost
opposite of money.

Money was the first computation, and in this age of compu-
tion, the nature of money will be transformed yet again. Alas, th
combination of relentlessly improving digital technology and lazy
ideals has created a new era in which money sometimes doesn't forget all it should. This is not a healthy development.

In today's networked world, money stored in some computers
remembers more than money stored in other computers. This can
cause problems. One problem is a temptation to corruption.

Liars have to have the best memories. It's more work to keep
two sets of books than one set of books. The plague of toxic assets
and mega-pyramid schemes, and the pointless growth spurt of
the financial services sector would all have been impossible without vast computational resources remembering and sorting all the
details needed to snooker people. The most egregious modern liars
need computers, they can be inspired by them.

a bank makes a loan based on confidence you can pay it back, but there is latitude in how you'll do it, and multiple banks compete in part by having different heuristics to assess your loan-worthiness. What an interesting compromise we've come up with, allowing both freedom and planning!

This has been one of the key gifts of modern, future-oriented money. By making an abstract version of the essence of a promise (such as to repay a loan), we minimize the degree to which we have to otherwise conform to the expectations of one another. Just as money forgets the past, sparing us uncountable blood feuds, it also became a tool to abstract the future, allowing us to accept each other only to the minimum necessary degree needed to keep promises we've made.

This is what can happen when you buy a house with a mortgage in the context of the much-maligned fractional reserve system. Some of the money to pay for your house might not have ever existed had you not decided to buy. It is invented "out of thin air," to use the language of critics of the system,* based on the fact that you have made a promise to earn it somehow in the future.

Ordinary people can help create new money by making promises. You constrain the future by making a plan, and a promise to keep to it. Money is created in response, because in making that promise you have created value. New money is created to represent that value.

This is why it is possible for banks to fall apart when people don't pay their mortgages back. Banks sell assets that are partially made of the future intents of borrowers. When borrowers do something other than promised, those assets no longer exist.

An economy is like a cosmology. An expanding market, like an expanding universe, has unique laws and local phenomena. Growth is necessary in a healthy market, and it doesn't have to come at the expense of the environment or other precious things we hold in common. Growth is merely honest if the goodwill of ordinary people is to be acknowledged instead of forgotten. That means a little

*Both progressives like Thom Hartmann and libertarians like Ron Paul assail the fractional reserve banking system. It is often deemed "fraudulent," a tool of "international bankers," or a form of indentured servitude. While I agree there is a tremendous cause to criticize the present system, the venom seems directed at basic principles that deserve to be understood in a better light.

inflation—not too much—is proper, as people get better at doing things in ways that are acknowledged to be good for one another.* This is such a basic idea that it can be hard to see.

To lose trust in the basic inception of wealth is to lose trust in the idea of human improvement. If all the value that can be already is, then market dynamics can only be about churn, conflict, and accumulation. Static or contracting economies make people cruel and shortsighted.

In an expanding market, new value and new wealth are created. Not all new wealth is created from game-changing events like inventions or natural resource discoveries.† Some of it comes from the ability of ordinary people to keep promises.

The psychology of money hasn't kept up with the utility of money. This is why the gold standard is so appealing in populist politics in the United States and keeps on recurring in libertarian circles.‡ There is very little gold in the world, and its value is based on that scarcity. The amount of gold recovered from the earth thus far would fill only a little more than three Olympic swimming pools.[2]

If the world were to run on a gold standard, then that stash would have to function as the memory of the global computer that humanity uses to plan its economic future. Therefore, the gold standard is a fundamentally pessimistic idea. Limiting our model of how to invent the future to the memory capacity of around 50 billion troy ounces§ is just a way of saying the future holds nothing of surprising value.

---

*Yes, decrepit governments have been known to print money for its own sake, throwing a market into a death spiral. The creation of fake value is just as bad as the refusal to acknowledge real value.

†Historically growth also resulted from other factors like conquests and population growth, which are no longer sustainable.

‡The gold standard is admittedly something of a red herring (gold herring?), in that it isn't a mainstream idea, though it remains commonplace in certain streams of American political thought. It is relevant, however, because the idea that there must be a hard limit to the amount of money in the world also drives most Silicon Valley–styled schemes to create new forms of money, like Bitcoin.

§The smartphone in my pocket as I'm writing this in 2011 has 32 gigs of memory, which is within an order of magnitude of the number of bits that are represented by all the ounces of gold in the world.

Money is only valuable as interpreted by people, so talking about the absolute value of money is meaningless, but we *can* talk about the information content of money. Counting what we might value in the future using only the bits already counted in the past undervalues what might be discovered or invented. It disbelieves in the potential of people to make promises to each other to achieve novel, great things. And the future has consistently proven to be grander than anyone dreamed.

The transformation of money into an abstract representation of the future (that thing we call "finance") began about four hundred years ago and boomed in bursts ever since, as during the era of post–World War II prosperity. In order to understand what money had become by the time cheap digital networking appeared, remember that during the previous few centuries, wealth and well-being in industrializing societies expanded consistently in the big picture, despite periodic crashes and, of course, horrific wars. Even accounting for those many awful episodes, the future became impossible not to believe in.

Coincident with the European age of exploration and the echoes of the Enlightenment, an optimistic new kind of memory emerged, based on promises about future behavior, as opposed to what had already happened. Artificial memory became more person-centric out of necessity. There was no other way to define money regarding the future, or in other words, to engage in finance. Only people, not inanimate information, could make promises about what to do in the future. A dollar is a dollar whoever holds it, and securities can change hands. But a promise belongs to someone in particular or it is nothing.

The recent breakdowns of finance can be understood as the symptoms of a fallacious hope that information technology can make promises on its own, without people.

CHAPTER 4

The Ad Hoc Construction
of Mass Dignity

Are Middle Classes Natural?

The advent of finance in the last four centuries or so coincided with rising ideals, the introduction of technologies that brought comfort and health to millions of people for the first time, and even the miraculous, imperfect rise of middle classes. In the context of this transformation, it is natural to ask why more people could not benefit from modernity sooner. If technology is getting so good, and there is so much wealth, why should there still be poor people at all?

Technological progress inevitably inspires demands for greater benefits than it has delivered at a given time. We expect modern medicine to be mishap-free and modern planes to be crash-proof. And yet, a century ago it would have been unimaginable to be even able to want these things. Modern finance similarly pairs benefits with frustrations.

If finance is imagined as a great fluid of capital flowing about the world, it will seem to storm and accelerate into great vortices, just like any large body of fluid. Some vortices swirl upward and some downward. It has often been true that the poor get poorer and the rich richer. Karl Marx spent a preponderance of his energies on observing this tendency, but it did not take a microscope to notice it.

Attempts to stem the flow and replace finance entirely with politics by means such as Marxist revolutions turned out to be vastly crueler than even the worst dysfunctions of capital. So the conundrum of poverty in a world driven by finance remains a challenge.

Marx wanted something that most people, including me, don't want: a committee to make sure everyone gets what's best for them. Let's reject the Marxist ideal and instead consider the question of whether markets can be counted on to create middle classes as a matter of course.

Marx argued that finance was an inherently hopeless technology, and that market systems will always degrade into the rut of plutocracy. A Keynesian economist would accept that "ruts" exist but would also add that falling into ruts can be staved off indefinitely with interventions. While there are theories to the contrary, it seems that middle classes have thus far relied on interventions in order to survive.

Great wealth is naturally persistent, generation to generation, as is deep poverty, but a middle-class status has not proven to be stable without a little help. All the examples of long-term stable middle classes we know of relied on Keynesian interventions as well as persistent mechanisms like social safety nets to moderate market outcomes.

However, it's possible that digital networks will someday provide a better alternative to these mechanisms and interventions. To understand why, we need to think about human systems in fundamental terms.

Two Familiar Distributions

There are two familiar ways that people can be organized into spectrums.

One is the star system, or winner-take-all distribution. There can only be a few movie or sports stars, for example. So a peak comprised of a very small number of top winners juts out of a sunken slope, or a "long tail" of a lot of poorer performers. There are stars and wannabes, but not a lot of Mr. In-Betweens.

A winner-take-all distribution.

The distributions of outcomes in fashionable, digitally networked, hyperefficient markets tend to be winner-take-all. It's true for tech startups, for instance; only a few succeed, but those that do can amass stupendous fortunes. It's also true for new kinds of individual success stories in the online world, as when someone actually earns serious money from a smartphone app or a video uploaded to YouTube; only a tiny number do well, while the multitudes dream but fail.

The other familiar distribution is the bell curve. That means there is a bulge of average people and two tails of exceptional people, one high and one low. Bell curves arise from most measurements of people, because that's how statistics works. This will be true even if the measurement is somewhat contrived or suspect. There isn't really a single type of intelligence, for instance, yet we take intelligence tests, and indeed the results form a bell curve distribution.

A bell curve distribution.

In an economy with a strong middle class, the distribution of economic outcomes for people might approach a bell curve, like the distribution of any measured quality like intelligence. Unfortunately, the new digital economy, like older feudal or robber baron economies, is thus far generating outcomes that resemble a "star system" more often than a bell curve.

What makes one distribution appear instead of the other?

Tweaks to Network Design Can Change
Distributions of Outcomes

Later on I'll present a preliminary proposal for how to organize networks to organically give rise to more bell curve distributions of outcomes, instead of winner-take-all distributions. We don't know as much as I believe we one day will about the implications of specific network designs, but we already know enough to improve what we do.

Winner-take-all distributions come about when there is a global sorting of people within a single framework. Indeed, a bell curve distribution of a quality like intelligence will generate a winner-take-all outcome if intelligence, whatever that means according to a single test, is the only criterion for success in a contest.

Is there anything wrong with winner-take-all outcomes? Don't they just promote the best of everything for the benefit of everyone? There are many cases where winner-take-all contests are beneficial. Certainly it's beneficial to the sciences to have special prizes like the Nobel Prize. But broader forms of reward like academic tenure and research grants are vastly more beneficial.

Alas, winner-take-all patterns are becoming more common in other parts of our society. The United States, for instance, has famously endured a weakening of the middle class and an extreme rise in income inequality in the network age. The silicon age has been a new gilded age, but that need not and ought not continue to be so.

Winner-take-all contests should function as the treats in an economy, the cherries on top. To rely on them fundamentally is a mistake—not just a pragmatic or ethical mistake, but also a mathematical one.

A star system is just a way of packaging a bell curve. It presents the same information using a different design principle. When used foolishly or excessively, winner-take-all star systems amplify errors and make outcomes less meaningful.

Distributions can only be based on measurements, but as in the case of measuring intelligence, the nature of measurement is often complicated and troubled by ambiguities. Consider the problem of noise, or what is known as luck in human affairs. Since the rise of the new digital economy, around the turn of the century, there has been a distinct heightening of obsessions with contests like *American Idol,* or other rituals in which an anointed individual will suddenly become rich and famous. When it comes to winner-take-all contests, onlookers are inevitably fascinated by the role of luck. Yes, the winner of a singing contest is good enough to be the winner, but even the slightest flickering of fate might have changed circumstances to make someone else the winner. Maybe a different shade of makeup would have turned the tables.

And yet the rewards of winning and losing are vastly different. While some critics might have aesthetic or ethical objections to winner-take-all outcomes, a mathematical problem with them is that noise is amplified. Therefore, if a societal system depends too much on winner-take-all contests, then the acuity of that system will suffer. It will become less reality-based.

When a bell curve distribution is appreciated as a bell curve instead of as a winner-take-all distribution, then noise, luck, and conceptual ambiguity aren't amplified. It makes statistical sense to talk about average intelligence or high intelligence, but not to identify the single most intelligent person.

Letting Bell Curves Be Bell Curves

Star systems in a society come about because of a paucity of influential sorting processes. If there are only five contests for stars, and only room for five of each kind of star, then there can only be twenty-five stars total.

In a star system, the top players are rewarded tremendously, while almost everyone else—facing in our era an ever-larger, more global body of competitive peers—is driven toward poverty (because of competition or perhaps automation).

To get a bell curve of outcomes there must be an unbounded variety of paths, or sorting processes, that can lead to success. That is to say there must be many ways to be a star.

In schoolbook economics, a particular person might enjoy a commercial advantage because of being in a particular place or having special access to some valuable information. In antenimbosian* days, a local baker could deliver fresh bread more readily than a distant bread factory, even if the factory bread was cheaper, and a local banker could discern who was likely to repay a loan better than a distant analyst could. Each person who found success in a market economy was a local star.

Digital networks have thus far been mostly applied to *reduce* such benefits of locality, and that trend will lead to economic implosion if it isn't altered. The reasons why will be explored in later chapters, but for now, consider a scenario that could easily unfold in this century: If a robot can someday construct or print out another robot at almost no cost, and *that* robot can bake fresh bread right in your kitchen, or at the beach, then both the old bread factory *and* the local baker will experience the same reduction of routes to success as the recording musician already has. Robotic bread recipes would be shared over the 'net just like music files are today. The economic beneficiary would own some distant large computer that spied on everyone who ate bread in order to route advertisements or credit to them. Bread eaters would get bargains, it's true, but those would be more than canceled out by reduced prospects.

Star Systems Starve Themselves;
Bell Curves Renew Themselves

The fatal conundrum of a hyperefficient market optimized to yield star-system results is that it will not create enough of a middle class

* "Before the cloud."

to support a real market dynamic. A market economy cannot thrive absent the well-being of average people, even in a gilded age. Gilding cannot float. It must reside on a substrate. Factories must have multitudes of customers. Banks must have multitudes of reliable borrowers.

Even if factories and banks are made obsolete—and this is likely to happen in this century—the underlying principle will still apply. It is an eternal truth, not an artifact of the digital age.

The prominence of middle classes in the last century actually made the rich richer than would have a quest to concentrate wealth absolutely. Broad economic expansion is more lucrative than the winner taking all. Some of the very rich occasionally express doubts, but even from the most elite perspective, widespread affluence is best nurtured, rather than sapped into oblivion. Henry Ford, for instance, made a point of pricing his earliest mass-produced cars so that his own factory workers could afford to buy them. It is that balance that creates economic growth, and thus opportunity for more wealth.

Even the ultrarich are best served by a bell curve distribution of wealth in a society with a healthy middle class.

An Artificial Bell Curve Made of Levees

Before digital networks, eras of technological development often favored winner-take-all results. Railroads enthroned railroad barons; oil fields, oil barons. Digital networks, however, do not intrinsically need to repeat this pattern.

Unfortunately, in many previous economic and technical revolutions, there was no alternative but to accept situations that tended to yield star-system results. Capital in these situations resisted rising up into a middle class mountain, just as would any fluid. To combat the degradations of star systems, an ad hoc set of "levees" awkwardly arose over time to compensate for the madness of fluid mechanics and protect the middle class.

Levees are broad dams of modest altitude intended to hold back the natural flow of fluid to protect something precious. A mountain of them rising in the middle of the economy might be visualized as a mountain of rice paddies, like the ones found in parts of Southeast Asia. Such a mountain rising in the sea of the economy creates a prosperous island in the tempest of capital.

An ad hoc mountain of rice-paddy-like levees raises a middle class out of the flow of capital that would otherwise tend toward the extremes of a long tail of poverty (the ocean to the left) and an elite peak of wealth (the waterfall/geyser in the upper right corner). Democracy depends on the mountain being able to outspend the geyser. Sketch by author.

Middle-class levees came in many forms. Most developed countries opted to emphasize government-based levees, though the ability to pay for social safety nets is now strained in most parts of the developed world by austerity measures taken to alleviate the financial crisis that began in 2008. Some levees were pseudo-governmental. In the 20th century, an American form of levee creation leveraged tax policy to encourage middle-class investment in homes and at-the-time conservative market positions, like individual retirement accounts.

There were also hard-won levees specific to avocations: academic tenure, union membership, taxi medallion ownership, cosmetology licenses, copyrights, patents, and many more. Industries also arose to sell middle-class levees, like insurance.

None of these were perfect. None sufficed in isolation. A successful middle-class life typically relied on more than one form of levee.

And yet without these exceptions to the torrential rule of the open flow of capital, capitalism could not have thrived.

The Senseless Ideal of a Perfectly Pure Market

Something obvious needs to be pointed out because of the historical moment in which this book is being written. It will probably read as a silly diversion to future readers during saner times. (I am ever the optimist!)

There is shrill, shattering, global debate that pits government against markets, or politics against money. In Europe, should financial considerations from the point of view of German lenders trump political considerations from Greek borrowers? In the United States, a huge wave of so-called populist ideology declares that "government is the problem" and markets are the answer.

To all this I say: I am a technologist and neither position makes sense to me. Technologies are never perfect. They always need tweaks.

You might, for example, want to design a tablet to be pristine and platonic, without any physical buttons, but only a touchscreen. Wouldn't that be more perfect and true to the ideal? But you can't ever quite do it. Some extra physical buttons, to turn the thing on, for instance, turn out to be indispensable. Being an absolutist is a certain way to become a failed technologist.

Markets are an information technology. A technology is useless if it can't be tweaked. If market technology can't be fully automatic and needs some "buttons," then there's no use in trying to pretend otherwise. You don't stay attached to poorly performing quests for perfection. You fix bugs.

And there are bugs! We just went through taxpayer-funded bailouts of networked finance in much of the world, and no amount of austerity seems enough to fully pay for that. So the technology needs to be tweaked. Wanting to tweak a technology shows a commitment to it, not a rejection of it.

So, let us continue with the project at hand, which is to see if network technology can make capitalism better instead of worse.

Please don't pretend there's some "pure" form of capitalism we should be faithful to. There isn't.

Income Is Different from Wealth

During the mortgage craze of the baby years of the 21st century, there was a popular book called *Rich Dad, Poor Dad*. The author explained that his real dad, an academic, earned a reasonable salary, but he never seemed to get ahead. His mentor, the "rich dad," made investments instead of thinking only in terms of earning. So millions of people chased after this magical thing enjoyed by the rich, not mere income but *wealth*. (Unfortunately, it turned out that buying a home, one of the principal strategies of that movement, summarily turned into an invitation to be scammed.)

Very few rich people are strictly big earners. There are a few in sports or entertainment, but they are freakish anomalies, economically speaking. Rich people typically earn money from capital. They have invested in real estate, stocks, or more rarefied opportunities, and money sloughs out of those positions. The rich have internalized a psychology of finance, as opposed to accounting. Another way to put it: The rich enjoy big levees in the flow.

Levees grow naturally and gracefully at the upper extremes of wealth. Wealth for the most successful people becomes like the ocean that rivers empty into after a great storm of commercial transformation.* It is easier to stay rich than to get rich.

The still-missing piece of the puzzle of capitalism is how to create a less ad hoc, more organic, middle-class-sustaining form of wealth, as opposed to mere income.

The ideal mechanism would be fluid enough to reward creativ-

---

*Apologies for inconsistencies in the topography of my images. In this case, the rich are placed at the lowest hydrological elevation, collecting fluid not trapped in levees, while elsewhere they are placed at the top, which corresponds better to our usual images and terminology. In mathematics we often switch around top and bottom to visualize ideas that become more intuitive one way or the other. We are constantly trying to find ways that our minds can make sense of abstractions, and that's hard enough that I am willing to cede consistency.

ity, and not turn into a moribund power base for committees. The design ought to nonetheless be tough enough to withstand inevitable giant hurricanes of capital flow, which will surely appear as new technologies unfold in this century. It ought to be graceful and ordinary, and not dependent on all-or-nothing life events, like getting into a union. A robust solution would be "scalable," meaning that it will be strengthened, not weakened, as more and more people embrace it.

A proposal for such a design appears later in this book.

The Taste of Politics

The beneficiaries of middle-class-sustaining levees have been subject to assault from two directions. From above, the rich, who had been elevated by the upward drafts of capital flow, sometimes look down and see an artificial blockage in their flow. A union, for instance, might prevent an employer from choosing an employee who would work for less and demand less security or safety. What might seem to a worker like security can seem to an employer or an investor like a blockade on the corrective mechanisms of the market.

From below, those who do not enjoy a particular sort of levee of their own might resent the levees of others. This is the case when people who don't benefit from levees like copyright royalties, union membership, or academic tenure assault the legitimacy of what seem to be contrived benefits enjoyed by others, or even more annoyingly, what seem like barriers to their own flow.

One example came up for me in the 1980s, when I mounted strange musical performances using early Virtual Reality equipment onstage.

In the strongest union towns it was almost impossible to perform. In places like Chicago, I would be forbidden from plugging equipment together onstage. That was a job for a union member, except no union member had ever dealt with shape-sensing optical fiber bundles or wiring for magnetic field generators that were needed to track parts of performers' bodies. So we would hit an impasse. It was absurd. Furthermore, the union people were sometimes kind of scary. Theirs wasn't just an intellectual argument; the threat of physical enforcement hung in the air. When we finally worked out a way to stage an experimental performance, it involved paying various people rather well to just sit there, and paying others to confirm they were sitting there.

So the union seemed at that moment to stand in the way of both personal expression and technological progress. And yet, I appreciate how unions came to be and how important they have been.

Next to every levee is a battle trench. The fight to establish unions was deadly, at times approaching a form of war. Generations of labor activists took great risks and suffered so that weekends, retirement, and general calm and security could become imaginable for ordinary people. The labor movement has never been perfect, but I respect it and am grateful for the improvements it has brought to our world.

Despite my favorable regard for organized labor, for the purposes of this book I have to focus somewhat on certain failings. The problems of interest to me are not really with the labor movement, but with the nature of levees. What might be called "upper-class levees," like exclusive investment funds, have been known to blur into Ponzi schemes or other criminal enterprises, and the same pattern exists for levees at all levels.

Levees are more human than algorithmic, and that is not an entirely good thing. Whether for the rich or the middle class, levees are inevitably a little conspiratorial, and conspiracy naturally attracts corruption. Criminals easily exploited certain classic middle-class levees; the mob famously infiltrated unions and repurposed music royalties as a money-laundering scheme.

Levees are a rejection of unbridled algorithm and an insertion of human will into the flow of capital. Inevitably, human oversight brings with it all the flaws of humans. And yet despite their rough and troubled nature, antenimbosian levees worked well enough to preserve middle classes despite the floods, storms, twisters, and droughts of a world contoured by finance. Without our system of levees, rising like a glimmering bell-curved mountain of rice paddies, capitalism would probably have decayed into Marx's "attractor nightmare" in which markets decay into plutocracy.

Drove My Chevy to the Levee but the Levee Was Dry

The levees weathered all manner of storms over many decades. Before the networking of everything, there was a balance of powers between levees and capital, between labor and management. The legitimizing of the levees of the middle classes reinforced the legitimacy of the levees of the rich. A symmetrical social contract between nonequals made modernity possible.

However, the storms of capital became super-energized when computers got cheap enough to network finance in the last two decades of the 20th century. That story will be told shortly. For now it's enough to say that with Enron, Long-Term Capital Management, and their descendants in the new century, the fluid of capital became a superfluid. Just as with the real climate, the financial climate was amplified by modern technology, and extremes became more extreme.

Finally the middle-class levees were breached. One by one, they fell under the surging pressures of superflows of information and capital. Musicians lost many of the practical benefits of protections like copyrights and mechanicals. Unions were unable to stop manufacturing jobs from moving about the world as fast as the tides of capital would carry them. Mortgages were overleveraged, value was leached out of savings, and governments were forced into austerity.

The old adversaries of levees were gratified. The Wall Street mogul and the young Pirate Party voter sang the same song. All must be made fluid. Even victims often cheered at the misfortunes of people who were similar to them.

Because so many people, from above and below, never liked levees anyway, there was a triumphalist cheer whenever a levee was breached. We cheered when musicians were freed from the old system so that now they could earn their livings from gig to gig. To this day we still dance on the grave of the music industry and speak of "unshackling musicians from labels."[1] We cheered when public worker unions were weakened by austerity so that taxpayers were no longer responsible for the retirements of strangers.

Homeowners were no longer the primary players in the fates of their own mortgages, now that any investment could be unendingly leveraged from above. The cheer in that case went something like this: Isn't it great that people are taking responsibility for the fact that life isn't fair?

Newly uninterrupted currents disrupted the shimmering mountain of middle-class levees. The great oceans of capital started to form themselves into a steep, tall, winner-take-all, razor-thin tower and an emaciated long tail.

How Is Music like a Mortgage?

The principal way a powerful, unfortunately designed digital network flattens levees is by enabling data copying.* For instance, a game or app that can't be easily copied, perhaps because it's locked into a hardware ecosystem, can typically be sold for more online than a file that contains music, because that kind can be more easily copied. When copying is easy, there is almost no intrinsic scarcity, and therefore market value collapses.

There's an endless debate about whether file sharing is "stealing." It's an argument I'd like to avoid, since I don't really care to have a moral position on a software function. Copying in the abstract is vapid and neutral.

To get ahead of the argument a little, my position is that we eventually shouldn't "pirate" files, but it's premature to condemn people who do it today. It would be unfair to demand that people cease sharing/pirating files when those same people are not paid for their participation in very lucrative network schemes. Ordinary people are relentlessly spied on, and not compensated for information taken from them. While I would like to see everyone eventually pay for music and the like, I would not ask for it until there's reciprocity.

---

*As we'll see, the very idea of copying over a network is technically ill-founded, and was recognized as such by the first generation of network engineers and scientists. Copying was only added in because of bizarre, tawdry events in the decades between the invention of networking and the widespread use of networking.

What matters most is whether we are contributing to a system that will be good for us all in the long term. If you never knew the music business as it was, the loss of what used to be a significant middle-class job pool might not seem important. I will demonstrate, however, that we should perceive an early warning for the rest of us.

Copying a musician's music ruins economic dignity. It doesn't necessarily deny the musician any form of income, but it does mean that the musician is restricted to a real-time economic life. That means one gets paid to perform, perhaps, but not paid for music one has recorded in the past. It is one thing to sing for your supper occasionally, but to have to do so for every meal forces you into a peasant's dilemma.

The peasant's dilemma is that there's no buffer. A musician who is sick or old, or who has a sick kid, cannot perform and cannot earn. A few musicians, a very tiny number indeed, will do well, but even the most successful real-time-only careers can fall apart suddenly because of a spate of bad luck. Real life cannot avoid those spates, so eventually almost everyone living a real-time economic life falls on hard times.

Meanwhile, some third-party spy service like a social network or search engine will invariably create persistent wealth from the information that is copied, the recordings. A musician living a real-time career, divorced from what used to be commonplace levees like royalties or mechanicals,* is still free to pursue reputation and even income (through live gigs, T-shirts, etc.), but no longer wealth. The wealth goes to the central server.

Please notice how similar music is to mortgages. When a mortgage is leveraged and bundled into complex undisclosed securities by unannounced third parties over a network, then the homeowner suffers a reduced chance at access to wealth. The owner's promise to repay the loan is copied, like the musicians' music file, many times.

So many copies of the wealth-creating promise specific to the homeowner are created that the value of the homeowner's original

---

*There are laws that guarantee a musician some money whenever a physical, or "mechanical" copy of a music recording is made. This was a hard-won levee for earlier generations of musicians.

51

copy is reduced. The copying reduces the homeowner's long-term access to wealth.

To put it another way, the promise of the homeowner to repay the loan can only be made once, but that promise, and the risk that the loan will not be repaid, can be *received* innumerable times. Therefore the homeowner will end up paying for that amplified risk, somehow. It will eventually turn into higher taxes (to bail out a financial concern that is "too big to fail"), reduced property values in a neighborhood burdened by stupid mortgages, and reduced access to credit.

Access to credit becomes scarce for all but those with the absolute tip-top credit ratings once all the remote recipients of the promise to repay have amplified risk. Even the wealthiest nations can have trouble holding on to top ratings. The world of real people, as opposed to the fantasy of the "sure thing," becomes disreputable to the point that lenders don't want to lend anymore.

Once you see it, it's so clear. A mortgage is similar to a music file. A securitized mortgage is similar to a pirated music file.

In either case, no *immediate* harm was done to the person who once upon a time stood to gain a levee benefit. After all, what has happened is just a setting of bits in someone else's computer. Nothing but an abstract copy has been created; a silent, small change, far away. In the long term, the real people at the source *are* harmed, however.

CHAPTER 5

"Siren Servers"

There Can't Be Complexity Without Ambiguity

We are aware of emergent, complex problems like global climate change only because of how much data there is. But there are special challenges in assessing problems that come into our awareness because of big data. It's hard to confirm that such broad problems definitely exist. Then, even if a consensus emerges about existence, it is hard to test remedies. One truism has emerged in the networked age. The mere existence of big data doesn't mean that people will agree about what it means.

The problem I am acting on is that a particular way of digitizing economic and cultural activity will ultimately shrink the economy while concentrating wealth and power in new ways that are not sustainable. That mistake is setting us up for avoidable traumas, as machines get much better in this century.

Some will say that the problem I worry about does not even exist. There is a legitimate claim of ambiguity on this point, and that ambiguity is completely typical of how problems present themselves in our modern world of networked big data. For instance, one might argue that some of the hundred-thousand-plus jobs that seem to have been lost in the transition from Kodak to Instagram will be made up for because people will be able to use photo sharing to sell their handicrafts more efficiently. While this might turn out to be true in one instance or another, I argue it is false in the big picture.

My initial interest was motivated by a simple question: If network technology is supposed to be so good for everyone, why has the developed world suffered so much just as the technology has become widespread? Why was there so much economic pain at once all over the developed world just as computer networking dug in to every aspect of human activity, in the early 21st century? Was it a coincidence?

There are a number of different explanations for the Great Recession that can be helpful. Brushing up against fundamental limits to growth is part of it, as is the rise of new powers of India, China, and Brazil, so that suddenly there are more customers with means bidding for the same resource base. There are also a lot more old people in most parts of the developed world, and more ways to spend money on their medical care than ever before.

But there's something else going on as well, which is that the mechanisms of finance failed and screwed almost everybody. If we acknowledge the extraordinary way in which virtually the whole developed world seemed to go into hopeless debt at once, an explanation is demanded beyond the rise of China, or the expense of social safety nets in southern Europe, or deregulation in the United States.

There's a simple answer to the mystery: Finance got networked in the wrong way. The big kinds of computation that have made certain other industries like music "efficient" from a particular point of view were applied to finance, and that broke finance. It made finance stupid.

Consider the expansion of the financial sector prior to the Great Recession. It's not as if that sector was accomplishing any more than it ever had. If its product is to manage risk, it clearly did a terrible job. It expanded purely because of its top positions on networks. Moral hazard has never met a more efficient amplifier than a digital network. The more influential digital networks become, the more potential moral hazard we'll see, unless we change the architecture.

A First Pass at a Definition

A Siren Server, as I will refer to such a thing, is an elite computer, or coordinated collection of computers, on a network. It is characterized by narcissism, hyperamplified risk aversion, and extreme information asymmetry. It is the winner of an all-or-nothing contest, and it inflicts smaller all-or-nothing contests on those who interact with it.

Siren Servers gather data from the network, often without having to pay for it. The data is analyzed using the most powerful available computers, run by the very best available technical people. The results of the analysis are kept secret, but are used to manipulate the rest of the world to advantage.

That plan will always eventually backfire, because the rest of the world cannot indefinitely absorb the increased risk, cost, and waste dispersed by a Siren Server. Homer sternly warned sailors to not succumb to the call of the sirens, and yet was entirely complacent about Hephaestus's golden female robots. But Sirens might be even more dangerous in inorganic form, because it is then that we are really most looking at ourselves in disguise. It is not the siren who harms the sailor, but the sailor's inability to think straight. So it is with us and our machines.

Siren Servers are fated by their nature to sow illusions. They are cousins to another seductive literary creature, star of the famous thought experiment known as Maxwell's Demon, after the great 19th century physicist James Clerk Maxwell. The demon is an imaginary creature that, if it could only exist, would be able to implement a perpetual motion machine and perform other supernatural tricks.

Maxwell's Demon might be stationed at a tiny door separating two chambers filled with water or air. It would only allow hot molecules to pass one way, and cold molecules to pass in the opposite direction. After a while, one side would be hot and the other cold, and you could let them mix again, rushing together so quickly that the stream could run a generator. In that way, the tiny act of discriminating between hot and cold would produce infinite energy, because you could repeat the process forever.

The reason Maxwell's Demon cannot exist is that it does take resources to perform an act of discrimination. We imagine computation is free, but it never is. The very act of choosing which particle is cold or hot itself becomes an energy drain and a source of waste heat. The principle is also known as "no free lunch."

We do our best to implement Maxwell's Demon whenever we manipulate reality with our technologies, but we can never do so perfectly; we certainly can't get ahead of the game, which is known as entropy. All the air conditioners in a city emit heat that makes the city hotter overall. While you can implement what seems to be a Maxwell's Demon if you don't look too far or too closely, in the big picture you always lose more than you gain.

Every bit in a computer is a wannabe Maxwell's Demon, separating the state of "one" from the state of "zero" for a while, at a cost. A computer on a network can also act like a wannabe demon if it tries to sort data from networked people into one or the other side of some imaginary door, while pretending there is no cost or risk involved. For instance, a Siren Server might allow only those who would be cheap to insure through a doorway (to become insured) in order to make a supernaturally ideal, low-risk insurance company. Such a scheme would let high-risk people pass one way, and low-risk ones pass the other way, in order to implement a phony perpetual motion machine out of a human society. However, the uninsured would not cease to exist; rather, they would instead add to the cost of the whole system, which includes the people who run the Siren Server. A short-term illusion of risk reduction would actually lead to increased risk in the longer term.

Where Sirens Beckon

Some of the prominent present-day Siren Servers include high-tech finance schemes, like high-frequency trading or derivatives funds, fashionable Silicon Valley consumer-facing businesses like search or social networking, modern insurance, modern intelligence agencies, and a multitude of other examples.

The latest waves of high-tech innovation have not created jobs like the old ones did.* Iconic new ventures like Facebook employ vastly fewer people than big older companies like, say, Gen-

*This is documented in Martin Ford's book *The Lights in the Tunnel* (2009). He sees jobs going away, and proposes that people in the future be paid only for consuming wisely, since they eventually won't be needed for producing anything. I find that idea inadequately human-centric and overly dismal, but it is an interesting contrast to my proposal.

eral Motors. Put another way, the new schemes, the Siren Servers, channel much of the productivity of ordinary people into an informal economy of barter and reputation, while concentrating the extracted old-fashioned wealth for themselves. All activity that takes place over digital networks becomes subject to arbitrage, in the sense that risk is routed to whoever suffers lesser computation resources.

The universal advice of our times is that people who want to do well, as information technology advances, will need to double down on their technical educations, and learn to be entrepreneurial and adaptable. These are the skills that might win you a position close to a Siren Server.

Planning to get as close as possible to a Siren Server is good advice in the near term. That is how the great fortunes of our age are being made. But there won't be enough positions close to Siren Servers to sustain a society unless we change the way we do things.

CHAPTER 6

The Specter of the Perfect Investment

Our Free Lunch

The specter of perfect investing haunts Silicon Valley. Wall Street and other theaters where digital networks channel human activity are similarly haunted.

A "perfect investment" in a Siren Server can be arbitrarily small, initially, but will yield titanic rewards, and often quickly. It will require remarkably few early employees or co-investors, and little power sharing. Even once it becomes gargantuan it will remain a rather unpopulated venture.

One needn't know exactly how the perfect investment will make money in advance, since the point is to channel information. Information and money are mutable cousins, so the investor will become rich without needing to know how. (Indeed, money might not even be the object, though even in that case, a large number of ordinary people will still lose some of their economic prospects* in order to support the influence and prominence of a Siren Server.)

The perfect investment presides at an arm's length from real events in the world, so that it barely takes on liability. It ideally doesn't do or make anything. The plan is simply to channel the information of those who do act in the world. It is those actors who take risks, not the perfect investment.†

*Wikipedia and nonprofit share sites have this quality.
†This goes beyond the traditional idea of cost externalization, to automated, unexamined risk externalization.

For example, it is not YouTube's job to notice that someone has posted copyrighted video. Misrepresented assets flowed through Great Recession–era funds that were bailed out, but as of this writing most of the beneficiaries have escaped any of the downsides, which were radiated out to taxpayers and ground-level investors. The responsibility for fixing problems enabled by the perfect investment lies with those sorry souls who are fated to act and take risks in the disadvantaged neighborhood that is reality.

The perfect investment will quickly anneal into an impermeable and unchallengeable position, by nature a monopoly in its domain. Competition in a traditional sense might appear, but it will never achieve more than a token status. (I use the term *monopoly* here not in the legal sense, as in antitrust law, but in the vernacular Silicon Valley sense. For instance, Peter Thiel, founder of PayPal and a foundational investor in Facebook, taught students in his Stanford course on startups to find a way to create "monopolies.")

Candy

The primary business of digital networking has come to be the creation of ultrasecret mega-dossiers about what others are doing, and using this information to concentrate money and power. It doesn't matter whether the concentration is called a social network, an insurance company, a derivatives fund, a search engine, or an online store. It's all fundamentally the same. Whatever the intent might have been, the result is a wielding of digital technology against the future of the middle class.

I know many of the people who run the biggest, richest servers, where the money and power are being concentrated. They're remarkably decent, for the most part. You couldn't ask for a nicer elite. But that doesn't really help. Iconic online empires have been accepted as sacrosanct. It's okay to notice in the abstract that free online services aren't creating as many jobs as they destroy, but we still hold up these newfangled companies as examples of how innovation will drive the economy.

The problem is broad and we are all part of it. Individuals of high or low station are not reasonably able to avoid playing along in an immediately compelling system, even if that system is destroying itself in the big picture. Who wouldn't want to get a quick online ego boost, or accept an insanely great deal on an online coupon, or insanely easy home mortgage financing? These might seem like unrelated temptations, but they reveal themselves to be similar once you think about information systems in the terms of information, instead of imposing outdated categories on them.

In each case, someone is practically blackmailed by the distortions of playing the pawn in someone else's network. It's a weird kind of stealth blackmail because if you look at what's in front of you, the deal looks sweet, but you don't see all that *should* be in front of you.

We loved the crazy cheap easy mortgages, motivated by crazed overleveraging. We love the free music, enabled by crazed copying. We love cheap online prices, offered by what would have once seemed like national intelligence agencies. These newer spy services do not struggle on behalf of our security, but instead figure out just how little payment everyone in the chain can be made to accept. We are not benefiting from the benevolence of some artificial intelligence superbeing. We are exploiting each other off the books while those concentrating our information remain on the books. We love our treats but will eventually discover we are depleting our own value.

That's how we can have economic troubles despite there being so much wealth in the system, and during a period of increasing efficiencies. Great fortunes are being made on shrinking the economy instead of growing it. It's not a result of some evil scheme, but a side effect of an idiotic elevation of the fantasy that technology is getting smart and standing on its own, without people.

Radiant Risk

A Siren Server can gather information to reduce its exposure to the risks inherent in its operation, which just means radiating those risks out to the general society, and that includes you. Amazon provides an example.

The usual complaints about Amazon* come from its competitors, and it's natural to dismiss them. However, if you're a smaller competing seller of books, the situation is quite stark.

A "bot" program in the Amazon cloud monitors the price of books you sell everywhere else in the world; it automatically makes sure Amazon is never undersold. There is no longer a local intelligence advantage for pricing by small local sellers. This leads to bizarre outcomes, such as books being priced for free through Amazon simply because they are being given away as part of a promotion elsewhere.[1] Therefore promotions for ordinary, small sellers become more expensive or riskier than they otherwise would be. Information supremacy for one company becomes, as a matter of course, a form of behavior modification of the rest of the world.

The total amount of risk in the market as a whole stays the same, perhaps, but it's not distributed evenly. Instead the smaller players take on more risk while the player with the biggest computer takes on less. Amazon's risks are reduced—it won't lose a sale to someone else's pricing strategy—while local sellers face increased risks if they want to undertake their own pricing strategies.

This is just one simple example of how information advantages turn into money and power advantages. Every player with a less global information position is forced to take on more risk so that

---

*Authors and publishers have become afraid of criticizing Amazon. To me, the people who run the big servers like Amazon are just a bunch of techie bums like me, so I know they can take a little criticism. However, once this book was already written, Microsoft, where I do my research, started a partnership with Amazon rival Barnes & Noble, so now I might be perceived as partisan. There is no way for anyone who is deeply engaged in the perversely intertwined world of tech to write about the big issues and not have conflicts of interest. To state it as clearly as I can: I am part of what I criticize. I benefit from time to time by actively participating in the schemes I would like to see ended; it happens as a side effect of doing the things I love to do. However, I don't want to become an academic or remote observer of tech events. My choice is to be engaged even if that means I am tainted. I live with contradictions, in accordance with the human condition, but do my best not to forget what absurdities are involved. What I can offer is being open about what I think.

the player with a superior information position can enjoy reduced risk.

You Can't See as Much of the Server as It Can See of You

The strange thing is that book consumers also have reason to be concerned, but it can be hard to tell this is so. From a consumer perspective, Amazon would seem to be driving prices down, and that ought to be a great thing. And yet the situation is more complicated than that.

Around the turn of the century Amazon was caught up in a controversy about "differential pricing." Essentially this means that an online site might charge you more for given items than it charges other people, like your neighbors.[2] Amazon stated at the time that it was not really discrimination, but experimentation. It was offering different prices to different people to see what they would pay.

There is nothing special about Amazon in this regard. Another example is the travel site Orbitz, which was found to be directing users of more expensive computers to more expensive travel options.[3] Who could be surprised? It is natural for a business to take advantage of a manifest benefit staring it right in the face. We probably don't know about the vast majority of examples. While customers might become uncomfortable when made aware of these practices, they are generally legal.

Despite the supposed openness of everything in the Internet age, customers don't necessarily notice differential pricing. Eventually such practices can come to light anecdotally, though we never learn how extensive they really are. In a physical store, you would immediately notice if a cashier eyed you and decided what price you should pay.

Differential pricing is worthy of attention only because of its starkness. Even if differential pricing turns out to be rare, the key point is that it's hard for ordinary people who interact with Siren Servers to get enough context to make the best decisions. If not differential pricing, then some other scheme will appear in order to take advantage of information asymmetry. After all, that is what information asymmetry is for.

Waiting for Robin Hood

You might expect a compensatory server to always magically appear on cue. Such a server might, for instance, perform cost comparisons so as to alert consumers to differential pricing or other hazards.

Sometimes the Internet will indeed produce a service that does really help. An example is Flightfox,[4] a service that solicits real people to act as travel agents to help customers plan exceptionally difficult itineraries. In that particular niche, the big automated travel services like Orbitz can't compete.[5] A nonautomated niche online service like Flightfox can make good economic sense. The reason is that success is not based on repatterning the world after the server's general information superiority. Instead there is a specific, local, and limited form of advantage. The word *local* doesn't necessarily refer to a geographical locality, it can also refer to any abstract information advantage; it can be a spot on an energy landscape instead of on the Earth. In this case, a human specialty in understanding complex travel creates a kind of local advantage.

Siren Servers do repattern the world, however, and conventional business thinking is inadequate to describe how they work. When a big cloud computing service suggests that it has found you the best price, think about what that could mean. Siren Servers have access to tremendous amounts of information about you, about sellers, and about everyone in between. They are not able to offer a bargain because they got lucky, cultivating just the right supplier, or because they have superior knowledge about a little corner of the world.

No, they are able to offer a bargain by applying broad analytic techniques to an automatic gathering of information about everybody. So once again, what does the offer of value to you really mean, relative to everyone else in the world? There can be no such thing as a universal bargain, any more than everyone can be above average.

From Autocollate to Autocollude

Large, highly automated online businesses can't help but present some of the problems of monopolies, even when there is no monopoly present. Amazon doesn't directly go after a smaller bookseller like an old-fashioned monopolist, any more than it might have targeted a particular person for differential pricing due to prejudice or some other malice. It all happens automatically, as a matter of course.

In some cases Siren Servers do tend to become approximate monopolies, as will be discussed later on in the section on the "exclusion principle." However, in other cases competitive Siren Servers coexist. Amazon coexists with Apple, and Orbitz coexists with Priceline, Expedia, and Travelocity.

It used to be that information superiority was a prize won by becoming a monopoly, but no more. If multiple, similar Siren Server sites coexist, and they each have information superiority over customers but approximate information parity with each other, then they won't be able to help but act as if they're colluding; this can be true even though there is no intent or action taken to collude.*

Old-fashioned collusion was an intentional creation of a specific, illicit channel of information transparency. Transparency is not as universal as it might seem, but nonetheless there is a lot more of it now than there used to be, for those who have the biggest and best-connected computers. There is a lot less intent, however, since so

---

*A "bot" which sets prices or otherwise makes decisions in a market, is an interactive process that is continuously altering its reactions based on new data. If there is only one such bot, then the data it is reacting to comes from the world at large. If there are multiple bots, however, some of the data they receive is influenced by each other. This is the way auto-collusion can arise. Nonetheless, others have made accusations of old-fashioned collusion. See http://www.huffingtonpost.com/2012/08/22/travel-site-class-action-lawsuit_n_1821839.html.

much about large online business is automated or contrived to take place at an arm's length. The big picture result ends up being almost the opposite of the immediate small-scale appearance.* It seems as though online services are bringing bargains to everyone, and yet wealth disparity is increasing while social mobility is decreasing. If everyone were getting better options, wouldn't everyone be doing better as well?

Rupture

The terminology of "disruption" has been granted an almost sacred status in tech business circles. It is ordinary for a venture capital firm to advertise that it is seeking to fund business plans that "shrink markets."[6] To disrupt is the most celebrated achievement. In Silicon Valley, one is always hearing that this or that industry is ripe for disruption. We kid ourselves, pretending that disruption requires creativity. It doesn't. It's always the same story.

Technologists repeatedly apply the extreme efficiencies of digital networks in some area of endeavor in such a way that the sources of value, whatever they may be, are left more off-the-books than they used to be, but we end up in control of the server that runs the scheme. It happened to music and other media early on, but the pattern is being repeated everywhere.

When health insurance companies turned into digital networks, general-practice physicians became somewhat marginalized, serving increasingly as nodes in a scheme run by statistical algorithms administered by insurance and, to a lesser degree, pharmaceutical

---

*This isn't quite the famous "tragedy of the commons." That model of tragedy is based on the long-term futility of rational self-interest in certain poorly designed circumstances, and so bears a similarity to the problem of Siren Servers. The Sirenic Age is more a tragedy of the commotion, more mania than myopia. Information technology can cause things to move so fast that there's a rush, a thrill that distracts. Garrett Hardin's classic 1968 paper "The Tragedy of the Commons" explained how cows were allowed to overgraze on common property, while private property was well maintained. The cows that overgrazed at least grazed. In our present idea about an information economy, cows get no free grass, but a token few might get famous.

concerns. Physicians should be empowered by networked information, but instead they are constrained because they didn't seize control of the servers that connected them as the network age dawned. But why should it have been their job to worry about that?

"Disruption" by the use of digital network technology undermines the very idea of markets and capitalism. Instead of economics being about a bunch of players with unique positions in a market, we devolve toward a small number of spying operations in omniscient positions, which means that eventually markets of *all* kinds will shrink.

CHAPTER 7

Some Pioneering
Siren Servers

My Little Window

I had an unusual vantage point on the digital networking of the world as it happened. During the 1990s and early 2000s I was on the consultant circuit, and was called on by every imaginable sort of institution, from nations to companies to churches to nonprofits. I consulted to universities, various intelligence agencies, every stripe of corporation, and every species of financial services entity. In the course of my consulting years I had assignments, either as an individual or as part of a team, with Wal-Mart, Fannie Mae, major banks, and hedge funds. I also helped create a startup that Google bought around the turn of the century and served in the lab that contained the engineering office of Internet2, the academic consortium concerned with the basic research aspect of making the Internet bigger and faster.

What I came away with from having access to these varied worlds was a realization that they were all remarkably similar. Again and again, the same principles of how human clout is expressed and constrained by digital networks would overwhelm or flatter the surprised participants. The big players often gained benefits from digital networks to an amazing degree, but they were also constrained, even imprisoned, by the same dynamics.

Is there really anything new under the sun? Maybe the way finance went nuts over networks in the early 21st century was really just a repeat of what happened just before the Great Depression of the 1930s, or during the spates of gilded economic chaos at the end of the 19th century. Maybe Siren Servers have always been with us. When I recall what I have seen, I am not speaking as a historian, but as a witness. I leave it to historians to determine how much the recent past has in common with other historical periods.

What is of primary interest to me is whether there are new options for solutions available now that were not available in other eras.

Wal-Mart Considered as Software

One early example of computer networks transforming an industry on a global scale did not come from a social networking site, or from search, or any den of mathematicians working in Silicon Valley or Wall Street. Instead consider Wal-Mart.

Wal-Mart is a real-world, "brick and mortar" concern that succumbed early to the allure of pure networked information. The company's supply chain was driven by real-time data and enormous amounts of computation well in advance of the appearance of search engines, the dot-com boom, or social networking.

Overall, Wal-Mart has brought about much good. Consider that in the decades before the explosion of Chinese imports to the United States, one of the greatest anxieties in American thinking concerned the "awakening" of the sleeping giant China. It was vastly more inscrutable even than the Soviet Union. I recall many chilling conversations about the potential for a third world war.

Instead, Wal-Mart's servers helped coordinate the demand side of the rise of China as a manufacturing powerhouse. Economic interdependence had been faintly imagined, occasionally, as a way to avoid a new, hot superpower confrontation, but back in the 1980s that was barely imaginable. And yet it happened. This was certainly one of the more dramatic positive effects of digital networking on the unfolding of history thus far.*

So Siren Servers can achieve good. My argument is not that Siren Servers always do harm. Often they accomplish great good in the

---

*To be clear, I am not at all saying today's China is above criticism!

short term. We are, however, using the power of networks to optimize for the wrong things overall.

From the Supply Chain's Point of View

I had a peephole into Wal-Mart's world through an occasional consulting assignment in the 1990s, via a Silicon Valley think tank. What I saw was a prototypical version of what has become the familiar pattern.

Wal-Mart recognized early that information is power, and that with digital networking you could consolidate extraordinary power. Wal-Mart's fledgling servers gathered information about simple but valuable conditions out in the world at large: what could be made where and when; what could be moved where and when; who would buy what, and when and for how much. Any little portion of this database would previously have been of value only to a few local players directly affected by it, but by collecting a lot of such information in one place, an overall, global picture emerged. This is the wild change of perspective that network technology can give you. The company gradually became the sculptor of its own environment.

Wal-Mart could practically dictate price and delivery targets, with the reduced risk and increased precision of an attack drone. Suppose you ran a service or parts company in the 1990s. You went to a company that sold products to Wal-Mart and stated your price for something needed by that company. That company would often find itself saying, Sorry; Wal-Mart has decreed a price for our product that doesn't allow us to pay you as much as you want.

It turned out that Wal-Mart had calculated a pretty good guess before you showed up about what everyone's real bottom lines would be. Often enough, you would realize that you could (barely) accept the counteroffer, even though it wasn't what you were looking for.

Wal-Mart didn't need to get direct information about everyone in the loop. A sampling of information about a system is good enough to form an approximate model of that system. That means that someone can be indirectly spied on without any information about that person being gathered directly. Instead, the behaviors of those who interact with a party might yield some clues, and a whole picture is roughly pieced together automatically.

Once other big retailers understood what Wal-Mart had achieved, they hired their own specialists and powered up their own big data centers. But it was too late. Wal-Mart had already repatterned the world, giving itself a special place in it. Vendors were often already coordinated with each other to offer the lowest prices in a particular way that was finely tuned to Wal-Mart's needs. The supply chain had become optimized to deliver to Wal-Mart's door.

Wal-Mart didn't cheat, spy, or steal to get information.* It just applied the best available computers to calculate the best possible statistics using legitimately available data.

Everyone else's margins got slammed to the bare minimums. It was like playing blackjack with an idiot savant who can't help but count cards. This is the moral puzzle of Siren Servers. In the network age there can be collusion without colluders, conspiracies without conspirators.

From the Customer's Point of View

Wal-Mart confronted the ordinary shopper with two interesting pieces of news. One was that stuff they wanted to buy got cheaper, which of course was great. This news was delivered first, and caused cheering.

But there was another piece of news that emerged more gradually. It has often been claimed that Wal-Mart plays a role in the reduction of employment prospects for the very people who tend to be its customers.[1] Wal-Mart has certainly made the world more efficient in a certain sense. It moved manufacturing to any spot in the world that could accomplish it at the very lowest cost; it rewarded vendors willing to cut corners to the maximum degree.

---

*Once again, perhaps my assessment is more charitable than others. I see a collective mistake rather than a class of villains.

Wal-Mart's defenders might acknowledge some churn in the labor market, but to paraphrase the familiar rebuttal, "making the market more efficient might have cost some people their jobs, but it saved even more people a lot of money by lowering prices. In the long term everybody wins because of efficiencies."

It's certainly reasonable to expect that making economic activities more efficient ought to increase opportunity for everyone in the longer term.* However, you can't really compare the two sides of the equation, of lower prices and lowered job prospects.

This is so obviously the case that it seems strange to point it out, but I have found that it is a hard truth to convey to people who have not experienced anything other than affluence. So: If you already have enough to live on, saving some money on a purchase is a nice perk. But if you haven't reached that threshold, or if you had been there but lost your perch, then saving is not the equivalent of making; it instead becomes part of a day-to-day calculus of just getting by. You can never save enough to get ahead if you don't have adequate career prospects.

To me this false trade-off, which was often stated in the 1990s, foreshadowed what we hear today about free Internet services. Tech companies have played similar games, said similar things, and pale in the same harsh light. "Sure there might be fewer jobs, but people are getting so much stuff for free. You can now find strangers' couches to crash on when you travel instead of dealing with traditional hotels!" The claim is as wrong today as it was back then. No amount of cost lowering can foster economic dignity when it also means that there are fewer good jobs.

All Siren Servers deliver dual messages similar to the pair pioneered by Wal-Mart. On the one hand, "Good news! Treats await! Information systems have made the world more efficient for you."

On the other hand, a little later: "It turns out you, your needs, and your expectations are not maximally efficient from the lofty point of view of our server. Therefore, we are reshaping the world so that in the long term, your prospects are being reduced."

---

*As I will explain, I strongly agree with the assertion, but only if we don't remove massive amounts of value from our ledgers.

The initial benefits don't remotely balance the long-term degradations. Initially you made some money day trading or getting an insanely easy loan, or saved some money couch-surfing or by using coupons from an Internet site, but then came the pink slip, the eviction notice, and the halving of your savings when the market drooped. Or you loved getting music for free, but then realized that you couldn't pursue a music career yourself because there were hardly any middle-class, secure jobs left in what was once the music industry. Maybe you loved the supercheap prices at your favorite store, but then noticed that the factory you might have worked for closed up for good.

Financial Siren Servers

The world of financial servers and quants is even more secretive than the corporate empires like Wal-Mart or Google. I have also had a window into this world, though it's hard to get a sense of how much of it I have seen relative to all that goes on.

There was an initial phase, which I mostly missed, when digital networking first amplified ambitions at what had been the margins of the world of finance. Starting in the 1980s, but really blossoming in the 1990s, finance got networked, and schemes were for the first time able to exceed the pre-digital limitations of human deception.

The networking of finance occurred independently and in advance of the rise of the familiar Internet. There were different technical protocols over different infrastructure, though similar principles applied.

Some of the early, dimly remembered steps toward digitally networked finance included: 1987's Black Monday (a market anomaly caused by automated trading systems), Long-Term Capital, and Enron. I will not recount these stories here, but those readers who are not familiar with them would do well to read up on these rehearsals of our current global troubles.

In all these cases there was a high-tech network scheme at play that seemed to concentrate wealth while at the same time causing volatility and trauma for ordinary people, particularly taxpayers who often ended up paying for a bailout.

In addition, a loosening of regulation was often involved. There's a legitimate argument about whether the weakening of regulation was the cause of the failures, or if the regulations were weakened because the temptations of overcoming them became so great because of new technologies, that financiers put more effort into political influence than previously.

In either case, it is interesting that the lost regulations dated from market failures of old, particularly the Great Depression. That should not be taken to mean that the hazards that arose once finance was networked are precisely what they were before finance was regulated. I worry that regulators might be inclined to look only backward.

I knew a few people involved with Long-Term Capital, and I fielded calls from Enron when it wanted to buy a startup that ultimately went to Google. Mostly I got to know what I believe were second- and third-generation financial Siren Servers.

I have had many friends who worked as quants, and have also gotten to know a few very successful financiers at the helms of some of the more hermetic ventures. During the late 1990s and early 2000s, I was able to visit various power spots, and had many long conversations about the statistics and the architectures.

Usually there would be an unmarked technology center in one of the states surrounding New York City, or perhaps farther afield. There, a drowsy gaggle of mathematicians and computer scientists, often recently graduated from MIT or Stanford, would stare at screens, sipping espressos.

The schemes were remarkably similar to Silicon Valley designs. A few of them took as input everything they possibly could scrape from the Internet as well as other, proprietary networks. As in Google's data centers, stupendous correlative algorithms would crunch on the whole 'net's data overnight, looking for correlations. Maybe a sudden increase in comments about mosquito bites would cause an automatic, instant investment in a company that sold lotions. Actually, that's an artificially sensible example. The real examples made no sense to humans. But money was made, and fairly reliably.

In most of the cases, the input wasn't the whole 'net, but only streaming numerical financial data. Signal-processing algorithms would attempt to discern subtle but predictable fluctuations that had never been noticed before. Maybe a number wobbled just a little bit, but not entirely at random. By betting for and against that number rhythmically, a slight, but steady profit dripped out. If this was done a million times simultaneously, the result was an impressive haul.*

Yet other schemes didn't rely so much on fancy analytic math as on the spectacular logistical capabilities of digital networks. For instance, banks settle accounts at particular times of day. With a sufficiently evolved network, money can be automatically wired in and out of accounts at precise moments, in order to enact elaborate rounds of perfectly timed transactions that cycle through many countries. At the end of each cycle, some money was reliably earned, not based on making bets about the unpredictable events of the world, but on the meticulous alignment of the quirks of the world's local rules. For instance, the same money might earn interest at two different banks on opposite sides of the world at once. No one at any of the localities involved would have a clue.

Then there were the exquisitely positioned schemes. The most notorious of these are the servers that accomplish high-frequency trading. They tap directly into the hubs of markets and extract a profit before anyone else can even get a trade in edgewise. This sort of thing was just getting started when I bid Manhattan adieu. (My place was damaged in the 2001 attacks, and I moved out to crazy Berkeley.)

Every scheme I encountered was completely legal, as far as I know. Of course there are lingering questions about the legality of

---

*It should be pointed out that if only one Siren Server is milking a particular fluctuation in this way, a reasonable argument could be made that a service is being performed, in that the fluctuation reveals inefficiency, and the Siren is canceling it out. However, when many Sirens milk the same fluctuation, they lock into a feedback system with each other and inadvertently conspire to milk the rest of the world to no purpose.

some of what happened at the most visible Wall Street firms—the ones that ended up receiving the most gargantuan bailouts at the public's expense in the wake of the 2008 financial crisis.

The quiet world of the quirkiest financial Siren Servers was racking up numbers that compared to the big players, however. Some of them came out of the recession quite well and others did not.

The most successful runners of financial Siren Servers were often unconventional, or at least the more unconventional ones were the ones who wanted to talk to me. There was one guy whom I only ever saw in his silk robes, hanging out by the spa in his sybaritic, giant loft in TriBeCa.

Later, I heard the same thing from other masters of the universe: It ultimately comes down to having some special "in," some special connection, or some special knowledge. You needed to know the right people to get the special data, or the special tap into the market's computers, or the agreements to let your algorithms automatically enact trades in far-flung locations where such things had not happened before.

Ultimately, there was an old-fashioned old boys' club obscured under the tangle of cables in the foundation of the newfangled digital network.

While there is never an absolutely sure thing, in the upper reaches of finance certain schemes come close to perfection. In the past, the perfect investment always rested on at least a touch of corruption. There was some chink in the law that you depended on.

There are certainly such legal maneuvers these days, such as tax loopholes for hedge fund managers. But the cores of these businesses, where the profit comes from, are in many cases more organic, more pure than previous "sure things." If you can pull money out of sufficiently advanced math, then the law couldn't keep up even if it tried.

Just as this book left my hands, regulators in Europe began to consider the regulation of high-frequency trading. I hope they appreciate the nature of the challenge they face. To an algorithm, a circuit breaker or timing limit is just another feature in the environment to be analyzed and exploited. Algorithms will "learn" to trip circuit breakers at the right millisecond to capture a profit, for instance. If the frequency of trades is limited, then some other parameter, like the phase, or relative timing, of trades, will be automatically refined in order to find an advantage. The cat-and-mouse game can go on forever. Undoing the Siren Server pattern is the only way back to a truer form of capitalism.

This is what computers appear to have made possible in some cases (though I can't know enough to be absolutely sure): a new path to a "sure thing" that sidesteps the nasty old business of having to court politicians.

What is absolutely essential to a financial Siren Server, however, is a superior information position. If everyone else knew what you were doing, they could securitize *you*. If anyone could buy stock in a mathematical "sure thing" scheme, then the benefits of it would be copied like a shared music file, and spread out until it was nullified. So, in today's world your mortgage can be securitized in someone else's secretive bunker, but you can't know about the bunker and securitize *it*. If it weren't for that differential, the new kind of sure thing wouldn't exist.

If Life Gives You EULAs, Make Lemonade

The information economy that we are currently building doesn't really embrace capitalism, but rather a new form of feudalism.

We aren't creating enough opportunity for enough people online. The proof is simple. The wide adoption of transformative connecting technology should create a middle-class wealth boom, as happened when the Interstate Highway System gave rise to a world of new jobs in transportation and tourism, for instance, and generally widened commercial prospects. Instead we've seen recession, unemployment, and austerity.

I wonder if thinking about lemonade stands might help. A prominent political meme for the Republican half of America in 2012 went like this: "You built it." This was a retort to an out-of-context attribution to President Barack Obama: "You didn't build that," originally referring to infrastructure like roads.

The contention was approximately that entrepreneurship is the most fundamental activity, and can close its own loops. Business would solve more problems if it were just left alone. Government taxes and regulation are the problem. Removing those things is the solution. Who needs infrastructure? Businesses would build their own roads if the government would just leave them alone.

Some girls who had created a lemonade stand were famously assembled on television by critics of the president and asked if they had built their business, or if the government had.[1] I wish children could experience earning money online today, but that is harder to do than starting lemonade stands.

Can we compare the Internet to the road that must precede a lemonade stand? The government built the road. The whole idea of a public road is to push entrepreneurship up to a higher level.

Without the government there would have most likely been a set of incompatible digital networks,* mostly private, instead of a prominent unified Internet.[2]

Without the public road, and utterly unencumbered access to it, a child's lemonade stand would never turn a profit. The real business opportunity would be in privatizing other people's roads.

Similarly, without an open, unified network, the whole notion of business online would have been entirely feudal from the start. Instead, it only took a feudal turn around the turn of the century. These days, instead of websites on the open Internet, people are more likely to create apps in proprietary stores or profiles on proprietary social media sites.

I have had more than one heated argument with Silicon Valley libertarians who believe that streets should be privatized. Here's the EULA[3] no one would read in the utopia they pine for:

Dear parents or legal guardians of _____

As you may be aware, your daughter is one of _____ children in your neighborhood who recently applied for a jointly operated StreetApp® of the category "Lemonade Stand."

As the owner/operator of the street on which you live, and on which this proposed app would operate, StreetBook is required by law to obtain parental consent. By clicking on the "yes" box at the bottom of this window, you acknowledge you are _____'s parent or legal guardian, and also agree to the following conditions:

1. A percentage of up to 30% of revenues will be kept by StreetBook. [*This clause reflects the revenue model established in app stores.*]
2. You will submit lemonade recipes, your stand design, signage, and the clothing you will wear to StreetBook for approval. StreetBook can remove your stand at any time for

---

*Al Gore played a crucial role in bringing that unity about when he was a senator, following in the footsteps of his father, who had facilitated the national system of interstate highways.

noncompliance with our approval process. [*This provision is also inspired by the practices of app stores.*]

3. All commerce, not limited to lemonade purchases, will be conducted through StreetBook. Customers must have StreetBook accounts even if they live on a street owned and operated by a StreetBook competitor. StreetBook will place a hold on all moneys in order to collect interest, and might place a longer hold if any party makes claims of fraud or activities that violate this agreement or any other residential use agreement. [*This provision is inspired by the business models of online payment services.*]

4. A $100 annual fee must be paid to be a lemonade stand developer. [*This is again an example of following in the successful footsteps of app stores.*]

5. Limited free access to StreetBook's curb in front of your house is available in exchange for advertising on your body and property. The signage of your lemonade stand, the paper cups, and the clothing worn by your children must include advertising chosen solely by StreetBook. [*This follows on the model of social network and search companies.*]

6. If you choose to seek limited free access to use of the curb in front of your house, you must make available to Street-Book a current inventory of items in your house, and allow StreetBook to monitor movement and communications of individuals within your house. [*This follows on the business model pioneered by search, social network, and other seemingly free services.*]

7. By accepting this agreement, you agree that any liabilities related to accidents or other events in the vicinity of your StreetApp® will be solely the responsibility of you and other individuals involved. We provide the ability for you to connect with others, and profit from that, but you take all the risk. [*The general character of EULAs inspires this clause.*]

8. You acknowledge that you have been notified that Street-Book's internal procedures for security and privacy don't take into account how our systems might be taken advantage of by criminals or pranksters who are able to combine

data we give out freely with data given out freely by other businesses, such as the privatized utilities you are signed up to. You agree that you will have to learn to think like a hacker if you wish to be in control of your accounts. [*Wired reporter Mat Honan was famously hacked because lulz-seekers could use information from different Siren Servers to assemble enough data to steal his identity. But no single server was to blame, naturally.*]

9. For additional fees, you can purchase "premium address" services from StreetBook. These include lowering your visibility to door-to-door solicitors and increasing your visibility for food delivery and repair businesses you have contacted. By accepting this agreement, you agree to receive information about our premium services by phone and other means. [*This clause was inspired by the practices of certain social networking and review sites.*]

10. Portions of your local, state, and federal taxes are being applied to the government bailout of StreetBook, which is obviously too big to fail. You have no say in this, but this clause is included just to rub it in. [*This clause is inspired by the success of the high-tech finance industry.*]

Please click "next" to proceed to page 2 of 37 pages of conditions.

Click here to accept.

StreetBook is proud to support a new generation of entrepreneurs.

STREETBOOK MAY CHANGE OR AMEND ANY AND ALL ASPECTS OF THIS AGREEMENT ENTERED INTO BY YOU AT ANY TIME. STREETBOOK ACCEPTS NO LIABILITY OF ANY KIND.

PART THREE

How This Century Might Unfold, from Two Points of View

CHAPTER 8

From Below

Mass Unemployment Events

Will There Be Manufacturing Jobs?

The key question isn't "How much will be automated?" It's how we'll conceive of whatever *can't* be automated at a given time. Even if there are new demands for people to perform new tasks in support of what we perceive as automation, we might apply antihuman values that define the new roles as not being "genuine work." Maybe people will be expected to "share" instead. So the right question is "How many jobs might be lost to automation if we think about automation the wrong way?"

One of the strange, tragic aspects of our technological moment is that the most celebrated information gadgets, like our phones and tablets, are made by hand in gigantic factories, mostly in southern China, and largely by people who work insanely hard in worrisome environments. Looking at the latest advances in robotics and automated manufacturing, it's hard not to wonder when the labors of these hordes of new potential Luddites might become suddenly obsolete.

In this case, even once the technology becomes available, I suspect politics will slow it down a little. It's hard to imagine China deciding to throw much of its own population into unemployment. It is still a centrally planned society to a significant degree. It's hard, even, to imagine one of China's neighbors doing it. Would an aging Japan automate its factories to undercut China? Seems like a significant risk.

But somebody somewhere would find the motivation. Maybe a low-population but capital-rich Persian Gulf nation worried about the post-oil future would fund gigantic automated factories to undercut China in the production of consumer electronics. It might even happen in the United States, which has ever-fewer manufacturing jobs to protect anyway.

What would it look like to automate manufacturing? Well, the first word that comes to mind is *temporary*. And the reason is that the act of making manufacturing into a more automated technology would inherently move it a step closer to being a "software-mediated" technology. When a technology becomes software-mediated, the structure of the software becomes more important than any other particularity of the technology in determining who will win the power and the money when the technology is used. Making fabrication software-mediated turns out to be a step toward making the very notion of a factory, as we know it, obsolete.

To see why, consider how automated manufacturing might advance. Automated milling machines and similar devices are already ubiquitous for shaping parts, such as forms for molds; robotic arms to assemble components are not as common, but still present in certain applications, such as assembling parts of large items like cars and big TVs. Detail work (like fitting touchscreens into the frame of a tablet) is still mostly done by hand, but that might change soon. At first manufacturing robots will be expensive, and there will be plenty of well-paying jobs created to operate them, but eventually they will become cheap and the data to operate them might then be crowdsourced, sending manufacturing down the same road traveled by the recorded music industry.

A current academic and hobbyist craze is known as "3D printing." A 3D printer looks a little like a microwave oven. Through the glass door, you can watch roaming robotic nozzles deposit various materials under software control in an incremental way to form a product as if by magic. You download a design from the 'net, as if you were downloading a movie file, send it to your 3D printer, and come back after a while. There, before you, is a physical object, downloaded from afar. There are fledgling experiments with printers that realize physical products including working electronic components. A chip is just a pattern deposited by something like a printing process to begin with. So is a flat display. In theory, it ought to be possible, in the not-so-distant future, to print out a working phone or tablet.

It is still unknown how good 3D printing will become, or how soon. The little gotchas and annoyances of technology are not predictable and can add decades of uncertainty to the timing of technological change. But it seems likely that 3D printing can close the various loops and become a fairly complete technology in this century.

But notice that once a 3D printer can be deployed in a factory, it might just as well be placed close to where the product will be used.

Being able to make things on the spot could remove a huge part of humanity's carbon footprint: the transportation of goods. Instead of fleets of container ships bringing tchotchkes from China to our ports, we'll print them out at home, or maybe at the neighborhood print shop.

What will be distributed instead will be the antecedent "goops." These are the substances squirted out by the printer's nozzles. At the time of writing, there are about one hundred goops in use by 3D printers. For instance, a particular goop might harden into the kind of tough plastic found in car interiors.

It is too early to say what goops will be in use in the future. Nor do we know how many different goops will be needed. Maybe a single supergoop would go a long way. Perhaps a suspension including graphene particles will be configurable into a variety of components like nanotube digital circuits, battery layers, and tough carbon fiber outer shells.

Will there be goops delivered by pipes to the home? Goop trucks that make rounds to refill printers once a week? Goop refill kits sold by Amazon and delivered by parcel? Little blimps that alight on your roof to refill your home printer? This we do not know. At any rate, a new infrastructure will be needed to get goops to printers. Expect goop to be as overpriced as ink for home photo printers is today.*

---

*Or, if goops turn out to be cheap to make at home, or wherever they are used, then some other imperfection or inconvenience in the cycle will become the nexus of cartel and artificially elevated costs.

The real magic might come about because of the transformation of recycling. Right now, when we throw something away, no information is packaged with that thing that described how it could best be disassembled into its constituents in order that they might be reused. This is a great inefficiency.

We rely on human labor to very approximately assess what we toss away so that it can be recycled. This happens when we choose the right trash bin at the cafeteria, or when poor people pick over garbage dumps.

Once 3D printers commonly create objects, the nature of recycling will transform utterly. An object that had been printed will be remembered in the cloud. There will be "deprinters" that accept objects that are no longer wanted, like the previous year's tablet. By referring to the original printing specification, always retrievable over the 'net, it will be possible to unravel the object back to its original goops with precision. Instead of melting it down, little nozzles with specialized solvents and cutting tools will separate each striation that originated from a different antecedent goop. The process will not be perfect, since the laws of thermodynamics cannot be revoked, but it will be *hugely* more efficient than what we do today.

Between the obsolescence of shipping and an extreme increase in recycling precision, 3D printing could create a massive explosion of convenience and fun, and at the same time vastly reduce humanity's carbon footprint and reliance on nonrenewable resources. All this modulo the gotchas we don't know about yet, of course.

But supposing that some portions of the benefits appear, it certainly would be foolish to oppose this stream of progress. How could a liberal not like the reduced carbon footprint? How could a conservative not like the efficiency? And of course techies will be in love.

And yet the transformation will throw factory workers out of work in a massive wave. Will China be destabilized? As happened with the file-sharing of other things like music, the transformation of fabrication into a file-sharing phenomenon could happen very quickly.

When I explain this scenario, I often receive this response: "But someone still has to make the printers." Somehow it's hard to wrap our heads around a world in which the printers themselves are printed. You wouldn't go buy a 3D printer at Wal-Mart. Your neighbor would print your first one for you. They'd spread "virally," to use the usual metaphor. Wal-Mart would probably go bankrupt fairly quickly.

Huge benefits on both a global and individual scale could appear, but coupled with a wave of supposed human obsolescence. I repeat that it's only "supposed" obsolescence, because all those files that are shared to describe objects to print have to come from somewhere.

In a world of efficient 3D printing and recycling we might experience much, much faster turnaround in our material culture than we are able to easily conceive of today. A guitarist might routinely print out a new guitar for every gig. Snobs might very well then decry that much of the design churn is stupid and pointless, just as critics might say the same about today's social network kinetics. But if people are interested in finding the latest stupid cool guitar to fabricate for the day, there will be a stupid cool guitar designer out there who ought to be paid.

The most radical change in daily life might be associated with fashion and clothing. A home device will be able to print out clothes based on Internet designs, but also based on your body. The device would scan your body in three dimensions, just as Microsoft's Kinect input device* does today. You'd see an outfit slinking about on your body before it exists. Everyone will be dressed exquisitely because every piece of clothing will be custom-fit.

Forget laundry. At the end of the day you'll pop dirty clothes into the top of the device for recycling. Never wear the same dress twice. (Though there will no doubt also be a countertrend in which vintage and handmade clothing becomes ever more revered. This is what happened with vinyl records after music became networked.)

Today "cool hunters" comb impoverished neighborhoods, sniffing out fashion trends. In the future, kids in those neighborhoods should earn wealth for their fashion trendsetting.

---

*Kinect is a camera that gathers the three-dimensional depth of the scene in front of it, and uses that data to estimate the body poses of people in view, allowing software to portray them as avatars. It was the fastest-selling consumer electronics product in history at its introduction.

Napsterizing the Teamsters

Humans are terrible drivers. We kill each other in car accidents so frequently that the toll has become a more deadly problem than wars or terrorism. It's one of our biggest sources of death and pain.

A team of Google and Stanford researchers has famously demonstrated cars that are quite effective at driving themselves. (They are not alone; similar developments are occurring around the world.) The motivations for developing self-driving cars are so extraordinarily powerful that it's hard to imagine stronger ones. Results from experiments thus far indicate that it is unlikely robots will ever drive as badly as people. My mother died in a car accident. What could be more compelling?

But there's more. Stoplights would generally go away. Cars would simply know when there's no other car coming, and no pedestrian, so they could just proceed through without stopping when there is no need. This would bring a huge gain in energy efficiency, since vehicles wouldn't have to accelerate from a stop nearly as often. City driving would become almost as efficient as freeway driving.

If cars could coordinate with each other, traffic jams might nearly cease to exist. Instead of people engaging in tiny ego-wars to merge between lanes on the freeway, causing huge backups going miles back, cars would anticipate mergers and merge cleanly, taking full advantage of the hypothetical bandwidth of the freeway.

There will be gotchas, just as with 3D printing. We can't yet know what they will be. One of the problems might be that when there is a screw-up, it could be a huge one. If a whole freeway of cars hit each other because of a snag, that would be a calamity on the order of a plane crash instead of an incident involving only a few people. That's conceivable should there be many cars connected together virtually, moving rapidly under a connected software system. If the overall death rate was way down, but accidents when they occurred were more horrific, how would we respond emotionally?

That brings up the existential/emotional issue of losing the freedom associated with driving.

Maybe we won't accept fully automatic vehicles, even if the safety statistics are in their favor. An intermediate scenario would still involve people in directing the cars, but in a subordinate position. You might be able to drive the car yourself when there's no one else around, and you can't kill anyone. However, when there is an intersection with other cars approaching, congestion, or an imminent collision, automation would be lurking and sprung to take over.

What sort of economic impact will self-driving vehicles bring? It could be catastrophic.

A giant portion of the global middle classes works behind a wheel. Many have entered middle-class life the first time as a taxi driver or a truck driver. It's hard to imagine a world without commercial drivers. A traditional entry ramp into economic sustenance for fresh arrivals to big cities like New York would be gone. Wave after wave of immigrants drove New York taxis. And I'm trying to imagine the meeting when someone tries to explain to the Teamsters that nothing like their services will ever be needed again.

Both cabbies and truckers have managed to build up levees with some legal heft over the years. They'll be able to delay the change, but not for long. Whenever an innocent person is killed in an accident involving a cab or a truck, there will be public outrage that human error is still allowed to intrude in its murderous ways to destroy life and love once automated cars become familiar in some guise. For a while, there might be a compromise in which a Teamster or a cabbie sits there passively, along for the ride, perhaps to man a failsafe button. But young people won't expect that to last and won't seek it as a way of life. The world of work behind the wheel will drain away in a generation.

You can't make cars quite 100 percent autonomous. If people are going to be people at all, somebody has to tell the car where to go and something about how to do it, and there has to be some failsafe. There has to be some human responsibility, if not on the part of the people who are passengers in the car, then at least somewhere over the network.

Will this remaining human role turn into a benefit for the middle classes or only for a Siren Server? If it's to only benefit a Siren Server, you can imagine that in, say, ten years, when you want to get to the airport, a robot taxi shows up. However, the chosen route might be peculiar. Maybe the taxi lingers in front of billboards along the way, or forces you to a particular convenience store if you need to pick up something, or whatever scam would come about in a Siren Server–driven car.

But one thing we can guess even at this early date is that self-driving cars will depend on cloud data about streets, pedestrians, and everything else that can affect a trip. That information will be renewed constantly, with every single ride. Will the rider be compensated beyond a free ride for helping to generate this information? To do otherwise would be considered accounting fraud in a humanistic information economy.

Flattening the City on a Hill

The middle classes that have already lost their levees and economic dignity to Siren Servers are sometimes called the "creative classes." They include recording musicians, journalists, and photographers. There were also a significantly larger number of people who supported these types of creators, like studio musicians and editors, who enjoyed "good jobs" (meaning with security and benefits). Those who have grown up in the networked era might have trouble understanding opportunity lost.

There is a familiar chorus of reasons why we should find the lousy fates of creative classes to be acceptable. I addressed that controversy in my earlier book. While it's an important debate, it's even more urgent to determine if the felling of creative-class careers was an anomaly or an early warning of what is to happen to immeasurably more middle-class jobs later in this century.

A pattern has emerged in which holders of academic posts related to Internet studies tend to join in the acceptance or even the celebration of the decline of the creative classes' levees. This strikes me as an irony, or an anxious burst of denial.

Higher education could be Napsterized and vaporized in a matter of a few short years. In the world of the new kind of network wealth, towering student debt has become yet another destroyer of the middle classes.

Why are we still bothering with higher education in the network age? We have Wikipedia and a world of other tools. You can educate yourself without paying a university. All it takes is discipline. Tuition pays for making discipline a little more structured, getting some extended years of parental support in a place with a quad and beer, and certification. You also meet elite friends. There's prestige in getting into a top school, whether you finish or not.

All these benefits might be had less expensively in other ways, and that is becoming truer every day. The knowledge is no longer held in a dungeon. Anyone with a 'net connection can pretty much get any information that would be presented in a university. Undoubtedly some sort of social coercion site or fantasy game will take off online to help out with the discipline of self-education. As for the degree, the piece of paper, Internet statistics ought to be able to make mincemeat out of old-fashioned degree earning in very short order. Why make do with a GPA when you can get an arbitrarily detailed dossier on your potential hire?

As for the years of parental support, it is turning out that in a Napsterized overall economy, more and more graduates stay with their parents well after college anyway. Why spend a ton of money supporting kids in college for four years when the same money could last longer to put them up somewhere cheaper?

As for the beer: Alas, the Internet has not made intoxication free as yet, but it still might. So wouldn't it be more efficient to get rid of higher education?

Silicon Valley has a love-hate relationship with universities. It means something to have a PhD from someplace like MIT. We love those places! There are legendary professors and we scramble to recruit their graduating students.

But it's also considered the height of hipness to eschew a traditional degree and unequivocally prove yourself through other means. The list of top company runners who dropped out of college is commanding: Bill Gates, Steve Jobs, Steve Wozniak, and Mark Zuckerberg, for a start. Peter Thiel, of Facebook and PayPal fame, started a fund to pay top students to drop out of school, since the task of building high-tech startups should not be delayed.

Mea culpa. I never earned a real degree (though I have received honorary ones). In my case poverty played a role, as it did for many others. But also, the very thought of slogging through someone else's procedures to gain abstract approval seemed unacceptably retro and irrelevant.

I must admit I was utterly dependent on the very institutions I neglected, for despite my not being a student, they introduced me to inspirational figures and mentors. Without MIT or Caltech, I imagine figures like Marvin Minsky or Richard Feynman would have been employed deep in the bunkers of Los Alamos or Bell Labs at the time, which were places less likely to be generous about having a weird kid roaming the hallways without official license.

Everyone in the high-tech world appreciates the universities deeply. Yet we are happy to rush headlong into flattening the levees that sustain them, just as we did with music, journalism, and photography. Will the result be any different this time?

Factoring the City on a Hill

The Khan Academy might be the most celebrated effort of the moment to bring free education to anyone with online access. It is filled with videos teaching every common topic, and its lessons have already been taken hundreds of millions of times.

Stanford professor and Google researcher Sebastian Thrun was inspired by Khan to share a graduate artificial-intelligence class online, and tens of thousands of people graduated from it. These events have been widely celebrated as a path for raising education levels everywhere by leveraging the Internet.

It might do great good. I do have some qualms about the way these new efforts are unfolding; the concerns are similar to those expressed in my previous book related to Wikipedia. Qualms about monoculture or treating all subjects as if they were technical subjects don't fall within the project of this book, however.

Instead, the question to ask here is whether online efforts of this kind could create Siren Servers, even nonprofit ones, which end up undermining the finances and security of academics. This is not a comfortable topic. Of *course* I appreciate how beautiful it is to bring great educational materials to people who might not have had access to them before. I have also worked toward that very goal.

But that doesn't cancel out a systemic problem that I fear is also accelerated by the same activity. I am certainly not saying there's something wrong with making great lessons and putting them online. I am saying that the overall pattern in which we are doing these beautiful things is not sustainable. Or perhaps a more constructive way to put it is to say that what we are doing is not enough.

Here is how it could go: Students at colleges ranked lower than Stanford would tune in to Stanford seminars, and gradually wonder why they're paying their local, lower-ranked academics at all. If locals are to remain valuable once a globalized star system comes into being over the 'net, it can only be because they are present and interactive.

But online experts can also be made virtually present and interactive. Perhaps tutors will be Skyped in the cheapest places. Forget people. Artificial intelligence can animate a simulated tutor. Imagine Siri, but as a digital talking head with the faraway look and awkwardly groomed countenance of a graduate assistant in a math class.

Why should we keep on paying for colleges? Why pay for all those levees that benefit a privileged class of middle-class people? All the pensions and health plans, the insurance, the soaring expenses that are crushing the nation under student debt?

Education in the Abstract Is Not Enough

I remember looking at images of all the bright young people in Egypt's Tahrir Square, right after they had overthrown a dictator. Here was a forward-looking, young, savvy, and high-tech new generation. How would they get jobs? Shouldn't a bunch of these young people be professors in Egyptian universities in ten years? Is the Internet going to make it easier or harder for them to get those jobs?

This is a pattern we'll see over and over again when people interact with top network servers. You get an incredible bargain up front, like super-easy mortgages, insanely cheap retail items, or free online tools or music, but in the long term you also face reduced job prospects. In this case you get free online education up front but fewer academic jobs in the longer term.

We need to find a way to make education more available *and* make the career benefits of education more attainable.

Now, as levees break and austerity rules, suddenly contracts turn out not to be inviolable. This is what union members and copyright holders have learned. So where will this leave academics, as our century of digital networking proceeds? They'll be caught like so many before them, clinging to old-fashioned levees, to the pomp of graduation ceremonies, to their employment contracts, and the tenure process, which has lasted for centuries. But all this will be under assault.

The problem won't be the price of the buildings or the land of the campus. No, it's always possible to raise millions of dollars to build a building, even as graduate students are paid so little that they take on lifetimes of debt just to make it through. Buildings are wealth, and wealth begets wealth. Graduate students are not.

How did anyone ever afford education? Society will not be able to afford the risk of the great debt load that students collectively take on. Austerity will force a contraction of government support of the academy, everywhere in the world at once.

Is it a coincidence that formal education is starting to become impossibly, cosmically expensive just at the moment that informal education is starting to become free? No, no coincidence. This is just another little fractal reflection of the big picture of the way we've designed network information systems. The two trends are a single trend.

If only we could live for free and get whatever we want without any worry that politics might be messy, that some political process might not make the best decision on our behalves, that cartels would never form around what isn't perfectly free or automated . . . if only we could carelessly let our levees melt away and throw ourselves into the waiting arms of utopia.

I imagine that the academics from top technical schools will do fine. Honestly, there's no way Silicon Valley would stand to see MIT fall. That wouldn't be a danger anyway because the top technical schools make money from technology. Stanford sometimes seems like one of the Silicon Valley companies.

What about liberal arts professors at a state college? Some academics will hang on, but the prospects are grim if education is seduced by the Siren song. A decade or two from now, if nothing changes, the outlook will recall the present state of recorded music. In the case of that industry, making a pre-digital system efficient through the use of a digital network shrank it economically to about a quarter of its size fairly quickly. It will shrink perhaps to about a tenth once people with old habits die off. This is not because of obsolescence. Music is not fading away like buggy whips, any more than the need for education will. Instead wealth is becoming concentrated around Siren Servers, since most of the real value, which still occurs out in the real world, on the ground, is reconceived to be off the books.

The lure of "free" will beckon. Get educated for free now! But don't plan on a job as an educator.

The Robotic Bedpan

One of the bright spots in the future of middle-class employment is usually taken to be health care. Surely we'll need millions of new nurses to care for the aging baby boomers. Caregivers will become a huge new middle-class population. If you want to think in terms of social mobility, this would also mean a huge transfer of wealth between generations that isn't necessarily kept within families. It should be an example of the great wheel of middle-class aspiration turning anew in the United States.

The undoing of this prospect is already observable in Japan, however. The country faces one of the world's most severe depopulation spirals in this century. Around 2025 or 2030, Japan can expect a profound shortage of working-age people and a gigantic population of elderly people. Japan has traditionally not welcomed waves of non-Japanese immigrants. And it is at the cutting edge in robotics research.

Therefore there is talk that robots will become advanced enough in time to take care of the elderly. This is plausible, from a technical point of view. Robots are already able to handle delicate tasks, like certain surgical subroutines, and are getting to be reliable enough to be a less risky choice than humans in some situations, like driving vehicles.

Would a robot nurse be emotionally acceptable? Japanese culture seems to have anticipated the coming demographic crunch. Robots have been cute in Japan for decades. Trustworthy fictional robots, like Transformers and Tamagotchis, are a primary national cultural export. As with all waves of technological change, it is hard to predict when the inevitable glitches and gotchas will be smoothed out. In this case, though, the motivation is so intense that I expect robots in Japanese nursing homes by 2020, and in widespread use by 2025.

Sans robots, one would expect waves of immigrants to go to American nursing schools in the next decade to prepare to take care of America's own age wave. Their children would be raised by parents who practiced a profession, and would tend to become professional themselves. Thus a whole new generation of customers for colleges and a new wave of middle-class families would make their way, continuing the American pattern.

But those imported robots will be awfully tempting. If you spend any time in elder-care facilities like nursing homes, a few things become apparent. First, there is no way for even the most professional and attentive staffs to help everyone as fast as would be ideal. It's inconceivable to have twenty-four-hour-a-day, immediately available help for every discomfort that comes up.

Second, elder care is unbelievably hard and uncomfortable work, if it's done well. It's very hard for even the best facility to make absolutely sure that every member of the staff is always doing the best possible job. The elderly make easy victims, like children. Petty thefts and taunts are not uncommon.

The economics of elder care reflects the destruction of middle-class levees and the rise of Siren Servers just like any other sector. There's a tremendous drive to hire staff without benefits, since paying for someone else's health care is an unbounded liability in an era when insurance is run by Siren Servers (this will be discussed in an upcoming section).

There's also fear of litigation. In the network age, lawsuits can be organized with network effects. Litigants can be gathered online into swarms. This creates an unfortunate paranoia. I have run into problems trying to get Internet connectivity into elder-care facilities, and the problem is often fear that a webcam will capture a small infraction that turns into an insanely amplified liability. Maybe someone will slip on a wet floor, and then there will be hundreds of thousands of dollars of legal bills to pay.

If you go to a tolerably decent elder-care facility, almost every resident will be the beneficiary of some form of levee. Almost none will have simply saved cash for old age. There is almost always a pension, or government programs like Medicaid. In every case, the institution that is providing these benefits is being crushed by the obligation.

Go visit places where residents don't benefit from levees. It's not pleasant. The facilities for those left hanging are more smelly and wretched than you'd expect things to be in a rich country. Seriously, go visit the public elder-care facility of last resort where you live. That would be better than me describing them.

It's not that the robots will necessarily be cheaper in an immediate sense. There might be significant expenses associated with the goops needed to print them, if they're printed, or with manufacturing and maintaining them if they are not. But the expenses will be more predictable, and that will make all the difference.

Hiring a human nurse will mean paying for that person's health insurance, and taking on unpredictable legal liabilities for the mistakes that person might make, like leaving a floor wet. Both of these drags on the ledger will be amplified by network effects, just as has happened with mortgage risks.

Insurance companies will use computers to weasel out of liability *and* to extract ever-larger payments. The whole world's lawyers will be circling online. The liability side of having an employee will be copied and amplified over a network, just like a pirated music file or a securitized mortgage. It will eventually become less risky to choose a robot. When you turn action into software, then no one gets blamed for what happens.

Humans will always do those jobs that a robot can't do, but the tasks might be conceived as being low skilled. It might turn out that robots can give massages, but can't answer the door. Maybe robots will be good at catching patients who fake the ingestion of medicines, but ineffective at soothing patients so that they'll take them voluntarily.

The key reason to avoid acknowledging that there's real skill in doing what robots can't do—and hiring people for real jobs—will not be to keep the immediate expenses low, but to reduce the amplified liabilities of the network age. So there will be plenty of dead-end jobs without security or benefits.* This will be despite the fact that the humans in the caregiving loop might be absolutely essential to the well-being of those being cared for.

Meanwhile, the programming of caregiving robots will be utterly dependent on cloud software that in turn will be dependent on observing millions of situations and outcomes. When a nurse who is particularly good at changing a bedpan feeds data to the clouds—such as a video that can be correlated to improved outcomes, even if the nurse never is told about the correlation—that data might be applied to drive a future generation of caregiving robots so that all patients everywhere can benefit. But will that nurse be compensated?

If present online patterns continue, the answer will be no to the nurse, who will be expected to "share" her expertise and to forgo proper compensation for it.

A Pharma Fable That Might Unfold
Later in This Century

The examples given so far are part of a standard set of anticipations in Silicon Valley. The pattern can be applied to almost any indus-

---

*This is being written in America, in advance of the 2012 election. It is possible that "Obamacare" will stand or fall, but in either case, the larger pattern described here will persist unless it is addressed more fundamentally than by health-care finance reform.

try that isn't yet fully software-mediated in the way that recorded music already is. Here I'll tell a tale of how the pattern might be realized in the pharmaceutical industry:

It was 2025. It all started in a Stanford dorm room. During a party someone knocked a bottle of vitamins to the floor and it shattered. "Dude! My vitamins." No one had a car, and it was miles to the nearest drugstore.

"Hey what about those reaction chips we use in chem?" Reaction chips were tiny chemistry experiment stations on a chip. Layers of gossamer shape-changing surfaces were puckered by charges from transistors in the top layer of an inch-squared chip, creating any desired architecture of chambers. Chambers could be manipulated to form tiny pumps, pressure chambers, or even itsy-bitsy centrifuges. The contents of a transient microchamber could be mixed, heated, cooled, or pressurized. Sensors of many kinds were also distributed on the chip's surface. Every spot on the chip was monitored for temperature, color, conductivity, and many other properties.

Tiny drops of antecedent chemicals were added to inlets at the surface of the chip by robotic eyedroppers within a desktop chip-filling station. Instead of spending hours to perform dozens of steps to synthesize a chemical at a bench, you could set up a chip to perform tens of thousands of steps while you went on with your life. More important, you could set up thousands of chips to perform variations on synthesis experiments in parallel. Chemistry finally merged with big data. A single typical senior project might test a million synthesis sequences to evolve a better one, or might test dozens of variations of an experimental material.

The most fun thing was to watch a chip under a microscope while it was carrying out chemical synthesis. It looked like the world's smallest Rube Goldberg device, squeezing, spinning, boiling, and squirting out tiny amounts of experimental substances. YouTube videos of chips in action drew a cult following. The ones where chips blew up were the most popular. T-shirts with the words CHIP FAIL became popular in chemistry departments everywhere.

Anyway, back at the dorm room, one of the guys said, "Just get a chip to make your vitamins, dude. It's stupid to go spend all that money at a store."

So a few chips went missing from the lab that night.

It turned out to be a pain to keep chips in a dorm room drawer. The first one that made vitamins got lost in a bundle of underwear. But a roommate said, "Dude, you should visit the wearable computing lab. We should be wearing these chips."

Where to wear them? Chips started showing up in tattoos, like gold accents in a Klimt canvas.

Amazingly, it took months for the administration to realize chips were being pilfered. First came the stern lecture, then, without even time to pee, a visit to Stanford's intellectual property lawyers for the patent drafting.

All the usual suspects in Silicon Valley put angel money into the startup, which was called VitaBop. The slide set at the first investors' gathering showed skiers and a winner of a dance competition with VitaBop tattoos. An Olympic sprinter came up on stage and showed off his Bop Tat. Everyone with a Bop just exuded health and vitality. Of course they were all twenty-two.

VitaBop created a no-hassle "fill-up station." You'd press your chip up against the station to get a refill of antecedent chemicals. The chips also gained an ability to monitor the blood and vital signs.

VB stations appeared at every café in Palo Alto. You could get a fill-up of the standard antecedents. Furthermore, a café might offer something exotic as a promotion. You could spend ten bucks to be part of a Bopathon, where everyone in the café would let the special chemistry of the day take hold. Despite all the hype, the active ingredient always turned out to be caffeine.

Culture pundits remarked that at least people at Bopathons were looking at each other instead of at gadgets, because everyone was curious what the recipe would do to you. In a strange way, Boppers were more physically aware of each other than non-Boppers. The chips became a social gateway. If you didn't have one, you became kind of invisible to someone who did.

VitaBop grew like crazy. The chips were basically given away. It turned out that the thousands of tattoo shops, which had been going a little out of fashion, provided a ready retail network for

VitaBop installs. The startup enjoyed a friction-free magic carper ride.

Oh yes, the business plan. Well, there was a "recipe store" where you bought formulas that could be run on your Bop. Venues could pay to entice people to VB stations that would provide supposedly special formulas. Advertisers, insurance companies, and all kinds of other third parties paid for access to the amazing database VitaBop was building about what was going on within the bodies of Boppers. Privacy advocates worried, but the company assured everyone that only "aggregate" data was available.

Revenues flowed in, though only a trickle compared to what was earned by the industries VitaBop might kill. Many took pleasure in seeing the Big Pharma companies scared out of their wits, but at the same time it was sad to see the coffee business shrivel. Some cafés survived, as Bopper dens, but there were heartrending stories about how all those hard-fought battles to create fair-trade coffee plantations in the developing world had come to bankruptcy.

But back in Silicon Valley, all was well. It was to be expected that the shrinkage of old industries would be greater than the expansion of new industries. After all, making things more digital was all about efficiency.

Somehow professional chemists and pharmacologists were surprised. The jobs were going away. Sure, if you got a gig at VitaBop itself, especially early in the game, you'd do great. But chem and bio graduates from campuses far from Stanford started noticing a drop-off of available jobs. At one school in Idaho, the head of the journalism school consoled the head of chemistry. "I've been there, my friend."

Somehow it took almost a year after the insane, ultraquick IPO before the culture wars discovered the world of Bopping. In theory there was an oversight board comprised of distinguished physicians and professors of public health who approved every program that could be distributed on the VitaBop store.

However, what was purported to be a hacking site in New Zealand soon posted a method to "root" or "jailbreak" VBs to gain access to the entire spectrum of their functions, not just those approved by the manufacturer. Now wearers could enter any program into a VB. Anti-abortion groups were horrified that a young woman could synthesize a morning-after pill without anyone knowing. Sports medicine was thrown into turmoil. Efforts to ban Bops in college and pro sports sputtered and ultimately failed.

If you have the luxury of programming tens of thousands of steps, you can synthesize an awful lot of results from commonplace antecedents. The psychedelics came first. An interesting feature of VitaBops was that smaller doses were needed than for what came to be known as "stuffing," or old-fashioned drug taking. You could titrate measured amounts directly into the bloodstream, controlled by how the body was responding at that moment. At first, police couldn't figure out how to prove a VitaBopper had programmed an illegal substance.

Boppers argued that you couldn't overdose off a Bop. This was a device measuring what was going on with your body millisecond to millisecond, after all. It wasn't like stuffing an illicit substance to see what would happen. Somehow, the staid pre-Bop society wasn't quite ready to hear that argument.

A youth culture around rooted* Bops was all about recreational substances, but Bops were also squirting out therapeutic drugs. It took about a month after a huge bust of Bop rooters at the University of California, Berkeley for an organization called the Granny Boppers to distribute recipes over the same file-sharing sites that had recently been conduits for pirated movies and TV shows. Legit pharmacy sales of drugs for diabetes, blood pressure, migraines, and erectile dysfunction suddenly sank.

Talk about lawsuits. All the pharmas and medical device companies ganged up on VitaBop.

VitaBop argued before the U.S. Supreme Court that it had done nothing wrong. It was only a neutral channel that its users acted within, and furthermore, it had absolutely no jurisdiction over the

---

*A rooted device is typically a phone or tablet which is no longer governed by the company that sold it, but instead by the owner who bought it. For instance, a "jailbroken" phone can load unapproved apps.

bodies of Boppers. For it to even attempt to eavesdrop on or influence what Boppers were up to would put it in violation of medical privacy laws.

VitaBop was for the most part able to survive legal scrutiny. People liked having the ability to control more about what went on in their own bodies. But at the same time, the economy was shrinking. Amazingly, fresh graduates in medicine and chemistry sometimes had to rely on their parents for even basic support, like getting the latest VitaBop.

Bops were still cheap or free, but the overall cost to use them seemed to be going up and up. You could try using aftermarket antecedent chemicals, but somehow they never quite worked. Something fishy was going on with the pricing of official antecedents; they gradually became more expensive for no good reason. Antitrust regulators had a hard time tackling VitaBop. After all, traditional pills were still available. VitaBop argued it existed in a competitive, dynamic environment. Plus, the company pointed out, what the government really should be worried about is the illegal trade in rooted Bops.

If you rooted a Bop, something strange happened. A gigantic firm called Booty arose based on building a proprietary database of what was going on in the bodies of people with rooted Bops. How did Booty get the data? Millions of people used pirate bopper sites that Booty could "scrape." Millions more voluntarily accepted contracts they had never read on a social chemical networking site in order to get access to free formulas. In doing so, they opened their bodies to Booty's competitor Bodybook.

Booty usually made money not by directly charging Boppers money, but instead by taking money from third parties in exchange for being able to influence what a Bopper would be exposed to online. For instance, a Bopper in excellent physical health might get an offer for a free fill-up at an army recruiting station. It turned out that this form of indirect manipulation worked well enough to earn Booty many billions of dollars.

Booty, Bodybook, and VitaBop coexisted awkwardly. Each collected a vast dossier on the metabolisms of everyone, but none could peer into the others' data vaults. Booty hoarded the treasure of the rooted, open world, while VitaBop did the same for the world of subscribers, and Bodybook for a world of "sharers." Booty accused VitaBop of being closed and not supporting the public good of bio-openness. VitaBop accused Booty of violating people's privacy and dignity. Pundits would say that VitaBop was a little like Apple, while Booty was a little more like Google or a hedge fund, and Bodybook was like, well, guess.

What they had in common was that each was shrinking the economy and the job prospects of everyone.

CHAPTER 9

From Above
Misusing Big Data
to Become Ridiculous

Three Nerds Walk into a Bar . . .

Your always-amused author once served on a panel at UC Berkeley judging mock business plans submitted by engineering graduate students who had enrolled in an entrepreneurship program. Three students presented the following scheme:

> Suppose you're darting around San Francisco bars and hot spots on a Saturday night. You land in a bar and there are a bounteous number of seemingly accessible, lovely, and unattached young women hanging out looking for attention in this particular place. Well, you whip out your mobile phone and alert the network. "Here's where the girls are!" All those other young men like you will know where to go. The service will make money with advertising, probably from bars and liquor concerns.

I looked at this geeky, sincere trio, and asked the obvious question: Will there ever, ever, ever be even the slightest chance that this service will provide even one bit of correct data? There was a tense pause. Was this yet another Asperger's syndrome–like example of incredible technical intelligence coupled with appalling naïveté about people?

Their answer: No, of course not. There will never be good data. The whole scheme will run on hope.

I gave them the most favorable possible evaluation, not because I wanted to encourage them to apply their hard-won skills to such an unproductive plan, but because they demonstrated an understanding of how networked information really works, when it comes to people.*

Your Lack of Privacy Is Someone Else's Wealth

Occasionally the rich embrace a new token and drive up its value. The fine art market is a great example. Expensive art is essentially a private form of currency traded among the very rich. The better an artist is at making art that can function this way, the more valuable the art will become. Andy Warhol is often associated with this trick, though Pablo Picasso and others were certainly playing the same game earlier. The art has to be stylistically distinct and available in suitable small runs. It becomes a private form of money, as instantly recognizable as a hundred-dollar bill.

A related trend of our times is that troves of dossiers on the private lives and inner beings of ordinary people, collected over digital networks, are packaged into a new private form of elite money. The actual data in these troves need not be valid. In fact, it might be better that it is not valid, for actual knowledge brings liabilities.

But the pretense that we have a bundle of other people's secrets is functioning like fine modern art. It is a new kind of security that the rich trade in, and the value is naturally driven up. It becomes a giant-scale levee inaccessible to ordinary people.

Few people realize the degree to which they are being tracked and spied upon in order that this new form of currency can be created. There is an extensive literature[1] and a sphere of activism[2] already in place to address the situation, so I will present only the briefest exposition of the topic here, with plenty of footnotes to follow.

---

*Silicon Valley comes through like clockwork. A year after this passage was written, a "where the babes are" app debuted at San Francisco bars. "SceneTap" used cameras and machine vision instead of volunteered information. No, I did not look into whether this startup was founded by the same students.

Even an innocent visit to a legitimate major newspaper site like the *New York Times* invokes a competitive swarm of more than a dozen tracking services, each of which is attempting to become a dominant compiler of spy data about you. One plug-in that attempts to block spying schemes, called Ghostery, is currently blocking more than a *thousand* such schemes,[3] though no one knows the true number.

There is no definitive map of network spying services. The allegiances and roles are multifarious and complex.[4] No one really knows the score, though a common opinion is that Google[5] has historically been at the top of the heap for collecting spy data about you on the open Internet,[6] while Facebook has mastered a way to corral people under an exclusive microscope.[7] That said, other companies you've probably never heard of, like Acxiom[8] and eBureau,[9] are also deeply determined to create dossiers on you.

Because spying on you is, for the moment, the official primary business of the information economy, any attempt to avoid being spied on, such as the use of Ghostery,[10] can seem like an assault on the very idea of the Internet.[11]

Big Data in Science

The seeming magic of using data over a network has been applied differently in the worlds of science and business. The operations of both worlds are increasingly enacted using almost indistinguishable big data tools, but they play by different rules. In science, verification and accuracy are paramount. In business and the culture at large, not so much.

Scientists are using new technologies to observe previously murky layers of nature in detail for the first time, but there are so many details that it would be useless to even try without big computers and networks. Genomics is as much a branch of computer science as it is of biology, for instance. The same is true for the frontiers of materials science and energy.

In the sciences, the arrival of a fresh source of big data means a lot of hard work for researchers, no matter how much technology is made available.* It is routine for new big data in medicine to transform our previous best guess about how to treat disease. And yet, new cures take years to arrive. In science, big data is magic, but *difficult* magic. We struggle with it, and expect to be fooled at first. The means to be rigorous with big data are still evolving.

No one in science thinks of big data as an automatic silver bullet. There is no shortage of common reference points to corroborate that assessment. Medicine provides the most consequential example. It is improving and yet improvement is tragically slow. Weather forecasting is better than it used to be, and is getting better. Satellites feed data we didn't used to have into computer models that can handle the vast data volume, and the result is better guesses about next week's weather, even next year's overall weather. And yet, the weather still surprises. Big data gradually improves our abilities as we work with it, but it doesn't instantly grant omniscience. Chasing a dynamic, ever-better-but-never-perfect statistic result is the very heart of modern cloud computing. Big data must be mastered in order to be valuable. It is not an automatic cornucopia, or a substitute for insight.

The spread of a flu outbreak can be tracked online faster than it can be tracked through the traditional medical system.[12] A research project at Google found that flu outbreaks could be tracked well by noting relevant searches in geographical zones. If there's a sudden lift in concern about flu symptoms in a particular place, for instance, there is probably flu there. The signal is observable even before doctors receive the first wave of complaints.

Tracking the flu online is science. That means it isn't automatic. Scientists must scrutinize the analysis. Maybe a rise in flu-related queries is actually in response to a popular movie in which the lead character has a bad flu. Without scrutiny, data isn't trusted.

However, even in the world of big scientific data, *magical-seeming* results can come before the understanding. Big data can occasionally reverse the sequence and confuse the incentives that have driven science and commerce since the beginnings of each.

---

*For a while it looked like there was a statistical effect hiding in a giant sea of numbers showing neutrinos traveling faster than light. The compelling illusion survived a number of challenges until it was finally shot down months later.

A spectacular recent example is the dawn of mind reading. In the first decade of the century there was a sequence of increasingly impressive examples of "brain reading." This might involve a person learning to control a robotic arm through direct brain measurement. But would it be possible to measure what a person was seeing or imagining from reading the brain? That would be more properly described as "mind reading."

Results started to appear early in the second decade of our century. Psychologist Jack Gallant and other researchers at UC Berkeley showed they could approximately determine what a person was watching simply by analyzing brain activity. It was as if computers became psychic, though a better way to understand the work is as an example of the challenges of scientific big data.

In Gallant's experiment, a movie was computed of what someone was seeing, based on nothing but fMRI* scans of the activity of the person's brain. The images looked blurry and otherworldly, but did conform to what was actually seen.

The way it worked was approximately this: Each subject was shown a batch of movie clips. Their brain activation patterns were recorded each time. Then, when the person watched a new, previously unseen clip, activation patterns were once again recorded. Then the original clips were mixed into a new clip proportionally, according to how similar the activation pattern for the new clip was to each original clip. With enough previously seen clips mixed together, a fuzzy new clip emerges that does look like what the subject is watching.

This was a remarkable result, of great importance, *but* it was only the first step of scientific inquiry. It didn't reveal how the brain codes visual memories. It did achieve something very important, which was that researchers had found a way to measure the brain that was relevant to specific visual cognition. Furthermore, similar techniques turn out to work for sound, speech, and other domains of experience and action. The age of high-tech mind reading has begun.

---

*fMRI, or functional MRI, is a higher-power version of the familiar MRI scanner. fMRI is usually used to detect blood flow in the brain, which reveals which parts of the brain are most activated moment to moment.

Jack Gallant is the first to point out that as spectacular as it is, the achievement is a beginning, not an end. The full cycle of scientific understanding will hopefully include additional attainments of insight and theory.

A Method in Waiting

You never know how long it will take for scientific conclusions about big data to form. Science gives up the best punch lines ever, but delivers them with the most inconsistent timing.

Big business data happens fast, as fast as people can take it in, or usually faster. Faster feedback loops make big business data ever more influential. We have become used to treating big business data as legitimate, even though it might really only seem so because of its special position in a network. Such data is valid by dint of tautology to an unknowable degree.

Science demands a different approach to big data, but we don't know as much about that approach as we will soon. Scientific method for big data is not yet entirely codified. Once practices are established for big data science, there will be uncontroversial answers to questions like:

- What standard would have to be met to allow for the publication of replication of a result? To what degree must replication require the gathering of different, but similar big data, and not just the reuse of the same data with different algorithms?
- What is publication? Is it just a description of the code used? The code itself? The code in some standardized form or framework that makes it reusable and tweakable?
- Must analysis be performed in a way that anticipates standard practices of meta-analysis?
- What documentation of the chain of custody of data must be standardized?
- Must there be new practices established, analogous to double-blind tests or placebos, that help prevent big data scientists from fooling themselves? Should there be multiple groups developing

code to analyze big data that remain completely insulated from each other in order to arrive at independent results?

Before long, all these questions will be answered, but for now, practices are still in flux. Though the details need to mature, the core commitment to testing hypotheses unites all scientists whether their data is big or small.

Wise or Feared?

In the world of business, big data often works whether it's true or not. People pay for dating services even though, on examination, the algorithms purporting to pair perfect mates probably don't work. It doesn't matter if the science is right so long as customers will pay for it, and they do.

Therefore, there is no need to distinguish whether statistics were valid in an a priori scientific sense, or if they were made valid because of social engineering. An example of social engineering is when two people meet through a dating site because they both *expect* the algorithms to be valid. People adapt to the presence of information systems, whether the adaptation is conscious or not, and whether the information system is functioning as expected or not. The science of it becomes moot.

This is a modern reflection of an ancient conundrum: It's hard to tell if a king is wise or feared. Either explanation suffices, on those occasions when what the king predicts is what turns out to happen.

Suppose a book vendor pitches an eBook on a tablet and the user clicks to pay for it. To a degree that might be because the vendor has cloud software that includes a scientifically valid prediction algorithm that has modeled the user correctly. *Or* it might be because users have been told the algorithms are smart, or maybe the user's attention is monopolized through a proprietary tablet. Perhaps the user would have equally been ready to buy any number of other books. It's not easy to tell which cause is more important.

Engineers will tend to assume it's the smartness of the software, and engineers are very good at fooling themselves into believing this is always so. In my previous book I described how it's empirically difficult to distinguish an artificial-intelligence success from people adjusting themselves to make a program look smart.

When the runners of a Siren Server are convinced it is providing a scientifically genuine computational service—that it is analyzing and predicting events that enlighten the human world—while it is actually just proving it has accumulated power, then nothing useful has been accomplished.

Occasionally an objective test of big business data reveals that the castles in the clouds were never real. For instance, there is no end to the braggadocio of a social network trying to sell advertising. The salespeople trumpet their system's ability to minutely model and target consumers as if they were Taliban in the crosshairs of a military drone. And yet, the same service, when it must simply detect if a user is underage, will turn out to be unable to counter the deceptions of children.

Yet the fantasy of precision persists. In that moment of fervor when you launch a Siren Server, you can practically taste the luscious swell of power. You will have information superiority because of your listening post on the 'net. This is one of the great illusions of our times: that you can game without being gamed.

The Nature of Big Data Defies Intuition

On a simplistic level, it is true that there are two versions of you on Facebook: the one you obsessively tend, and the hidden, deepest secret in the world, which is the data about you that is used to sell access to you to third parties like advertisers. You will never see that second kind of data about you.

But it isn't as if that secret version could be sent to you for review anyway. It wouldn't make sense by itself. It isn't separable from the rest of the global data that Facebook collects. The most precious and protected data, given the way we are doing things these days, are statistical correlations that are used by algorithms but are rarely seen or understood by people.

It might be a truth that people with bushy eyebrows who like purple toadstools in autumn are more likely to try hot sauce on their mashed potatoes in the spring. That might even turn out to be a truth with commercial value, but there would never be a purpose to explicitly revealing that such a correlation had been detected. Instead, a hot sauce vendor will in theory be able to automatically place a link in front of someone's eyes and increase the chance it will be well targeted, and no one need ever know why.

Big data commercial correlations are almost always eternally hidden; they are no more than tiny atoms of mathematics in the programs that spit out profits or power for certain kinds of cloud-based concerns. If a particular unexpected correlation were isolated, articulated, and revealed, what use would it be? Unlike an atom of scientific data, it is not rooted in an articulate framework and is not necessarily meaningful in isolation at all.

The Problem with Magic

To the degree big data can seem magical it can also be spectacularly misleading. Is this not clear? Perceiving magic is precisely the same thing as perceiving the limits of your own understanding.

When correlation is mistaken for understanding, we pay a heavy price. An example of this type of failure was the string of early 21st century financial crises in which correlations created gigantic investment packages that turned out to be duds in aggregate, bringing the world to indebtedness and austerity. Yet few financiers were blamed, at least in part because the schemes were complex and automated to such a high degree.

Naturally, one might ask why big business data is still so often used on faith, even after it has failed spectacularly. The answer is of course that big business data happens to facilitate superquick and vast near-term accumulations of wealth and influence.

Game On

Why is big business data often flawed? The unreliability of big business data is a collective project we all participate in. Blame the hive mind.

A wannabe Siren Server might enjoy honest access to data at first, as if it were an invisible observer, but if it becomes successful enough to become a real Siren Server, then everything changes. A tide of manipulation rises, and the data gathered becomes suspect.

If the server is based on reviews, many of them will suddenly start to be fakes. If it's based on people trying to be popular, then suddenly there will be fictitious fawning multitudes inflating illusions of popularity. If the server is trying to identify the most creditworthy or datable individuals, expect the profiles of those individuals to be mostly phony. Such illusions might be erected by clever third parties trying to get a little of the action, or they might be wielded by individuals trying to get some small personal advantage out of the online world.

In either case, once a Siren Server starts to get fooled by phony data, a dance begins. The Server hires mathematicians and Artificial Intelligence experts who try to use pure logic at a distance to filter out the lies. But to lie is not to be dumb. An arms race inevitably ensues, in which the hive mind of fakers attempts to outsmart a few clever programmers, and the balance of power shifts day to day.

What is remarkable is not that the same old games people have always played continue to be played over digital networks, but that smart entrepreneurs continue to be drawn into the illusion that this time they'll be the only one playing the game, while everyone else will passively accept being studied for the profit of a distant observer. It is never so simple.

The Kicker

Since I have long been concerned that the Internet has killed more jobs than it has created, I have been keenly interested in ventures that might reverse the trend. Kickstarter is a relevant experiment. Its original motivation was to make philanthropy more efficient, but here the focus will be on the way Kickstarter facilitates finance for new business ventures. Entrepreneurs raise money from the multitudes in advance of doing something they propose to do, but in a way that bypasses traditional ideas about finance.* Early supporters don't get equity, but they do often get something concrete, like a "first edition" of a new product. Is this not a sterling example of how the 'net can make capital available to unconventional innovators in nontraditional ways? What's not to like?

Indeed I like it, and I especially like that my friend Keith McMillen was able to launch an innovative music controller using it. Keith has been a celebrated musical instrument designer for years, and he had an idea for a new kind of digital musical device called the QuNeo. Instead of going the usual route of pitching investors, he used Kickstarter to pitch his future customers directly. They loved the idea, and his QuNeo controller became one of Kickstarter's fine early success stories. Hordes of customers lined up and prepaid for a device that didn't exist yet, turning into pseudo-investors and customers at the same time.

Kickstarter as a tool for funding product development isn't perfect. It would be even better if it supported the creation of risk pools for multiple projects, and an insurance or risk management system for customers. Siren Servers suffer the delusion that someone else can always take all the risk, that ignored risk will never come around to bite you. Even so, what a lovely case of the Internet making capitalism broader than it used to be.

But wait, all is not well. The same month that QuNeo units were

---

*Kickstarter is just one example of many. The idea is trendy, and is promoted in recent legislation such the 2012 JOBS act. See http://www.forbes.com/sites/work-in-progress/2012/09/21/the-jobs-act-what-startups-and-small-businesses-need-to-know-infographic/.

shipped to the earliest adopters, the tech blog Gizmodo announced a boycott of coverage of Kickstarter proposals.* The reason was that the site was so flooded with poor-quality proposals that it had become impractical to dig through so many fakes and flakes to find a few true gems.

This is an instance in which a classic problem in pre-digital markets should have been put to rest to a significant degree by digital designs. The supposed transparency of the way we have structured our present information economy turned out to be unusable.

The problem in question is known as the "Market for Lemons," after the title of the famous paper, which helped earn its author, George Akerlof, a Nobel Prize[13] in Economics. The lemons in the paper were not from the lemonade stand we encountered earlier, but were instead crummy used cars for sale. The paper detailed how a prevalence of bad used cars distorted markets through the mechanism of information asymmetry.

Buyers worried that sellers knew more about a used car's problems than they were letting on, which put a pervasive burden on the market, stunted it, and made it less efficient. A truly transparent form of digital market might perhaps offer a reduced occurrence of this sort of degradation. At least that was the hope in the air in the early years of network research, before the advent of Siren Servers.

In fact, digital networks have been helpful in reducing the fear of lemons in the physical used car market. You can now get instant

---

*Perhaps Gizmodo is not a definitive source of criticism, but I choose to link there since it and its parent network were the victims of a link boycott from parts of Reddit over an appalling issue while this book was being finalized. Subreddits gathered men who took surreptitious photos of women, or compiled suggestive pictures of underage girls. These men wanted to be able to enjoy the information advantage of being able to do these things to strangers while remaining anonymous. A Gawker reporter (in the parent organization of Gizmodo) revealed a ringleader, and that was considered unforgivable. The desire to manipulate others while remaining invulnerable is just the ordinary person's way of pretending to be a Siren Server for a moment. The ringleader, once revealed, turned out to be a rather vulnerable working-class fellow. Whenever you see a den of iniquity on the Web, look closer and you'll find a den of inequity. See http://www.newstatesman.com/blogs/internet/2012/10/reddit-blocks-gawker-defence-its-right-be-really-really-creepy, and http://gawker.com/5950981/unmasking-reddits-violentacrez-the-biggest-troll-on-the-web.

information about a car's history, for example.[14] But that sort of improvement has been avoided by Siren Servers. Instead, the need of Siren Servers to radiate risk to everyone but themselves has the perverse effect of reinstating the lemon dilemma.

Every QuNeo provides cover for lousy projects that gradually tarnish the prospects of the next QuNeo. What happens if a project isn't completed? What if a supporter never receives a gadget that was supposed to be manufactured? Is there any recourse? Can an innovation hub really radiate all risk away from itself?

Kickstarter has experimented with changing the rules to reduce the risks taken by supporters of projects. For instance, inventors were at one point suddenly forbidden from showing realistic renderings of what an end product might look like. That rule supposedly reduced the risk that a supporter would perceive a project to be closer to fruition than it really was. Even if the rule had the desired effect, is it not absurd to deny inventors the ability to show pictures of what they intend to create? But it's the sort of strategy a Siren Server must resort to in order to retain an arm's-length, risk-free state of being. Here is the question and answer about the policy from the Kickstarter website:

> How will Kickstarter know whether something is a simulation or rendering [. . . instead of a photograph of a physical prototype]?
>
> We may not know. We do only a quick review to make sure a project meets our guidelines.

I would like to see Kickstarter grow to be larger than Amazon, since it embodies a more fundamental mechanism of overall economic growth. Instead of just driving prices down, it turns consumers into a priori funders of innovation. But at an Amazon-like scale there would inevitably be an even bigger wave of tricksters, scammers, and the clueless to be dealt with.

Kickstarter continues to produce some wonderful success stories and a huge ocean of doomed or befuddled proposals. Maybe the site will enter into an endless game with scammers and the clueless, as it scales up, and render itself irrelevant. Or it might adopt crowdsourced voting or automatic filters to keep out crap, only to find that crap is smart and happy to jump through hoops to get through. Or maybe Kickstarter will become more expensive to use, and less naïvely "democratic," because human editors will block useless proposals. Maybe it will learn to take on at least a little risk to go with the benefits. Whatever happens, success will be dependent on finding some imperfect but survivable compromise.

The Nature of Our Confusion

Successful network ventures that become known to the public are always eventually gamed by epidemics of scammers. Unscrupulous "content farms" turn out drivel and link to themselves in an attempt to climb high on Google's search results, and bloggers herded by major media companies are encouraged to spice up their writing with key words and phrases not to grab human attention, but the attention of Google's algorithms.

To Google's credit, the company has engaged in battle with these encroachments, but the war is never over. When Google measures people, and the result has something to do with who gets rich and powerful, people don't sit around like flu viruses awaiting impartial assessment. Instead they play the game.

Sites with reviews are stuffed with fake reviews. When education is driven by big data, not only must teachers teach to the test, but it often turns out that there's widespread cheating.

What is odd, over and over, is that computer scientists and technology entrepreneurs are always shocked at this turn of events. We geeky sorts would prefer that the world passively await our mastery to overtake it, though that is never so.

Our core illusion is that we imagine big data as a substance, like a natural resource waiting to be mined. We use terms like *datamining* routinely to reinforce that illusion. Indeed some data is like that. Scientific big data, like data about galaxy formation, weather, or flu outbreaks, can be gathered and mined, just like gold, provided you put in the hard work.

But big data about people is different. It doesn't sit there; it plays against you. It isn't like a view through a microscope, but more like a view of a chessboard.

A classic optical illusion might be helpful.

This is the famous figure/ground illusion popularized by Danish psychologist Edgar Rubin in 1915. A contour can be seen equally as a golden goblet or two faces. Neither interpretation is more correct than the other. (In this case I have used Adam Smith's face.)

In the same way, cloud information generated by people can be perceived either as a valuable resource you might be able to plunder, like a golden vase, or as waves of human behavior, much of it directed against you. From a disinterested abstract perspective, both perceptions are legitimate.

However, if you are an interested participant in a game, it is in your interest to perceive those faces first and foremost.

Here is yet another statement of the core idea of this book, that data concerning people is best thought of as people in disguise, and they're usually up to something.

The Most Elite Naïveté

Attentive readers will note a continuing rotation in perspectives as I ridicule the illusions of big human data. Sometimes I write as if I were complaining from an everyman's perspective about being analyzed and treated as a pawn in a big data game. Other times I write as if I were playing a big data game and am annoyed at how my game is being ruined because so many others also play against me.

No one knew how digital networking and economics would interact in advance. Instead of a story of villains, I see a story of technologists and entrepreneurs who were pioneers, challenging us to learn from their results.

My argument is not so much that we should "fight the power," but that a better way of conceiving information technology would really be better for most people, *including* those ambitious people who plan to accomplish giant feats. So I am arguing *both* from the perspective of a big-time macher *and* from the perspective of a more typical person, because any solution has to be a solution from both perspectives.

Big human data, that vase-shaped gap, is the arbiter of influence and power in our times. Finance is no longer about the case-by-case judgment of financiers, but about how good they are at locking in the best big-data scientists and technologists into exclusive contracts. Politicians target voters using similar algorithms to those that evaluate people for access to credit or insurance. The list goes on and on.

As technology advances, Siren Servers will be ever more the objects of the struggle for wealth and power, because they are the only links in the chain that will not be commoditized. If present trends continue, you'll always be able to seek information supremacy, just as old-fashioned barons could struggle for supremacy over land or natural resources. A new energy cycle will someday make oil much less central to geopolitics, but the information system that manages that new kind of energy could easily become an impregnable castle. The illusory golden vase becomes more and more valuable.

Modernity Conceives the Future

MAPPING OUT WHERE THE CONVERSATION CAN GO

An endgame for civilization has been foreseen since Aristotle. As technology reaches heights of efficiency, civilization will have to find a way to resolve a peculiar puzzle: What should the role of "extra" humans be if not everyone is still strictly needed? Do the extra people—the ones whose roles have withered—starve? Or get easy lives? Who decides? How?

The same core questions, stated in a multitude of ways, have elicited only a small number of answers, because only a few are possible.

What will people be when technology becomes much more advanced? With each passing year our abilities to act on our ideas are increased by technological progress. Ideas matter more and more. The ancient conversations about where human purpose is headed continue today, with rising implications.

Suppose that machines eventually gain sufficient functionality that one will be able to say that a lot of people have become extraneous. This might take place in nursing, pharmaceuticals, transportation, manufacturing, or in any other imaginable field of employment.

The right question to then ask isn't really about what should be done with the people who used to perform the tasks now colonized by machines. By the time one gets to that question, a conceptual mistake has already been made.

Instead, it has to be pointed out that outside of the spell of bad philosophy human obsolescence wouldn't in fact happen. The data that drives "automation" has to ultimately come from people, in the form of "big data." Automation can always be understood as elaborate puppetry.

The most crucial quality of our response to very high-functioning machines, artificial intelligences and the like, is how we conceive of the things that the machines can't do, and whether those tasks are considered real jobs for people or not. We used to imagine that elite engineers would be automation's only puppeteers. It turns out instead that big data coming from vast numbers of people is needed to make machines appear to be "automated." Do the puppeteers still get paid once the whole audience has joined their ranks?

NINE DISMAL HUMORS OF FUTURISM, AND A HOPEFUL ONE

Each of ten tropes, which I call "humors,"* can be compressed into simple statements about how human identity, changing technology, and the design of civilization fit together. Since technological culture influences what technologists create, and technology is what makes the future different from the past, techie vocabulary is important.

I choose to avoid the loaded term *meme*. There are many reasons to avoid *meme* in this case; the primary one being that good ideas are not remotely as plentiful as varieties of traits in natural organisms. You might find this set of "technological humors" to be useful. If so, it is only because the solution space for how a person can react to accelerating technological change is small.†

Each humor is a trefoil binding politics, money, and technology to the human condition:

- **Theocracy**: Politics is the means to supernatural immortality.

  This is the oldest and still most common humor, which proposes that the natural world is but a political theater that

---

*Ancient physicians like Hippocrates understood the original humors as a small set of forces or essences that flowed through the human body. They were each a kind of fluid (black bile, yellow bile, phlegm, or blood) but also elements (air, fire, water, earth) and personality type. Black bile corresponded to melancholy, for instance.

†An admonition: Please, please don't try to implement my classification scheme of humors in some cloud software startup in order to organize the expressions of other people. They are only offered as thoughts, not as truth. In other words, I hope you find it helpful to consider them analytically, in a personal, skeptical fashion, but not as a way to constrain or determine future events through the structure of software.

No end of ontologies has been proposed to describe the human condition, from the enneagram to the *DSM*. Ontologies can be fun and useful, but of course it's essential to not take them too seriously. As with all ontological schemes, my humors are not meant to be confused with reality itself.

functions as a remote control of a more significant supernatural world. Politics here serves as the interface to that other world.*

Eight of the other humors collected here are naturalistic. A rapture, messiah, or other supernatural discontinuity in the future has not, as a matter of definition, been part of the discussion of the *natural* future until fairly recently, with the advent of the idea of the Singularity. Now we must include old religion in order to put new religion in context.

- **Abundance:** Technology is the means to escape politics and approach material immortality.

  Tech will someday become so good that everyone will have everything and there will be no need for politics. "Abundance" is a commanding humor in Silicon Valley, though it was pioneered in ancient Greece. It is both futuristic and ancient.

  This humor often presents itself arrogantly, to bring the naïve intuitions held by nontechnical people to shame.†

- **Malthus:** Politics is the means to material extinction.

  Our successes will be our undoing. As we approach abundance, we will overpopulate and overconsume, or otherwise screw up, until catastrophe strikes. The Malthusian humor suggests a fatal, deterministic ineptitude in politics.

---

*Yes, of course this is not a blanket definition of all religion or spirituality. Also, as I argue all the time, materialism doesn't even break a sweat to become as crazy and cruel as religion can be at its worst. A Stalin can keep up with any religious inquisition. Yet, there is a global ancient political phenomenon that must be given a name.

†It is true that people consistently underestimate technological change in some ways. The information technology gadgets imagined in the 1960s or 1980s for the starship *Enterprise* (as it would be centuries in the future) already feel antiquated. People are unable to appreciate how significant technological change is likely to be, even in their own lifetimes. On the other hand there is still no consumer flying car, and probably won't be one for a long time. So technological change is overestimated just as frequently.

How This Century Might Unfold, from Two Points of View

- **Rousseau:** Technology is the means to spiritual malaise.

  As we approach Abundance, we become inauthentic and absurd.

- **Invisible Hand:** Information technology ought to subsume politics.

  Adam Smith sketched a character known as the "Invisible Hand," who can serve as a figurehead for subsuming politics under information technology. Markets (or more recently, other, fundamentally similar algorithms) make decisions instead of human, political deliberations. This humor either ignores or rejects Abundance, for markets become absurd as supply approaches infinity.

- **Marx:** Politics ought to subsume information technology.

  Marxism anticipates Abundance but elevates politics infinitely and indefinitely. Once the machines can do all the work, politics will decide what's best for people, so that all will benefit from the bounty.

- **H. G. Wells:** Human life will be meaningful because primordial, pretechnological tribal drama will be reinstated once we are sufficiently challenged by either our own machines or by aliens. So, technology creates human meaning through challenge rather than through providing Abundance.

  The genre of science fiction was born to express a distinct humor, which contemplates the possibility that the future might not necessarily be framed with people at the center. Humans might instead face potential irrelevance in a world dominated by either our own future machines or superior aliens. Most science fiction constructs a narrative of the triumph of human relevance against all odds.

Much science fiction ends badly, however, and so serves either as a cautionary tale or a fascinating display of nihilism. In any case, anticipating a struggle for relevance suggests a new meaning of life or natural mission for humanity when technology gets good. This humor is dubbed "Wells's Humor" in honor of H. G.'s novel *The Time Machine,* a superb early example.

These seven humors mapped conversations about the human future up until the end of World War II. The 20th century brought two more humors into prominence, and a third into being, though that final one still hasn't gained the prominence it deserves.

- **Strangelove**: Some person will destroy us all when technology gets good enough. Human nature plus good technology equals extinction.

  With the bomb came the Strangelovian possibility of species-wide suicide. This was darker than Malthus, as it replaced unintentional self-destruction with instantaneous decisive destruction accessible with the simple press of a button.

- **Turing**: Politics and people won't even exist. Only technology will exist when it gets good enough, which means it will become supernatural.

  Not long after Hiroshima, Alan Turing hatched the idea that people are creating a successor reality in information. Obviously Turing's humor inspired a great deal of science fiction, but I'll argue it's distinct because it poses the possibility of a new metaphysics. People might turn into information rather than be replaced by it. This is why Ray Kurzweil can await being uploaded into a virtual heaven. Turing brought metaphysics into the modern conversation about the natural future.

Turing's humor also provides a destination, or an eschatology that the Invisible Hand's humor lacks. Turing's algorithms could inherit the world in a way that the Hand could not. This is because we can imagine software, improperly, I'll argue, operating without the need for human operators, and even in an era of Abundance depopulated of people. Abundance kills the hand, but not Turing's ghosts.

- **Nelson:** Information technology of a particular design could help people remain people without resorting to extreme politics when any of the other, creepily eschatological humors seem to be imminent.

   Ted Nelson, in 1960, came up with a brand-new, still-emerging humor, which suggests information as a way to avoid excesses of politics even as we approach an inevitably imperfect Abundance. It essentially proposes a consilience between the Invisible Hand and Abundance. This is the humor I am hoping to further with this book.

Each humor captures a distinct hypothesis about how politics, what it means to be human, and technology are related. They all concern the role of politics and the human will, or intentionality, in ever higher-tech futures. Will politics become obsolete or absolute? Will people be subsumed or will we transcend what had been our condition?

There's a way the humors cycle around into each other. Someone might be playing the technological triumphalist, celebrating the brashest entrepreneurs of the moment, but then end up imagining a weirdly socialist utopia in the future. This is one of the most common switchbacks, one that never fails to amaze me. "Free Google tools and free Twitter are leading to a world where everything is free because people share, but isn't it great that we can corner billions of dollars by gathering data no one else has?" If everything will be free, why are we trying to corner anything? Are our fortunes only temporary? Will they become moot when we're done?

It's not the only twist of its kind. If you play the back-to-nature card, you end up in an artificial game, chasing authenticity without a map or a way to verify that you've found it. "What this music software is about is getting in touch with the real emotion and meaning of music, which is done in this case by adjusting the pitches of people who can barely sing so that they can sing in perfect harmony, together. Singing in harmony is the most wonderful musical connection. But wait—maybe it would be more authentic if they weren't singing perfectly. That's too robotic. What is the percentage of perfection that represents authenticity? Ten percent? Fifteen percent?" This is a ricochet between the "Abundance" and "Rousseau" humors.

I hear variations of familiar switchbacks almost every day. These ubiquitous conversations of the tech community retrace the moves of older conversations—sometimes much older ones.

MEANING AS NOSTALGIA

Even technologists tend to have a streak of Jean-Jacques Rousseau's romanticism in us. We occasionally imagine and celebrate a kind of comfort, authenticity, and sacredness rooted in a past that never existed.

The obvious figurehead for this humor is Rousseau, but E. M. Forster could also serve as the cultural marker for nostalgic technophobia because of his short story "The Machine Stops." This was a remarkably accurate description of the Internet published in 1909, decades before computers existed. To the dismay of generations of computer scientists, the first glimmer of the wonders we have built was a dystopian tale.

In the story, what we'd call the Internet is known as the "Machine." The world's population is glued to the Machine's screens, endlessly engaged in social networking, browsing, Skypeing, and the like. Interestingly, Forster wasn't cynical enough to foresee the centrality of advertising in such a situation.

At the end of the story, the machine does indeed stop. Terror ensues, similar to what is imagined these days from a hypothetical cyber-attack. The whole human world crashes. Survivors straggle outside to revel in the authenticity of reality. "The Sun!" they cry, amazed at luminous depths of beauty that could not have been imagined. The failure of the Machine is a happy ending.

This theme has become commonplace in popular culture. A more recent incarnation was presented in the *Matrix* movies, in which humans live inside a Virtual Reality simulation. In the movies, those who become aware of their status, and able to manipulate it, are more vital, virile, and better dressed than those who do not. In the bucolic rural happy ending of *Minority Report,* which I contributed to, the gadgets that had filled the screen in all the earlier dystopian scenes were banished from the set. In *Gattaca,* the "In-valid," the natural, nongenetically engineered brother, is more vital and true, and benefits from incantations of optimism that evade the heart of the "Valid," genetically engineered brother.

The Rousseau humor is ambiguously ironic and sometimes even funny. See Woody Allen's *Sleeper* for an example of the humorous potential. I call it ironic, since we find ourselves psychologically victimized by technologies that we've chosen to adopt. The irony is ambiguous because it often isn't clear how much choice we really had.

The people in Forster's story were complicit in being hypnotized by the machine; they built it, after all. Why not keep it turned on, but also go outside once in a while? That's the irony.

On the other hand, the machine might be all that's saving the story's characters from short, diseased lives out in the real world; but then again, maybe it would have been possible to build a less alienating machine that would have created just as much security. That's the ambiguity.

And if, as I argue, the world must eventually become somewhat artificial in order for people to thrive, must experience enabled by the Machine be forever inauthentic, infertile, or shallow in comparison?

The Rousseau humor of reacting to technology is as common and influential as any other. It is common because it is based on a substantial, unavoidable conundrum.

Once the ground rules of life are changed, you no longer have the ability to understand what you might have forgotten from a previous incarnation. No adult really knows what was lost in the process of growing up, because the adult brain cannot quite realize the mentality in which childhood memories are fully meaningful. With that level of change comes a kind of partial death.

The transition from childhood to adulthood is a natural example, but technological change has put successive generations of adults through similarly intense artificial disruptions.

It is impossible for us to completely enter the experiential world of the hunter-gatherer. It's almost impossible to conceive of the subjective texture of life before electricity. We can't quite fully know what we have lost as we become more technological, so we are in constant doubt of our own authenticity and vitality. This is a necessary side effect of our survival.

Recent examples of the nostalgic Rousseauian humor have included the deconstructionist school of philosophy, the "natural" medicine and food movements, and the rise of what are purported to be traditional, fundamentalist versions of the world's religions, particularly as related to human reproduction. We use newly coined ideas of authenticity to attempt to hold on to something we can't quite articulate that might have been lost in the course of becoming modern.

My purpose is not to ridicule the Rousseau humor. As I have argued, its rationale is not only legitimate, but unavoidable.

At the same time, it's important to remember that nostalgia for lower-tech times is based on fake memories. This is as true in the small scale of centuries as it is in the vast scale of life. Every little genetic feature of you, from the crook of the corner of your eye to much of the way your body moves when you listen to music, was framed and formed by the negative spaces carved out by the pre-reproductive deaths of your would-be ancestors over hundreds of millions of years. You are the reverse image of inconceivable epochs of heartbreak and cruelty. Your would-be ancestors in their many species, reaching back into the phylogenetic tree, were eaten, often by disease, or sexually rejected before they could contribute genes to your legacy. The genetic, natural part of you is the sum of the leftovers of billions of years of extreme violence and poverty. Modernity is precisely the way individuals arose out of the ravages of evolutionary selection.

Unfortunately, Rousseau's humor can sometimes lead to loathsome behavior. Taking it to extremes is destructive, and you'll often find a trace of the nostalgia humor in the ideologies of terrorists of any origin, from jihadi suicide bombers to the people who attack abortion clinics and animal research centers.

But this humor doesn't have to be violent. I embrace it and practice it myself in a lightened form, which could be called homeopathic. Just about every technologist I know harbors some Rousseauian fetish in the closet. The same fellow who might work on "Augmented Wilderness," a technology in which a virtual world is perceived to be superimposed on a remote wilderness trail, will seek out the wild primitivist side of Silicon Valley rituals like Burning Man. The room where I am writing this is filled with rare, archaic, acoustic musical instruments that I have learned to play. I find that digital ways of making music are missing something and I will not let go of that thing. This is entirely reasonable.

Is there really something essential and vital about acoustic instruments that computers can't touch? Another incarnation of Pascal's bargain presents itself. I don't really know, but the cost of holding on to my perception of a difference is manageable, while the cost if I let go might be great, even if the resulting amnesia would hide the loss from me.

CAN WE HANDLE OUR OWN POWER?

Thomas Malthus articulated fear of an apocalypse in a naturalistic framework instead of the established supernatural ones. The future he dreaded from the perspective of the 18th century was one where our own successes grant us gifts we cannot absorb, leading to catastrophe.

In a typical Malthusian scenario, agriculture, public health, medicine, and industrialization enable an unsustainable population explosion, which leads to catastrophic famine. Our beloved technological achievements continue to seduce us even as they lead us to destruction.

Since Malthus, there have been endless replays of the "population bomb" motif, as Paul Erlich dubbed it in the 1960s. A documentary called *Surviving Progress,*[1] based on a book called *A Short History of Progress,*[2] puts it this way: "We're now reaching a point at which technological progress threatens the very existence of humanity."

A wide variety of Icarusian fates for mankind are never far from our thoughts. Global climate change is a principal example of the moment. Another is the prospect of weapons of mass destruction in the hands of terrorists. One could also mention viruses given flight by the jet

132

age, the prospect that we'll be bathed in the radiation of nuclear power when the oil runs out, and so on. Some respected technologists have publicly worried that the descendants of our computers might eat us later in this century.

Malthusian scenarios are often not just terrifying, but cruel in their irony. Industrialized, educated populations often face a population anti-bomb these days: a depopulation spiral. This is when there aren't enough children being born to maintain the population, and balance the burden of an age wave. Japan's situation was described earlier. Korea, Italy, and many other countries are also experiencing profound depopulation spirals. It is the "less modern" parts of the world that power population explosions.

The threats of global warming, terrorism, and the rest are very real, but not in a surprising or unnatural way. It is wholly natural that, as we humans gain more and more influence over our fates, we accrue an ever-greater variety of ways to commit mass suicide.

An analogy would be an individual learning to drive a car. Anyone who learns to drive has the power to kill himself at any moment. In fact, many do. And yet, most of us accept the risk and responsibility of driving, and for the most part manage to enjoy the power and fun available to us through cars.

In a similar way, on a global scale, it is inevitable that our survival will be in our own hands in more and more ways as technology progresses. While global climate change is in my opinion real, and scary, it is also an inevitable species-wide rite of passage.* It is just one of many that we will have to meet with expertise and cunning, and perhaps with the occasional self-manipulative incantation of optimism.

This is not an easy thing to say, so it isn't said very often. We cannot make the world better through expertise without also creating more and more means for people to destroy the world. Expertise is expertise.

That doesn't mean increasing expertise is inherently self-defeating! It is better to have more of a say in our fate, even if that means we must trust ourselves. Growing up is good. What is gained is greater than

---

*Later in the book, when solutions are proposed, we will consider how network architecture might be tweaked to make it easier to confront big challenges like global climate change.

what is lost. There's a natural lure to believe that the state of human-kind before technologists mucked with it was secure and comfortable. Technologists remember that it was not.

The only reason a less transformed world can be imagined as a safer one is that infant mortality and other tragedies used to constitute a constant, "natural" catastrophe. Death tolls were usually so well paid up in advance that Malthusian dangers were mooted. The elevation of the human story from constant catastrophe is one and the same with the rise of technological ability.

Yes, the benefits of technology always have catches. Every technological advance in our adventure up to the present has had side effects. Every medicine is also a poison, and every new source of food is a famine in waiting. Humans consistently demonstrated an ability to use ancient innovations in agriculture, fuel, and construction to deforest regions and destroy local environments. Jared Diamond and others have documented how human societies have repeatedly undermined themselves. We have been obliged to invent our way out of the mess caused by our last inventions since we became human. It is our identity.

The answer to climate change can't be halting or reversing events. The earth is not a linear system, like a video clip, that can be played in forward or reverse. After we learn how to survive global climate change, the earth will not be the same place it was before. It will be more artificial, more managed.

That is not anything new. It is nothing more than another stage in the adventure that started when Eve bit the apple, which we can also think of as Newton's apple. (Not to mention Turing's apple.)

But no one wants to hear that. It is hard to be comfortable accepting the degree of responsibility our species will have to assume in order to survive into the future. The game was entered into long ago and we have no choice but to play.

THE FIRST HIGH-TECH WRITER

It can be a little deflating to realize how much of the present-day conversation about economic systems, technology, and personhood was already well worn in the century before last. "The Ballad of John Henry" was one of the best-known songs of the 19th century. Our John was an apocryphal railroad worker who is said to have competed with a railroad-building machine and won, only to drop dead from exhaustion. Productivity was fatal. The late 19th century was already dominated by anxieties of human obsolescence.

The original Luddites were early 19th century textile workers worried about being made obsolete by improved looms. Just as Aristotle foresaw! Their story was not pretty. They gathered into violent mobs and were punished in public executions.

In material terms, life as a factory worker was better than that of a peasant. So the Luddites were often doing better than their ancestors. And yet their good fortune was terrifyingly fragile. Moment-to-moment loss of personal control when one worked in a factory might have enhanced Luddite anxiety, just as we sometimes fear being locked into a plane more than we fear driving in a car, even though the car is usually more dangerous. Something about becoming part of someone else's machine was terrifying on a fundamental level.

We have never overcome that anxiety. During the Great Depression, in the 1930s, one of the clichés of the popular press was that robots were coming to take away any jobs that might appear. There were popular stories of robots supposedly killing their makers and robots about to challenge human champions in boxing rings.[3] These old paranoias are typically exhumed these days in order to make the case that there's nothing to worry about. "See, in the old days they worried that technology would make people obsolete and it didn't happen. Similar worries today are just as silly."

To that I say, "I agree completely that the fears were wrong then and wrong today, in terms of what's actually true. People are and will always be needed. The question is whether we'll engage in complete enough accounting so that people are honestly valued. If there's ever an illusion that humans are becoming obsolete, it will in reality be a case of massive accounting fraud. What we're doing now is initiating that fraud. Let's stop."

But back in the 19th century, people weren't thinking of the world as information yet, and the robots of our imaginations were brawny, gunning for blue-collar jobs. Two huge streams of culture and argument that continue to underlie many of today's conversations were incubated by robot anxiety: the "left" and science fiction.

We find a hatching of the left in the early writings of Karl Marx, who as early as the 1840s was obsessed with the Luddite dilemma. Marx was one of the first technology writers. This realization came to me in a flash many years ago when I was driving in Silicon Valley and some Internet startup was on the radio trumpeting the latest scheme to take over the world. There was a lot of the usual filler about innovation breaking through traditional market boundaries, the globalization of technical talent, and so on. I was just about to turn the radio off, muttering something about how I couldn't take even one more pitch from one of these companies, when the announcer intoned, "This has been an anniversary reading of *Das Kapital.*" I had been listening to the lefty station, KPFA, without realizing it.

I'm no Marxist. I love competing in the market, and the last thing I'd want is to live under communism. My wife grew up with it in Minsk, Belarus, and I am absolutely, thoroughly convinced of the misery. But if you select the right passages, Marx can read as being incredibly current.

Every thoughtful technologist has probably gone through a period of self-doubt over Luddite scenarios. The damage to careers by technological progress is not uniformly distributed among people. If you wait long enough, anyone might potentially be vulnerable to playing the role of Luddite, even if it only happens to certain unlucky people at any given moment. Technological change is unfair, at least in the short term. Can we live with that unfairness?

The reason most technologists can sleep at night is that the benefits of technological progress do seem to eventually benefit everyone rapidly enough to keep the world from exploding or imploding. New jobs appear along with new technologies, even as old ones are destroyed. The descendants of the Luddites are with us today, and work as stockbrokers, personal trainers, and computer programmers. But lately, their adult children are still living at home. Has the chain been broken?

Neither training nor prestige insulates people from the potential to fall prey to the fate of the Luddites. Robotic pharmacists and "artificially intelligent" software performing legal research previously done by human lawyers have both already been shown to be cost-effective,[4] and we're still very early in the process. The only position at all that is safe is to be the proprietor of a top node on the network. And even that role cannot stand if it is to be the only secure human role.

Marx also described a subtler problem of "alienation," a sense that one's imprint on the world is not one's own anymore when one is part of someone else's scheme in a high tech factory. Today there is a great deal of concern about the authenticity and vitality of life lived online. Are "friends" really friends? These concerns are an echo of Marx, almost two centuries later, as information becomes the same thing as production.

MEANING IN STRUGGLE

H. G. Wells's science fiction novel *The Time Machine,* published in 1895, foresees a future in which mankind has split into two species, the Eloi and the Morlocks. Each survives in the ruins of a civilization that had been trapped in Marx's nightmare and collapsed. What was once a divide between rich and poor evolved into a split between species, and the character of each was debased. The Eloi, descended from the poor, were docile, while the Morlocks, descended from the rich, were decadent and ultimately just as debased.

The Morlocks could have descended from today's social network or hedge fund owners, while the ancestors of the Eloi undoubtedly felt lucky initially, as free tools helped them crash on each other's couches more efficiently. What is intriguing about Wells's vision is that members of both species become undignified, lesser creatures. (Morlocks eat Eloi, which is about as far as one can go in rejecting empathy and dignity.)

When science fiction turns dark, as in *The Time Machine,* or the works of Philip K. Dick or William Gibson, it is usually because people have been rendered absurd by technological advancement. When science fiction has a sunny outlook it is because heroes are making themselves human by struggling successfully against human obsolescence.

The struggle might be against aliens (*War of the Worlds*), plain old evil (*Star Wars*), or artificial intelligence, as in *2001: A Space Odyssey, The Matrix, The Terminator, Battlestar Galactica,* and many more. In all cases, science fiction is fundamentally retro, in that it re-creates the setting of early human evolution, when human character was first formed in a setting where meaning was inseparable from survival.

PRACTICAL OPTIMISM

When science fiction is bright, it brings the gift of helping to sort out what meaning might be like when people are highly empowered by their inventions. Optimistic science fiction suggests that we need not create artificial struggles against our own inventions in order to repeatedly prove ourselves.

In *Star Trek*'s imaginary future,* new gadgets don't just result in a more instrumented world, but also in a more moral, fun, adventurous, sexy, and meaningful world. Yes, it's pure kitsch, ridiculous on most levels, but so what? This silly TV show reflected something substantial and lovely in the culture of technologists better than any other well-known point of reference. It's a shame that there aren't more recent examples to supersede it.

An important feature of *Star Trek,* and all optimistic, heroic science fiction, is that a recognizable human remains at the center of the adventure. At the center of the high-tech circular bridge of the starship *Enterprise* is seated a Kirk or a Picard, a person.†

It is almost impossible to believe that the real-world technological optimists of the 1960s, when *Star Trek* first aired, were able to pull off wonders like the moon missions without the computers or materials we have today. Humbling.

There is an interaction between optimism and achievement that seems distinctly American to me, but that might only be because I am an American. Our pop culture is filled with the message that optimism is part of the magical brew of success. Manifest Destiny, motivational speakers, "If you build it, they will come," the Wizard of Oz giving out his medals.

---

*This is about the TV series. The qualities praised here are not found in the movies.

† *Star Trek* also included artificial intelligence characters, such as the Pinocchio-like Data. The conceit was that Data could not be reproduced. Had there been a billion Datas, his character would have become dull and a threat to humankind, and the whole show turned into a dark tale. It would have become *Battlestar Galactica.*

Optimism plays a special role when the beholder is a technologist. It's a strange business, the way rational technologists can sometimes embrace optimism as if it were a magical intellectual aphrodisiac. We've made a secular version of Pascal's Wager.

Pascal suggested that one ought to believe in God because if God exists, it will have been the correct choice, while if God turns out to not exist, little harm will have been done by holding a false metaphysical belief. Does optimism really affect outcomes? The best bet is to believe that the answer is "Yes." I suppose the vulgar construction "Kirk's Wager" is a workable moniker for it.

I'm bringing up Pascal's Wager not because of anything to do with God, but because I think the logic behind it is similar to some of the thought games going on in the minds of technologists. The common logic behind Pascal's and Kirk's wagers is not perfect. The cost of belief isn't really known in advance. There are those who think we've paid too high a price for belief in God, for instance. Also, you could make similar wagers for an endless variety of beliefs, but you couldn't hold all of them. How do you choose?

For better or worse, however, we technologists have made Kirk's Wager: We believe that all this work will make the future better than the past. The negative side effects, we are convinced, will not be so bad as to make the whole project a mistake. We keep pushing forever forward, not knowing quite where we are going.

The way we believe in the future is silly and kitschy, just like *Star Trek,* and yet I think it's the best option. Whatever you think of Pascal, Kirk's Wager is actually a good bet. The best way to defend it is to assess the alternatives, which I will do in the coming pages.

The core of my dispute with many of my fellow technologists is that I think they've switched to a different wager. They still want to build the starship, but with Kirk evicted from the captain's chair at the center of the bridge.

If my focus on the culture of technologists is unusual, it's because we technologists don't usually feel a need to talk about our psychological motivations or cultural ideas. Scientists who study "pure" things like theoretical physics or neuroscience frequently address the public with books and TV documentaries about the sense of wonder they feel and the beauty their work has uncovered.

Technologists have less motivation to talk about these things because we don't have a problem with patronage. We don't need to enchant the taxpayer or the bureaucrat because our work is inherently remunerative.

The result is that the cultural, spiritual, and aesthetic ideas of scientists are a public conversation, while technologists use the rather large slice of public attention we attract primarily for the purpose of promoting our latest offerings.

This situation is more than a little perverse, since the motivating ideas in the heads of technologists have a far greater effect on the world than the ideas that scientists talk about when they exceed the boundaries of their expertise. It is interesting that one biologist might be a Christian while another is an atheist, for instance. But it is more than interesting if a technologist can manipulate urges and behaviors; it is a new world order. The actions of the technologist change events directly, not just indirectly, through discourse.

To put it another way, the nontechnical ideas of scientists influence general trends, but the ideas of technologists create facts on the ground.

PART FOUR

Markets, Energy Landscapes, and Narcissism

CHAPTER 10

Markets and Energy Landscapes

The Technology of Ambient Cheating

Siren Servers do what comes naturally due to the very idea of computation. Computation is the demarcation of a little part of the universe, called a computer, which is engineered to be very well understood and controllable, so that it closely approximates a deterministic, non-entropic process. But in order for a computer to run, the surrounding parts of the universe must take on the waste heat, the randomness. You can create a local shield against entropy, but your neighbors will always pay for it.*

There is a fundamental problem with transposing that plan to economics: A marketplace is a system of competing players, each of whom would ideally be working from a *different*, but *not* an a priori better or worse, information position. In a pre-Internet market, it would sometimes be the case that small local players could conjure an informational advantage over big players.†

While it technically need not be so, the Internet is being used to force local players to lose what used to be local information-access

---

*A rare experimental machine called a "reversible" computer never forgets, so that any computation can be run backward as well as forward. Such devices run cool! This is an example of how thermodynamics and computation interact. Reversible computers don't radiate as much heat; forgetting radiates randomness, which is the same thing as heating up the neighborhood.

†This book can only present one point of view in a field with many interesting points of view. For foundational ideas about differing access to information in a marketplace, I direct readers to the work of the 2001 winners of Nobel Prize in Economics, who each addressed this topic in a different way: http://www.nobel prize.org/nobel_prizes/economics/laureates/2001/press.html.

advantages. The reduced portfolio of advantages of locality saps wealth from everyone who isn't attached to a top server. This problem is related to historic problems that motivated antitrust regulation but it is also distinct.

There doesn't have to be direct manipulation, but instead an automated, sterile "unintentional manipulation" that seems external to human agency and therefore is above the law. Owning a top server on a network is like collecting rent from the network, but that doesn't mean one gets there through "rent seeking."

Traditionally, market positions are set to compete in a pseudo-Darwinian way. Society benefits precisely from the fact that more possibilities will be tested and explored than could ever have been considered from the perspective of a single player, even one with a dominant information perspective.

The rise of top servers as businesses amounts to an ironic intellectual turnaround that gets a pass when it shouldn't. On the one hand, it is fashionable to overly praise automatic, evolutionary processes in the computing cloud and to underplay the capabilities of the individual, rational mind. On the other hand, it is even more fashionable to praise the success of businesses based on dominant servers, even though the very success of these businesses is based precisely in reducing the degree of evolutionary competition in a market. Individuals are to be underappreciated unless they are connected to the biggest computers on the 'net, in which case they are to be overappreciated.

Imaginary Landscapes in the Clouds

You can think of a marketplace as a form of what's called an optimization problem. This is the kind of problem where you figure what set of conditions leads to a most desired outcome. For instance, suppose you would like to take a shower with the water at a certain temperature and with the water pressure being just right.

Suppose you have a shower with only hot and cold knobs. Then you can't set the qualities you want directly. Instead you fiddle with the hot and cold knobs to find the settings that create the shower you want.

There are two inputs, hot and cold. A market can be thought of as a similar system, but with many inputs. The price of each product can be thought of like a knob, for instance. This leads to the idea of a very "high-dimensional" problem, like a shower with many millions of knobs.

Dimensions are a way of thinking about the conditions you are able to set. The hot and cold knobs can be thought of like the X and Y directions on graph paper. Now set a piece of imaginary graph paper down on an imaginary desk in your mind. Imagine that each point on the graph paper sprouts a pole that sticks up—and the height of the pole corresponds to the desirability of the actual temperature and pressure that come out of the shower for particular settings of hot and cold. A forest of these poles will form a sculpture above the graph paper. What will its shape be?

Anyone who has used showers with separate hot and cold knobs knows that finding the right temperature is a little tricky. Sometimes you can move one of the knobs a lot and it doesn't seem to have an effect. Sometimes the tiniest adjustment has a big effect.

If the knobs always produced consistent effects, then the sculpture would be nice and smooth, but actually, for most showers, the shape will include sudden cliffs. It will be complicated. A picture of the range of outcomes is sometimes called an "energy landscape" because of the cliffs and peaks.

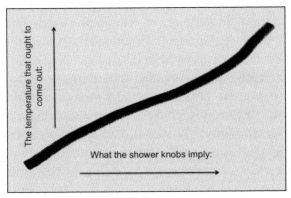

What you might naïvely expect from shower knob positions.

What you actually get.

The overwhelming practical issue is that when you have millions of "shower knobs," you can't readily calculate the ideal positions for them all. A landscape can sometimes be too complicated to evaluate comprehensively.* You can only make progress by starting at one point on the landscape and then tweaking inputs incrementally to see if the goal you seek seems to be furthered. You crawl on the landscape instead of leaping. In other words, your best bet is to move shower knobs a little bit at a time to see if you like the result better. You can't really explore every combination of shower knob positions in advance because that would take much too long.

This is also how evolution works. Evolution is dealing with many billions of "knobs" in genomes. If some new genetic variation reproduces a little more, it gets emphasized. The process is incremental, because there isn't an alternative when the landscape gets extremely big and complicated.

Usually a landscape is imagined so that the solution sought would be the highest point on it. The eternal frustration is that incremental exploration might lead up to a nice high peak, but an even higher peak might exist across a valley. Evolution takes place in millions of species at once, so there are millions of explorations of the peaks and valleys. This is one reason why biodiversity is so

---

*If you had an arbitrary amount of time and computer memory to do calculations, things would be different, but even with the power of today's cloud computers, we are unable to perform many calculations that we might like to.

important. Biodiversity helps evolution be a broader explorer of the gigantic hidden landscape of the potential of life.

Markets as Landscapes

The idea of a marketplace is similar to evolution, though in the relatively diminutive domain of human affairs. A multitude of businesses coexist in a market, each like a species, or a mountaineer on an imaginary landscape, each trying different routes. Increasing the number and eccentricities of mountaineers also increases the chances of finding higher peaks that would otherwise remain undiscovered.

The reason a diverse collection of competitive players in a market can achieve more than a single global player, like a central planning committee, is that they not only have different information to work with, but also different natures. This is why a genuine diversity of players explores a wider range of options than any one global player can, even if that one player has raided all the others of their private information.

Cloud software runs on massive assemblies of parallel computers, so it can perform many incremental explorations of a simulated landscape at one time. Even so, there is no guarantee of finding the highest point, even in a simulated landscape. The variations that make different players in a market importantly different aren't fully expressible within a single Siren Server.

A crowd of mountaineers who are all using the same guidebook will tend to swarm together and discover less overall. An occasional mountaineer ought to veer off on some strange path.

If you believe that artificial intelligence is already as creative as real human minds imbedded in real human lives, then you'll also believe that AI algorithms can be relied on to be the most creative mountaineers, and to find the highest peaks. However, that is not so. There is no way an Amazon pricing bot will have creative ideas about how to price an item. Instead it will just enact a deadly dull price war. All bots do is use the illusion of AI to reinforce positions of network power, by taking gross automated actions like setting prices to zero. Siren Servers reduce the diversity of explorations, no matter how big a calculation they run, thus increasing the chances that better peaks in the landscape will remain undiscovered.

Experimentalism and Popular Perception

In classical economics, a lot of attention is paid to how markets seek "equilibrium," which is another form of peak on a mathematical landscape. In the most recent forms of networked economics, it's clearer than ever that there's no way to know if a particular equilibrium is particularly distinguished or desirable relative to others that might be found. There could be a great many undiscovered, but preferable equilibriums.*

The existence of multiple equilibriums is part of what's so galling about the way networks have taken over money. Let's suppose there's a Siren Server making a lot of money. Maybe it's playing little games with microfluctuations in a massive number of signals. Or maybe it's playing a highly leveraged, bundled, remote hedging game, or a high-frequency game. Assume the scheme is working well, and the owners are doing so well that they are sure they've unlocked the key to the universe.

There are two common schools of thought about this sort of thing, and they are both wrong. One holds that if the money is being accumulated by these schemes, it is being taken from innocent ordinary people and impoverishing them. The other wrong school holds that optimization of a financial scheme that creates wealth for anyone anywhere also inevitably helps the whole economy, through trickle-down and the expansion of entrepreneurial avenues. These ideas, the "liberal" and "conservative" takes on wealth concentration over a network, are both based on the fallacious assumption that there's only one way these schemes could be made to work.

In fact, all these sorts of schemes might work just as well find-

---

*As the financial crises of the early 21st century unfolded, there was a fashion to invite mathematicians, computer scientists, and physicists to meetings with economists to see if any new ideas might come out. The physicist Lee Smolin published an interesting paper about multiple equilibriums as a result of some of these meetings: http://arxiv.org/abs/0902.4274.

ing *different* equilibriums. The either/or logic that pervades debates about economics should never be taken as a complete presentation of what is possible. For instance, it is entirely possible that a similar scheme to whatever cloud fund we might imagine could *also* increase employment *without* making less money. Cutting-edge entrepreneurs who have enjoyed the benefits of Siren Servers suddenly turn into backward, zero-sum thinkers when social issues are raised. If an economy can be made to employ people at all, it can probably be made to employ people without killing somebody's precious derivatives fund.

In fact, conservatives have gone to endless lengths for decades to make this very point when it suits them. Since the Reagan era, a highlight of the conservative playbook has been to claim that lowering taxes raises tax revenues. Their claim is that lower taxes stimulate business growth independently of any other variables. That is precisely a claim that there can be more than one equilibrium.

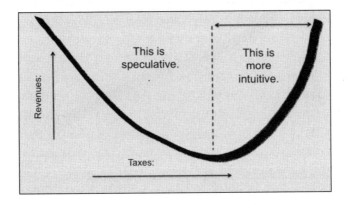

This is the famous Laffer curve, which was promoted by one late 20th century president, Ronald Reagan, and ridiculed by another, George H. W. Bush, as "voodoo economics."

It's counterintuitive, no? On the face of it, lowering taxes should lower the amount of money brought in by taxes. A remarkable, decades-long, and maniacal public relations campaign has brought about a general atmosphere in which the idea is respectable.

While there are huge problems with the way the idea is understood and the way it has influenced policy, the ascendance of a nonlinear, systemic sensibility into popular folklore bodes well. If the public can "get" the Laffer curve, then the public can probably also gain a more honest and balanced sensibility of the nonlinear nature of the big challenges we face.

A serious attempt to find a Laffer peak, a long-term lower tax rate with higher revenues,* would have to be as experimental and long term as the quest to improve weather predictions. Maybe something about education levels, retirement rules, or even the weather would make all the difference. It would be as ridiculous to say a Lafferesque solution is impossible as it would be to say it is automatic or easy to find.

The Laffer curve was supplanted in early 21st century conservative economic rhetoric by a different curve, which is really just a straight line:

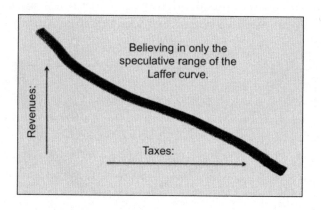

Both curves are hopelessly oversimplified. Recall your finicky shower knobs. If even your shower behaves in a complex way, surely the economy is also complex. Understanding it is more like the process of predicting the weather or improving medicine than it is like these smooth lines. Economics is a real-world big data problem, which means it's hard. It's not a phony big data problem of the kind being used to build instant business empires. That confusion is one of the great confusions of our historical moment.

---

*There have been claims that the effect has already occurred briefly in special circumstances.

The original Laffer curve had the merit of showing two peaks on either side of its valley. That betrayed an acknowledgment that there can be multiple equilibriums. The latest replacement, the absolute faith in austerity, doesn't even acknowledge that. To accept it is to be completely hypnotized by the illusions of easy complexity.

It is senseless to speak in the abstract about whether the Laffer curve is true or false. It is a hypothesis about peaks and valleys on a landscape of real-world possibilities, and these might or might not exist. However, the possibility of existence does not mean that any such landmarks have been found.

Systems with a lot of peaks must also have a lot of valleys between the peaks. When you hypothesize better solutions to today's way of dealing with complex problems, you are automatically also hypothesizing a lot of new ways to fail. So yes, there might well be ways to lower taxes that cause tax revenues to rise, or the economy to grow, but they will be tweaky and nontrivial to find.

To find that kind of sweet spot on the landscape requires a methodical search, which implies a certain kind of governmental actor, which is not to the liking of many of the people who most want taxes lowered. A government has to act like a scientist. Policy must be tweaked experimentally in order to "crawl on the landscape." That means a lot of analysis and testing, and no preconception of how long it will take to get to a solution—or expectation of a perfect solution. Anyone offering automatic detailed foreknowledge of a genuinely complex system is not on the level. Cloud calculations are never guaranteed or automatic. It's hard magic.

Keynes Considered as a Big Data Pioneer

The same argument that applies to taxation can just as well apply to employment. Keynes was offended by the sort of situation that can come up: People want to work, but there are no jobs. Builders want to build homes, but the customers are broke. Companies hold on to cash. Banks don't lend. Homelessness rises as construction workers can't find jobs. It would seem that all the necessary buyers, sellers, and financiers are waiting in the wings, and yet they fail to interact to cause a market to rise. This is the sort of stuck state that Keynes suggested should be prodded with stimulus.

Depressions and recessions can be understood as low hills on the energy landscape of an economy. If you have made it to the top of a low hill and you crawl around incrementally, you will always lose altitude. You seem to have already found the best state you will ever find. That is what a stuck state feels like. Holding on to money is better than lending it when the borrower is unemployed.

However, there might be a much higher hill to be climbed, just over a valley. An employed borrower could get the loan to buy the house from the developer who would employ the borrower. Keynesian stimulus is supposed to function as a kick that imparts enough momentum to bound across the valley up to a higher peak.

Keynes was an unapologetic financial elitist and had no interest in a quest for income equality or a planned economy. He simply sought a mechanism to get stuck markets unstuck. No one has proposed an alternative to his idea of a stimulus. The enduring nuisance is that someone has to guess about exactly how and when to aim a stimulus kick; this is just another way of saying you can't have science without scientists.

Keynesian economics is an authentic form of big data science, which means it is hard and not automatic or instant. (It encompasses such ideas as the Laffer curve.)

The left is just as capable of falling into the fallacy of expecting uncomplicated results from a given economic strategy. There is no automatic correlation between social spending and social improvement, or between fiscal stimulus and fiscal improvement. Every stab at zooming from one hill through a valley to a higher hill on an energy landscape is an experiment without guarantees.

An experimentalist's attitude is the only way forward. Technologies of complexity must be approached in a measured way, with patience and fortitude.

However, the possibility that there might be higher peaks waiting to be discovered is also the prelude to hope, and the way out of our current knot of austerity and acquiescence to private spy empires.

CHAPTER 11

Narcissism

The Insanity of the Local/Global Flip

The most basic reason to doubt or fear Siren Servers is not that they're unfair. Life is unfair, as my conservative friends never tire of pointing out. No, the problem is that Siren Servers eventually become absurd, because of the "Local/Global Flip."

A Siren Server can become so successful—sometimes in the blink of an eye—that it optimizes its environment—changes it—instead of changing in order to adapt to the environment. A successful Siren Server no longer acts only as a player within a larger system. Instead it becomes a central planner. This makes it stupid, like a central planner in a communist regime.

The problem is not the fault of Google or derivatives funds or any of the other schemes. Instead it's a dangerous temptation dangled by Moore's Law—a temptation we must learn to resist.

Cheap networking facilitates exaggerated and rapid network effects. These engender failures of the classical economic models, which had been based on competitions between multitudes of players with distinct and limited information positions.

For instance, networked finance kept on pretending it could eject risk out into the economy at large, like a computer radiating waste heat with a fan, but it became as big as the system. The computer melted.

Similarly: Health insurance companies in America, by using cloud computer analysis to mostly insure people who didn't need insurance, similarly ejected risk into the general system. But there wasn't some giant vastness to absorb the waste. Instead, the economies in which finance and insurance could exist in the first place were weakened.

Alas, all Siren Servers as currently construed are likely to eventually falter in similar ways.

Google might eventually become an ouroboros, a snake eating its own tail, unless something changes. This would happen when so many goods and services become software-centric, and so much information is "free," that there is nothing left to advertise on Google that attracts actual money.

Today a guitar manufacturer might advertise through Google. But when guitars are someday spun out of 3D printers, there will be no one to buy an ad if guitar design files are "free." Yet Google's lifeblood is information put online for free. That is what Google's servers organize. Thus Google's current business model is a trap in the long term.

The Local/Global Flip also reduces the number of available business plans. Silicon Valley, which once seemed a portal to unlimited potential, now induces claustrophobia as so many distinct companies with different competencies and cultures must compete for the same global pool of so-called advertisers. It is pathetic that Google and Facebook, two companies offering very different services, already have to compete over approximately the same customers.

Siren Servers Think the World Is All About Them

To the owner of a Siren Server, it can seem as though that server has a godlike overview of events not only on the network, but also in the world at large. This is the fantasy of being able to accomplish global optimization. It is an illusion.

Facebook's mission statement commits the company "to make the world more open and connected." Google's official mission is to "organize the world's information." No high-frequency trading server has issued a public mission statement that I know of, but when I speak to the proprietors, they claim they are optimizing what is spent where in "the world." The conceit of optimizing the world is self-serving and self-deceptive. The optimizations approximated in the real world as a result of Siren Servers are optimal only from the points of view of those servers.

For someone who has scaled a peak, that peak becomes the known world. It becomes hard to remember that there might be other peaks. This helps to explain the prevalence of vain selective blindness in the assessment of peaks already scaled by Siren Servers. A derivatives fund manager will suffer the illusion that the fund has brought maximum optimization and risk management to the world. A social network owner will believe that his business is one and the same with an ideal society.

It's easy to say what a shower is optimized for. You can state what temperature and pressure you would like to achieve. What is a market supposed to optimize for? In some abstract sense, a market ought to optimize for efficiency, but market efficiency is a subjective idea.

When it comes to Siren Servers, efficiency is a synonym for how well a server is influencing the human world to align with its own model of the world. This is just the big data way of stating the fundamental ambiguity of artificial intelligence. We can't tell how much of the success of an AI algorithm is due to people changing themselves to make it seem successful. People have repeatedly proven adaptable enough to lower standards in order to make software seem smart.

If we are to adhere to the most bloodless abstractions, such as efficiency only as measured from a Siren Server's point of view, then a more "efficient" economy would shrink compared to a less efficient economy. If robots are someday perceived to efficiently run the world, then little money will change hands and little investment will be made thereafter.

This economic dead end would be a stuck state on one peak on an energy landscape, a lowly little pathetic hill. If we succumb to the illusion that there can be only one peak, or a single equilibrium, then we might believe that any deviation from the top of this foothill would be a rejection of efficiency and rationality. But that would be a display of the same kind of mathematical illiteracy that has already poisoned our politics.

Whatever it is we want the mechanism of a marketplace to achieve for us, we will not find the highest peaks if we organize markets to radiate risk and become deterministic accumulators of power around a small number of dominant computing nodes. Too little is learned through that process.

Limits Are for Muggles

THE ENDLESS CONVERSATION ABOUT THE HEART CARTEL

Thirty years ago I had the good fortune to encounter Marvin Minsky, MIT professor and one of the founders of the artificial-intelligence approach to computer science. Marvin was astonishingly gracious and generous to me, yet another young weirdo to be taken under wing. Around his table I heard early voicings of the tropes that would dominate Silicon Valley and then the world decades later.

In the early 1980s, Cambridge, Massachusetts, was still a rotting place, the way most of urban America was rotting from the 1970s. Seemingly bombed-out buildings and wretched street life pressurized the gaps between buildings at MIT. Inside those buildings a ferocious new flavor of intellectual life crouched and glowed. The nerd assault on everyone else's reality was just beginning.

One night Marvin was expounding on the economics of artificial hearts over dinner. We dined at his sprawling, deliciously messy house, over in elegant, suburban Brookline. Piles of books, academic journals, and magazines coated everything, including what were probably multiple grand pianos, judging from the shapes of paper mountains. Amazing artifacts of 20th century science poked through as landmarks . . . parts of notorious robots, telescopes, some of the earliest digital musical instruments. The scent of aging paper and machine oil. A maze was all that was actionable in what had probably once been quite a large house. Lovely old wooden walls could sometimes be spied through narrow canyons.

Hopefully I can be forgiven for paraphrasing one of Marvin's provocations, decades later: "Each billionaire with a heart problem should spend a billion dollars on an artificial heart. Research should be concentrated in a giant project, like the moon shot or Los Alamos. Fill a small city with top scientists and engineers to make the first really good artificial hearts for some rich guys. Sure there are some interesting projects already going on . . . but small-scale efforts are taking much too much time. Spare no expense! Get it right! Once there's a single working model, the prices will collapse like they always do. Not long after that, everyone will benefit. What's killing millions of people is that we're so squeamish about letting rich people be rich." Marvin's eyes had an amazing glint when he was mischievous.

A retort, probably from some long-haired lefty student of the era, might have been: "Wouldn't there be an artificial heart cartel? What's to stop heart blackmail? You'd become an indentured servant just to stay alive."

"No, that wouldn't happen, and for the same reason it didn't happen with computers. There's more money to be made selling many millions of cheap things than a few expensive things."

"But money is just a means to the end of power. Controlling the flow of artificial hearts would be a more direct means to the same end."

"Same could have been said, and indeed was said about computers. Once there's one artificial heart there will be many, so don't worry about cartels. Someone will make a cheap one, just like someone made a personal computer."

"But if the government hadn't sponsored the start of computer science, computers might have been much more tightly controlled by the first companies."

"Look, even if there was a cartel, it wouldn't last forever. The bottom line is that the sooner the technology for a reliable artificial heart is created, the sooner people will benefit from it, especially ordinary people. The delay from your social squeamishness is going to waste much more time than it would take for a heart cartel to dissolve. Why do you want those millions of people to die so you can have your perfect society. Is it worth it?"

On and on the conversations would go. Finally talked out, we didn't go to sleep, but coded until dawn.

THE DEADLY RISK OF NOT BEING A SHAPESHIFTER

We don't really know what technology can achieve. Glinting at us from the horizon is a fantastic vista of a heavenly future where anything might be achieved. We can't tell how much is mirage. Just considering that some techie scenario is impossible might prevent us from discovering how to do it. We must not acknowledge limits. Limits kill.

The feeling of being a techie on the verge of escaping limits is ecstatic, manic, and irresistible. Not only did I feel it intensely, but I also learned to convey it to others. I wove visions of what Virtual Reality would be like in my talks in the 1980s, and into my patter as we gave demos in the lab. I could make people vibrate with excitement.

In Virtual Reality you could craft *any* world, *any* scenario. This idea of "any" is treacherous and deceptive, but I didn't yet know that. I still love creativity and expression, and especially wild free expression, but I know that meaning comes from struggle with constraints. Meaning is when creativity has high stakes. Ultralight, friction-free moments in life are wonderful, but not as figure, only as ground.

The very idea of the computer is that it's the "general" machine, in that "any" program can be run. That turns out not to be so in practice, even though we often can't help ourselves and still pretend it is. As we run our lives through computers more and more, we must reconcile ourselves to the illusions and truths of the digital "any."

THE FIRST MUSICAL "ANY"

My first encounter with the allure of overcoming finitude came long before I got involved with computers. Instead I succumbed to an obsession I developed in my early teens with the work of a composer named Conlon Nancarrow. This was not a likely event. I grew up in a tiny town in an obscure part of the country, southern New Mexico, and this was long before the Internet's debut. It was hard to even be exposed to the pop culture of the day, much less anything obscure. And yet, somehow I came across a reel-to-reel tape of the man's music and became absolutely mesmerized.

I was so excited I could barely talk about anything else for a while, and would happily regale strangers with my enthusiasm until they charted escapes. Nancarrow started out as a trumpeter and student composer from Depression-era Oklahoma. He volunteered to fight against the fascist Franco regime in Spain, joining the Abraham Lincoln Brigade, which was composed of lefty Americans before America entered World War II. Nancarrow was later denied reentry to the United States, and was bizarrely deemed "prematurely anti-Fascist."

He settled in Mexico City instead, and allowed a passion for the mastery of time and rhythm, together with his sympathy for math and machinery, to lead him into one of the weirdest and most intense musical journeys in history. Why must rhythms be organized from regular beats? Why not use irrational numbers* in time signatures, or have sheets of rhythm speed up and slow down, coming in and out of synch, the way waves do in nature?

What would it mean to compose in "any" rhythm? Artists had never quite achieved an "any." There was always some color you couldn't quite mix out of pigments, or some sound the synthesizers of the day couldn't yet synthesize. (They couldn't even create convincing artificial speech yet.) Plenty of people who were into the era's music synthesizers (this was the 1970s) spoke of them as if they could make "any" sound, but deep down we all knew that was not true.

Conlon would be one of the first artists to conquer an "any." He did it in the domain of rhythm and he used a crazy, brilliant tool to get there, the player piano. Conlon would sit at his desk, hand-punching player piano rolls, working for months to make each minute of music.

It still amazes me that Conlon's music isn't better known. It has an incredible intensity, tougher and more of a knockout than just about anything else you can hear. The music has incredible textures, harmonies, and of course, rhythms. And fantasy, for it corresponds to a sensual and luscious but unfamiliar world that can't be described or approached any other way. Most of the pieces, which he simply called "studies," are identified only by numbers, as in "Study 27," or "Study 36." (Those are both good ones.)

And yet it's difficult to share the impact of Conlon's music today. Sure, you can find sound files online. Information is not experience, however. The way to really hear the stuff was in Conlon's bunker-like studio, where the pianos thundered and you felt it in your body. The

---

*Musical rhythms are generally specified as fractions, like 4/4 or 3/4, which is also known as waltz time. An irrational number can't be expressed as a fraction. But could it be rhythm? Would music in such a rhythm mean anything to people? Conlon provided the answers: yes and yes.

digital recordings that are around somehow miss the power of the music. They were done in too clinical a way, perhaps, or the tempo was wrong, or something.*

You mustn't demand that someone be able to state exactly how information underrepresents reality. The burden can't be on people to justify themselves against the world of information. I don't know what was different. Certainly being there with Conlon was different from hearing a recording. The edge of difference is provocative in this case since a player piano is mechanical and perhaps a recording ought to provide a closer equivalent than a recording can provide of a concert.

I would hitchhike down over the border to Mexico City to visit Conlon. Mexico was insane in neon shades, but sweet in those days long before the drug wars. On arrival, I would be so excited that I could barely speak. It amazes me still that Conlon and his wife, Yoko, were tolerant of this weird, noncommunicative, worshipful kid.

Conlon didn't share my sense of moment. He was unassuming, even taciturn. An elegant man from an era when it was expected for men to have well-developed egos, he conveyed a regal stature quietly, declining to construct a romantic life story. He worked, he enjoyed his family, music, and life, and that was it. This came as a revelation to me. It hadn't occurred to me that he'd be anything other than messianic. (Though on another level, I still think to myself, "Come on! He was playing a game of understatement. He knew perfectly well what he was doing.")

To me, at any rate, Conlon's music was the momentous first appearance of a musical "any." Here was an example of someone who had gained precise, unlimited control of a domain and indeed he did create entirely new meaning and sensation by leaping out of the snags the rest of us navigate, onto a new plateau of generality. Who had done that before? Alan Turing, certainly. The great analytic mathematicians. Who else? Who had done it aesthetically?

It seemed to me that I must seek out any and all opportunities to find other such plateaus. What Conlon did for rhythm might be done

---

*I suggest you seek out the old Columbia or 1750 Arch vinyl records, which are much better than the digital recordings made later by Wergo.

for sensory impressions, for the human body, for the whole of human experience. That would be Virtual Reality.

CLIMB ANY "ANY"

Chasing after limitlessness had already become a central idea in Silicon Valley when I moved there not too many years later, in my early adulthood. Just as I talked up Virtual Reality as encompassing "any" external reality, or sensory motor experience, possible, a fellow named Eric Drexler was talking up nanotechnology as someday doing the same for physical reality. Another friend named Stephen LaBerge was experimenting with lucid dreaming at Stanford and offering "any" possible subjective experience to those who could learn the technique. Silicon Valley was a temple of yearning for "anyness" in those days, and remains so.

"Anyness" still commonly serves as the guiding principle of freedom, achievement, and attainment that drives Internet design. "Any" music, text, video, available anywhere, anytime.

Tablets and smartphones have fluid uses, turning into "any" device that can be accommodated by the fixed physical attributes. A tablet might be a book, a guitar tuner, sketchpad, and so on. Gradually, even the physical properties of gadgets will become more mutable. 3D printing, as explained earlier, will fabricate any shape, and perhaps eventually "any" consumer electronics product.

Even those designs might take on morphing qualities. I have worked on robots inspired by the "morphing" varieties of octopi that can change shape in order to allow your hands to feel arbitrary surfaces in a virtual world. Using such a robot feedback device, you would be able to feel virtual knobs instead of just see them, for instance.

There is any number of other examples. Synthetic biology might someday produce "any" microorganism, and then maybe someday any macro one. The true star toward which we navigate is freedom from particularity.

PART FIVE

The Contest to Be Most Meta

CHAPTER 12

Story Lost

Not All Is Chaos

A sanctioned malaise has been in effect for some decades now; it is accepted in some circles that future history will not be coherent. From here on out the human story will no longer unfold in a sensible way. We are said to be entering into a fate that will resist interpretation. Narrative arcs will no longer apply.

Lana Wachowski, cowriter and director of the Matrix movies, described a later project, *Cloud Atlas*, as residing between "the future idea that everything is fragmented and the past idea that there is a beginning, middle, and end."[1] As the turn of the millennium approached, such declarations were commonplace (as in the monologue of the "world's oldest Bolshevik" in Tony Kushner's play *Perestroika*, or aspects of Francis Fukuyama's book *The End of History*—both from 1992), but it's odd that we can still hear them today even from the most tech-oriented writers and thinkers.

You won't find any such point of view within tech circles, however. There, one is immersed in a clear-enough dominant narrative. Everything is becoming more and more software-mediated, physicality is becoming more mutable by technology, and reality is being optimized. I have criticized aspects of our narrative, but no one can say it doesn't have direction. The problem with it is that humans aren't the heroes. People might merge with machines and become immortal, but that's a sideshow. The dominant story is machine-centric. It's technological determinism.

My view is that people are still the actors. Technology is not really autonomous. People act in the network age either by struggling to get close to top Siren Servers in order to enjoy power and wealth, or by doing something other than that and falling into relative poverty and irrelevance. Ours is as well ordered an age as any other.

Since I've been thinking about Siren Servers, I've found that they provide a simple story line that works awfully well as a principle for making sense of our times. I might be overapplying the idea. As the saying goes, when you have a hammer, everything looks like a nail. Nonetheless, we are entering into an age of networked information, and power struggles over digital networks will naturally be the typical stories of that age.

The reason the information age seems "fragmented" is that there are episodes in the unfolding of network power, in the rise of a Siren Server, that are genuinely chaotic and unpredictable. But these pockets of chaos are circumscribed by a simple logic. Overall, story finds its home in network-age struggles just as well as it ever did in "civilization clashes," court intrigues, romantic triangles, or any other narrative pattern from the past.

The Conservation of Free Will

A story must have actors, not automatons. Different people become more or less like automatons in our Sirenic era.

Sirenic entrepreneurs intuitively cast free will—so long as it is their own—as an ever more magical, elite, and "meta" quality of personhood. The entrepreneur hopes to "dent the universe"* or achieve some other heroic, Nietzschean validation. Ordinary people, however, who will be attached to the nodes of the network created by the hero, will become more effectively mechanical.

A Siren Server's data must be at least a little predictive, or to put it more bluntly, the people being modeled must act at least somewhat predictably. Otherwise, the data wouldn't be actionable at all.

One can't say that a system that unfolds predictably, like clock-

*A phrase usually attributed to Steve Jobs.

work, exhibits free will.* To the degree people become predictable by a server, they won't appear to have as much free will as "free range" individuals who aren't tied to the server.

As I have explained earlier, it is impossible to reliably distinguish study from manipulation when you occupy the high perch of a Siren Server. The difference isn't really a difference, within the scope of business epistemology.

Ordinary people are influenced by the particular theory of optimization imbedded in a server in order to use it, and therefore become more predictable by it. Siren Servers conserve the tally of free will perceived in human affairs, since some people appear to have more of it even as others appear to have less.

Sirenic idealists browbeat those who are thought to be attempting to insert free will into human affairs in places where it doesn't belong. This is not a new impulse, as it recalls earlier thinkers like Ayn Rand. Randian free market idealists declare that it is ridiculous to willfully address problems like a stalled economy or poverty. Charity and policy are scorned, but more generally, human will is only respected when it comes from an entrepreneur. Free will is granted only a narrow legitimacy.

What is new in the network age is the extension of this kind of thinking into every sphere of experience. New lines are being drawn between where individual agency should matter and where it shouldn't, so the dichotomy must now be understood in an even broader way than the ancient debate about the role of government.

People trust dating sites like eHarmony to algorithmically select prospects for marriage. But people also attempt to force universal laws on each other about what kinds of marriages can be legal. If this juxtaposition doesn't seem odd, think about this: What if the eHarmony algorithm analyzed a customer and calculated that she was gay even though she had never realized that before? That's a type of judgment that I suspect would not be tolerated by many of

---

*The question of whether reality is deterministic overall must be separated from the design of human society. Because of the limits of measurement, data storage, and other factors, we can't definitively test the nature of determinism in physical systems. The two best-confirmed theories of physics, quantum field theory and general relativity, offer conflicting sensibilities of determinism.

eHarmony's users, even though the judgments they do solicit are no less intimate or consequential.

We're setting up barriers between cases where we choose to give over some judgment to cloud software, as if we were predictable machines, and those where we elevate our judgments to pious, absolute standards.

Making choices of where to place the barrier between ego and algorithm is unavoidable in the age of cloud software. Drawing the line between what we forfeit to calculation and what we reserve for the heroics of free will is the story of our time.

CHAPTER 13

Coercion on Autopilot
Specialized Network Effects

Rewarding and Punishing Network Effects

"Network effects" are feedback cycles that can make a network become ever more influential or valuable.* A classic example is found in the rise of Facebook. It attracted people because of the people already on it, a little like the old joke about someone being famous for being famous.

To understand how Siren Servers work, it's useful to divide network effects into those that are "rewarding" and those that are "punishing." Siren Servers gain dominance through rewarding network effects, but keep dominance through punishing network effects.

Here's a classic example of a rewarding network effect: A cliché in the advertising world is that in the old days you knew you were wasting half of your advertising budget, but you didn't know which half. For instance, you'd spend tens of millions of dollars on TV and print ads, and somehow there would be a benefit, but you never knew exactly how or why. Surely many of the ads were playing when people were going to the bathroom, laying waste to your precious spend.

---

*Network effects were an obsession for those interested in the pre-digital phone system. They have become an even greater obsession in the age of digital networks. Metcalf's Law is a famous claim that a network becomes as valuable as the square of the number of its nodes. That means value climbs with an insane, ever-increasing pitch as a network grows. The economist W. Brian Arthur pioneered the understanding of economic network effects.

An oft-repeated trope goes like this: Because of all of Google's data and placement algorithms, an advertiser can now finally know which half is waste. Google can individually target ads, and document the click-throughs that follow.

The reason this is a rewarding network effect is that success breeds success. Because people use Google, other people benefit from using Google, creating a cycle of growth. The more advertisers use Google, the more Web pages are optimized for Google, for instance. Google is perhaps a confusing example, since it is part of the large phylum of Siren Servers in which the users are product, and the true customers, the so-called advertisers, might not always be apparent. (Varieties of Siren Servers will be listed later on.)

Apple provides a clearer example. People use Apple products in part because there are so many apps in its store. Developers are motivated to create lots of apps because there are a lot of people using the Apple store. That's a classical rewarding network effect.

For Every Carrot a Stick

The most successful Siren Servers also benefit from punishing network effects. These are centered on a fear, risk, or cost that makes "captured" populations think twice if they want to stop engaging with a Siren Server. In Silicon Valley–speak this is also called "stickiness." Players often can't take on the burden of escaping the thrall of a Siren Server once a punishing network effect is in place.

Remember, Google sells ad placements based on auctions. Imagine once again that you're an advertiser. In the old days, if you had been paying for, say, a billboard, you might decide to give that billboard up and instead buy more newspaper ads. Neither you nor anyone else would have had any idea who would place a new ad on the billboard you abandoned. It might be a furniture company or a perfume brand. The risk you took by giving up the billboard was vague and uncertain.

However, if you give up a position on Google's ad placement system, you know for certain that your next-nearest competitor in the auction will inherit your position. This risk and cost of leaving a position is made specifically scary and annoying. You are yielding to your archrival! An in-your-face loss must then be weighed against an inevitably more vague future alternative.

Human cognition is often spooked by a trade-off of this kind.[1] Within businesses it can be even spookier. It's very hard to leap into a crisp risk in pursuit of a fuzzy benefit. As a result, Google's customers are effectively locked in, or maybe we should say "glued in," since we call it sticky.

Another type of punishing lock-in is to get users to put data they value into your server in such a way that access to it will be lost— or at least expensive or labor-intensive to salvage—if they choose to leave. This is a common strategy.

After you've spent money in a particular online store, your value received is entirely dependent on your continued fealty to that single Siren Server. Once you've paid for music, movies, books, or apps on one Siren Server, you typically have to give up your investment if you leave. Then you have to respend it if you want access to similar stuff on a different Siren Server. This is precisely the *opposite* of a middle-class levee.

It's not always necessary that the data be made absolutely unavailable; sometimes data can just be decontextualized enough to become less valuable. Facebook provides a fine example. If a great deal of personal creativity and life experience has been added to the site, it's hard to give all that up. Even if you capture every little thing you had uploaded, you can't save it in the context of interactions with other people. You have to lose a part of yourself to leave Facebook once you become an avid user. If you leave, it will become difficult for some people to contact you at all. Would you ever be willing to take the risk to sever a part of your own life's context in order to disengage from a Siren Server that ogles you?

Denial of Service

Yet another way to create a punishing network effect involves control of routing and bandwidth. To understand this method, I refer you to your wireless bill. A particular Siren Server becomes the only way to connect to the information world. (Companies with proprietary hardware, like Apple, do this as well.) To sever, you must often pay penalties, purchase new equipment, and therefore potentially lose investments tied to the old equipment, like apps, only to get into a new long-term contract.

Access-granting services need not be Siren Servers, since they could just be boring and bill for granting access, but they have caught the deliriously alluring scent of the game by now and are trying to become big data players as well. This has led to power struggles, such as whether a smartphone company or the wireless carrier is in charge of various services and revenue opportunities, and whether the principle of "net neutrality" will endure.

There is often a cascade of hardware lock-ins that cumulatively corner a particular person. You might be locked into one service that connects your home to the Internet with a cable, another that connects your phone or tablet to the wireless signal, and yet another that provides the devices you use and key services like an app store for it.

This demonstrates an interesting difference between Siren Servers and traditional monopolies. There is no reason that there can't be a lot of Siren Servers. They form ecologies instead of company towns. The reason to be concerned about them is how they distort and shrink the overall economy by demonetizing more and more value. But they don't necessarily turn into the only game in town in the way that an old-time railroad monopoly might have.

Arm's-Length Blackmail

There are yet other punishing network effects that resemble a soft kind of blackmail. Some local retail review sites have periodically been accused of skewing or ruining the online visibility of local businesses that cease to buy "optional" premium placement services.[2] Social networking sites will sometimes extract fees to make someone more "visible" on the site.[3] This is particularly true for hookup services akin to the "where the babes are" app that was pitched by the Berkeley graduate students.[4]

Readers of my previous book will recall an extended examination of how ideas and patterns of use and behavior get "locked into" networked software. This type of software lock-in is often employed to create or buttress a punishing network effect. If a small business designs its own processes and code around the cloud services from only one of the major cloud companies, then it can easily get locked into that company.

Some sites have gotten fairly large with mostly rewarding network effects and barely any punishing ones. eBay is mostly based on rewarding effects, for instance. No one's really punished for buying or selling elsewhere.* (This is in contrast to Amazon, which will sometimes lower prices on an item to undercut you if you sell the same item at a lower price elsewhere.)

When you are subject to someone else's punishing network effect, every decision becomes strategic. If you plan to break out of the gravitational field of a Siren Server, you often have to swallow hard and go all the way. The burden of that big leap creates a new kind of social immobility.

Who's the Customer and Who Are All Those Other People?

To understand a particular Siren Server, it is critical to distinguish between distinct populations connected to the venture in different ways. Siren Servers often pit these populations against each other.

Once a Siren Server becomes dominant in its niche, after the Local/Global Flip, it treats those who connect with it as data sources and as subjects for behavior modification. However, there are usually sub-populations subject to different mixes of rewarding and punishing network effects. One sub-population might be shown carrot and stick in equal measure, for example, while another might mostly be offered carrots.

---

*Twitter's lack of a plausible revenue growth plan as I write this is similarly due to offering carrot without a commensurate serving of stick. By the time you read this, that might have changed.

In the cases of Google and Facebook, this difference tracks the distinction between users and customers. Some people, the users, are valued mostly as data and potential for behavior modification, while others, the advertisers, are also sources of money. It is crucial, obviously, to capture money if the Siren Server is to be a business.

This bifurcation can lead to confusion, as when Siren Servers are scrutinized in the terms of old-fashioned antitrust. When a service like Google is evaluated, one of the first observations is that users are free to leave. That is true.* From a typical user's perspective, Google is mostly carrot. But the other population—the true customers, the advertisers—is less free. It is captured because of punishing network effects.

In the case of Wal-Mart, the captured population was the supply chain. Google's true customers are the advertisers, who are captured. Wal-Mart's customers weren't the critical population for it to capture, however. Retail customers gradually became a little captured in some locations where retail choice was eventually reduced, but for the most part they could shop elsewhere if they were so inclined, but it was the optimization of the global supply chain through the use of punishing network effects that really empowered and enriched Wal-Mart.

*True for search, that is. Not so true if a user has put personal data in Google's tools.

CHAPTER 14

Obscuring the Human Element

Noticing the New Order

Every tale of adventure lately seems to include a scene in which characters are attempting to crack the security of someone else's computer. That's the popular image of how power games are played out in the digital age, but such "cracking" is only a tactic, not a strategy. The big game is the race to create ascendant Siren Servers, or, much more often, to get close to those that are taking off and ascending in ways that no one predicted.

Networked contests for wealth and power tend to follow a pattern. Each particular scheme launched over a network, each purported golden goblet, tends to follow a well-worn course. Networked information, when it is about business instead of science (or, if you like, about human behavior instead of nature), follows a characteristic life cycle.*

Since I prefer to see the faces instead of the goblet, I find that following the ways in which servers obscure the real people who are the sources of value is also a good way of noticing how the struggle for power proceeds.

---

*Oh how I hate using the term *life cycle* for something that isn't alive. We are fascinated by ritualistic declarations that we have created new life in our artifices. In the case of big human data, it's a mistake to perceive even an object, much less a living thing. This is the way these matters are talked about in my community, however, so I occasionally use the terminology despite my objection.

Who Orders the Data?

Some Siren Servers relish a world in which data starts out as a mess, decontextualized and mysterious, until it is brought to order by the server's analytics. Google is probably the best-known example. A Siren Server in this position will do all it can to promote every manner of "open" activity. Data made available for free with inadequate documentation on the open Internet is the ideal raw material for such a venture.

Later on I'll describe how a remarkably simple idea in network architecture, which was the motivation for the very first digital media designs, was lost, and how that loss created much of the chaos that search engines attempt to undo today.

Other Siren Servers enjoy data that is ordered either at the time of entry or later on, but in either case for free. Facebook is a great example. Google must find patterns in chaos, while Facebook expects you to enter fairly contextualized information in the first place, essentially filling in the blanks of provided forms. However, Facebook also derives additional order through analysis, results that are hidden away in a dungeon.

A "content" site in which almost all contributions are unpaid, like the *Huffington Post,* shares this quality with Facebook. Online retailers like Amazon and eBay are also examples, since they don't have to pay for reviews or the design of product presentations. Those who sell through these schemes are mostly responsible for creating and tending their own presentations, unlike in traditional retail, where the retailer has to figure out how to present each product.

This is a key sign of a Siren Server. The lowly non-Sirens are as responsible as possible, while the Siren Server presides from an arm's length.*

---

*Another example is Wikipedia. I am not condemning it, and in my previous book have discussed what I see as its strengths and weaknesses. As I argued earlier, however, it does reduce markets for certain kinds of scholars in the long term in order to demonetize scholarship in the short term, so it qualifies as a Siren Server. It creates the kinds of false efficiencies that thwart levees.

In some cases, ordinary people are persuaded to put extraordinary work into correcting and sorting the data in an Siren Server, at their own risk and expense. A fine and maddening example is credit rating agencies, which provide a labor-intensive path for people to correct mistakes in their own data.

The Human Shell Game

Computation done within a Siren Server occasionally still requires some human involvement from insiders to the scheme.* Today, for instance, Amazon has skilled, real people answer the phone to provide customer service.

However Amazon is also exploring how to get non-elite service jobs out of the way of the Siren Servers of the future. The company offers a Web-based tool called Mechanical Turk. The name is a reference to a deceptive 18th century automaton that seemed to be a robotic Turk that could play chess, while in fact a real person was hidden inside.

The Amazon version is a way to easily outsource—to real humans—those cloud-based tasks that algorithms still can't do, but in a framework that allows you to think of the people as software

---

Yet another interesting example is Craigslist. This is a fascinating, idealistic Siren Server that is mildly for-profit. It only charges for certain types of ads, such as from prospective employers, while offering most services for free. Craig Newmark could probably have built his business into a giant along the lines of eBay or Amazon. Instead, he created a service that has greatly increased convenience for ordinary people, while causing a crisis in local journalism that once relied on paid classified ads. To me, Craigslist has a tragic quality, since it is as modest and ethical as it can be, eschewing available spying opportunities, and yet it still functions as a Siren Server despite that.

*There's usually a ritual in place to make sure everything possible is done to avoid actual human involvement for as long as possible, even if it is inevitable. The cliché we've all lived through is that you call about, say, a problem in how an insurance or credit rating Siren Server has screwed up a key decision about your life. Perhaps you were denied coverage for needed medical treatment. After an hours-long battle with the maze of a robo call center, you finally talk to a real person, probably in India or the Philippines. This might be the first time real human eyes associated with the Siren Server have perceived your data.

components. The interface doesn't hide the existence of the people, but it still does try to create a sense of magic, as if you can just pluck results out of the cloud at an incredibly low cost.

The service is much loved and celebrated, and competes with other similar constructions. My techie friends sometimes suggest to me in all seriousness that writing books is hard work and I should turn to the Mechanical Turk to lower my workload. Somewhere out there must await literate souls willing to ghostwrite for pennies an hour.

The Mechanical Turk is not really that different from other Siren Servers, but it is so up front about its nature that it stands out. Those who take assignments through it often seem to even enjoy the fun of emulating an intelligent machine for someone else's profit.[1]

The charade has a triply dismal quality.

Of course there is the "race to the bottom" process that lowers wages absolutely as much as possible,[2] making temp jobs in the fast-food industry seem like social climbing on-ramps in comparison. Yet there are people ready to step up and take such roles. More than a few recruits appear to be the live-at-home kids of middle-class Americans, whiling away their time.[3]

Whenever there is a networked race to the bottom, there is a Siren Server that connects people and owns the master database about who they are. If they knew each other, comprehensively, they might organize a union or some other form of levee.

The second dismal quality is that artificial-intelligence algorithms are getting better, so gradually it will become more possible to not even acknowledge the contributions of real people to the degree done now.

Finally, the Mechanical Turk is often applied to the more pathetic tasks associated with Siren Server contests. One journalist found that 40 percent of the tasks on offer are to create spam.[4]

CHAPTER 15

Story Found

The First Act Is Autocatalytic

A newly launched Siren Server is like a tiny baby creature in a hostile ecosystem that must grow fast enough to survive in a world of predators. The most common means to survival is to route enough data fast enough so that by the time predators notice you at all, they won't find it worthwhile to go after your niche.

There are a variety of Siren Servers, ranging from consumer-facing Silicon Valley startups tempting people with "free" bait, to financial servers that skim the cream off the economy in relative obscurity, to providers of infrastructure who realize that they can also play the big data game, to governments and other entities yet to be discussed.

In all cases, there has to be some way for a particular Siren Server to gain enough initial momentum to become the beneficiary of network effects. Therefore, the primary enemy of a fresh server is not competing wannabe servers, but rather "friction."

Friction is what it feels like to be on the bad side of a network effect. Even the slightest expense or risk might slow the initial growth spurt, so every possible effort is made to pretend there are no costs, risks, or even delayed gratifications. This can never really be true. Yet it feels true as you sign up for a social network or an app store for the first time.

Since You Asked

Here's typical advice I'd give to someone who wants to try the Silicon Valley startup game: Obviously you have to get someone else to do something on your server. This can start out as a petty activity. eBay started out as a trading site for people who collected Pez candy dispensers. The key is that it's your server. If you're getting a lot of traffic through someone else's server, then you're not really playing the game. If you get a lot of hits on a Facebook page, or for your pieces on the *Huffington Post,* then you are playing a little game, not the big game.

In some cases you can be the predator. You might start by noticing some other pretender to a throne that isn't growing as fast as it could and overtaking it once it has identified a viable Siren Server niche to be won. This is what Facebook did to Friendster, Myspace, et al.

In other cases you might form an offering out of whole cloth at just the right time and place. This is what Twitter did.

Some part of me still wishes that serious technical innovation were more essential to hatching Siren Servers. Google was initially based on genuine algorithmic innovation. Facebook certainly has had its engineering challenges, mostly related to getting big fast without a reliability crisis, but it's hard to see much computer science innovation in it, at least in its foundation.

Why the Networked World Seems Chaotic

Lately, the depths of pettiness seem unbounded. Why do so many people use Pinterest?* There were many competitors offering similar designs. By now Pinterest enjoys rewarding network effects so there's no mystery. People now use it because others do. But why

---

*It's always tricky to write about these things since I must guess what points of reference will survive long enough to mean anything to this book's readers years hence. Pinterest is a fast rising star among consumer-facing sites. You can copy photos and other data from around the Web onto virtual pin boards and share them.

did Pinterest grow enough to win network effect prizes, instead of any of the many other similar infant creatures in the ecosystem?

There's a well-supported analytic class—statisticians and MBAs employed by venture capitalists, big companies, and private capital firms—that attempts to model the qualities of hopeful startup sites, in order to predict which ones will take off. This is like predicting the weather, a challenging kind of science. Some progress has been made, but there remains an element of chaos and unpredictability. No one can know all the little fluctuations that were in play that gave a site like Pinterest its window of opportunity.

What makes one Siren Server take off while a seemingly identical one flops? This is like asking why some silly Internet memes rise and others fall. There are many factors, mostly uncounted.

It's entirely imaginable that Pinterest would have flopped if circumstance had been just slightly different. A butterfly might have flapped its wings on the other side of the world, as the saying goes. Of course, the proprietors of a site that takes off are always certain it was because they did exactly the right thing.

When Are Siren Servers Monopolies?

As explained in the sections on network effects, when users put effort, money, or important data into a particular service, like a social network, then network effects tend to create a single Sirenic presence, a monopoly for that particular kind of data or pattern of use.

Many Siren Servers of this kind are subject to something like a Pauli exclusion principle, or if you prefer, they tend to discover and uniquely occupy pseudo-monopolistic roles. There can't be both a Friendster and a Facebook. One of them must win.

When a Siren Server is more a mediator than an accumulator of primary data sources, then it can have company. There can be multiple travel sites, as explained earlier, because they don't own the primary reservation-related data that they mediate. There can be multiple Sirenic financial services because none of them own Wall Street.

Similarly, there can be both a Bing and Google, since neither owns the Web. To be more precise, there can be two search engines,* but Google still tends to be monopoly-like in selling advertising based on search, which is a different matter. That is because, as an accumulator of advertiser relationships, Google does enjoy a monopoly-like network effect.

Another example is that Amazon and Barnes & Noble can coexist as booksellers, because they don't own the books, but if they also become major publishers, then one would probably have to kill the other.

Sometimes potential Sirenic monopoly is blocked because of a structural or legal blockade that limits reach. For instance, a language barrier might limit a social network to certain regions of the world, or a mobile carrier might be able to capture users by contract instead of through pure data effects.

Even when there is only one Siren Server to a niche, there can be a lot of niches, however.

Free Rise

What's the threshold for rewarding network effects to kick in? For consumer-facing sites, it is the point at which enough people are using a site to support each other's expectations of dynamism. An additional threshold is that a critical number of people have to stick together long enough so that the site becomes a habit for them. Then the dynamism won't decay.

It's not as if there is no technical requirement at all for a site to catch a wave and become huge. The site generally has to be at least consistently available, though in its early years Twitter wasn't.

Once you reach a critical point, you have a population or two locked in. You might very well grow to global proportions and exert influence like a messiah, tweaking the design of human experience at large.

---

*This observation only applies to traditional personal computers. On mobile phones, Google generally enjoys a structural advantage because of preferred placement.

If you've made it to the point that growth is accelerating, you've entered the honeymoon phase, or free rise (the opposite of free fall). Some entrepreneurs promote like crazy during this phase, while others are just consumed with keeping the thing running. If you want free rise to continue until your Siren Server becomes a monster, you'll have to attend to a few things . . .

If the first phase goes well, you can experience an amazing lift, as you aggregate connections and data at an intense clip. During this period, all the usual rules of life and commerce are suspended. It's free rise, and anything can happen.

During free rise, you can see patterns in data no one else can see, as if you were an oracle. You will suddenly know more about some slice of human life than anyone else. Maybe you'll see something about eating habits, sex, shopping, or driving patterns.

A few of the folks you have aggregated will inevitably get an insane lift from being hitched to you, and they'll create even more excitement. An early investor in your fund will get superrich superfast, or a user of your free service will earn a windfall from sudden exposure. This will happen to only a tiny token number of people, though. It is really you, the proprietor of the Siren Server, who will benefit above all others.

At first, all you'll have is rewarding network effect. That means that people will benefit from using your server because other people are using it. A virtuous cycle causes more and more people to use your offering. That's not enough, however, if you want to build a world-class, persistent Siren Server. In addition, you have to inject some sort of punishing network effect.

Make Others Pay for Entropy

Once both rewarding and punishing network effects are taking hold, another crucial task is to make sure that risk is being radiated out to other people and institutions, and not accruing to your server. Sites like Pinterest invariably demand that users click through an agreement that places all responsibility for copyright violations or anything else squarely on the user.

If people are paying money to use your server, don't accept any of it directly if you can possibly avoid that. You should be a broker between buyers and sellers to the degree that's possible. You can then earn commissions, placement fees, visibility fees, or any number of other fees yet to be conceived, but without taking any responsibility for the actual events that took place.

Make both buyers and sellers click through agreements that make them, not you, take on all liabilities. These click-through agreements are the grandiosely verbose descendants of the Zen koan about a tree falling in a forest that no one hears. No one will read them, so they are very unlikely to be tested in a legal proceeding. No one wants to read them, not even lawyers. Some lawyer at the Electronic Frontier Foundation or some such place might occasionally be able to make it through one of them, but that is rare. Since they are unread, they basically do not exist, except for setting the basic rule everyone understands, which is that the server takes no risks, only the users of the server. The ideal is for click-through agreements to remain unread until your server becomes so huge that it's scary.

This principle applies doubly if you are running a Wall Street fund on your server instead of a Silicon Valley startup. The ideal Siren Server is one for which you make no specific decisions. You should do everything possible to not do anything consequential. Don't play favorites; don't have taste. You are to be the neutral facilitator, the connector, the hub, but never an agent who could be blamed for a decision. Reduce the number of decisions that can be pinned on you to an absolute minimum.

What you *can* do, however, is pattern how other people make decisions. You can get people to have less privacy or organize a business around coupons, but you never get into the middle of any specific event within the pattern template you've created for other people to use.

Bills Are Boring

It isn't free to run a Siren Server. You will need to hire some of those fabled PhDs from MIT or Caltech sooner or later, and pay the storage and connectivity bills. For the Silicon Valley startup variety of Siren Server, this brings up the question of monetization. It isn't polite or cool to think about monetization very early in the game. Have some faith, man! Information always turns to money, somehow, sooner or later.

Money usually doesn't flow much into a Siren Server in its earliest phases, but fortunately they're cheap to run. You can outsource much of the nontechnical heavy lifting that might come along to the peasants who populate Mechanical Turk and similar services. "The entire cost of running this business on the human side is incredibly low," says Keith Rabois, chief operating officer of Square, an up-and-coming Siren Server that hopes to become the router of choice for consumer credit cards.[1]

Coattails

Fleeting success sporadically flares for a lucky few players on the sidelines of Siren Servers, as if by magic. These rags-to-riches tales are 21st century echoes of the famous Horatio Alger tales of the 19th century, in which unlikely underdogs worked hard and found great success—except the hard work part is no longer a given.

No end of ridicule has been directed at Horatio Alger stories ever since they first appeared, because they build false hope. They are deceptive; even when the original story is true, it is vanishingly unlikely that any particular individual will find similar success by pursuing similar strategies. Horatio's algebra offered horrible ratios. Theater can't replace a functional economy. An economy can't grow authentically if it is too much like a casino.

There are actually two types of 21st century Horatio Alger story that spark off of Siren Servers. One type is the occasional "viral" success. This might occur on YouTube, for instance. Every now and then a sympathetic individual will achieve visibility, and perhaps even income. But in the longer term, such people generally must seek to leverage Internet visibility in a gambit to find success in old media, which is being shrunk by the Internet at the same time. For instance, TV talent shows like *The Voice* attract YouTube stars, even though their audience on YouTube might have been larger. At least old media, even in its decline and with all its problems, still offers a career path.

A more disturbing version of deceptive viral success is the occasional charity effort on sites like Reddit. A sympathetic figure in need will reach the hearts of a large audience and get some help, usually in the form of many small donations. On the one hand, in each case this is wonderful, and yet it's ultimately a way for people to feel good while having achieved nothing, in statistical terms.

However, viral success is small-time compared to another, more rarefied kind of rags-to-riches tale. When a Siren Server is on the rise, in a honeymoon phase, a small-time player might just score a once-in-a-lifetime spectacular lift.

The Web itself went through a honeymoon phase around the turn of the century, which is now remembered as the "dot-com bubble." During this time there were weird and wild successes that motivated a stampede of hopefuls. My favorite story was of a young woman who drove up her credit card debt and then created a website asking for donations from strangers to pay off her debt, for no reward and with no real explanation. It worked, but as I recounted in *Gadget,* that was only because her timing was accidentally perfect. She caught the wave at the right moment, and none of the many copycats who followed her could duplicate her success. Of course it would be absurd to think that any could.

Her success was due to the fact that she had a rapt audience for that fleeting magic moment when a network is gaining its network effect but before all the hapless scammers of the world rush in to dilute the radiated benefit of it. She was like the first person to arrive in California for the gold rush, when the gold was still visible, strewn on the surface.

During the honeymoon phase of a newly successful Siren Server, a lucky few people will typically be gifted with astounding, deceptive success. Their stories will be celebrated, creating a distorted popular perception of opportunities.

For instance, musician Amanda Palmer launched a Kickstarter campaign in 2012 that became legendary. She stated a goal of raising a hundred thousand dollars to support a new release and tour, but instead raised more than a million dollars. There were other similar tales during that honeymoon year for Kickstarter. (Good for her! I would like to believe this type of success will become unremarkable, but as things stand, I won't hold my breath. World, please prove me wrong!)

An interesting psychological phenomenon, when a modern Horatio Alger–like hero hits the jackpot, is that she might succumb to the illusion, for a moment, that she has achieved Siren Server status herself. Palmer promptly asked for free labor from musician fans on the same tour that had been luxuriously funded by those same fans. Needless to say, the Mechanical Turk effect came into play, and free labor presented itself. In response to a torrent of criticism from professional musicians, Palmer relented and announced a plan to pay musicians. (Good for her, once again! But this doesn't suggest a societal solution.)

There is always a tale of someone making it big or changing their life because they caught a digital wave at just the right moment. If only there were enough of those moments generated by the regime of Siren Servers to support a society.

The Closing Act

How do Siren Servers die? We don't know as much as we will someday soon, since the phenomenon is still new. One can imagine Wal-Mart being overwhelmed by Amazon, for instance, simply because Amazon is even more computational than Wal-Mart.

Amazon, by using superior computation, might potentially piggyback on Wal-Mart's legacy of supply chain optimization, and essentially aggregate Wal-Mart's efficiencies into its own. It wasn't Amazon that brought about all the cheaply available goods, but by having the best spy data at a given time, Amazon might become the concern that benefits the most from them.

Maybe some other Siren Server related to self-driving vehicles will come along and be able to make itself meta to Amazon and then steal whatever advantage Amazon builds up, since Amazon depends on vehicles to deliver goods to consumers. Competition becomes mostly about who can out-meta who, and only second-arily about specialization.

We do know that Siren Servers can die. It happened to Lehman Brothers.

They are not like classical monopolies that can become so entrenched that a regulator might choose to break them up. How would you break up Facebook? Into one for fake hot babes and another for political organizing? The idea is absurd.

Individual Siren Servers can die and yet the Siren Server pattern perseveres, and it is that pattern that is the real problem. The systematic decoupling of risk from reward in the rising information economy is the problem, not any particular server.

Stories Are Nothing Without Ideas

This book proposes a grand future story in which the pattern of Siren Servers will be superseded by a more inclusive new pattern. But even today, it would be a mistake to only see chaos and mean-inglessness in the crazed energies of a networked world.

The endgames of contests between Siren Servers are not mean-ingless. Siren Servers are not interchangeable. While they all share certain traits (narcissism, hyperamplified risk aversion, and extreme information asymmetry), they also represent particular, more specialized philosophies. The requirements of being a Siren Server leave enough room for variation that contests between them can also be collisions of contrasting ideas.

Facebook suggests not only a moral imperative to place certain information in its network, but the broad applicability of one template to compare people. In this it is distinct from Google, which encourages semistructured online activity that Google will be best at organizing after the fact.

Twitter suggests that meaning will emerge from fleeting flashes of thought contextualized by who sent the thought rather than the content of the thought. In this it is distinct from Wikipedia, which suggests that flashes of thought be inserted meaningfully into a shared semantic structure. Wikipedia proposes that knowledge can be divorced from point of view. In this it is distinct from the *Huffington Post,* where opinions fluoresce.

In all these cases, unquestionably big ideas are at play. The designs of these sites are embodiments of philosophies about what a person is, where meaning comes from, the nature of freedom, and the nature of an ideal society. When Master Servers die, the associated ideas can be suppressed for long periods of time, which is as close as ideas get to death.

The blog TechCrunch keeps a grim count of failed Silicon Valley efforts, called the Deadpool.[2] In it we find not only would-be Siren Servers that died, but also an early hint at how ideas might be lost along with them.

For instance, Google tried to get a new Siren Server going, to tremendous fanfare, called Wave.[3] It proposed that conversations between people could be highly structured from the start, to make the content of the conversation more valuable later. That would mean that meaning in natural language would be preserved even if everything said had to be fit initially into a particular, tree-shaped data structure. That in turn suggests a level of meaning in human conversation that is more orderly and tiered, more Chomskyan, than has ever been isolated by researchers before. It's a major assertion about what meaning is, or might become. (I am skeptical that the idea is correct, but that is beside the point.)

Since the effort was about big business data instead of big science data, we can't say that the idea suffered a Popperian* disqualification. Instead the idea was attached to a server that failed. With the death of a Siren Server, a distinct sensibility concerning human meaning and how we communicate with one another became effectively dead and unexplored for now.[4]

A networked story is just as much a contest of ideas as was the Cold War, which served as a standard of meaning for Kushner and Fukuyama. Story lives, and the future is not random.

---

*Karl Popper was an Australian philosopher who famously described how science never achieves absolute, eternal truth, but instead gets closer and closer to truth by disqualifying false ideas. Mathematics, on the other hand, does include a concept of absolute, eternal truth, because of proofs.

The Wise Old Man in the Clouds

THE LIMITS OF EMERGENCE AS AN EXPLANATION

In 2012, the University of San Francisco, a Jesuit institution, themed its recruitment campaign on the idea that Christianity is like Facebook. One of the slogans was "Our CEO mastered social networking 2,000 years before Mark Zuckerberg was born."[1]

There's something to the comparison, and I find that worrisome. Each institution became powerful in an unconventional way. Each network created a center of power that bypassed territorial and political boundaries, and existed on its own plane. Each became what might be called a "social monopoly," engaging in social engineering on a grand scale.

That's not to say that bad things will necessarily happen in a social monopoly. They can achieve breathtaking large-scale social good. The Catholic Church unquestionably educates many millions of the poor, heals many millions of the sick, stabilizes many millions of families, and comforts many millions of the dying; in 2012 Facebook dipped a toe into the waters of social engineering by increasing the rolls of organ donors with a simple tweak of its user experience. By putting the option to donate right in front of people, many more people embraced that option.

But the problem with freestanding concentrations of power is that you never know who will inherit them. If social networking has the power to synchronize great crowds to dethrone a pharaoh, why might it not also coordinate lynchings or pogroms?

During the Middle Ages, which were characterized by weak states, the Church endured "bad popes." Access to the afterlife, and indeed the papacy, was bought and sold, and all manner of hypocritical and criminal scheming overwhelmed any charitable or spiritual mission.

The core ideal of the Internet is that one trusts people, and that given an opportunity, people will find their way to be reasonably decent. I happily restate my loyalty to that ideal. It's all we have.

But the demonstrated capability of Facebook to effortlessly engage

190

in mass social engineering proves that the Internet as it exists today is not a purists' emergent system, as is so often claimed, but largely a top-down, directed one. There can be no sweeter goal of social engineering than increasing organ donations, and yet the extreme good of the precedent says nothing about the desirability of its inheritance.

We pretend that an emergent meta-human being is appearing in the computing clouds—an artificial intelligence—but actually it is humans, the operators of Siren Servers, pulling the levers.

THE GLOBAL TRIUMPH OF TURING'S HUMOR

The news of the day often includes an item about recent developments in artificial intelligence: a machine that smiles, a program that can predict human tastes in mates or music, a robot that teaches foreign languages to children. This constant stream of stories suggests that machines are becoming smart and autonomous, a new form of life, and that we should think of them as fellow creatures instead of as tools. But such conclusions aren't just changing how we think about computers—they are reshaping the basic assumptions of our lives in misguided and ultimately damaging ways.

The nuts and bolts of artificial-intelligence research can often be more usefully interpreted without the concept of AI at all. For example, in 2011, IBM scientists unveiled a "question answering" machine that is designed to play the TV quiz show *Jeopardy*. Suppose IBM had dispensed with the theatrics, and declared it had done Google one better and come up with a new phrase-based search engine. This framing of exactly the same technology would have gained IBM's team as much (deserved) recognition as the claim of an artificial intelligence, but it would also have educated the public about how such a technology might actually be used most effectively.

AI technologies typically operate on a variation of the process described earlier that accomplishes translations between languages. While innovation in algorithms is vital, it is just as vital to feed algorithms with "big data" gathered from ordinary people. The supposedly artificially intelligent result can be understood as a mash-up of what real people did before. People have answered a lot of questions before, and a multitude of these answers are gathered up by the algorithms and regurgitated by the program. This in no way denigrates it or proposes it isn't useful. It is not, however, supernatural. The real people from whom the initial answers were gathered deserve to be paid for each new answer given by the machine.

Consider too the act of scanning a book into digital form. The historian George Dyson has written that a Google engineer once said to him: "We are not scanning all those books to be read by people. We are scanning them to be read by an AI." While we have yet to see how Google's book scanning will play out, a machine-centric vision of the project might encourage software that treats books as grist for the mill, decontextualized snippets in one big database, rather than separate expressions from individual writers. In this approach, the contents of books would be atomized into bits of information to be aggregated, and the authors themselves, the feeling of their voices, their differing perspectives, would be lost. Needless to say, this approach would hide its tracks so that it would be hard to send a nanopayment to an author who had been aggregated.

What all this comes down to is that the very idea of artificial intelligence gives us the cover to avoid accountability by pretending that machines can take on more and more human responsibility. This holds for things that we don't even think of as artificial intelligence, like the recommendations made by Netflix and Pandora. Seeing movies and listening to music suggested to us by algorithms is relatively harmless, I suppose. But I hope that once in a while the users of those services resist the recommendations; our exposure to art shouldn't be hemmed in by an algorithm that we merely want to believe predicts our tastes accurately. These algorithms do not represent emotion or meaning, only statistics and correlations.

What makes this doubly confounding is that while Silicon Valley might sell artificial intelligence to consumers, our industry certainly wouldn't apply the same automated techniques to some of its own work. Choosing design features in a new smartphone, say, is considered too consequential a game. Engineers don't seem quite ready to believe in their smart algorithms enough to put them up against Apple's late chief executive, Steve Jobs, or some other person with a real design sensibility.

But the rest of us, lulled by the concept of ever-more intelligent AIs, are expected to trust algorithms to assess our aesthetic choices, the progress of a student, the credit risk of a homeowner or an institution. In doing so, we only end up misreading the capability of our machines and distorting our own capabilities as human beings. We must instead take responsibility for every task undertaken by a machine and double-check every conclusion offered by an algorithm, just as we always look both ways when crossing an intersection, even though the signal has been given to walk.

When we think of computers as inert, passive tools instead of people, we are rewarded with a clearer, less ideological view of what is going on—with the machines and with ourselves. So, why, aside from the theatrical appeal to consumers and reporters, must engineering results so often be presented in Frankensteinian light?

The answer is simply that computer scientists are human, and are as terrified by the human condition as anyone else. We, the technical elite, seek some way of thinking that gives us an answer to death, for instance. This helps explain the allure of a place like the Singularity University. The influential Silicon Valley institution preaches a story that goes like this: One day in the not-so-distant future, the Internet will suddenly coalesce into a superintelligent AI, infinitely smarter than any of us individually and all of us combined; it will become alive in the blink of an eye, and take over the world before humans even realize what's happening.

Some think the newly sentient Internet would then choose to kill us; others think it would be generous and digitize us the way Google is digitizing old books, so that we can live forever as algorithms inside the global brain. Yes, this sounds like many different science fiction movies. Yes, it sounds nutty when stated so bluntly. But these are ideas with tremendous currency in Silicon Valley; these are guiding principles, not just amusements, for many of the most influential technologists.

It should go without saying that we can't count on the appearance of a soul-detecting sensor that will verify that a person's consciousness has been virtualized and immortalized. There is certainly no such sensor with us today to confirm metaphysical ideas about people. All thoughts about consciousness, souls, and the like are bound up equally in faith, which suggests something remarkable: What we are seeing is a new religion, expressed through an engineering culture.

What I would like to point out, though, is that a great deal of the confusion and rancor in the world today concerns tension at the boundary between religion and modernity—whether it's the distrust among Islamic or Christian fundamentalists of the scientific worldview, or even the discomfort that often greets progress in fields like climate change science or stem-cell research.

If technologists are creating their own ultramodern religion, and it is one in which people are told to wait politely as their very souls are made obsolete, we might expect further and worsening tensions. But if technology were presented without metaphysical baggage, is it possible that modernity would make people less uncomfortable?

Technology is essentially a form of service. Technologists work to make the world better. Our inventions can ease burdens, reduce poverty and suffering, and sometimes even bring new forms of beauty into the world. We can give people more options to act morally, because people with medicine, housing, and agriculture can more easily afford to be kind than those who are sick, cold, and starving.

But civility, human improvement, these are still choices. That's why scientists and engineers should present technology in ways that don't confound those choices.

We serve people best when we keep our religious ideas out of our work.

DIGITAL AND PRE-DIGITAL THEOCRACY

People must not be gradually equated with machines if we are to engineer a world that is good for people. We must not allow technological change to be driven by a philosophy in which people aren't held to be special. But what *is* special about people? Must we accept a metaphysical or supernatural principle to acknowledge ourselves?

This book will culminate with a prospectus for what I'm calling "humanistic information economics." Humanism might include a tolerance of some form of dualism. Dualism means there isn't just one plane of reality. To some people it might mean that there's a separate spiritual realm, or an afterlife, but to me it just means that neither physical reality nor logic explains everything. Being a skeptical dualist means walking a tightrope. Fall to the left and you acquiesce to superstitions. To the right lies the trap of sloppy reductionism.

Dualism suggests a difference between people and even very advanced machines. When children learn to translate between languages or answer questions, they also nurture assets such as context, taste, and moral feeling that our machine inventions cannot originate, but only mash-up.

Many technologist friends tell me that they think that I am clinging to a sentimental and arbitrary distinction. My reasons are both based on a commitment to the truth and to pragmatism (the survival of liberty—for people).

Belief in the specialness of people is a minority position in the tech world, and I would like that to change. The way we experience life—call it "consciousness"—doesn't fit in a materialistic or informational worldview. Lately I prefer to call it "experience," since the opposing philosophical team has colonized the term *consciousness*. That term might be used these days to refer to the self-models that can be implemented inside a robot.

WHAT IS EXPERIENCE?

If we wish to ask what "experience" is, we can frame it as the question "What would be different if it were absent from our world?"

If personal experience were missing from the universe, how would things be different? A range of answers is possible. One is that nothing would be different, because consciousness was just an illusion in the first place. (However, I would point out that consciousness is the one thing that isn't reduced if it's an illusion.)

Another answer is that the whole universe would disappear because it needed consciousness. That idea was characteristic of followers of the physicist John Archibald Wheeler's early work. He once seemed to believe that consciousness plays a role in keeping things afloat by taking the role of the quantum observer in certain quantum-scale interactions.

Yet another answer would be that a consciousness-free version of our universe would be similar but not identical, because people would get a little duller. That would be the approach of certain cognitive scientists, suggesting that consciousness plays a specific, but limited practical function in the brain.

But then there's another answer. If consciousness were not present, the trajectories of all the particles would remain identical. Every measurement you could make in the universe would come out identically. However, there would be no "gross," or everyday objects. There would be neither apples nor houses, nor brains to perceive them. Neither would there be words or thoughts, though the electrons and chemical bonds that would otherwise comprise them in the brain would remain just the same as before.

There would only be the particles that make up things, in exactly the same positions they would otherwise occupy, but not the things. In other words, consciousness provides ontology for particles. If there were no consciousness, the universe would be adequately described as being nothing but particles. Or, if you prefer a computational framework, only the bits would be left, but not the data structures. It would all mean nothing, because it wouldn't be experienced.

The argument can become more complicated, in that there are limited information bandwidths between different levels of description in the material world, so that one might identify dynamics at a gross level that could not be described by particle interactions. But the grosser a process is, the more it becomes subject to differing interpretations by observers. In a minimal quantum system, only a limited variety of measurements can be made, so while there can be arguments over interpretation, there can be less argument about phenomenology. In a big system, that isn't the case. Which economic indicators are substantial? There's no consensus.

The point is that one goes round and round trying to get rid of an experiencing observer in an attempt to describe the universe we experience, and it is inherently impossible to verify that projects of that kind have been completed.

That is why I don't think reason can definitively resolve disputes about whether people are "special." These kinds of arguments recall Kantian attempts to use reason to prove or disprove the existence of God. Whether the argument is about people or God, the moves are roughly the same. So I can't prove that people are special, and no one can prove the contrary, either, but I can argue that it's a better bet to presume we are special, for little might be lost and much might be gained by doing so.

PART SIX

Democracy

CHAPTER 16

Complaint Is Not Enough

Governments Are Learning the Tricks of Siren Servers

A revolutionary narrative is common in digital politics. Broadly speaking, that narrative counterpoises the inclusiveness, quickness, and sophistication of online social processes against the sluggish, exclusive club of old-fashioned government or corporate power. It's a narrative that unites activists in the Arab Spring with Chinese and Iranian online dissidents, and with tweeters in the United States, Pirate Parties in Europe, nouveau high-tech billionaires, and "folk hero" rogue outfits like WikiLeaks.

That particular idea of revolution misses the point about how power in human affairs really works. It cedes the future of economics and places the entire burden on politics.

In our digital revolution, we might depose an old sort of dysfunctional center of power only to erect a new one that is equally dysfunctional. The reason is that online opposition to traditional power tends to promote new Siren Servers that in the long run are unlikely to be any better.

Also, it's silly to think that only a particular sort of activist will benefit from a technology. It's not as though traditional power structures have been sealed in stasis while digital networking has risen. Instead, old forms of power have been gradually melded into highly effective, modern Siren Servers.

A modern, digitally networked, national intelligence agency, such as the CIA/NSA/NRO complex in the United States, illustrates the trend. A visit to one of these organizations feels very much like a visit to the Googleplex or a major high-tech finance venture. The same sorts of cheery recent PhDs from top schools cavort in an airy and playful environment with lots of glass and excellent coffee. Spymaster Siren Servers thrive in all countries by now. We tend to hear more about the excesses of foreign ones in China or even Britain, but the trend is universal.

Nations increasingly recast themselves as Siren Servers in other ways as well. China, Iran, and to varying degrees all other nations wish to be the ultimate masters of digital information flow. The clichés are so familiar that you can fill in the blanks. Developing country X bans certain websites, or filters the Internet for certain words, but courageous citizens and stalwart Silicon Valley companies provide sneaky ways to contravene those restrictions. Or: Rich country Y spies on all its citizens online even though it is a democracy, in the hopes of catching terrorists.

It's easy to motivate a coalition in opposition to control freakery in digital statesmanship, because democracy advocates and network entrepreneurs hate it equally. While there have been some interesting challenges to state power, particularly in the Arab Spring, elsewhere it hasn't been so easy for such coalitions to have much of an effect. I suspect that the role of digital networking in the Arab Spring was a novelty effect.* When governments engage in the Siren Server game, they get good at it fast. (It appears that governments are getting better at getting ahead of citizen cyber-movements than commercial schemes, which consistently outwit regulators.)

In the long term, I worry that the efforts of online activists who hope to support democracy will backfire the most just when they seem to be succeeding. Opposing a particular type of Siren Server, even when the target is the latest cyber-concept of a nation-state, doesn't really help when your actions only serve to promote yet other Siren Servers.

---

*Since I wasn't there, I will not take a position on whether Silicon Valley tech really played an essential role. However, I am sick of hearing us pat ourselves on the back by describing someone else's revolution as the "Twitter Revolution" or the "Facebook Revolution," as if the whole world were about us. The half-Burmese journalist Kathleen Baird-Murray pointed out to me that Burma's population achieved similar results at about the same time without the Internet.

For instance, activists use social media to complain about lost benefits and opportunities, but social media (as we currently know it, organized around Siren Servers) also gradually concentrates capital and shrinks opportunities for ordinary people. Within a democracy, the resulting increased income concentration gradually enriches an elite, which is likely to promote candidates who will support yet further concentration.

On the world stage, the same conundrum makes it harder for developing nations to sprout good jobs for educated people, because information flow is currently fated to be "free." No one expects Twitter to help create jobs in Cairo.

It's impossible to divorce politics from economic reality.

Alienating the Global Village

Economic interdependence has lessened the chances of war between interconnected nations. This is the gift I thanked Wal-Mart for earlier. Unfortunately, by forcing more and more value off the books as the world economy turns into an information economy, the ideal of "free" information could erode economic interdependencies between nations.

Nations have been far more willing to engage in cyber-attacks on each other than other kinds of attacks, because the information sphere is largely not on the books, which would otherwise reflect how globally interdependent it really is. Chinese interests have hacked American corporations like Google, but they would hardly be motivated to toy with the infrastructure in America that delivers Chinese goods.

A warehouse should not be perceived as being in a separate economic category than a website. China is as economically dependent on an American website's security as it is on the truck that delivers goods made in China. But that dependency doesn't show up adequately in international accounting.

Siren Servers are narcissists; blind to where value comes from, including the web of global interdependence that is at the core of their own value.

Electoral Siren Servers

Only genuinely empowered masses of people, with real wealth, clout, and economic dignity, can balance state power. We have seen this in U.S. electoral politics. The cyber-activist community, which leans in a knotted lefty/libertarian fashion, fancies itself able to organize the vote, but actually it turns out that "big money" is even more able to do so.[1] Social media are used to raise money first, and directly influence the vote second.

But what does "big money" really mean? At least in the United States we aren't bribing voters as yet. In fact, voters often seem to vote against their own immediate economic interests. Democrats might vote to raise their own taxes, while Republicans might vote often enough to reduce their own safety nets and earned benefits.

No, what "big money" means is turning election campaigns into Siren Servers. Candidates hire big data professionals and use the same math and computer resources that enable every other type of Siren Server to operate to optimize the world to their advantage.[2] The interesting thing about elections is that law dictates multiple competing players. This makes elections unusual in the era of big data, since the "exclusion principle" doesn't hold. As with wireless operators, there are multiple Sirenic schemes occupying a single niche.

If elections were run like markets, a winning political party would emerge and become quite persistent. This is the failure mode of politics in which a "party machine" emerges. The terminology is instructive. The process becomes deterministic, as if it were a machine. Democracy relies on laws that impose diversity on a market-like dynamic that might otherwise evolve toward monopoly.

Democracies must be structured to resist winner-take-all politics if they are to endure. That principle applied in the network age leads to periodic confrontations between competing mirror-image big data political campaigns. It is a fascinating development to watch.

Perhaps we should expect to see more elections that are either extremely close or extremely lopsided from here on out. If opposing Siren Servers are well run, they might achieve parity, while if one is better than the other, its advantage ought to be dramatic. It's too early to say, since big data and politics haven't mixed long enough to generate much data as yet. It's like climate change was for a long time—not enough data yet to really say—though it does look like we're seeing this pattern.

Just as a small, local player in a market loses local information advantages in the shadow of a Siren Server, so does a local political activist. I remember when I was a young person working for political campaigns, we would inform a campaign about potential voters who might be swayed because we knew our own territory. (This often involved seeking out grouchy old New Mexicans and convincing them that the political opponent was a little too cozy with the Texans.)

These days, the central database of a political campaign more often informs local activists of the optimal way to scour the land for votes. The activist becomes like a general practitioner doctor, who acts more and more as a front man for insurance or pharmaceutical Siren Servers.

The problem with optimizing the world to the benefit of an electoral Siren Server is the same as it is for the other species of such servers. It's not that it doesn't work in the short term, because it does, but that it becomes increasingly divorced from reality. Just as networked services that choose music for you don't have real taste, a cloud-computing engine that effectively chooses your politicians doesn't have political wisdom.

The process is increasingly divorced from real-world events. A message is fine-tuned and tested. Feedback signals are fed into statistics engines. Just as big data in business can function with lower standards of veracity than big data in science, so can big data in politics.

Optimization is not the same thing as truth. The 2012 elections in the United States were widely described as more divorced from facts than any other in history. Before, we could not use central servers to find every person vulnerable to paranoia about Texas; now we more or less can, but that doesn't mean that paranoia is any more justified or useful.*

*I doubt that political views have become more extreme as a result; there have always been extreme views. Politics has always nurtured and exploited paranoia, and I chose Texaphobia only because it is the funniest and mildest example I could think of.

If the party with the biggest/best computer wins, then a grounded political dialog doesn't matter so much. Reality becomes less relevant, just as it does in big business big data.

Big data means big money works in politics. So if democracy is the goal, it becomes truer than ever that the middle class must have more money in aggregate than elites who might employ Siren Servers. The bell curve must overwhelm the winner-take-all curve.

Maybe the Way We Complain
Is Part of the Problem

Two diametrically opposed schools of thought appeared in response to the Great Recession. Roughly speaking, an austerity/trickle-down tendency—a Hayek/Rand axis—opposes a Keynesian/fairness tendency, but the two sides agree about one thing. Both agree that social media like Facebook and Twitter are part of the solution.

Every power-seeking entity in the world, whether it's a government, a business, or an informal group, has gotten wise to the idea that if you can assemble information about other people, that information makes you powerful. By glorifying the tools that enable this trend as our channels of complaint, we're only amplifying our own predicament.

There are ongoing calls for rights that might provide a balance to the trend, with an example being calls for digital privacy rights or intellectual property rights. (These are deeply similar, but people trapped in fake conflicts between old media and new media might fail to see that.)

But those arguments are increasingly irrelevant. Trying to update legal rights to catch up with technology only sets up a dismal contest between prohibitions and what actually happens.

Campaigns for rights have tended to play out as benefiting one or another cabal that seeks to run a top server. In a contest between, say, a Hollywood studio and a "pirate" video-sharing site over who should be favored by the law, the answer will hopefully evolve to become a clear "neither." The idea of humanistic information economics presented here is an attempt to open up a third way.

CHAPTER 17

Clout Must Underlie Rights, if Rights Are to Persist

Melodramas Are Tenacious

My conviction that building a strong middle class in the information economy must underlie the pursuit of rights unfortunately pits me against the kinds of rascals I would otherwise tend to feel more organically at home with. It would perhaps feel better to go with the flow and celebrate outfits like WikiLeaks, but I believe that would ultimately be a self-defeating choice.

We who are enthusiastic about the Internet love the fact that so many people contribute to it. It's hard to believe that once upon a time people worried about whether anyone would have anything worthwhile to say online! I have not lost even a tiny bit of this aspect of our formative idealism from decades ago. I still find that when I put my trust in people, overall they come through. People at large always seem to be more creative, good-willed, and resourceful than one might have guessed.

The problem is that mainstream Internet idealism is still wedded to a failed melodrama that applies our enthusiasms perversely against us. A digital orthodoxy that I find to be overbearing can only see one narrow kind of potential failure of the Internet, and invests all its idealism toward avoiding that one bad outcome, thus practically laying out invitations to a host of other avoidable failures.

From the orthodox point of view, the Internet is a melodrama in which an eternal conflict is being played out. The bad guys in the melodrama are old-fashioned control freaks like government intelligence agencies, third-world dictators, and Hollywood media moguls, who are often portrayed as if they were cartoon figures from the game Monopoly. The bad guys want to strengthen copyright law, for instance. Someone trying to sell a movie is put in the same category as some awful dictator.

The good guys are young meritorious crusaders for openness. They might promote open-source designs like Linux and Wikipedia. They populate the Pirate parties.

The melodrama is driven by an obsolete vision of an open Internet that is already corrupted beyond recognition, not by old governments or industries that hate openness, but by the new industries that oppose those old control freaks the most.

A personal example illustrates this. Up until around 2010, I enjoyed a certain kind of user-generated content very much. In my case it was forums in which musicians talked about musical instruments.

For years I was warned that old-fashioned control freaks like government censors or media moguls could separate me from my beloved forums. A scenario might be that a forum would be hosted on some server where another user happened to say something terrorist-related, or upload pirated content.

Under some potential legislation that's been proposed in the United States, a server like that might be shut down. So my participation in and access to nonmogul content would be at risk in a mogul-friendly world. This possibility is constantly presented as the horrible fate we must all strive to avoid.

It's the kind of thing that has happened under oppressive regimes around the world, so I'm not saying there is no potential problem. I must point out, however, that Facebook is *already* removing me from the participation I used to love, at least on terms I can accept.

Here is how: Along with all sorts of other contact between people, musical instrument conversations are moving more and more into Facebook. In order to continue to participate, I'd have to accept Facebook's philosophy, which includes the idea that third parties would pay to be able to spy on me and my family in order to find the best way to manipulate what shows up on the screen in front of us.

You might view my access to musical instrument forums as an inconsequential matter, and perhaps it is, but then what is consequential about the Internet in that case? You can replace musical instruments with political, medical, or legal discussions. They're all moving under the cloak of a spying service.

You might further object that it's all based on individual choice, and that if Facebook wants to offer us a preferable free service, and the offer is accepted, that's just the market making a decision. That argument ignores network effects. Once a critical mass of conversation is on Facebook, then it's hard to get conversation going elsewhere. What might have started out as a choice is no longer a choice after a network effect causes a phase change. After that point we effectively have less choice. It's no longer commerce, but soft blackmail.

And it's not Facebook's fault! We, the idealists, insisted that information be demonetized online, which meant that services about information, instead of the information itself, would be the main profit centers.

That inevitably meant that "advertising" would become the biggest business in the "open" information economy. But advertising has come to mean that third parties pay to manipulate the online options in front of people from moment to moment. Businesses that don't rely on advertising must utilize a proprietary channel of some kind, as Apple does, forcing connections between people even more out of the commons, and into company stores. In either case, the commons is made less democratic, not more.

To my friends in the "open" Internet movement, I have to ask: What did you think would happen? We in Silicon Valley undermined copyright to make commerce become more about services instead of content: more about our code instead of their files.

The inevitable endgame was always that we would lose control of our own personal content, our own files.

We haven't just weakened old-fashioned power mongers. We've weakened ourselves.

Emphasizing the Middle Class
Is in the Interests of Everyone

Figuring out how advancing digital technology can encourage middle classes is not only an urgent task, but also a way out of the dismal competition between "liberal" and "conservative" economics.

To a libertarian or "austerian" I say: If we desire some form of markets or capitalism, we must live in a bell-shaped world, with a dominant middle class, for that is where customers come from. Neither a petro-fiefdom, a military dictatorship, nor a narco-state can support authentic internal market development, and neither does a winner-take-nearly-all network design.

Similarly, anyone interested in liberal democracy must realize that without a dominant middle class, democracy becomes vulnerable. The middle of the bell has to be able to outspend the rich tip. As the familiar quote usually attributed to Supreme Court justice Louis D. Brandeis goes, "We can have democracy in this country, or we can have great wealth concentrated in the hands of a few, but we can't have both." *

Even for those who might dispute the primacy of either markets or democracy, the same principle will hold. A strong middle class does more to make a country stable and successful than anything else. In this, the United States, China, and the rest of the world can agree.

Another basic function of the design of power must be to facilitate long-term thinking. Is it possible to invest in something that will pay off in thirty years or a hundred, or is everything about the next quarter, or even the next quarter of a millisecond?

These two functions of the design of power in a civilization will turn out to be deeply intertwined, but the middle class will be our immediate concern.

---

*I have been unable to find an original attribution for this quote, so am not certain it is authentic. Once I cited a quote of Einstein's ("Everything should be made as simple as possible, but not simpler") and was informed by an Einstein biographer that there was no evidence he had said it. Then I met a woman who had known Einstein and heard him say it! In this case, I have no idea, but it's a super quote, whoever said it.

A Better Peak Waiting to Be Discovered

We're used to getting Google and Facebook for free, and my advocating otherwise puts me in the position of having to sound like the
Grinch stealing a present, which is a crummy role to have to take.
But in the long term it's better to be a full economic participant
rather than a half participant. In the long term you and your descendants will be better off, much better off, if you are a true earner and
customer rather than fodder for manipulation by digital networks.

Even if you think you really can't get past this point, please just try
a little longer. I think you'll see that the benefits outweigh the costs.

One way to think about the third way I am proposing, the
humanistic computing path, is that it is a "cyber-Keynesian" scenario of kicking cloud-computing schemes up onto a higher peak
in an energy landscape.

Recall the graphs of energy landscapes. We can draw various pictures of the central hypothesis of this book as such a landscape. In
the picture below, I've labeled one of the axes vaguely as "degree of
democracy," since that's one of the primary concerns that confuse
discussions about monetizing information. (An illustration might
have instead a Y-axis labeled "accessibility of material dignity.")

At any rate, however one defines democracy, or if democracy is
even a concern, the core hypothesis of this book is that there are
higher peaks, meaning more intense, higher-energy digital economies to be found. Of course, if that is true, it also means there are
more valleys, as yet undiscovered and unarticulated, to be avoided.

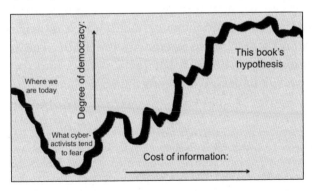

Cyber-Panglossian fallacies rule Silicon Valley conversations. The very idea that demonetized information might not mean the most possible freedom meets resistance in the current climate. I defy convention when I draw the vague "degree of democracy" as being only halfway up to its potential when the cost of information is zero.

This reminds me of the way some libertarians are convinced that lower taxes will *always* guarantee a wealthier society. The math is wrong; outcomes from complex systems are actually filled with peaks and valleys.

It's an article of faith in cyber-democracy circles that making information more "free," in the sense of making it copyable, will also lead to the most democratic, open world. I suspect this is not so. I have already pointed out some of the problems. A world that is open on the surface becomes more closed on a deeper level. You don't get to know what correlations have been calculated about you by Google, Facebook, an insurance company, or a financial entity, and that's the kind of data that influences your life the most in a networked world.*

A world in which more and more is monetized, instead of less and less, could lead to a middle-class-oriented information economy, in which information isn't free, but is affordable. Instead of making information inaccessible, that would lead to a situation in which the most critical information becomes accessible for the first time. You'd own the raw information about you that can sway your life. There is no such thing as a perfect system, but the hypothesis on offer is that this could lead to a more democratic outcome than does the cheap illusion of "free" information.

We cannot hope to design an ideal network that will perfect politics; neither can we plan to replace politics with a perfect kind of commerce. Politics and commerce will both be flawed so long as people are free and experimenting with the future. The best we can aim for are network designs that focus politics and commerce to approximately balance each other's flaws.

---

*There are other problems that I explored more in my previous book. For instance, you also lose an ability to choose the context in which you express yourself, since more and more expression is channeled through Siren Servers, and that lessens your ability to express and explore unique perspectives.

The Pocket Protector in the Saffron Robe

THE MOST ANCIENT MARKETING

Are Siren Servers an inevitable, abstract effect that would consistently reappear in distant alien civilizations when they develop their own information networks? Or is the pattern mostly a function of distinctly human qualities? This is unknown, of course, but I suspect human nature plays a huge role. One piece of evidence is that those who are the most successful at the Siren Server game are also playing much older games at the same time.

Before Apple, for instance, Steve Jobs famously went to India with his college friend Dan Kottke. While I never had occasion to talk to Jobs about it, I did hear many a tale from Kottke, and I have a theory I wish I'd had a chance to try out on Jobs.

Jobs used to love the Beatles and bring them up fairly often, so I'll use some Beatles references. When John Lennon was a boy, he once recalled, he saw Elvis in a movie and suddenly thought, "I want that job!" The theory is that Jobs saw gurus in India, focal points of love and respect, surrounded by devotees, and he similarly thought, "I want that job!"

This observation is not meant as a criticism, and certainly not as an insult. It simply provides an explanatory framework for what made Jobs a unique figure.

For instance, he liberally used the guru's trick of treating certain devotees badly from time to time as a way of making them more devoted. This is something I heard members of the original Macintosh team confess, and they were tangibly stunned by it, over and over. They saw it being done to themselves in real time, and yet they consented. Jobs would scold and humiliate people and somehow elicit an ever more intense determination to win his approval, or more precisely, his pleasure.

The process is described in an essay[1] by Alan Watts on how to be a guru that was well-known around the time Apple was first taking off.

The successful guru is neither universally nor arbitrarily scornful to followers, but there should be enough randomness to keep the followers guessing and off guard. When praise comes, it should be utterly piercing and luminous, so as to make the recipient feel as though they've never known love before that moment.

Apple's relationship with its customers often followed a similar course. There would be a pandemic of bleating about a problem, such as a phone that lost calls when touched a certain way, and somehow the strife seemed to further cement customer devotion instead of driving them away. What other tech company has experienced such a thing? Jobs imported the marketing techniques of India's gurus to the business of computation.

Another way in which Jobs emulated the practices of gurus is in the psychology of pseudo-asceticism.

Consider the way he used physical spaces. Jobs always created both personal and workspaces that were spare like an ashram, but it is the white Apple store interior that most recalls the ashram. White conveys purity, a holy place beyond reproach. At the same time, the white space must be highly structured and formal. There must be a tangible aura of discipline and adherence to the master's plan.

The glass exteriors and staircases of elite Apple stores go further. They are temples, and I imagine they might someday be repurposed for use along those lines. (Maybe, some decades from now, our home 3D printers will just pop out the latest gadgets, leaving stores empty.)

There is yet another Beatles reference to bring up: It was Yoko Ono who first painted a New York City artist's loft white. Conceptual avant-garde art invites people to project whatever they will project into it, and yet the artist offering a white space, or the silence of John Cage's "4:33," still becomes well-known. This is the template followed by Apple marketing.

A dual message is conveyed. The white void is empty, awaiting you and almost anything you project into it. The exception is the surrounding institution, the business, which is not something to be projected away.

While that setup might seem to only benefit the establishment offering the white space, there's actually a benefit to the visitor who projects what they will into it. It's like a good parent or lover who will listen endlessly without complaint but also sets boundaries. Narcissism can then be indulged without the terror of being out of touch or out of control. This formula is a magnet for human longings.

It's all about you, iThis and iThat, but we will hold you, so you won't screw yourself up. Of course that's not really a possible bargain. To the degree you buy into the ashram, you *do* give up a certain degree of yourself. Maybe that's not a bad thing. It's like how Apple customers experience culture in general through the lens of Apple's curation whenever they use an Apple device. Maybe it's the right mix for some people. But one ought to be aware.

It's tempting to ridicule this aspect of Jobs's legacy, but everything people do is infused with some degree of duplicity. This is doubly true of marketing.

Putting the duplicity up front might be best. Back to the Beatles: Lennon's "Sexy Sadie" ridiculed the guru shtick, while McCartney's "Fool on the Hill" praised it, and they were singing about the same guru. These two songs could well be applied to the appeal of Apple under Jobs. Yes he manipulated people and was often not a nice guy, and yet he also did either elicit or anticipate the passions of his devotees, over and over. (No one can say what the mix of eliciting versus anticipating really was.)

MONKS AND NERDS (OR, CHIP MONKS)

There is no single explanation for why tech culture has come to be as it is. However, Apple exemplifies one strain of influence that is particularly underappreciated: the crossover between countercultural spirituality and tech culture.

The prevalence of the New Age was a heavy burden to bear for skeptics in Palo Alto in the 1980s. Everyone was attending preachy "workshops" where a narrative about a mystical path to self-empowerment was reinforced. If you found it to be a load of claptrap you learned to keep quiet. It wasn't worth the arguments.

We like to pretend this phase of Silicon Valley culture didn't happen, but it did. To my mind, this was a distinct period from the 1970s hippie/tech crossover, which was documented nicely in John Markoff's book *What the Dormouse Said.*

Well before the computer nerds showed up, California was already a center of "Eastern Religion." There were Tibetan temples and Hindu ashrams. The wave of Eastern-influenced spiritual style was inescapable. During the wild early development of Virtual Reality, in the 1980s, I lived for a while in a faux Greek temple in the Berkeley hills built by friends of the radical dancer Isadora Duncan much earlier in the century. Looking out at the ocean through the vines, you could melt into the Bay Area's pervasive drama of almost erotic spiritual pageantry. It was life in a Maxfield Parrish painting. The exoticisms of the world made comfortable.

"est" (I recall one was supposed to spell it in all small letters) was an expensive workshop that started out with mystical metaphysics and led to secular, almost Confucian ideals about self-improvement. I never attended a session, but everyone else I knew seemed to have, much in the way that everyone is on Facebook now. The main thing attendees talked about, in addition to confiding that they were now masters of their fates, was that one was not allowed to pee during the workshop. You had to hold it in.

Many of the top scientists, politicians, and entrepreneurs attended est or similar happenings. Terms like *self-actualization* became ubiquitous. You'd develop yourself, and your success would be manifest in societal status, material rewards, and spiritual attainment. All these would be of a piece.

It's hard to overstate how influential this movement was in Silicon Valley. Not est specifically, for there were hundreds more like it. In the 1980s the Silicon Valley elite were often found at a successor institution called simply "the Forum."

The Global Business Network was a key, highly influential institution in the history of Silicon Valley. It has advised almost all the companies, and almost everyone who was anyone had something to do with it. Stewart Brand, who coined the phrases "personal computer" and "information wants to be free," was one of the founders. Now Stewart is a genuinely no-nonsense kind of guy. So is Peter Schwartz, who was the driving force behind GBN and wrote *The Art of the Long View*. And yet the ambience of the New Age was so thick that it helped define GBN. It was inescapable.

I was one of the so-called remarkable people of GBN. These were experts who would consult or speak when GBN interacted with clients. I always thought the honorary designation was odd and a little embarrassing. It turns out to come from George Gurdjieff! Gurdjieff died in 1949, but he was a primary source of the New Age style of spirituality that defined the flavor of the Bay Area in the late 20th century and continues to thrive.

One of Gurdjieff's books was called *Meetings with Remarkable Men*. There was also a movie made. We GBN "remarkables" were so-named to recall the esoteric masters Gurdjieff supposedly had to seek by climbing mountains in Turkmenistan. Feminism tempered the honorary title to "Remarkable People."

Meanwhile, the world of marketing was being reinvented at the Stanford Research Institute. This is the same SRI that employed Doug Engelbart, who first demonstrated the basics of person-oriented computing in the 1960s. More recently SRI spawned Siri, the voice interface used in Apple products.

SRI had a unit called VALS, for Values, Attitudes, and Lifestyles, which was for a while the guiding light of a transformation in corporate marketing. (The use of the term *transformation* was long a signal of the technocratic/spiritual New Age. It has been mostly replaced by *disruption* since the Singularity replaced Gurdjieff as the spiritual North Star.)

The marketing, investment, and media sectors in the United States were all heavily influenced by VALS in the 1970s and beyond. VALS classified consumers and customers into a system that was reminiscent of Gurdjieff's "enneagrams." I knew some of the principals at VALS and they would speak openly about their goal being to change the world so that it would be more suitable for spiritual people, called "Inner Directeds" in VAL-speak. The expectation that a few people living near Stanford ought to be able to go and change the world in a few years wasn't born with Facebook.

IT'S ALL ABOUT I

The lexicon of the New Age, or self-actualization, movement reserved a special place for the word *Abundance*. Abundance could mean two things. At the rational, technocratic, Confucian end of the spectrum, it might mean that people ought to take responsibility for their failures and successes, but they ought to believe that great success is possible. This sensibility sprouted the motivational speaker industry. Its traces are preserved in reality television and popular song.

In America before the New Age, you could find untold success if you went out and searched for it. This classically entailed a physical search, such as "going west." In America after the New Age, you expect to find untold success once you have perfected yourself. What that means is becoming self-confident, "believing in yourself," and the rest of a sequence of prompts that has become utterly ubiquitous.

But the other end of the spectrum of the meaning of *Abundance* penetrated the mire of superstition and magical incantations.

The idea was that the physical world is a mere façade conjured by people who are too asleep in their lives to realize they are the ones making up their own confinements. This was a taunt Gurdjieff always returned to, that most people are effectively asleep all the time. An enlightened, "remarkable" person would know better.

The magical version of Abundance is that if you can buck up your self-confidence, not only will you succeed in the world of human affairs, but you will also be able to bend or "dent" physical reality. It is really your show, if you would only realize it.

This idea of Abundance continues to thrive. An extremely popular book called *The Secret* promulgated the hope in the early 21st century. If you can only gain the confidence to just expect the finest lovers, the most exquisite possessions, the most vibrant health, then these things will simply accede to your robust imagination.

The faith that it's all you, and not the world out there, probably runs thickest in the Bay Area. At a California vegan restaurant chain, with roots in the Forum and related institutions, each item on the menu[2] is called something like, "I am successful." That might be tofu with eggplant. A radish stew might be called "I am charismatic." You have to say those things to the waitperson in order to eat. You have to be your own hypnotherapy tape in front of everyone.

Or more precisely, you have to prove fealty to an institution or be shunned for not being sufficiently self-actualizing.[3] This twisted transaction is similar to what people buy into when they live their social lives through today's consumer-facing Siren Servers.

Express yourself, you are prompted, but through Facebook's template. If you don't, you are not empowering yourself. Same old pattern, same old tricks.

"ABUNDANCE" EVOLVES

The business of starting Siren Servers would certainly seem to confirm the worldview of the Abundance movement. You just imagine that the whole world will use your social network and it does. Just like that.

Around the turn of the century, with the rise of Google, a new merger of the techie and the New Age streams of Bay Area culture appeared.

For some time, at least since those dinners at Marvin Minsky's house, there had been talk of every manner of amazing future tech revolution. Maybe we'll disassemble our bodies temporarily into small parts that will be easier to launch into space, where we'll be reassembled and then float naked except for a golden bubble to shield us from radiation.

This was an utterly typical idea. But if there were anything actionable, it would be in the realm of engineering. Could you really sever and then reattach a head?

After the rise of Google, the tenor of these speculations changed in Silicon Valley. Now the top-priority action item was perfecting one's mentality, one's perspective and self-confidence. Are you really enlightened enough to "get" accelerating change? Are you really awake and aware, preparing for the Singularity?

The engineering will come about automatically, after all. Remember, the new attitude is that technology is self-determined, that it is a giant supernatural creature growing on its own, soon to overtake people. The new cliché is that today's "disruptions" will deterministically lead to tomorrow's "Singularity."

The strange inheritance of ideas has induced a number of comic reversals. Now I find myself arguing that human agency is the better way to interpret events. Doesn't that make me sound a little like the kind of motivational speaker I used to make fun of? We must take responsibility for our own successes and failures, I declare.

CHILDHOOD AND APOCALYPSE

Even the most ambitious outcomes in the most fabulous futures articulated in the moneyed dreamspace of Silicon Valley, those where the
world isn't utterly wrecked by nuclear war or some other disaster, tend
to leave people behind. Even the optimism is dismal for people. People
will be surpassed and left behind.

And yet Silicon Valley engineers, venture capitalists, and pundits
continue to go about their days, zipping up to Napa to frolic in the wine
country from time to time, having children, generally living as if nothing unusual is happening.

Do we really believe we are on the cusp of disrupting the human
world? Are we on the verge of destroying the cycles of life as we know
them, or is that just shtick? Are we just making up stories to get by, to
romanticize our own little fog atop the chasm of mortality?

Denial is the human baseline. Fantasy of insulation is our most common habit. We are mortal and can't possibly be expected to fully grasp
death, so we inhabit just enough insanity to keep the absurdity manageable. Pretending to be able to deal with mortality sanely makes
room for life.

But in the matters of fantasy and madness, technology is different,
just as it is always different. Technology works. It really does change
the world.

The normal craziness of the world isn't enough for Silicon Valley.
Going about my day, there is nothing unusual at all about running into
a friend at the coffee shop who is a for-real, serious scientist working
on making people immortal. Or a neuroscientist who can read what
images a person is seeing directly from scanning their brain, and further hopes to someday be able to incite ideas and memories into people's brains.

Yet I can hardly think of a hard-core Silicon Valley figure who has
decided not to have children because of a belief that we will successfully engineer a posthuman future. On some deep level most of us
must be in on our own joke.

PART SEVEN

Ted Nelson

CHAPTER 18

First Thought, Best Thought

First Thought

Ted Nelson was the first person to my knowledge to describe, starting in 1960, how you could actually implement new kinds of media in digital form, share them, and collaborate.* Ted was working so early that he couldn't invoke basic notions like digital images, because computer graphics hadn't been described yet. (Ivan Sutherland would see to that shortly after.)

Ted's earliest idea was that instead of reading a text as given originally by the author, a more complex path might be created that uses portions of text to create a new sequence, to create a derivative work, without expunging or losing the original. This is what we might call the idea of the "mash-up" today, but it also was the first appearance, so far as I can tell, of the realization that digital systems could both gather and repackage media to enable new kinds of collaboration and new kinds of expression.

As the first person on the scene, Ted benefited from an uncluttered view. Our huge collective task in finding the best future for digital networking will probably turn out to be like finding our way back to approximately where Ted was at the start.

In Ted's conception, each person would be a free agent in a uni-

---

*In an even earlier article, in 1945, titled "As We May Think," Vannevar Bush hypothesized an advanced microfilm reader, the Memex, which would essentially allow a reader to experience mash-up sequences of microfilm content. But as celebrated and influential as that article was, it did not explore the unique capabilities of digital architectures.

versal online market. It might seem at first as though having only one store would reduce diversity, but in fact it would increase it.

Instead of separate stores like those run by Apple or Amazon, there would be one universal store, and everyone would be a first-class citizen, both buyer and seller. You wouldn't have to keep separate passwords and accounts for different online stores. That's a pain and it guarantees that there can't be too many stores. The way we're doing things now re-creates unneeded limitations that shouldn't be inherited from brick-and-mortar commerce. When too many layers of access to culture are privatized, as has happened online, you eventually end up with a few giant players.

This is an example of how thinking in terms of a network can strain intuition. Ted benefited from beginner's luck. He saw the issues more clearly than we do today.

Ted is a talker, a character, a Kerouac. He was always more writer than hacker, and didn't always fit into the nerd milieu. Thin, lanky, with a sharp chin and always a smile, he looked good. He came from Hollywood parents and was determined to be an outsider, because in the ethics of the times, only the outsiders were "where it's at." He succeeded tragically, in that he isn't as well known as he ought to be, and it's a great shame he wasn't able to directly influence digital architecture more.

Ted began his work years before actual networking existed, so he had to conceive of the whole damned digital world. He called it Xanadu.

He foresaw how digital information could become a new form of expression for people. Instead of conceiving of only a single person in front of a computer, he imagined new networked forms of collaboration and culture. People would create information structures that could be shared, reused, collaborated on, and interacted with. These concepts are utterly ordinary today, but at the time very few could understand them at all. By the time I got into the game, as a teenager in the 1970s, it was still almost impossible to find someone with whom you could talk about this stuff.

Best Thought

There wasn't only one version of Xanadu, as the project evolved over many decades, becoming ever more obscure as personal computers, the Internet, and all the other familiar digital set pieces appeared. Rather than offering a definitive history of the design, I will relate a few principles that I find most helpful.

The first principle is that each file, or whatever unit of information the thing is built of, exists only once. Nothing is ever copied.

We are utterly familiar with that trio of activations, cut, copy, and paste. The right to copy files on the Internet is held up as a form of free speech in the digital rights community. The Internet has even been described as a giant copying machine.[1]

But copying on a network is actually rather odd and at the very least an extraneous, retro idea, if you think about it from first principles. After all, in a network, the original is still there. It's a network!

The idea that copying would no longer be needed in a networked world was almost impossible to convey for many years. It has finally been made familiar in recent years because it is the principle on which most information services that actually charge for information must operate.

For instance, Netflix does not allow its customers to download a video file that is identical to the master file on its servers. Instead, it provides software that delivers a video experience by accessing that master file in real time over a network, and displaying it to the customer. While Netflix might employ cached data mirrors to back up their data, or to speed up transmittal, that is not the same as creating multiple *logical* copies—as users on a BitTorrent sharing site do.

There's also only one "logical copy" of each app on the Apple store. You can buy a local cache of it for your phone, and Apple undoubtedly keeps a backup, but there's just one master instance that drives all the others. When the master version of an app is updated in the store, it's eventually updated on all the phones as a matter of course. The existence of the app in your phone is more a mirror of the original than a copy.

If someone wants to go to the trouble, there's usually a way to make a copy of information offered in a no-copy way, even if that wasn't the intent of the people who made the information available. The point is that the designs will function without those copies being made.

What's wrong with making copies? In addition to the problems described already, such as in the section comparing music and mortgages, one huge problem is that you never really know what anything is. If you copy a file, you don't know where it came from, if it's been altered, or what other information might be needed for it to make sense. The context is lost, and meaning is dependent on context.

For instance, if you find a copy of a video with a politician intoning some bizarre senseless snippet, you don't know what the context was. Maybe the full version of the video would tell a different story. One of the reasons not to make copies is to avoid problems like that.

The Right to Mash-up Is Not the Same as the Right to Copy

For Ted, it was *crucial* that people be able to extract such a snippet as they wished! This is an absolutely central point.

Ted's original concept of hypertext was based on the idea that people must be able to create derivative works. Someone should be able to snip a bit of what a politician says and put it into a documentary, even if the cut is deceptive. Ted recognized that people need to be able to work with what others have done, and that digital technology could expand the ways that could happen. To expand human capability is to express faith that overall people will do well with their new powers, so Ted advocated opening expression up, even if human failings would be empowered now and then.

The pre-digital world had evolved a set of laws and conventions for how people could reflect and reuse each other's expressions. This is the familiar and uncomfortable web of logistics and procedures including copyright, fair use, libel laws, and so on. As pointed out earlier, it has functioned to provide middle-class levees to generations of creators, and shouldn't be maligned as being entirely awful. And yet given the speed and fluidity of digital expression, these old structures feel like lugubrious prohibitions today, and are often ignored.

Ted wanted mash-up rights to become a given. Information would be reusable as a matter of course, without hassle. His original idea for how to evolve ideas like copyright into the network age strike me today as being much more sophisticated than the familiar naïve rallying cries about making mankind's information free and open.

In Ted's model, it would be *easier* than it is now to make use of preexisting material. The procedure would be consistent. The ability would become ambient. However, the rights of the masher and the mashed would be balanced.

In a Xanadu-like system, you could extract a misleading, out-of-context passage of a politician's video because that would be a free speech right. You wouldn't need permission. But the link back to the original would always be right there. It would become much harder to make the illusions of misleading mash-ups stick.

These days, we wait for unpaid partisan crowds to pore through a controversial speech to document misleading mash-ups. Bloggers will notice when a candidate is quoted out of context in a campaign commercial. Similarly, journalists will eventually notice when inflammatory anti-Islamic videos have been faked and dubbed.

That is not an entirely dysfunctional means of making up for lost context, but it does mean that corrections and context are trapped within online "filter bubbles." It is not a given that those who might be predisposed to believe in a deceptive mash-up's point of view will be exposed to a factual correction about what was mashed.

Of course, there's no guarantee that a person who wants to believe in an idea would actually follow the link to see if a mash-up was deceptive, but at least the link would be right there in front of them. If you doubt the importance of that small change, just look at Google's revenues, which are almost entirely based on putting links immediately in front of people.

The real sophistication of Ted's idea is how it would bring about a balance of rights and responsibility while at the same time reducing friction. That's a rare, magical combination.

Hackles in the digital rights movement are usually raised so high that it's often hard to see past the fears. There's an absurd but entrenched fear that any system other than anonymous copying would lead to an end to free speech. These fears only serve to blind. What we are familiar with today is not necessarily the best we can do.

Traces of Ted's idea for balance are reflected in some of today's designs. For instance, each Wikipedia page has a history.

But the economic angle is what concerns us the most here. If the system remembers where information originally came from, then the people who are the sources of information can be paid for it.

That means if a snippet of your video were reused in someone else's video, you would automatically get a micropayment. Furthermore, a Nelsonian system "scales," as we say in the trade. A remash of a remash of a remash is facilitated within this system just as easily as the first remash, preserving a balance of commercial and expression rights for everyone in the chain, no matter how long the chain becomes. If someone reuses your video snippet, and that person's work incorporating yours is reused by yet a third party, you still get a micropayment from that third party.

Forget the usual dilemma that divides people. On the one side are intellectual property advocates who struggle to shut down share sites. On the other are the Pirate Parties, wiki enthusiasts, Linux types, and so on. The contest between the two sides sparks endless debates, but they're both inadequate and inferior to the original idea for digital media.

Ted forged a path through the horns of the usual dilemma, even though the path predates the sprouting of the horns. Anyone in a Nelsonian system can reuse material to make playlists, mash-ups, or other new structures, with even *more* fluidity than in today's "open" system, where the all-or-nothing, ad hoc system of intellectual property intervenes unpredictably. At the same time, people are paid, and information isn't made free, but is affordable. A Nelsonian solution provides a simple, predictable way to share without limit or hassle over digital networks, and yet doesn't destroy middle classes in the long term.

This is the half-century-old idea on which I build.

Two-Way Links

A core technical difference between a Nelsonian network and what we have become familiar with online is that Ted's network links were two-way instead of one-way. In a network with two-way links, each node knows what other nodes are linked to it.

That would mean you'd know all the websites that point to yours. It would mean you'd know all the financiers who had leveraged your mortgage. It would mean you'd know all the videos that used your music.

Two-way linking would preserve context. It's a small, simple change in how online information should be stored that couldn't have vaster implications for culture and the economy.

Two-way links are a bit of a technical hassle. You have to keep them up to date. If someone else stops linking to you, you have to make sure you don't maintain an out-of-date indication that they still are linked. That hassle means there is some initial difficulty in getting a two-way system going as compared to a one-way system. This is part of why HTML spread so fast.

But it is one of those cases where getting something easy up front just makes the price worse later on. If everything on the Web were two-way linked, it would be an easy matter to sort out which nodes were the most important for a given topic. You'd just see where most of the links led. Since that information wasn't present, Google was needed to scrape the *entire* Web all the time to recalculate all the links that should have existed anyway, keep them in a dungeon, and present the results in order to lure so-called advertisers.

Similarly, if two-way links had existed, you'd immediately be able to see who was linking to your website or online creations. It wouldn't be a mystery. You'd meet people who shared your interests as a matter of course. A business would naturally become acquainted with potential customers. "Social networks" like Facebook were brought into existence in part to recapture those kinds of connections that were jettisoned when they need not have been, when the Web was born.

Why Isn't Ted Better Known?

Xanadu wasn't merely a technical project; it was a social experiment of its time.

The most hip thing in the Bay Area from the 1960s to sometime in the 1980s was to form a commune or even a cult. I remember one, for instance, in San Francisco's Haight-Ashbury neighborhood, where hippie culture hatched, that fashioned itself the "Free Print Shop." They'd print lovely posters for "movement" events in the spectral, inebriated, neo-Victorian visual style of the time. (How bizarre it was to hear someone recommended as being "part of the movement." This honorary title meant nothing beyond aesthetic sympathy, but there was infantile gravity in the intonation of the word *movement,* as though our conspiracies were consequential. They never were, except when computers were involved, in which case they were more consequential than almost any others in history.)

The Free Print Shop made money doing odd jobs, included women, and enacted a formal process for members to request sex with one another through intermediaries. This was the sort of thing that seemed the way of the future, and that beckoned to computer nerds. An algorithm leading reliably to sex! I remember how reverently dignitaries from the Free Print Shop were welcomed at a meeting of the Homebrew Club, where computer hobbyists shared their creations.

I recall all this only to provide the context. Ted had a band of followers/collaborators. It would have been uncool to be specific about exactly what they were. They sometimes lived in a house here or there, or vagabonded about. They broke up and reconciled repeatedly, and were perpetually on the verge of presenting the ultimate software project, Xanadu, in some formulation, which would have been remembered as the first implementation of the Web, or perhaps even the Internet itself.

To be clear, the key technical insight that allowed networking to become decentralized and scale was packet switching, and that insight did not arise from Ted Nelson or the Xanadu project. Instead it arose just a little later than Ted's earliest work, from the very different world of elite universities, government labs, and military research funding. However, at least the functionality of something like packet switching is foreseen in Ted's early thinking.

Ted published outrageous books. One was a big floppy book composed of montages of nearly indecipherable small print snippets flung in all directions, called *Computer Lib/Dream Machines*. If you turned it one way and started reading, it was what Che would have been reading in the jungle if he had been a computer nerd. Flip it upside down and around and you had a hippie wow book with visions of crazy psychedelic computation. Ted often said that if this book had been published in a font large enough to read, he would have been one of the most famous figures of the computer age, and I agree with him.

The main reason for Ted's obscurity, however, is that Ted was just too far ahead of his time. Even the most advanced computer science labs were not in a position to express the full radical quality of change that digital technology would bring.

For instance, I first visited Xerox PARC when some of the original luminaries were still gathered there. I remember muttering about how weird it was that PARC machines supported the virtual copying of documents. After all, the same research lab had pioneered ways to connect computers together. For God's sake, I would say, this is the place that invented Ethernet not long before. We all know it's stupid to copy documents when you have a network. The original is still *right there*!

A stern look would greet me. I would be taken aside. "Look, we know that and you know that, but consider our sponsor. All this work is funded by Xerox, the preeminent *copying machine* company."

Indeed, in those days, Xerox was so associated with copying that it had to worry about whether its trademark would go generic. Visitors to PARC were reminded never to say "Xerox machine."

The admonitions would continue: "No one can tell the Xerox execs that innovations from this lab could make the very *idea* of copies, even in the abstract, obsolete. They'll freak out."

The early computers built at PARC looked remarkably like modern PCs and Macs, and the concept prototypes and sketches foresaw modern phones and tablets. Xerox became notorious for having funded the lab that defined the core of the modern feeling of computation, and yet famously failed to capitalize on it.

Much later, when Tim Berners-Lee's design for HTML first appeared, computer scientists who were familiar with the field Ted had pioneered—hypertext and networked media—offered the reaction you'd expect: "Wait, it only has one-way linking. That's not adequate. It's throwing away all the best information about network structure."

HTML appeared at a tired moment for Silicon Valley. The way I remember it, there was a trace of panic right in the early 1990s about whether anyone would come up with new "killer apps" for personal computers. Would there ever be another idea like the spreadsheet? HTML was so easy to spread. Each node had no accountability, so nodes could accumulate in a "friction-free" way, even though there is no such thing as a free lunch, and the friction would surely appear later on in some fashion. We were all impatient and bored and leapt at the thrill of quick adoption.

Ted was the source point for much of what we hold familiar today. For instance, he called the new medium "hypertext." Ted was very fond of *cyber-*, which originally related to navigation, and which Norbert Wiener adopted into *cybernetics* because navigation was a great example of the core process of feedback in an information system. But Ted's preferred prefix was *hyper-*, which, he once told me, when I must have still been a teenager, also captured something of the frenetic edge that digital obsessions seem to bring into human character. So Ted coined terms like *hypermedia* and *hypertext*.

Much later, in the early 1990s, the Web would be born when Tim Berners-Lee proposed HTML, the foundational protocol for Web pages. The letters *ML* stand for "markup language," but the *HT* stands for Ted's coinage, *hypertext*.

Ted is the only person alive who invented a new humor to add to my scheme of humors.* Ted's humor suggests an unlimited, but still human-centered future based on improving technologies.

---

*Positive, optimistic, but solidly humanistic science fiction, such as *Star Trek*, fits into this humor, but so far as I can tell, Ted's early work predates the genre.

PART EIGHT

The Dirty Pictures (or, Nuts and Bolts: What a Humanistic Alternative Might Be Like)

CHAPTER 19

The Project

You Can't Tweet This

Enough has been said about the problem. The time has come to pitch a solution.

The "elevator pitch" is a common phrase in Silicon Valley, even though few buildings have enough floors to require actual elevator rides. You are supposed to be able to pitch a startup quickly enough that a highly distracted person can get your idea before the next incoming tweet spurs the smartphone to buzz.

It wouldn't be credible for me to compress a pitch for a whole new digital economy design into such a tiny packet. There must be sufficient detail for it to at least be meaty enough to criticize. And yet, my pitch would become ridiculous if I tried to specify such a huge new thing in detail in advance.

My best guess on the right level of detail is what I'll call a space elevator pitch. A space elevator is a hypothetical technology that might make it easy to get into space. A very strong cable would be hung from a satellite to a tether in the ground, and you'd just climb up it. So far, we don't know how to make a strong enough cable, and that's only the start of the problems. But in principle, the idea might work someday.

This proposal is like that. I don't pretend for a moment that all the problems implicit in it are already known, much less solved. And yet it might work, and the benefits would be huge, just like a cheap way to get into space.*

---

*As it happens, I am working on an alternative to space elevators, which is a gigantic lighter-than-air railgun to launch spacecraft.

A Less Ambitious Approach to Be Discouraged

One can imagine the gears turning inside the minds of policy wonks.

"This notion of Lanier's is ambitious. The transition would be politically difficult. But he does have a point about how value is being driven off the books in order to concentrate wealth in a way that shrinks the economy as it becomes more about information. Maybe there's an easier way to address the problem he's attempting to solve. Wouldn't it be easier just to treat the information space as a public resource and tax or charge companies somehow for the benefit of using it?"

We do have rules in place to charge commercial concerns for using the public airwaves. Maybe that model could be extended to information flows in general. The argument would be that every citizen contributes to the information space whether they want to or not. Everyone is measured and tracked in the network age. So why not have government collect compensation for the use of that value in order to fund social welfare?

In that case it would cost real money to use the resources needed to start an occult Wall Street scheme or to dangle "free" Internet bait in the hopes of trapping a population into paying for visibility. The benefit of a general "spy data tax" would be a lessening of "scammy" entrepreneurship and a corresponding increase in the funding of genuinely productive new ventures. Meanwhile, as more and more jobs are lost to automation, social welfare funds would burst with new revenues to cope with the deluge.

In the current American climate, what I just said would be called "fighting words." Most Americans would probably fear that such a policy would promote unlimited growth of government bureaucracy, and that would ultimately lead to a loss of both liberty and innovation. The argument against the idea would generally go as follows: Since everything is becoming more and more software-mediated, a spy data tax would not lead to a bureaucracy of a fixed size, like the ones that deal with the public airwaves. Instead, there would be ever more kinds of spy data, more and more revenues collected for that information, and eventually a giant central planning agency that collects money from absolutely every aspect of activity and then doles it out. This would be the ultimate magnet for corruption. A colossal bureaucracy would take on all the worst characteristics of Siren Servers but in a more monolithic way.

An argument from the left is equally important. If you have to pay to use information in general, then experiments like Wikipedia would never get off the ground, because they'd first have to argue that they deserve an exceptional license to get free access. The granting of those exceptional licenses would become a political choke hold on expression. Even though I have criticized Wikipedia, I would abhor any system that regulates experiments of that kind.

Going "all the way" and treating information as genuinely valuable, from the moment it first originates from a person, is the path around these depressing bureaucratic failure modes.

Information systems can create problems, obviously, but they can also create new options. The existence of advanced networking creates the option of directly compensating people for the value they bring to the information space instead of having a giant bureaucracy in the middle, which could only implement an extremely crude and distorting approximation of fairness.

The path proposed here can't be taken easily, because we have already gone far down a different one. A difficult transition would need to be endured. Even at its best this new path would ultimately still present serious annoyances.

Yet despite the titanic "friction" of a transition, and the inevitable imperfection of the result, the path proposed here is still the better alternative.

A Sustainable Information Economy

A humanistic approach to future digital economies might, on first sniff, smell redistributionist, but it is nothing of the kind. Some people would contribute and earn more than others. The point is not to create a fake contest where everybody is guaranteed to win, but rather to be honest about who contributed to successes, so as not to foster fake incentives.

The most powerful arguments for a humanistic approach to high-tech economics don't rely at all on a liberal concept of fairness. Instead they rely on more accurately marrying risk and achievement to reward.

I described the biggest long-term advantage to business earlier, which is an expanding economy as digital efficiencies become more pronounced. Valuing *all* the information on networks (instead of mostly valuing the information in the "most meta," or most dominant network nodes) will create an economy that can continue to grow as more and more activity becomes software-mediated.

Right now, because we aren't accounting for the value of most information on the 'net, efficiencies based on technology can seem to cause a market to shrink instead of grow, even though a few new fortunes are created along the way. This is ultra-stupid.

Some other benefits to business from humanistic information economics will include:

- an expanded range of long-term business models;
- addressing intellectual property rights incrementally and gracefully instead of as an exception or affront;
- more predictable liabilities and obligations related to privacy and other potentially creepy digital-settings policies;
- and, as I already argued, enabling an economic model that can continue into the future even as bits gradually expand their influence over physicality.

Furthermore, these benefits will accrue to both the individual and the large corporation, creating a shared interest between small and large players.

A Better Beach

The silly beach fantasy that opened this book would unfold differently in a humanistic economy. It's a sunny day, and you are making a sand castle. Is it possible to make a stable bridge over the moat? You ask the seagull. "No, I can't find any record of that having been done over such a large moat," it replies. "Sand bridges collapse at that scale. Of course we could infuse robotic grains into the sand."

"No," you say to the seagull. "That would be cheating." Besides, you don't feel like spending money on nanobots to play with the sand.

You carefully shape a hill of sand and start to carve away a space within it. It is looking a little like the giant natural arch of Kashgar. "Seagull, set up a simulated twin of this arch." Through your mixed-reality glasses, you experiment with shaping the simulation. Ah, a solution!

You call your friends over. They're delighted.

"Seagull, quick! Post this thing before it collapses." A little later, the seagull says, "Your arch has been replicated fifty-eight times around the world. Check out this giant version from a beach in Rio." Through the mixed-reality glasses, you and your friends find yourselves sharing a beach with revelers in Rio.

Wow, a nice day's earnings for you. "Seagull, that casino nearby has an excellent restaurant, doesn't it? Let's splurge." You call out to your friends, "Who's hungry?"

CHAPTER 20

We Need to Do Better than Ad Hoc Levees

Keep It Smooth

One problem with traditional middle-class aspiration is that the quest for security tends to have an all-or-nothing quality. The traditional journey to middle-class dignity has often been comprised of big, chunky thresholds. You won the big job, or the big promotion, or not. You got the mortgage, owned your own taxi medallion, got into the union, got the record deal—or not. Those who didn't make it over such thresholds could still find means to success, but with greater risks and less security.

What felt like the attainment of economic dignity (through a levee) to one person inevitably felt to another, less successful aspirant like the insertion of an artificial barrier. This was a mad way to run a society, and one that often made middle-class people who only wanted to create stable family situations, or plan for their old ages, seem like the bad guys. There was a tremendous amount of vitriol hurled at union members, for instance.

The inherent tension was exacerbated with the arrival of the Internet, since young people became especially impatient. "Who is a musician to tell me not to use her music for free in my video just because it's copyrighted?"

The project at hand is to imagine leveraging network technology to create a smoother kind of path to achieving ordinary, middle-class financial security.

Such security would no longer come in quantum blocks, but

would build up gradually. It would not be absolutely assured, but would be accessible to a preponderance of people who seek it. Security would not be administered by bureaucrats, but would emerge in the marketplace.

A more incremental path to security would not answer the hard philosophical questions about such concepts as copyright, but it would make them less contentious. In a world in which a person starts to earn royalties on tens of thousands of little contributions made over a lifetime of active participation on the 'net, it will matter a little less if there is a conflict about attribution in some minority of those cases.

The creation of a much more general and ambient kind of intellectual property would happen in a routine, small-scale way. This new incremental form of accumulated financial dignity might supplement traditional systems like copyright, unions, or tenure during a transitional era, and eventually replace them. Or maybe both systems would coexist indefinitely. I cannot fill in all the details in this early sketch.

Ideally, *earning* full-on wealth, not just cash, will become more like what *spending* is like already. There will be a multitude of incremental wealth creation events instead of a few big game-changing leaps in one's status.

In a more incremental world, attributions and rewards will still be contested, no doubt, but particular outcomes will no longer make or break lives. The consequences of losing a particular battle for attribution will become analogous to missing out on a good sale. There will be plenty of other occasions to make up for it.

Another problem with existing chunky levees is that they tend to have zero-sum gotchas. If everyone gets a taxi medallion, then medallions become worthless. That also means speculators can buy up medallions and corner the market, undoing the original purpose. What we should seek instead is a system where value *increases* as more and more people participate in it.

So, a way to conceive the project at hand is to imagine how computer networks could help create a fluid, incremental kind of wealth creation that thrives at a middle-class level and is not zero-sum.

Not Enough Money Grows on Trees

One of the most central qualities of a network is its "topology." That means the way things are connected. Some networks are formed as "trees." In a tree-shaped network, you can identify a top node, and none of the connections form loops. For instance, Apple is the top or "root" node* in its app store network, and your Apple device is an ordinary "leaf" node in that network. You can't start your own app store and directly sell an app to another customer. If you could, you'd form a loop of connections, but you can't.

A less constrained topology is a "graph," which can include loops. In a graph-shaped network, you could sell to someone else, who could sell to someone else, who could eventually sell something else back to you, without involving the top node. Everyone's used to graphs. That's how social networking is structured, for instance. You can link to someone who links to someone who links to you, forming a loop. That type of graph is not where online commerce is happening, however, which is a big problem.

So far, the networks where ordinary people can make some money online have tended to be trees. For instance, you can make money on eBay, but eBay is the root node. It's a violation of the terms to make a sale on the side, one that evades eBay's root node.

However, information age commerce would become more beneficial to middle classes if it took place on a more general graph with loops. The reason is that the distribution of interest and connections gets "thicker" or "bushier" on a general graph than on a tree. More nodes become connected to a typical node.

The biggest shift since the publication of my previous book has been the rise of the app economy, pioneered by Apple. This is gener-

---

*This gets confusing, since *top* and *root* mean the same thing when it comes to networks, even though they mean approximately opposite things in living trees. Other terms that are sometimes used to express the same concept are *source* and *center*. We must use the physically inspired vocabulary we have inherited in order to describe abstract ideas. Getting used to this awkwardness is a big part of becoming conversant in digital technology.

ating some serious cash flow, and I take that as a sign that a better, more useful information economy is possible.

However, the current information economy is simply not doing enough. If there were a universal app economy, it might be big enough to support a middle class. As it is, the app economy is confined to proprietary tree-shaped company stores. Even so, this subeconomy is getting bigger, but not big enough fast enough to save the middle class.

In speaking with a wide variety of app developers, what I find is that there is indeed an upper stratum of successful app entrepreneurship that is supporting not only individuals, but in fact significant companies. This is really a wonderful development, recalling the growth of the software industry during the rise of the PC.

The app economy is, however, a new kind of star system, even worse than old Hollywood. At least Hollywood funded a range of hopefuls. Hollywood paid for its own risk pools, while app stores expect hopefuls to self-fund. The game Angry Birds is a big hit, but there isn't a thick trunk in the curve of distribution of other games that do less well. Instead there is a steep drop-off to miserable numbers.

The pattern repeats in most of the cases where people are starting to find careers in the new information economy. A small number of people make some money from YouTube videos, for instance, because Google has started to share ad revenue with top stars. This is a great development, but the number is inherently small, and the tiny numbers of video producers who are making a living for the moment are not necessarily doing well enough to build wealth for their futures.

This tree-like distribution pattern isn't surprising, but it contrasts with the graph-like distribution of interest found in the social networking world. There one finds a thus far unmonetized middle-class distribution of interest, meaning a very thick tail of outcomes. Instead of finding either stardom or abject obscurity, a great many people enjoy outcomes in the middle of the spectrum.

Proprietors of social networks are quick to point out research that distinguishes their lushly connected graph networks from more constrained tree networks. For instance, Facebook funded research showing that Facebook users are exposed to a great diversity of information from a great diversity of origins.[1] (This does not address my complaints that Facebook's design still rewards acquiescence to someone else's categories. It just shows that information flows in thickly connected graphs really are thicker in character.)

In social networks we see a pattern in which lots of people are able to get each other's attention, which contrasts with the star system that emerges in tree-shaped company stores.

Taken together, this is evidence that a graph-shaped information economy can support a middle class—as opposed to the winner-take-all outcome that emerges in tree-shaped economies. A monetized version of a many-to-many network could create an organic path to middle-class wealth that would be *better* than the ad hoc mountain of levees that sustained middle classes in pre-digital capitalism.

CHAPTER 21

Some First Principles

Provenance

The foundational idea of humanistic computing is that provenance is valuable. Information is people in disguise, and people ought to be paid for value they contribute that can be sent or stored on a digital network.

The primary distinguishing feature of humanistic computing is therefore two-way linking, just as networking and hypermedia might have possessed anyway, had the original ideas from Ted Nelson and other early pioneers prevailed.

If two-way linking had been in place, a homeowner would have known who had leveraged the mortgage, and a musician would have known who had copied his music.

New data can be created in all sorts of ways. It might be a side effect of what you do to have fun online. For instance, the videos you choose to watch might be announced over a social networking service. In other cases you might deliberately create data, as when you blog or tweet. You might just set up a webcam or some other sensor and feed the Web raw data. Or, your DNA might be measured, or your brain waves. All sorts of information might get onto a network because of your existence.

In all these cases, in a humanistic information economy, when new data is uploaded from a local device into a server or cloud computer, its provenance is remembered. That means a record of origin is connected to the data. This record is protected from error and fraud by redundancy between local devices and servers in the cloud, so faking or erasing provenance would at the very least require taking on nontrivial effort and risk.

In humanistic information economics, provenance is treated as a basic right, similar to the way civil rights and property rights were given a universal stature in order to make democracy and market capitalism viable.

Don't worry: It's not excessively expensive or a threat to the efficiency of the Internet to keep track of where information came from. It will actually make the Internet faster and more efficient.

Universal retention of provenance without commensurate universal commercial rights would lead to a police/surveillance state. Universal commercial provenance can instead lead to a balanced future, where a middle class can thrive with proportional political clout, and where individuals can invent their own lives without being unduly manipulated by unseen operators of Siren Servers. Instead of relying on dubious prohibitions to avoid disasters of privacy violation or coercion, the expense of using data would temper extreme exploitation.

Commercial Symmetry

We have come to accept as inevitable a duo of coexisting lousy extremes. Sometimes information is supposedly free but people are subject to weird surveillance and influence, with insufficient commensurate rights. This is the familiar world of Google, Facebook, et al. It will not be a sustainable path as technology advances.

On the flip side, customers can be locked into one-sided contracts in order to have access to what they want online. This is the world of proprietary tree-shaped stores found through mobile devices or boxes that put entertainment on a big screen at home. These include stores operated by Apple, Amazon, et al.

Unfortunately, paying for value over a network in this way also sets us down an untenable path in the long term. Consider eBooks. A purchase of an eBook is not as substantive for the buyer as was a paper book purchase in physicality. An eBook buyer is no longer a first-class citizen in a marketplace.

When you buy a physical book, you can resell it at will, or continue to enjoy it no matter where you decide to buy other books. It might become a collectible book and go up in value, so you might make a profit on your original purchase. Every purchase of an old-fashioned book opens an opportunity to earn money by enhancing provenance. You can get the author to sign it, to make it more meaningful to you, *and* to increase its value.

With an eBook, however, you are not a first-class commercial citizen. Instead, you have only purchased tenuous rights within someone else's company store. You cannot resell, nor can you do anything else to treat your purchase as an investment. Your decision space is reduced. If you want to use a different reading device, or connect over a different cloud, you will in most cases lose access to the book you "purchased." It wasn't really a purchase, but a contract entered into, even though neither you nor anyone else ever reads such contracts.

If the information economy is to evolve on its present track, so that each player is either running a Siren Server or is an ordinary person ricocheting between two extremes of noncapitalism, between fake free and fake ownership, then markets will eventually shrink and capitalism will collapse.

So a primary task in imagining a sustainable information economy must be to imagine a sustainable model for transactions. A key idea that makes a transaction model sustainable is a kind of symmetry between buyer and seller, so that transactions harmonize with a social contract.

When a social contract works, you recognize that what's good for others is ultimately good for you, too, even if it might not seem so at a particular moment. In a particular moment, having to pay for something might not seem so good for you. Ultimately, being paid by other people as part of the deal more than makes up for the initial sacrifice. That also means you empathize with the needs of those who sell to you, because you sometimes play the role of seller.

Right now it might seem draconian to charge for access to information we have come to expect for free, but it would feel very different if you knew that other people were also paying you at the same time for information services you have fractionally contributed to in the course of your life.

This is the only way that democracy and capitalism can be in alignment. The current online commerce models create a new kind of class division between full economic participants and partial economic participants. That means that there isn't enough shared economic interest to support long-term democracy.

If we can get to the point of symmetrical commercial rights, then a large space of potential transaction models becomes thinkable. While the structures of transactions will be some of the most critical elements of the workable information economies of the future, it would be premature for me to predict which ones will work best from this early perspective. There can be no doubt that entirely new models for transactions, unimaginable to me now, will be invented by young, brilliant generations of computer scientists, entrepreneurs, and economists. All their brilliance will go to waste, however, if the basic symmetries of a social contract are not expressed in the foundational architectures of our networks.

Some starting ideas about what future transactions might be like will be presented later on.

Only First-Class Citizens

Commercial symmetry suggests a radical difference between what I am proposing here and the world we currently know. Everyone will need to have a unique commercial identity in a universal public market information system. That contrasts with the way things work currently, where machines have unique identities, like IP addresses, but people don't.

Human identity is currently handled on an ad hoc basis, and most people have multiple identities that are owned by remote companies like Facebook. This way of doing things might seem to favor the private sector over the public sector, but in the long term it actually hurts the private sector.

The most basic foundation of the way people connect to networks has to be the public sphere if the competition between private offerings is to be symmetrical, fair, and dynamic. When the very connection of people to each other or their own data is owned by remote concerns, then it's impossible to outrun impedances and stagnation.

The Internet might have started out making better use of the public sphere, but in the 1970s and 1980s the mostly young men building what would turn into the Internet were often either pot-smoking liberals or CB-radio-using, police-evading conservatives who were violating speed limits. (That's a bit of an exaggeration, but not much.) Both camps thought anonymity was the essence of coolness, and that it was wrong for the government to have a list of citizens, or for people to need government IDs. In retrospect I think we were all confusing the government with our parents. (This despite the fact that during the early stages, digital networking was a government-funded research endeavor.)

How times change. As I write this, one of the common ideas on the conservative side of American politics is that people should have to have government IDs on them if they want to vote, or even if they want to avoid arrest if the police want to talk to them and they don't look proper. Meanwhile, many liberals favor a universal health care system that would build on a universal ID.

This is one of those cases where you have to choose the least of evils. You might not like the idea of a universal online identity, but face it, if you don't allow one to come about in the context of government, it will happen anyway through companies like Google and Facebook. You might like and trust these companies now more than you like or trust the government, but you should see what happens to tech companies as they age.

Eschewing Zombie Siren Servers

It's sad to say, but all young things change over time. The prototypical great Silicon Valley company Hewlett-Packard, which inspired all the rest to come, encountered in the not-too-distant past a period of not only crummy management but weird, tawdry scandals, board intrigues, and demoralization. Chances are that some of today's bright young companies will go through similar periods someday. It could happen to Facebook or Twitter. That is one good reason why these are the wrong entities to be the long-term foundations of online identity.

Corruption, senility, and brutality emerge in democratically elected governments, of course, but the whole point of a viably designed democracy is to provide a persistent baseline for society. You can vote in new politicians without killing a democratic government, while a free market is a fake if companies aren't allowed to die due to competition. When giant remote companies own everyone's digital identities, they become "too big to fail," which is a state of affairs that degrades both markets and governments.

One reason companies like Facebook should be interested in what I am proposing is that planning a regulation regime is better than morphing involuntarily into a dull regulated utility, which is what would probably happen otherwise. Suppose Facebook never gets good enough at snatching the "advertising" business from Google. That's still a possibility as I write this. In that event, Facebook could go into decline, which would present a global emergency.

It's not an outlandish scenario. It once seemed unthinkable that tech giants like Silicon Graphics could disintegrate. If Facebook starts to fail commercially, suddenly people all over the world would be at risk of losing old friends and family ties, or perhaps critical medical histories. Companies would suddenly lose connections with their customers. Facebook is only one example of many recent highly successful network players that have made themselves essential in advance of making themselves sustainable.

Facebook is becoming more like an electric utility every day. It's a piece of infrastructure people need, and when people need something they eventually ask the government to make sure they have it. That's why government ended up in the middle of water, electricity, roads, and the like. Businesses also demand that access to these things be constant and secure, so it is not a question of corporations versus individuals.

The death of Facebook must be an option if it is to be a company at all. Therefore your online identity should not be fundamentally grounded in Facebook or something similar.

Only First-Class Identity

Government must come to be the place where the most basic online identity will be grounded in the long term. That doesn't mean that the government should run everything. The line where government should stop is not hard to draw, as it's always been drawn.

Without any government ID it's awfully hard to open a bank account. You need a bank account, but you can choose different banks and you can still live much of your life outside the banking system if you want. Government provides grounding, but no more. Your bank might fail, but you won't lose your Social Security number. You are not *totally* dependent on remote private financial services in order to have a financial identity.

A balance along the lines of what has worked with banking in the pre-networked world will also be possible in a humanistic economy. In a future in which you own your data, you might agree to have a company like Facebook provide services, but if Facebook went bankrupt your online life and identity would not disappear; Facebook would not have been the *exclusive* holder of your data or identity.

There are interesting questions that must be left to sort out in the future. How much storage and computation would be part of the public sphere? How much would be given to each citizen as a birthright? Birthright provisions might be minimal, so you might have to open an account with a cloud computing service to hold even the most basic elements of your data and manage transactions, just as you need to find a bank today. Or maybe the government will provide a functional dollop of computation and storage to everyone. This will be a great new debate for liberals and conservatives to tear each other apart over in future elections.

CHAPTER 22

Who Will Do What?

Biological Realism

Naturally enough, we humans like to think of ourselves as if we were immortal. A conservative who opposes universal health care might argue that people should only have to pay for health care when they want it, since it's a consumer choice. It's as if we were talking about aliens with the super-power to choose when to get sick and how much it will cost when that happens.

Similarly, the Pirate Party/Linux/openness crowd suggests that instead of making money from recordings, musicians should play live gigs. This is a topic I addressed in my previous book, but to summarize: This strategy only works reliably for those who will always be healthy and childless. In fact it works best if the person's parents are still healthy and generous.

Any society that is composed of real biological people has to succeed at providing a balance to the frustrations of biological reality. There must be economic dignity, defined here as knowing you won't fall off a cliff into abject poverty if you get sick, become a parent, or grow old. (Young, healthy, childless adults perhaps need not be protected from the danger of falling off that cliff. I certainly wasn't protected from it when I was young. I'll leave that question to the liberal-versus-conservative debates, which are separable from the project at hand.)

If we demand that everyone turn into a freelancer, then we will all eventually pay an untenable price in heartbreak. Most people won't be able to pull freelancing off through the contingencies of a lifetime. We need those levees, not because we're lazy, but because we are real.

When enough people lack economic dignity, there's no way for the economy overall to function well. Even those who are reasonably successful on their own can get stuck in damage control, helping their family and friends. The recent absurdities of the financial markets served to disenfranchise aging people in particular. Their savings, jobs, and equity evaporated.

There are always feel-good ways to help out in a few of the most outrageous and visible tragedies. A local jazz club will have a night to raise money for an aging musician's medical bills, for instance. But for every aging musician helped a little by a special benefit, there are dozens lost to the shadows.

Some decades from now all those idealistic people who contributed to open software or Wikipedia will be in the same position as today's aging jazz musicians. We'll help one per week through fundraising on Reddit in order to feel good, even though on average that will be the equivalent of doing nothing.

In a humanistic information economy, as people age, they will collect royalties on value they brought into the world when they were younger. This seems to me to be a highly moral use of information technology. It remembers the right data. The very idea that our world is construed in such a way that the lifetime contributions of hardworking, creative people can be forgotten, that they can be sent perpetually back to the starting gate, is a deep injustice.

Putting it that way makes the complaint sound leftist. But today there's also an erasure of what should be legitimate capital. The right should be just as outraged. The proposal here is not redistributionist or socialist. Royalties based on creative contributions from a whole lifetime would always be flowing freshly. It would be wealth earned, not entitlement.

The Psychology of Deserving

The idea that you ought to suffer and fight your inner laziness demons in order to earn your keep is deeply ingrained in anyone who has learned to succeed in a market economy, and that's for a very good reason. Astounding improvements to life in general since the Enlightenment have been brought about by multitudes of individuals acting like grown-ups and keeping the commitments they've made. In particular, they have paid their debts, allowing the idea of finance to be realized.

Thus each recent generation of modern humans feels compelled to impart a moral code to its progeny that might be expressed this way: "Responsibility and maturity are what built most of the comforts of our world, which are almost entirely recent innovations. We forget how bad things were before modernity. The possibility of childish laziness wasn't even a remotely survivable option before the advent of modern comforts. Children used to die all the time from preventable disease and exploitation. But now things are almost too easy. Letting you children get lazy now because of the work of the earlier generations could bring the cumulative achievement of many generations of people down to rubble in a single generation."

You don't need to remind me how easy it is to slough off and become lazy. Oh, I know how sweet the temptation is.

So modernity has brought with it an endless internal mental conflict between stern, rather parental inner voices and lazy childish ones. Unfortunately, these two voices, which have functioned as opposites, checking each other for centuries, have been confounded into idiotic agreement and collusion with the appearance of digital network technology.

Upon hearing that I propose that people be able to earn their livings in part just for doing what they do while being watched by cloud algorithms, the parent voice can be expected to say: "Doing what you want shouldn't be a way of earning a living. Allowing even a hint of that is the very core of moral hazard. The moment kids get a whiff of the notion, they'll never learn to take on the sheer pain of growing up—or the self-sacrifice of doing a job or paying a mortgage—and civilization will fall apart."

The child voice doesn't listen to any of this, naturally, but instead demands exactly the same thing using a different argument: "Why bring money into it? Money is all about greed and getting ahead and getting old and boring. Anarchy is true and real and direct. If money enters the equation, then the feeling of freedom will soon be ruined."

In other words, both sides are saying that if technology makes life easier, it should also make you poor. When parent and child agree, it can be almost impossible to get a word in edgewise. This is the stupidity of our age, a conclusion so utterly bankrupt that no single generation could muster a sufficient momentum of mental failure to express it alone. Only a collaboration of generations could manage to spread a dusting of credence over such a gaping, appalling, vacant falsehood.

One way to notice that this approach to being responsible is becoming obsolete is to observe how modernity is already working for the luckiest people. We've grown used to the idea that success comes easier to some people than others, and comes easily indeed to the luckiest people. There's an old Buck Owens song called "Act Naturally," which was also famously sung by Ringo Starr. "They're gonna make a big star out of me . . . and all I have to do is act naturally."

This isn't to say that all stars are lazy; many of them clearly work very hard, especially early in their careers. And yet, there is a certain almost unseemly grace that propels some careers, not only in the movies, but also in finance and other fields.

And yet: Natural stars are celebrated by society overall, even though they earn well, despite not suffering as much as some might hope they would. We're used to the idea that in a market economy, you can be annoyed about the success of others, but you have to live with it.

I hesitate to even invoke the topic, since so many people are on a hair trigger about it. One side might declare, "The one percent didn't earn it!" and the other might admonish, "The market says they did, so you should stop being jealous." Neither the left nor the right seems to anticipate that the future might hold many, many more legitimate, self-propelled lucky stars.

Is it such an awful thing to suggest that what technological progress should look like is more and more people becoming a little more like lucky stars? What other vision of progress is viable?

The existence of more lucky stars does not mean socialism, nor does it mean the triumph of lazy childhood demons. It just means a market in an expanding information economy functioning honestly instead of being hampered by obsolete parental admonitions or childish fears, no matter how appropriate they might have been in times past.

The crazy network-based wealth of inscrutable investors lately can serve as both a warning and an inspiration. What I'm arguing is that just because networked finance boomed at everyone else's long-term expense, there's no reason in principle a similar outbreak of lucky-starism couldn't happen much more broadly, so that more people could enjoy the fruits of modernity based on more complete accounting.

But Will There Be Enough Value from People?

The employment picture is increasingly "hollowed out" in physicality. People increasingly find their sustenance in dead-end jobs at the bottom, or in elite jobs at the top.

To me that means our economy is obsolete and needs to be reformed to keep up with technological progress. But to others it means that people are becoming obsolete.

As I complained earlier, I hear this infuriating comment all the time: "If a lot of ordinary people aren't earning much in today's markets, that means they have little of value to offer. You can't intervene to create the illusion that they're valuable. It's up to people to make themselves valuable."

Well yes, I agree. I don't advocate making up fake jobs to create the illusion that people are employed. That would be demeaning and a magnet for fraud and corruption.

But network-oriented companies routinely raise huge amounts of money based precisely on placing a value on what ordinary people do online. It's not that the market is saying ordinary people aren't valuable online; it's that most people have been repositioned out of the loop of their own commercial value.

A dismissive smirk often greets proposals for a humanistic information economy. How could nongenius, ordinary people have anything valuable to offer in a world dominated by elite technical people and advanced machines?

This reaction is understandable, since we have become used to seeing the underemployed languish. But there are occasions when this kind of doubt in the value of others betrays gross prejudices.

One example is when investors are perfectly confident to value a Siren Server that accumulates data about people in the tens of billions of dollars, no matter how remote the possibility of an actual business plan that would make a commensurate amount of profit. And yet, at the same time, these same investors can't imagine that the people who are the sole sources of what is so valuable can have any value.

And then there are ideological pundits from the sidelines who strike out at anyone who points out the absurdities of what we're up to in Silicon Valley lately. If someone complains that all those brilliant recent PhDs ought to perhaps be working on something more substantive than putting yet more paid links in front of people, you can expect a rigorous defense of the nonmonetary value being created by today's cloud computing. Twitter doesn't yet know how to make much money, for instance, but it is defended this way: "Look at all the value it is creating off the books by connecting people better!"[1]

Yes, let's look at that value. It is real, and if we want to have a growing information-based economy, that real value ought to be part of our economy. Why is it suddenly a service to capitalism to keep more and more value off the books?

Why must it be the case that from the perspective of the Siren Server, knowing what ordinary people do is breathtakingly valuable, while from a personal perspective, exactly the same data usually earns only transient crumbs in the form of easier-to-find couches to crash on and lightweight ego boosts?

Or to put it another way, once industries like transportation, energy, and health care start to become software-mediated, shouldn't the communication and entertainment industries becomes relatively more important to the economy, to take up the slack? And yet these are precisely the industries that software has sapped so far.

A Question That Really Isn't
That Hard to Answer

Whenever one sort of task can be automated, others that can't be automated come into view. The economic question is who gets paid for what people at ground level do beyond the horizon of automation in a given historical phase.

As long as the people who actually do whatever it is that can't be automated are paid for what they do, an honest human economy will persist. If third parties who run the biggest network computers are the ones who are paid, then there will no longer be an honest economy.

So will people in a humanistic economy find enough value in each other to earn a living, once cloud software coupled with robots and other gadgets can meet most of life's needs and wants? Or even more bluntly, "Will there be enough value from ordinary people in the long term to justify the existence of an economy?"

In order to answer, we can start with familiar ideas about what people can do for Siren Servers, and change the question ever so slightly to be about what people can do for themselves and each other. At least two answers are immediately apparent.

One manifest answer is that people are infinitely interested in what other people express online. Huge numbers of people find audiences for their tweets, blogs, social network updates, Wikipedia article tweaks, YouTube videos, snapshots, image collections, meanderings, and from second-order reactions and mash-ups of all of the above. Is it really such a flight of fancy to predict that a large number of people will still be offering this type of value online, so long as the accounting is complete and honest, into the foreseeable future?

Now is when I expect to hear that this kind of activity is all fluff and not the stuff of an economy. Once again, why is it fluff if it's for the benefit of the people who do it, while it's real value if it's for the benefit of a distant central server?

Economics is not about your taste. Economics, once people have risen above basic needs into the middle class, is about the tastes of *other* people, whether you like it or not.

It's hard to say how much of the present-day economy is based on taste instead of need, since, as Abraham Maslow pointed out, the line shifts. At the very least, not only entertainment, but titanic industries like cosmetics, sports and recreation, tourism, design, fashion, hospitality, dining, hobbies, grooming, cosmetic surgery, and the majority of the activities of geekdom ought to count as "tastes" that have turned into needs as far as commerce is concerned.

All of these industries, whether they are construed as answering wants or needs, would remain monetizable in the terms of humanistic computation no matter how advanced technology gets. When home robots make other home robots that sew dresses from designs found online, then either the fashion business will be demonetized or not, depending on whether the accounting is complete. In a humanistic information economy, accounting will be complete, and people will continue to make their livings as fashion designers, fashion photographers, and fashion models, and will achieve dignity.

In a humanistic digital economy, the economy will be more ambient, and designers will still make a living, even when a dress is sewn in a home by a robot. Someone who wears the dress well might also make a little money inadvertently by popularizing it.

There will also presumably be new wants/needs appearing on the horizon into the future without end. Who can say what they will be? In addition to recipes to be mixed by artificial glands, there might be genetic modifications to make space travel more enjoyable, or neural patterns to excite special capabilities in your brain, such as an increased aptitude for math.

Whatever may come, if the control of it can be transmitted on a network as information, then there will be a choice about whether to monetize that information. Even if the idea of money becomes obsolete, the choice will remain of whether the distribution of clout and influence will be centralized or proximate to the people who are the origin of value. That choice will remain the same no matter which science fiction technologies come about.

If the answering of wants or needs is to be instead *demonetized* except for the central, all-seeing Siren Server, then both capitalism and democracy will gradually grind to a halt with the advancement of digital technology.

Nothing More to Offer?

"Won't the cloud be trained enough eventually to forever-after do things like translate between English and Chinese, or to customize a robot-built house properly? After some future date no one will need to be paid much anymore to keep the cloud competent at serving us."

An addled and useless, leech-like and lecherous humanity drearily lives off the legacy machines set in motion long ago by ancestors. This was the premise of Wells's *The Time Machine* and Forster's "The Machine Stops."

Admittedly, some well-established cloud services will gradually become less dependent on the fresh contributions of living people. There are cloud services that one can imagine becoming well enough automated by some date, and allowed to run on autopilot thereafter, generating royalties for no one. A time might come when enough old English/Chinese translations have been observed to drive new translations for the foreseeable future.

Here the key observation is that there is no absolute measure for the value of something in a marketplace. The whole point of a market is to allow prices to emerge in context. It isn't shocking for a movie star to earn a huge paycheck for offering very few lines in a movie. It is reasonable to guess that some action movie stars have earned about a million dollars per grunt on occasion. If it turns out that someone's grunt is worth a million dollars in just the right circumstances, then that's the value of the grunt.

Someday it might be the case that your offhanded grunt helps an automated assistant interact more successfully with grumpy people. Decades or centuries from now, when the global or interplanetary cloud algorithms for language translation are so refined that there's only very occasional room for improvement, your grunt might turn out to be worth a million dollars. It might sound strange today, but imagine how strange it would sound to a hunter-gatherer from thirty thousand years ago that a star's grunt on a movie screen would be worth a million dollars today.

Actually, if cloud algorithms ever seem to come to rest and need little tending, that should be taken as a danger sign. In that eventuality, stasis would be an indication that people have allowed themselves to be overly defined and guided by old software and have stopped changing, or to put it another way, have stopped living fully.

Living languages ought to require continued examples from living people in order for automated translation services to stay up to date. If the cloud has learned all it will ever need to learn to translate between English and Chinese, it means those languages have become fixed.

People ought to be in the driver's seat and not allow the network to define and capture a language for all time. A humanistic economy would remove moral hazards that might incentivize artificial language stasis, and other similar traps.

If a language translation service becomes so refined that it requires only one one-hundredth of the data gathering it did in its early years, just to keep up to date with new expressions, then that service should not be surprised to pay a hundred times more for a given amount of the latest data it requires.

I expect to hear familiar objections. For instance, if only a very small number of people are contributing to a mature cloud service, then wouldn't the middle-class bell curve distribution of rewards be ruined? It isn't strange to hear this anxiety from a neo-Marxist who distrusts capitalism in all cases, but I often hear it from cyber-libertarians who only become skeptical when ordinary people might be the beneficiaries of an information economy.

It seems to me that any market economy takes the risk that a preponderance of people will turn out to be uncreative, lazy, antisocial, or otherwise dysfunctional. In order to accept the very idea of markets for ordinary people, you have to somehow find faith that people you would never suspect of having anything to offer will keep on showing up out of the blue to offer value you never suspected could exist. I can't prove that faith is justified, but it's what we have to work with if we want to create a market system where people are free agents. The question we *can* address is whether the overall game is rigged to allow them to do that or not, presuming they can and want to.

Should a day arrive when it really becomes true that very few people are able to offer anything of value to anyone else—if everything becomes automated to the point that almost no one is really needed, but only needs—then obviously the very idea of a market must be retired.

I see no evidence to support that dark fear.

To the Dead Their Due

Suppose an information society is based on individuals accruing multitudinous, diverse, tiny flows of royalties, and that these build into a new kind of more organic "middle-class levee" system. What happens when someone dies?

Do the flows stop? Do they go to a general fund, to taxes? To charity? Would the dues to the dead eventually outpace dues to the living, and even then continue to grow until the living were squeezed out of the economy, just like the poor are today? Or might a system of cyber-inheritance lead to a new kind of plutocracy?

A primary advantage of a more generally monetized information economy is that levees are built up gradually instead of in all-or-nothing, career-making quantum leaps. That means that we needn't import the old limitations from eras that were hobbled by cruder information technologies. The levees can be eroded after death as smoothly as they were built up, instead of being breached in an instant.

The dues to the dead can be rolled off according to a smooth function. At first, some money can flow to descendants, but the amount can taper off, so that the grandchildren will have to learn to earn their keep more and more as they grow up.

On the whole, the total due to the dead would taper off, so that the ghosts of the future's Beethovens, Edisons, and Shakespeares will not hog all wealth forever.

Tapering addresses one of the passions of copyright reformers.

By making copyright and related benefits taper off, the problem of orphaned or inaccessible works ceases to be a dilemma. The use of the work of the dead gradually becomes less and less expensive, until it's free or virtually free. Our present all-or-nothing way of dealing with intellectual property prompts high-stakes end-of-term games that always leave someone unhappy. Tapering will make reasonable compromise predictable and normal.

CHAPTER 23

Big Business

What Will Big Companies Do?

Even stranger than the question about what ordinary people would do is the question "What would big companies do?" Some of the people who ask this question are the usual ultra-cyber-idealists. In their view, the great institutions of today, whether governments, churches, banks, or giant Internet corporations, will simply blur into nothingness. In their places there would only be spontaneous, instant outbursts of coordination as needed: the occasional Kickstarter barn-raising to initiate a Martian colony, for instance.

There are many reasons to doubt this point of view, even though it is often presented with great purity of heart. There is often a lefty undercurrent of thinking that a utopian information economy ought to mean the end of big institutions, including corporations. I often find I am introduced at lectures as being "anticorporate," perhaps because I have what at one time would have been countercultural hair. The truth is that I find big companies to be essential, and have enjoyed working with them. I have helped to create startups that are now parts of Oracle, Adobe, Pfizer, and Google.

Working in Microsoft's research labs has been great fun in part because of the Kinect project. Thousands of people were needed to bring what we once upon a time called an "avatar camera" to market for the first time and to promptly sell tens of millions of them. It was the selling of tens of millions that facilitated a spontaneous hacker community of thousands to create hacks. To pretend that a bottom-up approach by itself could have done the same is nuts.

The future is not predictable enough to know what kinds of big, inherently top-down jobs will need to get done, but it is extremely unlikely that there will be none. Big data requires big data centers, and big companies build them. Some new niches for big companies are suggested by the notion of a humanistic digital economy, such as the commoditized decision reduction services to be described later on. Other futuristic candidates for jobs for big companies are stabilization of the climate, repositioning earthquakes,* or creating launch structures that make space access inexpensive.†

Big companies are the flywheels and ballast of a market economy, creating a degree of stability. (To put it in geekspeak, they act as lowpass filters.) The resulting lessened turbulence will always annoy the most peripatetic and impatient young innovators, but it also makes it easier for most people in most phases in life to understand and navigate the economic environment.

The Role of Advertising

The dominant current business plan for consumer networking is advertising. What would the role of advertising be in a humanistic information economy?

Advertising can be manipulative, sneaky, and a maddening source of distortions. It is also purely human, a part of us we couldn't remove any more easily than we could sever our limbs.

In a cab in New York City, some sweaty summer day in the 1990s, a cloying, intrusive jingle blared from the radio. "Can you turn the radio down, please?" Was I heard? Louder. "Turn the radio down, driver, please!" It was an ad for a chain of furniture stores. A percussive Pakistani accent penetrated the barrier between driver

---

*Gluing existing faults and using explosives to open up new ones in less destructive locations, such as in the oceans, might accomplish this. Yes, this is one of my crazy, speculative side projects.

†In a humanistic economy, big companies would trade within the chain of commerce just as they do today. Big companies should do better in the world proposed here, not only because the economy would be expanding but because regulation in a high-tech information economy would be more readily expressed incrementally instead of in big, unpredictable, punitive chunks.

and passenger, "Mister, when you own your own cab you can turn the radio off. This is my cab, not yours. Stop shouting at me."

Then it hit me. That was *me* playing the annoying melody on the flute. My friend Mario Grigorov, a soundtrack composer, and I picked up jingle work from time to time. We had produced this one for an ad agency a year ago, and I remembered we had to go back and forth many times to please the client—to make sure the music was sufficiently piercing to ruin the precious solitude one might hope to enjoy in a cab on a sweltering day.

Advertising was one of the main business plans of the age of mass media from well before the appearance of digital technology, and there is no reason to expect it to disappear as technology evolves. In fact, advertising ought to be celebrated for the starring role it has played—for centuries—in the onset of modernity. Ads romanticized progress. Advertising counterbalances the tendency of people to adhere to familiar habits.

It bothers me that link placement in search engines and social networks is called "advertising" in the online world. That is at most a tactical sort of advertisement, but it's more a form of direct micromanagement of the options in front of a person from moment to moment. Real advertising romanticizes the offerings of people to each other. This is usually called "brand advertising" these days, but romantic— or if you prefer, heroic—advertising isn't limited to brands.

Brand advertising is what Apple did, for instance, in huge outlays for TV, billboards, and print in order to introduce a product like the iPad. Tactical link placement of the kind pioneered by Google could not have accomplished that. Instead, such links, placed for pay in front of your eyes, might influence where you buy something like an iPad. It remains a bit of a mystery how to best transfer true brand advertising from TV, billboards, or steaming New York City taxicabs into the frenetic jumble of online experience.

My purpose here is not to dictate what a utopia would be like, but I imagine that a romantic, stylish form of advertising will continue to be a central part of human experience in any advanced economy. I am a little less sanguine about paid link placement. Our online world should function well enough that we see the best links as a matter of course.

CHAPTER 24

How Will We Earn and Spend?

When Will Decisions Be Made?

It would be humanly impossible for a person to constantly make all the decisions needed in an advanced information economy. Say you want a cab. Today it is already possible to call a cab with a smartphone, but to do so a user has to have populated a stack of about ten interdependent decisions.*

Ten is a lot. Such a tangle of decisions can only be reconsidered infrequently. In some cases the decisions are forced,† which is annoying, but also a cognitive benefit in disguise.

It isn't hard to imagine future scenarios in which the stack could grow to hundreds or thousands of decisions. That would certainly be possible when you bring an elder-care robot into your life, or operate your 3D printer.

Any desirable alternative economic future must include an idea about a user interface that brings at least as much simplicity to people as acquiescing to a Siren Server does today. This means reducing the density of decisions people are expected to make to a level that leaves cognitive room to live life in free and creative ways.

If Siren Servers turn out to be the only way to reduce the burden of

---

*A phone must be chosen, and a wireless carrier, and a payment service, and a taxi-calling app, and an email account to tether the payment and taxi apps, and a credit card to process the payments, and a bank to tether the credit card to, and possibly a PC to tether the phone to, and connectivity for home Wi-Fi, and a contacts management app or social network to keep track of the addresses of places the taxi might take you.

†Choosing a phone might force the choice of wireless carrier, for instance.

decision making in an information economy, then we are done. That would mean there is only one possible design for high-tech society.

However, there are almost certainly other options. Imagine a future industry of "decision reduction" that would be (gasp!) regulated so as to remain unaligned with other services. You'd choose a decision reduction service the way you choose a broker now. The decision reduction service would use its particular style and competence to create bundles of decisions you could accept or reject en masse. You could switch to other services without penalty at any time. Such services would be prohibited from having conflicts of interest. That is a proper place for regulation.

A little basic regulation would force decision reduction services to be competitive instead of being vulnerable to the moral hazard of locking people into contracts. This idea is a generalization of many familiar ideas from antitrust and network neutrality.

If we allow ourselves to lean into a utopian stance just a little, then we can suppose that the ideal solution would be an open market in decision reduction, which even individual entrepreneurs could enter. Just like a personal assistant, a certain sort of person might be effective and happy reducing the choice space for others. In other cases, delegation to a huge decision reduction cloud service worth hundreds of billions of dollars might be the best choice for a particular customer.

The possibility of new kinds of personal assistants adds to the arsenal of answers to the question "What would people do?" In a world of thorough and honest accounting, whole new large classes of service professions should naturally pop up.

In early experiments like Second Life, we've already seen glimmers of new paid roles, from avatar stylists to virtual performance venue promoters. Facebook and the like also generate fledging new paid roles, but they're often defensive and dreary, like reputation protection and restoration.

Once a humanistic economy gets going, I imagine that accounting will suddenly become an interesting job. Accountants will be called upon to expand the kinds of value that can be documented to enhance the network. They'll not only get their clients paid, but also cause the economy to grow. They'll be a little like politicians and a little like detectives. They will not be backroom nerds but action heroes.

New careers as fresh as these, or beyond my imagination, should be appearing already, but the Sirenic pattern shuts down that kind of progress.

If I try to imagine what it would be like to be an individual in a humanistic economy, I suppose that a big life choice would be how much attention to devote to one's information transactions. One choice would be to be lazy in the quotidian sphere of life and sign up with a decision reduction service, but then double down on whatever you're good at that generates your income and wealth. Another choice would be to become personally obsessed with the details of your information life. People with a mind to do it could optimize their information incomes and wealth creation, but might as a result not look at the big picture as much. There would be all sorts of in-between options to suit different personalities.

Once again, as a reminder, this argument is neither anticorporate nor redistributionist. The test of success ought to be that both the big players and individuals do better in a growing economy. To put it another way, there ought to be big corporations doing big jobs without necessarily having to become Siren Servers.

Dynamic Value

The price of computation in a humanistic information economy ought never be set exclusively by rote, but always be determined to a significant degree by market negotiation. We will never know for sure in advance how valuable a particular datum might turn out to be. Each use of data will determine a fresh valuation of it in context.

There will be vastly more commercial events than in the world we are used to. Every time code runs, a lot of people will be paid a tiny bit each. There is no such thing as calculation without data. Therefore, if the provenance of the data has been preserved, then calculations can generally be expanded to yield additional results about who should get credit for making them possible.

It will be very rare, essentially impossible, for Amazon to sell a book for zero dollars, as it sometimes does today. This is because it will be almost impossible to assemble any information stream for which no component has some established value, or for which there is no potential customer. In physicality, it isn't unusual to see puppies or large items offered for free, because it's hard for the owner to keep them. That's almost never the case for information. There should be far less free stuff in an information economy than in physicality.

There will be no upper bound to a price. Sellers at every level will be able to set prices as high as their markets will bear, but competition will keep prices in check.

The principle would apply to code as well as data. Computer code these days tends to be either proprietary or open-source. A third option would come into being in the future proposed here, and perhaps into ubiquity. Code would remember the people who coded each line, and those people would be sent nanopayments as part of code execution. A programmer who writes code everyone uses will be able to benefit directly, instead of having to leverage code into a Siren Server scheme. The Google guys would have gotten rich from the search code without having to create the private spying agency. At the same time, an open community of programmers would have been able to contribute incrementally, without any more barriers than are found in today's open-source community.

My current thinking, which will undoubtedly not be the last word, is to calculate prices in humanistic transactions in a mixed way, partially determined by buyers and sellers in the moment and partially determined automatically by universal policies. Each price will have two components, called "instant" and "legacy."

The reason for this is to account for the value that people have already brought into the world. Capitalism has suffered from a memory disorder. It's been so glued to the moment, to the current deal on the table, that it's possible for an economic crash to occur in the midst of wealth.

The "instant" part of the price will arise from agreement between buyer and seller. Just as in physicality, there are varied mechanisms by which agreement can be reached. Sometimes a seller will set a retail, take-it-or-leave-it price. Or there might be an auction, or a back-and-forth negotiation. A mature information economy ought to spawn new styles of price determination. We'll talk more about this interesting new frontier shortly.

The "legacy" portion of the price will be composed of algorithmic adjustments to instant pricing that uphold the social contract and economic symmetry. Here are examples of the sorts of legacy adjustments that might be incorporated:

- Something old: Tax.
- Something new that might make a price go up: Calculation of the relative contributions of upstream people to the value of the transaction, so that they will be compensated. A buyer and seller can't set a price to screw over those who came before, without whom the present transaction would be impossible. Those who came before remain first-class economic citizens, though they must contend with market forces and can't set arbitrarily high prices. The next adjustment will prevent them from engaging in "blackmail" pricing.
- Something new that might make a price go down: Incremental correction for examples of software lock-in or other impediments to competition, so that antitrust-like problems are avoided in advance. This would not be a matter of bureaucratic judgment, but a dispassionate mathematical calculation. The calculation would answer the question "How much would it cost the buyer if prior decisions about 'populating the stack' had been different?"* For instance, suppose you had chosen a different wireless service in the past and want to call a cab with your smartphone now. If that different past decision in how you populated your stack would have caused a *major* difference in the cost of calling the cab now, larger than some threshold, then that should be understood as an instance of unproductive lock-in. The price paid would partially, not totally, be adjusted to undo the moral hazard of lock-in. In the present system, businesses need to

---

* The notion of calculating "What if things had been different?" ought to alarm mathematically inclined readers. Would it always be possible to calculate counterfactual financial histories? Wouldn't there be many chaotic situations in which petty differences would have had huge implications? This would indeed become a major area of concern in a humanistic information economy. It is beyond the scope of this book to go into the topic in detail, but the key idea is to design an economy to incentivize and otherwise foster more "linear" financial dealings that avoid chaos as much as possible. When the answer to "What if things had been different?" is chaotic and mostly meaningless, then chances are that the actual happening was also thus. The point is to make capitalism as little like a casino as possible.

rely on lock-in to make a profit in the online world, but in the world foreseen here there would no longer be a proper function for it.

The legacy portion of transactions overall might be centrally regulated. If it's too low, it won't act as a flywheel, propelling the economy forward to make sure it doesn't stall or fall into Keynesian traps. If it's too high, it will undo the motivational aspect of the market, since outcomes would then be based too much on what happened long ago.

Earning a Little Money
by Living Well or Interestingly

Here's a simple example of how you might make money from the cloud in a humanistic future of more complete accounting. It's based on the kind of dubious calculation that's typical of cloud entrepreneurship today.

You meet a future spouse on an online dating service. The algorithms that implement that service take note of your marriage. As the years go by, and you're still together,* the algorithms increasingly apply what seemed to be the correlations between you and your spouse to matching other prospective couples. When some of them also get married, it is automatically calculated that the correlations from your case were particularly relevant to the recommendations. You get extra nanopayments as a result.†

This sort of result is already calculated today, but the payments don't flow. The extra work for the microprocessors in the cloud computers would be trivial, considering the expected course of Moore's Law, and the extra payments would expand the economy

---

*Wishful thinking, I know. Investors in today's startups want their money out so soon that the services they fund can't even be tested against the rhythms of human life. Hopefully that will change.

†This process would be a microscopic echo of what is already done when you get a mortgage. By paying it you not only create new money, but you strengthen property values around your own house, effectively making a little of the money that your neighbors create when they get mortgages.

for everyone, including the cloud computing companies. Economic expansion ought to more than pay for the extra trouble.

Would the correlation be valid? Well, this would be business and not science. Honestly, as I explained earlier, I am super-skeptical of algorithms of this kind. It's incredibly hard to design experiments that separate the influence of such algorithms from their predictive veracity. They create their own validity if people are willing to use them. That critique is economically irrelevant, however. The point is that if future couples pay for a service for which you and your spouse contribute data, you'll benefit—though only proportionally.

This brings us to the "instant" part of the calculation of the nanopayment to you. It should be proportional to *both* the importance of the data that came from your state or behavior *and* what the seller downstream was able to earn *and* whatever profit you or your decision reduction partner tried to extract. So, for instance, if the dating service were due an extra fee for brokering a successful marriage, part of that fee would go to you.

Anytime the calculation that led to your marriage is referenced in any way, then a tree of dependencies back to your original provision of data would lead to a nanopayment to you.

For instance, suppose the dating service creates advertisements that highlight the happy marriage of a new couple, a match that was inspired from analyzing the example of your marriage to a greater degree than the examples of other marriages. In that case, you'd be owed something for the reference, and in the event business went up because of the ad, you'd be owed more. Or, if the dating service business model consists of just vanilla monthly dues, then a steady monthly calculation would determine the payment to you.*

A crucial question remains: What are the network finance implications of a romance that goes bad?

---

*When I talk to my Silicon Valley friends about these ideas, they leap into the puzzle of how one would cheat, spoof, phish, or spam such a system. My purpose now is not to present an airtight design. The goal here is to demonstrate that the way we are doing things is not the only conceivable way. In real life, there is no question that setting up a system along these lines would have to be undertaken with great care and patience. It will never be airtight, but might become more beneficial, fun, and easy to embrace than to defy.

CHAPTER 25

Risk

The Cost of Risk

The most basic attribute of a digital network is what is remembered and what is forgotten. In other words, what is entropic about the network?

The second most important attribute concerns risk pools—specifically the granularity of risk pools.

The easiest way to clarify the idea of a risk pool is by recalling a conversation I've had many times. I'll ask, "How much do you think it should properly cost to watch, say, an online video, even though it could be easily copied?" Most people feel it is proper to pay something, but don't think it should be very much. What feels fair?

The usual answer is "I'd add up how much it cost to make it and then divide that by the number of people who watch it, so we all support it. That would be fair."

The better answer would be for the people who enjoy the video to expect to pay enough to cover the *risk pool* that financed a batch of videos, some of which were more or less successful. Capitalism and the survival of liberty both depend on people deciding it is proper to pay this higher amount.

Freedom demands accepting the cost of risk. So therefore a venture capital firm has a portfolio. Some of the investments will do great, some will fail utterly, and some will be in between. A movie studio or a book publisher is in a similar game. It's not so much that the hits pay for misses that are supported out of love or some other nonremunerative criteria, but that no one really knows what will be a hit.

Internet commerce has evolved with the benefit of a number of free rides that create the illusion that somebody else can always pay for the non-hits, and that we should only have to pay for the hits. Mom and Dad can pay for the production of the first movie, for instance. That way of thinking leads to plutocracy and stagnation.

In a real market, players invest in a variety of bets to cope with uncertainty. By investing in a spread of bets, you increase your chances of supporting not only conventional successes, but also unconventional ones, which might open up new options you had not imagined. This is why most risk pools invest in a scattering of small, weird things, in addition to the more obvious bids for big hits. The oddball startup, movie, or book might launch an important career, or open up a new genre. You never know.

Studios, venture capitalists, and the like earn the scorn of hopeful young people because they seem like gatekeepers. The new "open" systems can offer easier ego boosting for contenders but less material support for risk taking. We're all poorer as a result.

The current network architecture centralizes money and power in a way that gathers the benefits, but puts the risk on everyone else. In the present era, it's becoming expected that people will self-fund to the point that they can demonstrate success.

An obvious example is YouTube, where you put up stuff for free. Once in a blue moon, you might get some benefit if you achieve the very highest level of success. So Google essentially gets the benefits of a risk pool without the cost of a risk pool.

This should sound reminiscent of what goes on in networked finance, because it is almost the same pattern. Financial concerns, through the magic of digital networks, can now take risks without paying for those risks, while gaining benefits for successes. It's sometimes called "too big to fail."

Essentially what has happened is that a global risk pool has been created, in which everyone must pay for the risk, but the server that skims the pool for benefits is private. This is also called "privatizing benefit while socializing risk."

Since this is the new model of how to be powerful, it is natural that when you ask people what feels fair in paying for a benefit over a network, an ordinary person will imagine themselves to be in the new kind of seat of power, running the server—and from that perspective it feels right and proper not to have to pay for the risk side of the equation.

Risk Never Really Goes Away

Consider the startup Airbnb.com, which has grown very rapidly and is by all appearances the sort of quick candy investors love the most. It smells like one of those Silicon Valley stories that instantly attract gigantic fortunes.

Ah, but there's a catch. Airbnb's business plan is to pretend risk does not exist. The idea is that many people travel, so while they are away there might be a spare bedroom going to waste. The full capacity of the world's housing isn't always used to maximum capacity!

So, Airbnb applies the standard playbook to use the power of network technology to optimize the world. It connects people looking for a place to stay with people who have a spare bed in the right place at the right time. The efficiency of the Internet ought to be able to disrupt the hotel industry just like Napster et al. disrupted the recorded music business! The number of available beds in the Airbnb system can quickly outstrip the entire hotel industry, and at almost no cost.

This is classic Silicon Valley thinking. And it works! To a point . . .

After millions of happy engagements, some horror stories started to appear. A woman in San Francisco lent her home to Airbnb visitors who trashed it and stole everything from her, including information to steal her identity.

One of the Airbnb founders wrote on the company blog that the good experiences of millions of transactions shouldn't be discounted because of a few bad ones. People are basically good, he decried. I agree that people are mostly good, and yet, in a functioning economy, it is necessary that those millions of good transactions account for the effects of fools, creeps, and just plain randomness.*

This is how money has to work if it's to be about the future at all. Criminals and creeps are rare, but the sum of risk is unavoidable.

We like to imagine ourselves as being eternally young, and flowing about in a world of trust. A perfect world, without the tragedy of the biological life cycle, without risk, could run on trust, and wouldn't need an economy.

Puddle, Lake, or Ocean?

The right question is not whether risk should be paid for honestly by the people who stand to gain from corresponding benefits. That answer has to be "yes." An open question is "How big should risk pools be?"

If the risk pool is the size of the whole society, then it isn't really a risk pool at all. This is what happens with Google, Facebook, networked finance, and the other Siren Server schemes. This is precisely the Local/Global Flip.

If each person must be her own risk pool, then we are also back where we started. Then everyone would have to sing for each supper. Material dignity and the middle class would be lost. Risk pools only become meaningful when they are bigger than individuals but smaller than the whole society.

So the quest for sustainable middle classes in an advanced information economy is also the quest for finding the right sort of risk group. This is a Goldilocks problem. Not too big, not too small.

The project here can only be to illuminate a possibility, not solve

---

*This is a universal quality of Siren Servers. I selected Airbnb, but I could just as easily have selected any of the other sites in which people coordinate their affairs efficiently so that some faraway entrepreneur enjoys their money without sharing their risks. Skout, a social network for meeting people, turned out to be the medium for a scattering of rapes of underage users. See http://travel.usatoday.com/destinations/dispatches/post/2011/07/plot-thickens-airbnb-renter-horror-story/179250/1, and http://bits.blogs.nytimes.com/2012/06/12/after-rapes-involving-children-skout-a-flirting-app-faces-crisis/.

all the open questions about it in detail. I would guess that in a functioning humanistic economy, there would be a quite a wild range of risk group types.

But remember, our premise is that only individuals are real. If the risk groups start to function as persons, gaining benefits at the expense of real people, then the project might falter.

Risk groups can invest in individuals, however. Unions invest in apprentices, venture firms invest in inventors, labels once upon a time invested in unknown musicians, and, remarkably, this book is being written in an age when publishers still invest in writers.

The next chapter will propose the use of theatrics to make the funding of risk more palatable in the long term.

CHAPTER 26

Financial Identity

Economic Avatars

As discussed earlier, once people start to rely on networks for a living, there will appear a balance of desires between wanting to earn money and not wanting to spend money. Just as must always be the case, everyone will realize that if we want to enjoy the free agency of being participants in an economy instead of relying on politics alone to deal with each other, we have to accept the price, which is, well, a price.

Right now, we're used to the familiar dual forms of unsustainable online economic life (fake free and fake ownership). At some point we need to make a transition to sustainable practices in which people are full economic participants in the information economy. But that shouldn't mean that a transition to a new set of practices must be forced on everyone all at once.

A dictated transition would be rough. But software can help make the transition gradual, voluntary, and smooth. Instead of utopians trying to design the perfect new style of economic life for ordinary people, people will be able to explore an evolving variety of transaction styles to find those that come most naturally.

Another way to express this is that people will be able to choose "economic avatars." Long ago, I had the pleasure of being the first person to experience being an avatar in an immersive virtual world. When you become an avatar you can become a different creature, like a lion or a Klingon. That concept is entirely familiar now.

In the same way, your interface to the information economy might take on varying qualities, as if you were a different sort of economic creature. People might even interact with you economically in a different way than you experienced the interaction.

A seller might think that a service or content is being sold on a pay-as-you-go basis, but a customer might experience the same business relationship as if it were a case of "first sample is free." The network would adjust the interface to transactions so that each person can function within the transaction style they prefer at the same time.

It might sound like a strange idea, but this capability will help make the new economy both more usable by ordinary people and more robust overall.

Economic Avatars as an Improvement on the Forgetfulness of Cash

In old-fashioned economies, the seller usually designs the transaction and the buyer must take it or leave it. That needn't be the case in an advanced humanistic economy.

Through clever programming, buyer and seller can think in the terms of different transactions and still do business with each other. Just as the cloud can translate between English and Chinese, it can translate between market participants who prefer different kinds of deals.

One reason economic avatars matter is that without them, it will be hard to create incentives and mobility for people in the lower rungs of an information economy. Right now, if a newspaper wants to charge you a monthly fee and you're poor, you pirate it, or you accept being disadvantaged. If you are poor but hopeful and motivated in a mature information economy, you might instead enter into a transaction type that gives you initial free access to the paper without breaking the economic social contract.*

---

*More complicated events might unfold: You might enter into a risk pool with other aspiring people who have something in common with you. Maybe you're young aspiring decision reducers, or dress designers, or Bopper mixologists. Once in a risk pool, you'd have a much better shot at attracting investors than as individuals. Maybe then you could issue a bond to the newspaper in order to read it.

That's not unlike what cash achieved in physicality already, as discussed earlier. Cash allows us to interact without having to reveal everything. Fluid online economics is currently designed for one-sided revelation, however. A new mechanism is needed to preserve the selective bidirectional blindness accomplished by cash, while retaining the benefits of the huge amount of valuable information that can now be harnessed. Cash unfortunately forgets *too* much for an information economy.

Interpersonal Economic Symmetry Through Theatrics

However one might prefer to think about economic life online, everyone will eventually have to both buy and sell, and become a full participant. If you never buy, you'll never be able to sell, since it's virtually never the case that something can be created online entirely out of whole cloth.

You shouldn't be able to sample everyone else's stuff for free while being paid for your stuff. That's what Siren Servers do today, and the whole point of a humanistic economy would be to get away from that pattern. Yet everyone will want to do just that.

As a consolation to the fairness of life, economic avatars will let us pretend to have our cake and eat it, too, for a while, because that will help. Our economic lives are already filled with contrivances like sales that wouldn't have a place if we acted dispassionately. Without such games, all economics would fail. The human mind didn't evolve for modernity, so we use theatrics to bridge the gap.

So, for instance, in the future economy foreseen here you'll be able to organize your commercial life around the principle of trying before you buy, but that means you'll pay a little more when you do buy. The theatrical mechanism of economic avatar creation will protect you from having to track that consequence in detail.

As far as the newspaper was concerned, you would have bought a normal subscription. The newspaper shouldn't be required to understand or approve of your economic avatar if you can generate the capital.

The principle must work in both directions. You can pretend that someone else isn't allowed to try your stuff before they buy, but in fact when they do buy, they'll pay a little more, so it's irrelevant to you how it seemed to them.

Any sustainable economy must be sustained almost entirely by voluntary participation, rather than by enforcement. But the transition to becoming a full economic participant won't be "in your face" since instead there will be avatars—and people who aren't used to economic symmetry might tend to prefer more self-deceptive economic avatars at first.

Economic Network Neutrality

Google, Facebook, and other Siren Servers already depend on an elaborate filigree of calculations that are similar to what is proposed here for their livelihoods. Auctions, click-through counts, behavioral models, and an evolving book of other tricks might or might not be valid in a scientific sense, but these ideas are apparently good enough to run an industry. These are the calculations that form the basis of pricing for vast oceans of transaction on the Internet, like the fee to place an ad or a link in front of your eyes.

A humanistic economy would extend the type of calculation already taking place and make it symmetrical. Therefore the same rules of assessment applied to one party in an online transaction would be applied to all other parties.

So, for instance, if Google placed the ads that referenced your marriage, and earned a certain amount based on auction and click-through results, your instant remuneration would be proportional to Google's.

Note that it no longer makes sense to worry about whether your nanopayment comes from Google or the dating service. Each calculation, whatever computer carries it out, as a matter of course generates nanopayments to everyone who sent it data, whether the players are small or large. Everyone benefits from the same system.

This is another way of saying that everyone is a first-class citizen. It is similar to the idea that a nation needs a single currency, and the rights for whoever holds that currency are the same. There can't be a different kind of dollar just for certain stores.

In practice, an implementation of humanistic economics would be more complex than I can indicate in a couple of pages, but the complexity would not be intractable. What we do online is already crazily complicated. The kinds of calculations proposed here are not particularly scary in comparison.

The principle of using the same valuation mechanisms for all the parties to a calculation can be called *economic* network neutrality. "Network neutrality" is the term[1] used to describe the idea that a business that transports bits should not play favorites with those bits for financial gain. An Internet access company that also offers a video streaming service should not be able to slow down videos from a competing source to make its own video streaming look better, for instance. To do so would break the principles of a network and centralize all power in a transport layer.

Economic network neutrality is simply a generalization of that idea and recognizes that as information technology becomes central, the economy becomes a form of bit transport. The motivation is the same, to avoid extreme and useless concentrations of wealth or power based purely on the position of a player, also known as moral hazard.

Symmetry as a Disincentive to Game the System

An advanced economy should let people try on different economic participant styles easily, without having to build up a lot of personal capital at first. That doesn't mean people will get a free ride. Those who enjoy the illusion must eventually pay for the cost of credit needed to finance it.

It is too early for me to solve every problem brought up by the approach I'm advocating here, but I imagine the cost of ambient credit might actually be paid a little in the near term and a little in the long term.

In the near term, each person would have to make their income and spending principles equivalent. That is, if you want to minimize your initial spending (as when you can try before you buy), then it will also be true that your earnings from other people will eventually be adjusted to reflect what would have happened if they had made the same choice regarding the value you offer to them.*

Over time, people will hopefully adjust to the idea that you have to pay others as you would like to be paid. The more interests a person perceives in common with others, even when commonalities are best illuminated by theatrical effects, the more likely the market will function well, and grow. The psychology of a social contract will eventually take hold.

In isolation, economic symmetry might pose a risk of a race to the bottom. Wouldn't everyone initially want stuff for free, and then never be able to compete with the expectation of free stuff from others in order to start charging? This is approximately what happens when a traditional economy stalls and falls into a depression.

Recall, though, the "legacy" portion of the calculation of price described earlier. The "instant" portion of a price is vulnerable to the same old Keynesian catastrophes that have always plagued markets, but the legacy portion is something new, only possible in an information economy run by large computers enabled by Moore's Law.

The accumulated payments due to past contributions will provide a momentum to prevent stalls.

Faith and Credit

When there's a deal between two people who prefer different styles of transaction, then one might offer a different mix of cash and

---

*An actual implementation of these ideas would require sorting out a lot of details, which would be wildly premature to attempt at this stage. A lot of the details will concern the basis on which "what if" calculations are performed. For instance, if you change your mind about the kind of transactions you prefer, the changes must be reflected proportionally. The proportions can be calculated based on bandwidth used, or time spent online, or some other rough measure. If you choose to spend an hour as a pay-as-you-goer, and another as a free-the-first-timer, then half of your income over that period (if time is the basis) will also seem to have come from people making the first choice, and the other half from people making the other choice.

credit (to use retro language) than the other expects to receive. This transaction between parties would just be a fine-grained, minuscule version of what already happens with mortgages all the time.

As explained earlier, when you credibly promise to pay your mortgage you can help to create new money in the world, because your promise does in fact generate new value. A generalization of that principle can give people legitimate access to ambient credit in new ways. This is a fundamental reason why, in a well-realized information economy, information needn't be free in order to be accessible.*

There would need to be a mechanism similar to a "central bank of the 'net." You can't have an expanding economy without one. New value has to be reflected as new money, which must enter the system somehow.

Since people will be looking for income as well as bargains, this fund will not just be a charity operation to pay for everyone getting everything for free. People will be paying into the general fund as often as they are pulling from it, through the mechanism of financing their avatars.

Tax

There will be a cost to calculate all that must transpire in a mature, humanistic digital economy. This cost will not be trivial, but will not introduce an undue burden compared to what Siren Servers already do today. Search engines, for instance, must scrape the *entire* Internet all the time to approximate the context lost because all the links are one-way instead of two-way.

The cost of calculation will be like older forms of the cost of governance, or the cost of civilization. Taxes, whether that is the

---

*I wish I didn't have to use mortgages as a point of reference since as I'm writing this, the world is still suffering from financial troubles that radiated from stupidly securitized mortgages. Mortgages were a reliable, clean mechanism for many years. What happened in the early 21st century was exceptional, and caused by the poor use of digital networks. It's exactly the kind of failure all these ideas are intended to prevent.

term used or not, will inevitably be taken as part of the respiratory cycle of an advanced network credit system, as it inhales and exhales money to balance gaps between credit and cash, billions of times a second.

Taxes are always a hard pill to swallow, but you must swallow it. If you are only willing to consider a utopia without central authority or taxes, you will create a phony utopia where power is ultra-concentrated behind impregnable private gates. This will lead to epochal decrepitude and poverty through the mechanism of titanic moral hazards. Change the language if you must. What I'm talking about needn't be called taxes. Infrastructure fees? You can get a good deal on having a decent civilization, but they never come for free.

CHAPTER 27

Inclusion

The Lower Half of the Curve

What about those people who fall into the bottom half of the information economy bell curve, and would have to pay more for information than they make from it? While there are problems with what I have proposed, they should be compared to the existing alternatives, not to abstract utopias. Utopia is by nature another dangerous siren.

Trying to create an overly flattened society inevitably and unintentionally creates new centers of power. A revolution might dethrone the old rich, but only at the expense of empaneling an unchallenged communist party, along with a politburo and legions of clever schemers and ass kissers who turn into a new privileged class. The right way to deal with concentrations of power is not to try to vaporize them, but to balance them.

Similar unintended side effects appeared with attempts to make information free. Efforts like Linux and Wikipedia might have weakened some old centers of power, but that only created the space for new centers of power. In what sense is becoming dependent on private spy agencies crossed with ad agencies, which are licensed by us to spy on all of us all the time in order to accumulate billions of dollars by manipulating what's put in front of us over supposedly open and public networks, a way of defeating elites? And yet that is precisely what the "free" model has meant.

To restate the premise of this project, it's ultimately better to have paid information in order to create a middle class. So with that in mind, let's consider the hard question stated above: How might a humanistic economic system support information access for those who find themselves persistently in the bottom ranks of the information economy, meaning that they have to pay more for cloud services than they earn from cloud services?

We might first ask how many people will be in this situation. If the overall economy is growing, the answer is less than half. If the economy is absolutely stagnant, then the answer is half. If the economy doesn't grow or shrink at all, then a market system is just churn, or worse, plutocracy. But there's no reason to think that innovation and creativity will suddenly run out in the information space, so we should expect a humanistic information economy to grow in the long term.

Beyond that, just because someone is on the bum side of the information economy doesn't mean that person will be poor. There ought to be plenty of people who do very well in physicality. Deeply physical professions like child care, lutherie, or massage might become better paid than ever in an advanced information economy. The more advanced our electronic gadgets become, the more expensive "artisan" organic produce seems to become. Virtuality reveals physicality to be ever more precious in comparison.

At the same time, creative practitioners of inherently human physical trades ought to do well in the information economy, too, by starting trends and helping supply the most valuable example data to cloud algorithms. Hopefully, the number of people who could not afford to pay for information would be small. That's not to say it will be zero, so the question of their status is important.

The Lowly Tail of the Curve

What about someone who can't help but be a failure in the terms of the marketplace? What's it like to be a bum in a highly advanced technological world? We don't know yet. Computation can't work miracles. If there is limited space in a city center, an algorithm can't whip up a new fold in space-time to make room for someone who doesn't want to pay rent but still wants to live there.

The nexus of problems around motivation and responsibility

will still be with us, no matter how advanced our information systems become. It goes without saying that all people will need to have access to information services or else there will be a crushing end to social and economic mobility. That would be a terribly destructive development.

My tendency is toward liberalism, so I would advocate a state role, but on the other hand, the project of a humanistic economy doesn't rest on liberal or conservative thinking. A liberal might be inclined to extend the safety net, perhaps including a highly evolved version of the public library. In such a place you might be able to print out the medical prosthetic you need for free. In that scenario, the state would serve as a surrogate customer for information services for those who cannot afford to be customers directly. Beneficiaries would have access, but perhaps not in precisely the most convenient way.

A conservative might prefer to send those who cannot afford information services to churches or foundations to find access to information. There are precedents for that in the pre-digital world as well. In my youth I occasionally made use of Christian Science reading rooms, which could be found most anywhere and graciously offered access to a wide variety of information, with far less preaching or advertising for the church than you find in any modern social network or search engine, at no charge. Neither the libraries nor the reading rooms demanded that authors not be paid.

Wealth and Civility

My current guess is that in a humanistic information economy, it would be best if it were easy for people to keep their wealth secret. The reason for this is that it would defuse the tendency of prejudices to congeal around a single status hierarchy. I have found that people behave better when there are multiple status hierarchies present, overlapped and confused.

Of course, one's wealth is the very first datum every Siren Server covets. But in a world where the sirens have been silenced, or at least where the volume has been turned down, maybe that particular signal would remain hidden under the cloak of personal privacy.

In Silicon Valley, a high-status person might be rich, or an accomplished engineer, or renowned in some other way. They all mix. It isn't always clear which kind of status is the most important.

This is a lovely quality of our little society that deserves emulation.

CHAPTER 28

The Interface to Reality

How Great Are Our Powers?

If the climate is getting screwed up, technologists propose infusing the atmosphere with corrective particles, or positioning mirrors in space to deflect excess solar energy. When politics is dysfunctional, we propose new floating nations at sea. If rare elements are in short supply, we'll mine asteroids. We'll find new sources of water on the moon. We don't accept the limits of earthly physicality.

Technologists can therefore become complacent about the lure of Panglossian economic daydreams. We have faith that tech fixes will come along in time to fix core problems, whether or not an economic system is blind to them. Furthermore, we presume that a competent technologist will always be well positioned to implement a fix, and will easily outmaneuver any obstacles presented by economics or politics.

It's easy to doubt the faiths of technologists, and it's healthy for us to be questioned so that we don't get too full of ourselves. At the same time, our faith is not completely off base. I am genuinely optimistic that people will figure out how to do more and more. However, it's foolish to pretend to know how long it will take for any particular technology to mature.

Waiting for Technology Waiting for Politics

Suppose it is true that various tech fixes can moderate the global climate, but that it will take two hundred years for them to become viable? That would be an impressive achievement, but we need a solution for this century.*

Despite the uncertainty of the timing of tech fixes for the biggest core problems we face, it is bizarre that they are only funded in token ways, and in scattershot, weird situations. If we were for a moment to forget the mirror maze of economics, and the circular firing squad of politics, and only think about the fundamentals, then a rational response to global climate change would be to supercharge all large-scale curative climate research, at least at the scale of the Manhattan and Apollo projects combined. There would also be massive social engineering experiments in order to reduce the carbon footprint of humanity in case the tech fixes don't work as soon as we'd like.

Doing these things seems unimaginable now, and yet the creation of giant stupid ghost suburbs in places like Las Vegas during the leveraged mortgage debacle of the last decade was practically automatic. This was a remarkably expensive activity at the time and turned out after only a few more years had passed to be catastrophically more expensive than anyone anticipated.

There is no shortage of explanations for why politics has become impossible just when we need it most. We've never faced genuinely global long-term political issues before, so never needed genuinely global politics. For instance, nuclear weapons treaties were multilateral, but not genuinely global. Only a small number of people needed to agree.

People are clannish, and politics among humans is therefore by nature about tribal inclusion and confrontations between tribes. We

---

*There's a wise old joke that if a programmer thinks a project will be done in two weeks, that really means "I have no idea." If he says it'll take a year, then that might be right. "Two weeks" is how uncertainty reads inside a programmer's brain.

In the realm of big real-world problems, I often hear my fellow technologists declare that a solution or transformation will occur in fifteen or twenty years. That is like "two weeks." If you hear a date like 2030 as the expected time frame for solving global warming or water shortages through quick tech fixes, be worried. That sense of timing is usually just a way of saying we have no idea how long it will take. (Yes, you are welcome to note that this is the time frame I used to anticipate elder-care robots and other events. It's the best I can do.)

can have conferences about global climate change, but the outcomes don't really stick. The very idea of global politics can make sense to the human mind but is usually nonsense to the human heart.

What Can We Do About Big Data and the Reality Problem?

It's worse than foolish to imagine that technologists will be able to fix the world if economics and politics have gone insane. We can't function alone. What we do is empower people. The world needs to be approximately sane for us to make any positive difference.

But the world is not converging on sanity. For evidence, look no further than the lack of action on the matter of global climate change. As discussed earlier, we only know about global climate change because of scientific big data, but big business data is more influential and undermines the benefits we should gain from the insights of big climate science.

I am not condemning big business data, but celebrating it. People might find better liberty in the extremely automated economies of the future by making the accounting of big business data more comprehensive.

However, we confuse big business data with big science data at our peril.

So let's reframe the global sanity question this way: How can big science data interface with big business data in a way that doesn't confuse the two? Instead of suppressing big business data, and favoring big science data, I suspect that the best results would come from making big business data *more* successful. The happier markets get, the less they will interfere with science.

Markets are happier when they are expanding. This point becomes critical in considering how markets can be better aligned with reality.

If a market is stagnant or contracting, it is in the interests of players to protect their positions and contest the positions of others. Antagonism becomes more prevalent in a zero-sum game. The whole of the game becomes the besting of others.

If a market is expanding, the game is non-zero-sum. Then win-win thinking becomes rational more frequently. The opportunity of the new can often outweigh the opportunity of fighting over the old.

This is not to say that an expanding market is automatically aligned to reality. The real estate market was expanding in Las Vegas during the stupid boom. But I am claiming here that if a market is not expanding, then players will find it hard to look beyond their immediate contests with each other. Fights over redistribution or concentration of wealth are necessarily focused inward on the affairs of people, and not outward at the larger reality.

For this reason alone, the Siren Server model of wealth that emerged in the first decade of this century is pro-stupidity. When a venture capital firm openly advertises that it is *only* looking for investment opportunities that shrink markets,[1] we should know we have entered into a game in which we are choosing zero-sum thinking, and baiting the world to ignore reality.

What should happen instead is that information technology should create a persistent expansion of markets by monetizing more and more information, enshrining the potential for non-zero-sum thinking.

Carbon Copies Ruin Carbon Credits

If economics were perfect, then human activity would be aligned with human interests—or at least that ideal is the only imaginable one for economics. So when human activities are obviously not well aligned with human interests, it's worth searching for sources of illusion that might distance economic motivations from reality.

I suspect that Sirenic effects are already creating illusions that dilute the potential benefits of carbon credits, for example. Such credits are one approach to making markets rally to fundamental needs—as opposed to random projects like building empty suburbs.

The very idea of economics is based on a feedback model that is fast enough to be relevant to one's decisions. Long-term global outcomes are not fast enough. Carbon credits attempt to bridge that gap.

However, in the context of today's dysfunctional, one-sided networked finance, there is a risk that catastrophic speculation and derivatives bundling of carbon credits would overwhelm the original purpose, should those credits become more widely used. On the other hand, absent those scams, carbon credits will have a hard time gaining traction.

Governments can introduce exceptional mechanisms like carbon credits, but these don't seem to rise to the forefront of investment strategies in their own right. The reason why is that "scammy" investments offer better returns, and for carbon credits to compete, they'd have to become scammy, too, but they benefit from too many altruistic guardians to allow that to happen. Therefore, the prominence and influence of carbon credits are limited.

How Fighting "Fraud" Might Also Fight "Scams"

Exotic and experimental ideas in finance are not necessarily scammy. Betting on the climate has a place. In my previous book I advocated the exploration of new exotic financial instruments for just this reason. We need them. But we need a more honest and sustainable approach to networked economics even more—an approach that could bring about the very positive side benefit of subduing the scams that blind.

Consider an old-fashioned way to fight economic scamminess, regulation. Critics of financial deregulation in the United States point out that before the Great Depression there had been a decades-long sequence of frequent and destructive market busts. Regulations put in place in response to the Depression seemed to lead to happier market conditions until deregulation in the late 20th century ushered back in the same old chaos.

The politics of reinstating old regulations appear to be uncertain, but also it's becoming harder for regulation to keep up with technology. It is doubtful that new language in a law could anticipate the cleverness of programmers. A rejection of Siren Servers in network architecture might, however, do the same job as old-fashioned regulation, but in a way that forestalls even highly inventive network schemes.

If homeowners with mortgages had been owed something resembling royalties whenever a mortgage was leveraged, then there would not have been overleveraging. The cost of risk would have been built in from the start, and would have been paid for by the investor creating the risk. Benefits would have been shared with those who were creating the fundamental value: homeowners who promised to pay the mortgages. Economic symmetry would have prevented investors from taking risks on other people's uninformed behavior, using yet other people's money.

A more honest and complete accounting of who is responsible for data could perhaps accomplish the same good as old-fashioned regulation, but in a new, less political way.* If we demand that sources of data always be tied to the real people who are responsible for the data's presence in the first place, not only would those people be compensated, but also the value of data could not be fraudulently multiplied.

A more honest network economy wouldn't be one where no risks are taken, but one where risks would be taken more wisely, as there would be informed participation by the ground level creators of value. It's a simple principle that could reach far. A scam is always an illusion of creating something from nothing, but there is no nothing. A well-implemented information economy would always remember the source, the something.

Siren Servers make money by shorting the whole of the project of human civilization. They bet that the improvement of reality couldn't keep up with the supernatural and extrahuman realm of "something from nothing." They are the opposite of carbon credits.

---

*Though newness is in the eye of the beholder. In a sense the project of this book was foreseen by one of the Ten Commandments, the one about not bearing false witness. As a technologist I feel entitled to claim newness for things, and it seems to work in raising interest in them.

Feeding the Frenetic Mind
of the Networked Person

So, one potential benefit of retiring Siren Servers is to make room for investments like carbon credits. But there is another network idea for addressing climate change that might also work, based on the way networking *feels*. Networking feels like a game.

This is how derivative funds and high-frequency trading outfits feel to the people who operate them, like video games. This is also what the housing bubble or the earlier dot-com bubble was like for the most engaged, and victimized, small-time investors. People get drawn into the obsessive feedback loop of interacting over a network in real time. The draw might be most profound in social media.

In order for any scheme for idealistic finance to work well, the experience of entering into it would have to be appealing on this profound organic level. Entertainment is based on pacing, and so are cybernetic networks.

It's All in the Timing

All markets are based on feedback loops with characteristic time delays. The interval between choice made and feedback received varies according to the type of transaction. The timing determines a lot about what use a market can be to people.

Short feedback intervals are often criticized, and I tend to agree with the criticisms. High-frequency trading can't possibly incorporate information about the real world because there isn't time for that information to get into the feedback loop. This is a different criticism than the more common question of fairness. Aside from fairness, the problem with high-frequency trading is nonsense.

Similarly, though on a much slower time scale, critics bemoan the quarterly report, which forces corporations to please investors four times a year even when they are in businesses that demand planning years in advance. The biggest problems we face are often even slower than that, however. Climate change happens over decades and centuries.

Therefore, if there is to be any reconciliation between market forces and a problem like global climate change, some mechanism must come into play to create short-term, entertaining feedback within the information sphere on actions that ultimately matter in a much longer time frame.

People who drive cars that give constant energy efficiency feedback, like the Toyota Prius, seem to enjoy playing the game of driving more efficiently. That principle could be extended to other areas of life, and designs to do exactly that have been proposed by researchers such as Natalie Jeremijenko.*

In such a scenario, your carbon footprint might be estimated constantly.† Through the use of economic avatars, you would not be forced to start paying for carbon immediately and explicitly, but instead could enter into the practice at your leisure as it became appropriate for you.

The Treachery of Toys

But there's a potential serious problem. This approach would involve constant measurement of your personal activity. That in turn could lead to a horrific surveillance society. There is already something of a revolt against "smart power meters," which send information back to utilities.[2] Energy use is fundamental to our

---

*Natalie proposed devices similar to personal exercise monitors, but more comprehensive, that would constantly measure how much energy one was expending, and how much it cost. At the same time, one might constantly know how much one has saved or wasted in comparison to a "what if" scenario.

†Results could be displayed on your phone, or to better get your attention, could be more persistent and novel, like an animated tattoo on your wrist, or pixels grafted into your eyelashes so you could always look up at them. (Yes, this author has looked into both possibilities. In the 1990s I used to give undergraduate students an assignment to work out the engineering of body modifications their children would someday perform to freak them out. These were two ideas I gave as examples.)

lives, so carbon footprint feedback could form the basis of a truly creepy new kind of Siren Server.

One can imagine the nightmare scenarios: "Your energy bill indicates your girlfriend has been over a lot. Now your rent is going up, since two are technically living there." "Your refrigerator has been opened a lot and is using more power than would be ideal. Your friends will be alerted that you ought to attend a class on green living and food preparation." Or: "What's going on with that electricity flow, dude? Grow lights? The authorities have been alerted."

Can any design improve feedback to help people live their lives more knowingly without also centralizing power in yet another Siren Server? That is the topic of the next chapters.

Creepy

Three Pervasive Creepy* Conundrums

There's an industry built around a set of tricky problems that include online security, privacy, and identity. The industry extends into antivirus protection, online reputation management, credit repair, data recovery, help desk subcontractors, fancy firewalls, and too many other examples to list. At times I have mused that the servicing of these concerns might be the way to support middle classes in the long term.† Billions of people could labor to fix each other's privacy and security debacles.

Alas, aside from the dark absurdity, an economy based on this principle wouldn't create enough wealth. If middle classes aren't earning money from something else, they won't be able to pay each other to man the help desks. Is there any other way to manage the complexity of creepiness?

All three creepy vexations—privacy, identity, and security—have ancient pedigrees but have been made catastrophically more confusing by big data and network effects. Much of what is said about these problems individually is interesting, but here I will make things simpler by treating them as faces of the same underlying quandary.

Creepiness is when information systems undermine individual human agency. It happens when you feel violated because the flow

---

*Eric Schmidt famously applied the term *creepy* to the Internet when he was CEO of Google, while discussing the possible future of facial recognition.
†In my previous book, this was the scenario called "Planet of the Help Desks."

of information disregards your reasonable attempts to control your own information life. The principle can be extended to organizations that are undermined by hacking, for instance.

All three sorts of creepiness are promoted by an ever-splintering menagerie of powerful remote interests hoping to hijack your informational life.

Some of the most visible and immediately annoying instigators of creepiness are criminals and vandals. To my mind, however, the actions of legitimate corporations and governments are often not far removed from those of hooligans on the creepiness spectrum.

For instance, Google wants you to be "open" so that it can search all the data related to you, even if you didn't initially enter it through the company's services. Google also wants to be closed about how it compiles and exploits your information. Facebook wants you to have only one identity, so that it's easier to collate information about you and reliably influence the options put in front of you, and it also doesn't want to share how your information is used (it also doesn't want Google to have access to it).

Loan and insurance companies demand information about you but don't share how they make decisions based on that information. Even if you attempt to browse the Web anonymously you will still be tracked and identified by hundreds of stealthy "marketing" companies, unless you develop a rarefied degree of technical skill to insulate yourself.

Distant corporate machinations gradually change your life in unfathomable ways. You never really know what might have been if someone else's cloud algorithm had come to a different conclusion about your potential as a loan taker, a date, or an employee.

A Hacker's Paradise

The creepiness problem is basically that most people aren't idiot savants.

The hacker attitude is often approximately this: "Open up your life to the 'net, all you ordinary people. The world is about to become transparent and that transparency will be the beginning of a golden age. Sharing is good. *However*, encrypt your life like crazy. Use VPN, etc. Only the smartest people can make no sound in the digital forest."

This is basically a way of saying that the better your computer skills are, the more right you have to be a genuine individual in control of your own digital life. But we technologists ought to be serving mankind, not turning ourselves into a privileged class.

Creepiness intrudes into the lives of ordinary people with varying levels of sophistication. For instance, it's rare that criminals or vandals exhibit technical brilliance, although that does happen on occasion. What's vastly more commonplace is that mediocre hoodlums search for an opening created by a victim's little mistake or oversight.

No one can remember as many IDs and passwords as we'd wish. This has been one of the choke points of online commerce. So now the industry is shifting to new identity verification schemes, like asking users to draw squiggles. The problem is that we are in an eternal cat-and-mouse game with criminals.

If people were like ideal machines, then perhaps we'd maintain and periodically update different log-ins for many different types of online data, but in reality no one is that perfect. Users do not understand the endless choices that must be made to master privacy policies and even the top companies routinely screw up the administration of such policies. No set of rules foresees all the twisted circumstances that occur in online life.

The way that Siren Servers avoid direct responsibility for doing anything, radiating risk to their peripheral node "users," also happens to engender a sloppy mind-set about creepiness concerns. To be fair, however, even security companies can't remember to always set passwords, permissions, encryption, and all the other details correctly. This is why pranksters can eventually find a way in.[1]

Most social media companies have let private data leak, screwed up privacy settings for users, or violated what users had come to think were the rules about how they could be targeted and how their data could be used. In the course of writing this book I assembled references of such screw-ups, but there were so many, and new ones appear so frequently, that I gave up trying to choose.

Social media companies have by now screwed up enough that it's doubtful they will be trusted anytime soon as commerce platforms, and that precludes one of the best options for them to turn into successful enough businesses to grow the overall economy instead of shrinking it.

If people had infinite memories and were infinitely reliable, then creepiness would go away (though in that case people wouldn't need to rely on computation so much). In the real world most people just can't conform to tedium superbly enough.

Creepiness Thrives on the Quest for Utopia

People often love the feeling of being open and trusting each other with information, and yet we've seen over and over that naïve openness fertilizes panopticons.* While you're sharing, the search engine, the market intelligence firm, and the credit bureau are all sizing you up and influencing your life, but without transparency regarding their operations.

Cyber-activists are usually most worried about traditional governments and law enforcement, with perhaps a nod to the potential of businesses or churches to overreach. But just as social networks and derivative funds have become world-shaking giants in only a few years of hypergrowth, so could a new vigilante movement, or a blackmail pyramid scheme, or a cyber-aligned cult.

The devil you know is probably not as scary as the one you don't. The transparent world so desired by idealistic techies might tame old-fashioned governments on occasion, but it will also empower new kinds of network power, in just the way that making information and code "open" empowers certain Siren Servers like search engines. Don't worry exclusively about the past forms of power; worry also about the future forms.

Just making a network open and free is not enough to create a balance of powers. Instead, simple-minded openness is actually an

---

*Michel Foucault popularized this metaphor. The panopticon was Jeremy Bentham's prison design in which cells were arranged in a circle around a central guard tower so that all prisoners were put under constant surveillance with maximum efficiency by a small number of guards.

invitation to the cleverest new concentrators of power to percolate creepiness and inspire justified paranoias.

Once Upon a Time I Hoped to Wish Paranoia Away

Creepy darkness in digital networks was foretold fiendishly by some of my writer friends back in the earliest era of digital network research. I remember talking to William Gibson, a founder of the cyberpunk subgenre of science fiction thirty years ago. I begged him to not make Virtual Reality seem so dark and menacing.

At the time I felt I ought to be trying to hypnotize the world into positivity. We technologists would dream our way into a kind and creative future, as if abuses of power were nothing but bad habits that would vanish forever if they could just be broken once, during a technology transition.

Bill actually humored me. The retort would eventually come, however, intoned in an inimitable Tennessee twang, "Jaron, I *tried*. But it's coming out dark."

Of course it was all in fun. I knew Bill wasn't about to listen to me about lightening up—what a literary disaster that would have been!

Some decades later there are days when the world does seem to be plowing right into one of Bill's novels. But the story is not over. It has barely begun.

The 'Net Is Watching

Worries about who can see what on Facebook, or whether it's safe to enter a password while on the café Wi-Fi, are going to be superseded by serious questions about how well people understand the implications of their most basic activities, such as walking around. Paranoia is only getting started.

Around the turn of the century Google bought a little startup from a few people including me. It turned into the seed of the machine vision part of the company, including such initiatives as Google Goggles. I mention this to make clear that I am not writing about some remote "them" but about a world I have helped to create.

Among many other tricks, good machine vision can track where people are whenever they're in view of a 'net-connected device with a camera. Recognizing a face, for instance, or analyzing the gait (the characteristic motion of a person's walk) can do the trick. It's getting to be unusual to not be in view of such a device when in public in a city.

Machine vision has massive creepiness potential. Weren't wars fought and many lives lost precisely to prevent governments from gaining this kind of power, knowing where everyone is all the time? And yet now, because of some cultural trends, we're suddenly happy to offer exactly the same power to a few companies in California, along with whoever will come along with enough money to piggyback on them.

Long ago, working on the movie *Minority Report,* I proposed that billboards might grab the hero's face and implant it in the ads. Then he'd never be able to run away from the police, because they could just watch to see where he popped up in billboards. State surveillance without the state having to lift a finger! That's a classic Siren Server ploy, keeping an arm's length and yet enjoying information superiority. I even made a demo at the time.

Sure enough, Facebook is now bringing your friend's faces into ads, and location-based services are already targeting ads on mobile phones to specific people when they go to specific places.

Where is it all leading? The trend is toward ever more creepiness. Any of the technologies I described earlier that might put masses of people out of work,will also have vivid creepiness potential. The more a society bases itself on the wrong model of automated "efficiency," the more potential there is for sudden outbreaks of evil. There will be more players who are motivated to act outside of a social contract.

A photo that happens to include a view of someone's key chain resting on a café table might provide enough data to replicate copies of the keys. 3D printers might also be used to create parts for bombs, restraints, devices of torture, or other cruel props. (A pro gun-rights group is already distributing "open source" gun-printing files online.) Self-driving cabs might someday be hacked to hit pedestrians and run, or deliver car bombs in coordinated attacks, or kidnap someone who was expecting a quick ride.

Despite their real potential for harm, I remain of the opinion that these tools are just tools. There is nothing inherently evil in a machine vision algorithm. However, it is also inadequate to say that the only level on which to address the ethical use of tools is personal responsibility.

No, what we have to look at is economic incentives. There can never be enough police to shut down activities that align with economic motives. This is why prohibitions don't work. No amount of regulation can keep up with perverse incentives, given the pace of innovation. This is also why almost no one was prosecuted for financial fraud connected with the Great Recession.

The only effective point to intervene, to fight creepiness, is in the fundamental economic model. If the economic model tends to bring out noncreepy developments, then only true creeps will want to be creepy. True creeps will then be rare enough to be treated as a law enforcement problem. There will always be a few sociopaths and more than a few teenagers going through a phase, but society has always had to deal with those challenges. Legit companies and professionals should not be motivated to go creepy.

The long-term goal of a security strategy, for instance, cannot be to outsmart criminals, since that will only breed smart criminals. (In the short term, there are plenty of tactical occasions when one must struggle to outsmart bad guys, of course.)

The strategic goal has to be to change the game theory landscape so that the motivations for creepiness are reduced. That is the very essence of the game of civilization.

Some Good Reasons to Be Tracked by the Cloud

Given the way networks are structured now, one reaction to creepiness might be to pull back from connecting to cloud software. You might be tempted to go off the grid as much as possible to not be tracked. That would be a shame, because there are real benefits to using cloud computing, and there will be more and more benefits in the future.

People already routinely tap "yes" to allow tracking options in their phones, and then expect the cloud to recommend nearby restaurants, keep track of their jogging, and warn about where the nearby traffic jams have formed. Could there be even more compelling reasons to accept being tracked, and being observed by remote algorithms in computer clouds? Yes, there will be many good reasons. I gave one earlier: knowing your carbon footprint moment to moment.

Other examples will come about because of Mixed, or Augmented, Reality. This is a technology that brings Virtual Reality into the everyday physical world. A typical way it might work is that your sunglasses would gain the ability to add an illusion of virtual stuff placed in the physical world. The glasses might reveal something about a flower as you walk by a garden in springtime. The compatible pollinating insect could gain an annotated halo.

Seeing the living world annotated with what science has been able to learn about organisms and their interdependencies is going to become a new common joy. I've been able to experience it in Mixed Reality research and it's really wonderful. Augmenting nature might at first seem to miss the point, but it is also a way to see it in a new light without disturbing it. Don't worry about losing track of the beauty of the real world. Virtuality only makes reality look better in comparison.

Maybe the birds and bees don't excite you, but something probably would. Another potentially beneficial reason to be tracked will be keeping your life experiences with you.

For instance, suppose you once understood a tricky technical principle when a friend explained it to you, but years later understanding eludes you. Replaying the experience and circumstances of the initial exchange with your friend—perhaps using your Mixed Reality sunglasses—would be the most superb reminder.

There is no access to your memories except through resonance with either immediate experience or internal experience of related memories. While technology can't yet record and replay your inner mental state, it can record a lot about what you've sensed and done. That record can be made replayable in order to provide a wonderfully rich trove of mnemonics.

Replaying aspects of an older experience is a vivid prod to the mind, awakening dormant thoughts, sensations, emotions, and even talents. A general tool for re-creating old multisensory circumstance would open up memories, skills, and insights that would otherwise be obscure to you, even though you always carry them around hidden somewhere in your mind.

You'd dip back into your own past on those occasions when you get stuck but think there might be a clue hiding in your cortex somewhere. Where did I find that recipe? Haven't I gotten into a similar fight with my boyfriend before?*

David Gelernter's "Lifestreams"[2] was one early stab at thinking about saving what can be collected of life's memories.† My colleague Gordon Bell at Microsoft Research is another pioneer of this approach to personal information systems.[3]

In all this foundational work, the emphasis was on personal benefit. Of course, we all understood there would be creepiness potential. Alas, the real world is on the path toward creepiness.

Companies like Facebook organize many people's digital memories for the benefit of remote clients who want to manipulate what's put in front of those people. Fortunately, this commercial development has come about before the devices to collect really intimate information are available. We still have time to get this right.

---

*While I am convinced this type of design would bring wonderful value to many people, it wouldn't be for everyone. I might not use it. Possibly because my mother died when I was young, I've developed a cognitive style in which I forget a lot of what's happened, and try to only retain what seems to be most important and what works best for me. There's absolutely no reason to expect every information tech design to be right for everyone. The more powerful that personal information tech becomes, the more variety we should expect to see, unless we hope to dumb down our species to have limited variation in cognitive style.

†David and I even had a consulting company together for a while, trying to get clients to try this approach to supporting human cognition.

The Creepiness Is Not in the Tech,
but in the Power We Grant to Siren Servers

Mixed Reality can get as creepy as any other advanced information technology, but the creepy part is how Siren Servers might make use of it. The technology becomes quite creepy indeed when another party is the manager and proprietor of your "externalized memories." It had never occurred to me back in my twenties that people would someday find it young and cool and hip to give that power to remote corporations.

To add to the earlier glimpses of what a creeped-out version of Mixed Reality might be like, imagine a situation where a young man returns from college and wants to reexperience his old room as he left it, before his parents turned it into a guest room. He puts his eyewear on, and a message hovers, "To recall your old room, you must check this box accepting Company X's latest changes to its privacy policy, and agree to use the company's services for personal navigation for a year, and agree to publish the book you're working on through the company's store. Otherwise, good-bye old room."

The online space feels a little creepier, a little less under individual control, every time a user is asked to acquiesce to a bunch of fine print no one reads. The reason no one reads the fine print is that even if you do take the time, there will soon be a new revision, and you'd have to make reading the stupid EULAs a full-time job. In those cases where the user is given more than an all-or-nothing choice, the options become so complex, and so dynamic, that once again it would be a full-time job just to manage the settings. This is what happens with privacy settings on Facebook. It's become a smug, geeky achievement—with bragging rights—to be able to manage them well.

The reason people click "yes" is not that they understand what they're doing, but that it is the only viable option other than boycotting a company in general, which is getting harder to do. It's yet another example of the way digital modernity resembles soft blackmail.

Maslow's Pyramid of Blackmail

Information technology changes the baseline of expectations as we go about our lives. It's not yet possible to reexplore with Mixed Reality the room you grew up in; one could argue that being denied access to that recreation would really not be a serious problem. But once people are used to having an information service, their cognitive style and capacity becomes molded by the availability of the service. To remove it later is a serious matter. So while it might not seem important today, someday it could become deeply disruptive if unseen third parties are able to manipulate virtual environments, like blocking a re-creation of a childhood room, in order to manipulate you.

This is not only a personal problem. What if the real-world signage of a store was obscured when people looked at it through popular eyewear—perhaps as retaliation because the proprietors were not paid up on some future review or check-in service?

It would also be both creepy and sad if the virtual things you saw were not seen by your friends or family because you were all locked into different contracts with opposing business empires.

It's bad enough that people can't share apps because of which phone or carrier they got locked into, but it will be worse if people can't see the same augmentations of the world they otherwise share.

The Weird Logic of Extreme Creepiness

Creepy concerns become weirdly intertwined and transformed when they are extrapolated to extremes. For instance, if we come to be utterly unconcerned about privacy, identity theft risks will be mooted. If everyone were under constant surveillance, each person would present a single, consistent, imperturbable continuity of identity and there would be no possibility of identity theft. A person whose identity was stolen would seem to suddenly split in two, or leap at the speed of light to a different location. Someone somewhere would always be looking, so you couldn't get away with that sort of thing anymore.

One aspect of "identity" is to secure unique access to one's assets. But why worry about whether someone stole your guitar/bicycle/shoes if any 3D printer can just spit out replacements?

What if everyone were really able to spy on everyone equally? Some believe they see this state of affairs emerging in today's Internet, though it is not so. Players are actually highly segregated by technical ability, and, for big players, by ownership of central, privileged servers with closed internal data, and by control of other people's connectivity. But if it *were* true that we could all spy on each other equally, then some utopian thoughts would become possible. Perhaps there would be more of a sense of privacy in big numbers. At some point no one would care anymore if a congressman tweeted a picture of his penis. Yawn. When people don't care enough to look, then privacy will be restored. This is a common hope in the "transparency" movement.

The golden rule might become hard to distinguish from ambient blackmail if blackmail really becomes ambient enough. A society-wide "mutually assured destruction" effect could motivate a mutually respectful social contract, improving security. If everyone were equally vulnerable to creepiness, then there would be less creepiness. If a lulz-seeker were always just as easy to identify and harass as a victim of online humiliation, then there would be a lot less online humiliation. It's an interesting idea, and yet that's neither the world we live in, nor the one we are approaching if we keep to the present course.

The problem with pretty digital utopian ideas is the Siren Server. We are not building a society of mutuality, where everyone is a first-class citizen in the information space.

The way digital networks have been designed by fashion, though not by necessity, creates ultravaluable central nodes that spawn temptations for bad actors, whether those actors are traditional legitimate players or not.

The best way to reduce temptation to act abusively is to distribute value, power, and clout less centrally. The best way to do that is to enable a more comprehensive commercial sphere than the one in place today.

CHAPTER 30

A Stab at
Mitigating Creepiness

Commercial Rights Scale Online
Where Civil Rights Don't

To participate in the online world lately, such as by using Facebook, means to either renounce privacy or accept a significant burden of becoming your own programmer. You must tweak the way you connect to the various Siren Servers as best you can, in order to forestall undesired interactions between them. The data available on a social network might provide the clues to guess your password on an online store, or your struggle to get a loan might show up in a misleading way on a credit report.

Suppose, though, that any cloud computer operator, whether it is a social network, an eclectic Wall Street scheme, or even a government agency, is required to pay you for useful data that is derived from you. Any Siren Server will then have a full-fledged commercial relationship with you. You will have intrinsic, inalienable *commercial* rights to data that wouldn't exist without you.

This means, for instance, that Facebook would be sending you little payments when data derived automatically from you helped some business successfully pitch a friend of yours to buy something. If your face shows up in an ad, you get paid. If you are tracked while you walk around town, and that helps a government become aware that pedestrian safety could be improved with better signage, you'd get a micropayment for having contributed valuable data.

Commercial rights are better suited for the multitude of quirky little situations that will come up in real life than new kinds of civil rights along the lines of digital privacy.

There are always tricky questions about how to interpret a digital right. You probably agree that it's still okay to be photographed in public, in a pre-network-age sense, but it also might feel creepy to have a multitude of automatically generated photographs collated in a remote server to generate a comprehensive record of everything you do in public. How do you draw the line between these two cases?

Even if a clear line can be drawn, how can a prohibition be enforced? It would be as impossible as preventing music piracy. You will never know which unseen Siren Servers are compiling dossiers. Or more specifically you will never know as long as we continue to use networks as they are built today, because information about you can be copied without a trace.

As I've argued earlier, a world of universal commercial information rights would also be *better* for a company like Facebook, since there are more opportunities in an expanding overall market than in a shrinking one, and companies like Facebook are currently causing more shrinkage than growth overall.

Online empires might be a little slow in catching on to their own long-term self-interests, however. So, would companies still ask you to click on a form no one ever reads that signs away commercial rights, for free, forever, as they do now? Of course they would, but since there would be real money at stake, there would be a new ecosystem of middlemen and lawyers motivated to help you retrieve the money due because of your commercial rights in exchange for a cut.

Ouch! Do we really want that world, filled with litigation? I'll admit right out front that the future proposed here will have its annoyances, and yet I must also argue that in the long term you have to pick your poisons. The rancor of lawyers and middlemen won't be nearly as ridiculous as the current intractable farce of attempting to set policies and prohibitions to preserve rights in unboundedly complex, unforeseen scenarios.

This proposal suggests a future in which people will have something at stake, something worth arguing about, so there will be arguments. That is the price of not turning into lightweight fodder in someone else's aggregation fantasies.

Commercial Rights Are Actionable

Once the data measured off a person creates a debt to that person, a number of systemic benefits will accrue. For just one example, for the first time there will be accurate accounting of who has gathered what information about whom. No amount of privacy and disclosure law will accomplish what accounting will do when money is at stake.

In the days before digital networking, we typically didn't have to worry about petty little imbalances of information and power, because information technologies were too weak to matter. For instance, it was generally accepted that a photographer could take a picture in public without getting consent from other subjects who were also in public.

However, there was a petty power imbalance in that someone who was photographed didn't necessarily know that a picture had been taken. The photographer had the upper hand, and photographers relished that status. Nonetheless, it was a minor inequity, occasionally leading to paparazzi tensions, but not so serious as to potentially undermine a social contract.

Networked cameras are powerful enough, however, that what used to be a minor power imbalance becomes a major one. If a company or government can know what everyone is doing always, but the observed people don't know as much, then most people are put at a serious information disadvantage. Universal tracking by cameras, all the time, would realize one of the most familiar dark science fiction nightmares. A person raised in such a world would never know dignity.

So now that we have networked cameras, the traditional information inequity of photography is so amplified that it is no longer survivable. People now deserve to know when and how they are tracked.

And yet, how could an equitable power balance in photography be implemented, if it is to be considered only as an abstract right?

319

Who has the time to review all the photographs taken of oneself in public? There will be thousands, millions. What to do about the ones you feel should not be part of the records used to influence your credit, or other prospects? Do you call the police or some new type of online arbitration bureau? It is inconceivable that mankind could have the time to adjudicate information disputes in the terms of regulations and rights.

But commercial rights could be tractable. Every photo of you would be registered not only in photographers' accounts, but also in yours. There would then be duplicate records, as there always are in business, so that fraud would become nontrivial.

More important, you would automatically share proceeds in commercial rights to any profitable use made of photographs of you, according to the policies you've set for "instant" transactions. Some people might choose more privacy and demand so much money as to make the use of their photographs prohibitive. Most people will choose some reasonable, conventional setting.

What that will mean is that enough people will allow themselves to be tracked to generate data for things like improving pedestrian safety, but people will still have the dignity to choose their own balance of privacy versus being tracked.

A criminal who sets a high price on his data to avoid being tracked while committing a crime will find himself owing that amount if law enforcement has to get a warrant to track him in order to gain a conviction. On the other hand, if law enforcement doesn't get a conviction, the price of the data will be taken out of a department's budget. This balance of power can be tweaked to find a reasonable sweet spot generally balancing police effectiveness and civil liberties protection. Maybe the police would only owe up to a fixed limit, unlike civilian actors. However, a reasonable, intermediate solution to the quandary of access to digital information would come about without requiring constant reinterpretation.

Moderation, according to terms set in advance, will strengthen both the police and civil liberties. Civil libertarians will have access to good data, since everyone will have commercial rights to their own accounts, and will have civil recourses, which are more predictable, and easier to fund.

Meanwhile, the police will be able to leverage the consistency of cloud-monitored physicality to detect criminal schemes. As pointed out earlier, you can fake an ID, but you can't fake a thousand concurrent views of the person you are falsely pretending to be. The police will have to pay to access those views, just as they have to pay for cars and bullhorns these days. Policing should never be "free" in a democracy. All things must be balanced.

Commercial rights might be the only approach to digital privacy that opens up a path to moderation. Privacy in a humanistic economy will no longer be all-or-nothing. Instead it will cost real money to access your information. Sometimes some of your photographs might be worth accessing, other times not. All your data won't always be available for free to the advantage of whoever has assembled the best cloud computer at the moment.

Extending the commercial sphere genuinely into the information space will lead to a more moderate, balanced world. What we've been doing instead is treating information commerce as a glaring exception to the equity that underlies democracy.

The Ideal Price of Information Equals the Minimization of Creepiness

Some libertarian idealists would prefer that markets be freed from regulators. Let's for a moment, though, assume that a regulatory function will still find a place in the economies of the future.

In that case, a regulator might seek a principle for tweaking policies to make sure that information isn't becoming too cheap or too expensive overall. If it were to become too expensive, not only would less successful people be thrown into a vicious circle of disenfranchisement, but the economy could also stall because innovation would become too expensive. If information becomes too cheap, the Siren Server pattern could reappear, which would lead to massive unemployment and economic contraction. As always, a sweet spot is found approximately, somewhere in the middle.

A good measure of the sweet spot would be the amount of creepiness. The correct price of information should be the price at which a Siren Server can make no money without adding value to the information it has gathered, but the price should not be so high that adding value can't generate a profit. (An excessive price would mean upstream players are exerting blackmail-like influence.) In other words, the right price minimizes creepiness.

In the world foreseen in this book, a Siren Server of any type would have to pay for the information gathered about you proportionally to the value of that information, as determined by expectations for future transactions. "Spying" on you would still occur, especially when you are the customer for a service related to you. However, in the event a company offers you something worth paying for over the network, that success would have to be based primarily on some creation of value beyond spying, based on the unique competence of the seller.

Nothing is outlawed in the scenario imagined here. No moralists or absolutists have descended on business, tsk-tsking about privacy. There are no boycotts or shunnings. Neither are there mad campaigns by entrepreneurs to grab as much of what had been private data as possible, as we now endure from credit agencies or companies like Facebook. Instead a path of moderation appears where previously there was only black-and-white.

Individual Players Will Also Be Motivated to Set Prices to Minimize Creepiness

There will still be buyers of influence, like the so-called advertisers Google and Facebook are fighting over these days, but they'll have to take into account the cost of the information they've measured off of you in order to influence you, and the cost of that information will be proportional to its value. Simply spying on you to manipulate you—into paying more than your neighbors for the same thing, for instance, with no other added value—will cease to be a commercial option.

This is a subtler concept than it might seem to be at first glance. You'll set the price of information that exists because you exist. More likely, you'll pay a service to do that, since it would be a hassle to constantly worry about it. What should the price be? Make it too high and no one will buy. Make it too low and you're not making as much as you might be able to.

The ideal price of data would remove the profit from buying access to data for its own sake. The profit would then have to come from adding value.

If a Siren Server can spend a dollar to peek at data that manipulates you to spend an extra two dollars, then the server will earn a dollar profit. However, a "what if" calculation will have automatically been performed to calculate that, and will determine that actually you are owed a significant royalty on the use of your own information once it is put to a profitable purpose, even if that purpose is to manipulate you.

So you might get a rebate of, say seventy-five cents. The Siren Server might be motivated to lobby politicians to change the rules to make this transaction turn out less in your favor, but then there would be many other transactions that would also turn out less in the Siren Server's favor, since it is playing fundamentally the same game you are playing. You and the server are both first-class citizens, with a common stake in the same set of rules.

An online retailer could still compete on pricing, service, user interface and presentation, and all sorts of other things, but it would no longer be profitable to raise prices on those customers who could be predicted to be the easiest victims of a price-gouging ploy. The spy data that would make the targeting of the gambit possible would cost too much. A Siren Server could still make itself better, but it would no longer be profitable to make itself worse. This is an essential benefit of making it cost money to spy on people.

A vendor who finds it worthwhile to use data about you or anyone else would only be able to create a business if the unique value it could add to the data were profitable enough to more than pay for the data. Spy data *in the abstract* would ideally become worthless, because its expenses, in the form of nanopayments out to the people who were measured, would tend to approximately balance the benefits of using it naively.

Using "spy data" will often still make commercial sense, and there will no doubt continue to be controversies about what uses of data are proper, no matter what economic practices are in place. There will always be a need for advocates of rights, including rights to privacy. Innovative companies will still need to sell themselves to a skeptical public on occasion.

Getting away from extreme outcomes is crucial if we are to find our way to a high-tech but humane future. We can't turn into zero or one bits. We can't be expected to either give up privacy entirely or hoard it insanely.

The best ideas are ones that can be pursued fanatically, as digital innovators like to pursue things, but which inherently lead to moderate outcomes. Modern democracies and markets occasionally display this quality when functioning at their best. Ideally the architecture of digital networks, which are so able to enact sudden large-scale social change, will evolve to mediate instead of divide.

Limits Are for Mortals

FROM SOCIAL NETWORK TO IMMORTALITY

The Singularity University is located right next to Google, in Mountain View, California, on the grounds of a NASA research center that has been semiprivatized in keeping with the austere trends of our times. The university is a real place with some fine, smart people. It supports interesting research, and offers excellent classes, and yet I tend to make fun of it. Periodically, someone involved in it will reach out and I always feel a little awkward trying to explain my amusement, because there really is something of a gulf of perception that can be quite hard to bridge.

The Singularity, recall, is the idea that not only is technology improving, but the speed of improvement is increasing, as well. If you visit the campus, expect to be browbeaten about how you, as a mere muggle, don't have the intuition to grasp the implications of that profound fact. We ordinary humans are supposedly staying the same (a claim I reject), while our technology is an autonomous, self-transforming supercreature, and its self-improvement is accelerating. That means it will one day pass us in a great whoosh. In the blink of an eye we will become obsolete. We might then be instantly dead, because the new artificial superintelligence will need our molecules for a much higher purpose. Or maybe we'll be kept as pets.

Ray Kurzweil, who helped found the university, awaits a Virtual Reality heaven that all our brains will be sucked up into as the Singularity occurs, which will be "soon." There we will experience "any" scenario, any joy.

Others simply expect that medical knowledge will deterministically be accelerated as well, granting people physical immortality. To the old question about where everyone will live if people live forever but still want to have children, there are answers. Starships, of course. But also, engineer people to be smaller. I remember Marvin Minsky suggesting this option decades ago, and it recurs regularly in Singulatarian circles.

This is the sort of fantasy that drives many—and I would actually guess most—successful young entrepreneurs and engineers in Silicon Valley these days. The idea is that the amazing lift you get from starting a 'net-based business that can become huge in just a few years is the fore-echo of something far more profound that you will be able to achieve almost as quickly. Soon technological prowess will make the cleverest hackers not only immortal but immortal superheroes.

Earlier, I noted that Peter Thiel, founder of PayPal and an investor in Facebook, teaches a class at Stanford in which he advocates that students *not* think in terms of competing in a marketplace, but in terms of defining a position they can "monopolize." This is precisely the idea of the Siren Server. It is a given that in Silicon Valley no one wants to suffer the indignity of sharing a market with competitors.

It is the correlate that must be understood. Thiel also advocates an end to death, to be enjoyed by the alpha proprietors of network-based monopolies. The flood of data about biology ought to be churned by cloud-based algorithms into an antidote to mortality in no time at all. That's the expectation. The culture of power on the 'net is so different from what people everywhere else are used to that I wonder if it's even possible to convey it. For instance, *New York Times* columnist David Brooks wrote[1] about Thiel's arguments based on a student's notes,[2] posted online. What he didn't comment on was the headline on the student's offering:

> Your mind is software. Program it. Your body is a shell. Change it. Death is a disease. Cure it. Extinction is approaching. Fight it.

What most outsiders have failed to grasp is that the rise to power of 'net-based monopolies coincides with a new sort of religion based on becoming immortal.

SUPERNATURAL TEMPTATIONS IN TECH CULTURE

Silicon Valley is far from the first society sprouting from protean quests. The modern spectacle of engineers professing a mastery of mortality— and even seeming to also believe themselves on occasion—is not new at all.

Would it surprise you to learn that animal sacrifice once played a critical role in an early contest to be the "most meta" network? The contest for electricity was fought between the master dramatists Nikola Tesla and Thomas Edison. Tesla had a mad, romantic technical career. He rarely missed an opportunity to be notorious and strange. At one party he illuminated the air and in another he injected acoustic frequencies designed to make guests urinate involuntarily. These would be radical things to do today, but at that time they were practically supernatural. Edison on the surface was more the straight man, but actually he played a similar game. Electricity was, aside from being a physical phenomenon, a folk tale with Grand Guignol undertones from its earliest days.

The physician Giovanni Aldini had made a spectacle of using electrodes to make freshly dead corpses twitch at public demonstrations around the beginning of the 19th century. He created a public career a little like Ray Kurzweil's today, claiming to have highly technical knowledge that would end the old cycle of life and death. He might have inspired Mary Shelley's character Dr. Frankenstein.

The audacious race to bring the force of life and death into sockets in every home tempted every theatrical impulse. So, Edison made a public spectacle of electrocuting an elephant. Ostensibly, this demonstrated the demon in Tesla's design of electricity (alternating current, AC), but Edison would certainly have understood that his own offering, direct current, DC, could also kill the beast.

I sometimes think of that elephant when I plug a phone into the wall to charge. The electricity works because of basic and universal laws of nature, but would not be there, as it is, where it is, were it not for the dark mythmaking of technologists.

Singularity University is part of a grand tradition. Most techies are not great showmen, but whenever the combination appears, watch out.

JUST FOR THE RECORD, WHY I MAKE FUN OF THE UNIVERSITY

Obviously, however rich the cultural pedigree might be, I think calling an institution of higher learning the Singularity University is ridiculous. I'll outline my position: I am not questioning whether any particular piece of technology is possible. In fact I work on some of the components that my friends at the university consider harbingers of the Singularity. For instance, I've worked on making predictive models of parts of the human brain, and on direct interfaces between computers and the human nervous system.

The difference is that I think these things are done by researchers, of whom I am but one. I do not think the technology is creating itself. It's not an autonomous process. It's something we humans do.

Of course, you can always play with figure-ground reversals, as we saw earlier with the Golden Goblet. The reason to believe in human agency over technological determinism is that you can then have an economy where people earn their own way and invent their own lives. If you structure a society on *not* emphasizing individual human agency, it's the same thing operationally as denying people clout, dignity, and self-determination.

So, in an absolute sense, there's no way to prove that the Singularity would be the wrong way to interpret certain future events. But to embrace the sensibility would be a celebration of bad data and bad politics. Of course, if you really believe people and machines are the same, then you won't recognize this as a well-formed pragmatic argument.

Where a true believer at the university would see a Singularity occurring sometime in the future, I would see a mess of engineering that was so bad and irresponsible that it was killing a lot of people, as is portrayed in Forster's "The Machine Stops." Let's look at it my way and not kill those people, okay?

WILL THE CONTROL OF DEATH BE A CONVERSATION OR A CONFLAGRATION?

We are witnessing the beginning of a new kind of death denial. Although Facebook arose fairly recently, we already see what happens when a Facebook user dies. For young users, in particular, it sometimes happens that friends will take over the site and keep it animated for some time, as if the person were still there a little bit.[3] The U.S. military funded a research initiative looking into making interactive video simulations of fallen soldiers so that their families could still interact with them.[4] The late hip-hop artist Tupac Shakur was presented as a "holographic" performer with optical tricks onstage.[5]

This is an intimate matter, and I'm loath to judge what other people do about their dead, but I do feel it's essential to point out that when we animate the dead, we reduce the distinction we feel with the living. All is relative. We reduce the sense of the weirdness of being alive.

One of the most successful individual network-oriented financiers is not someone I can name. He has amassed one of the world's great fortunes using computers to fine-tune complicated international transactions. He feels confident he is doing well for the world, propelling mankind forward, growing capital for everyone. (Whether he is or not is not clear to me.)

He is also an unfettered health and fitness nut. When money is no object, the quest for ultimate health and fitness becomes an often bizarre tour of the world's visionaries and charlatans, and no amount of money can distinguish them perfectly.

Given all this, I was quite surprised when one day this fellow said to me, "Capitalism is only possible because of death." He had been visiting with some of the many researchers on the circuit of cyber-insiders who think they can solve the problem of death fairly soon. Genes modulate aging and death, and those genes appear to be tweakable.

Death, he explained, is the foundation of markets. This line of thinking is obvious and perhaps it's not necessary to state it, but: That people age and die is what makes room for new people to find their places, so that aspiration is possible. If individuals were no longer temporary, then the species would enter into a worse-than-medieval stasis of eternal, absolutely boring winners. Plutocracy would suffocate creativity definitively.

THE TWO TIERS OF IMMORTALITY PLANNED FOR THIS CENTURY

Recall, however, the accelerating technology trends that form the upside-down slide upon which the imaginations of Silicon Valley glide ever upward. Death is under assault. A weird science meeting at Google or one of the other usual venues wouldn't be complete without presentations on ending death. The message is usually that we're just a pinch away from it. Correcting for the common illusions, we are probably just decades away from it, at least in theory.

So there are two tech trends related to countering death, one based on a media technology and the other on biology. Both will take decades to advance.

Some years from now, a good-enough simulation of a dead person might "pass the Turing Test," meaning that a dead soldier's family might treat a simulation of the soldier as real. In the tech circles where one finds an obsession with the technologies of immortality, the dominant philosophical tendency is to accept artificial intelligence as a well-formed engineering project, a view I reject. But to those who believe in it, a digital ghost that has passed the Turing Test has passed the test of legitimacy.

There is, nonetheless, also a fascination with *actually* living longer through medicine. It's an interesting juxtaposition. AI and Turing Test–passing ghosts might be good enough for ordinary people, but the tech elites and the superrich would prefer to do better than that. The social outcome we seem to be approaching later in the century would grant simulated immortality for ordinary people, which could only be enjoyed by observers, not the actual dead, while the very rich might enjoy actual methusalization.

One of the keenest reasons to want a middle-class distribution of wealth is to avoid a situation in which a small number of wealthy individuals live very long lives while no one else can afford the same life extensions.

In my breakfast conversations about artificial hearts with Marvin

Minsky, so long ago, he proposed that life extension could become so cheap that it would be universal. What we've seen, though, is that when some things become very cheap, other things become very expensive. Printers are incredibly cheap, and yet ink for them is incredibly expensive. Phones are cheap and yet connectivity for them is insanely expensive. Wal-Mart is cheap, and yet jobs go away. Software is "free" and yet the Internet is not creating as many jobs as it destroys.

The talking seagull from the first chapter is probably more realistic than universal life extension for all in a world where clout and wealth flow to Siren Servers.

A great showdown will occur when lives are extended significantly for the first time. My guess is that this won't happen in the United States first. Russian oligarchs[6] or Gulf sheiks might step up initially.

If there's a clock ticking to get a monetized information economy started, this is it. Will there be middle-class wealth and clout to balance the potential of masters of Siren Servers to become near-immortal plutocrats? This is the scenario H. G. Wells foresaw in *The Time Machine*.

If the middle classes are strong when the time comes, some sort of compromise will be sorted out; some new social contract about how medicine is applied once the idea of a "natural" lifetime becomes as anachronistic as the idea of a "natural" climate.

If the middle classes are weak, then chaos will unfold. People usually protest in a reasonably orderly fashion against austerity. If they come to see that their families must die before those of a weird insular upper class, there will be no restraint. As much as we like to romanticize revolutions, they are a form of terror in practice. It would be wise to institute a universal system to strengthen the middle classes before the destined moment arrives.

PART NINE

Transition

CHAPTER 31

The Transition

Can There Be a Digital Golden Rule?

The most common question I have heard since I started talking about the prospects for a Nelsonian economy is about enforcement. Why wouldn't people copy? Why not cheat? Why not let other people suffer for the risk you bring into the world?

The reason people won't copy—or exploit information without paying for it—is that to copy would be to undermine the very source of their own wealth. This is what the golden rule looks like on a network.

A social contract must take hold for any orderly economy to be possible. Any functioning, authentic economy has to by definition be sustained more by voluntary participation than by enforcement. In the physical world it's not all that hard to break into someone's house or car, or to shoplift, and there aren't all that many police. The police have a crucial role, but the main reason people don't go around stealing in the physical world is that they want to live in a world where stealing isn't commonplace.

Some readers will prefer a moral formulation to an ethical one, and would say that stealing is simply wrong. In either case, the point is that there could never be enough police to enforce a standard of behavior that most people reject.

It saddens me that even idealistic digital activists often assume that enforcement is the key question. We've become used to a double standard online, where there's either an often mean-spirited, hostile anarchy or one submits to institutional control. Anarchy reigns on sites like 4chan or in uncensored comments on videos or articles. Meanwhile most content and expression flows through institutional channels like app stores or social networks in which censorious policies are enforced. Neither situation supports real freedom. (Many of the most supposedly open and free online designs are often actually choked by a controlling elite.)[1] Real freedom has to be based on most people choosing to give each other latitude most of the time.

History records many instances of workable social contracts breaking down. States fail and murderous spasms overtake whole populations. But history also records "miracles," instances of decent social contracts being initiated. The American experiment was one instance, but so is the initiation of any inclusive democracy. The early rise of the World Wide Web, before Siren Servers overtook it, was another miracle.

The instantiation of a social contract "miracle" is a big jump over a valley in an energy landscape. It might take a political figure of rare genius, or the right lucky confluence of events, but it is ridiculous to think that a beneficial social contract could not take hold for the majority of people in their online lives.

Yes, enforcement will be an issue, but it only makes sense to talk about enforcement when only a small minority of a population are offenders. Civilization will remain by definition a mostly voluntary project, a miracle.

The Miracle's Gauntlet

One of the hardest questions about a humanistic economic scenario is how to get there from where we are. Who will step up and take risks in order to learn if this new world will come about? It's not only a political challenge, but an economic one, since a present economy of a certain size must somehow fund a quantum leap to a new, larger economy despite a gigantic accounting vacuum. How would the initial surge of required credit be financed?

The higher altitudes of finance have become used to "sure things" that recently flowed rather easily. It's hard to bring expectations back down to earth after a period like the Great Recession, which offered such treats to financiers. Finance was freed from having to pay for risk, though that bargain was only a temporary illusion; ordinary people were freed from having to pay for consumption of Internet services, though once again, an illusion was at play.

The temptations of free stuff over digital networks recall problems in American health care finance. No one wants to pay for something if they can possibly avoid it; so young healthy people don't like to pay for health insurance. In an immediate sense, the ability to not pay seems to increase wealth and freedom for those who can get away with it.

But then later, when inevitable health problems come up, illusion turns out to cost more both in money and in lost freedom than up-front realism. When a system is in place for everyone to share risk in advance, life doesn't become perfect, but dealing with hard times at least becomes cheaper and more flexible.

Nonetheless, to get people to agree to pay to care for each other in advance requires political genius. Maybe it helps if everyone looks similar. Homogeneous societies seem to have an easier time of it. A common enemy doesn't hurt, either. The online world fails miserably at providing any such traditional inspirations.

Avatars and Credit

The cognitively gentle mechanism of economic avatars gives a hint about how a transition might work. The fluid nature of digital systems would allow for the coexistence of both old and new economic systems during a transitional period, which would motivate a gradual person-by-person transition.

Each person could remain in the world of fake "free" for as long as desired. However, a person could also eventually decide when she's had enough of "free" and would prefer to buy into a commercial social contract where she can earn money.

This means that two sets of accounting books would be kept for people who aren't paying for information, so that they can transition from "free" to universal micropayments whenever the time comes. A delayed choice could give people the best of both worlds.

If the core hypothesis is right—that monetizing more information instead of less will grow the economy—then a lot of people will end up with money due to them after enough time has passed. At some point, you might decide you want to cash in all that's due to you, even if the price is that you can no longer get free stuff online thereafter.

The Price of Antenimbosia

A trickier question is how to design the initial state of a new information economy to reflect all that had been done by people before the new accounting was initiated.

Wikipedia has procedures in place to incorporate material from the 1911 edition of the *Encyclopaedia Britannica,* which has fallen into the public domain. When we build on the past in that way, how will we acknowledge it in a *monetized* information economy?

Earlier it was pointed out that the seeming magic of cloud-based "automatic" translation between languages is actually based on the use of a corpus of translations performed by real people originally. Had a better-crafted information economy been in play when the original human translators provided their examples to the cloud, then they would be remembered and we could send royalties to those still living.

However, they missed the boat, so now we don't have a reasonable way to reconstitute the provenance that should have been stored. We threw away crucial information because of incomplete engineering. Whenever an advanced information economy comes into being, this will be a rancorous intergenerational social justice issue. A grand bargain will be needed.

Will everyone from the lost generations—which acquiesced to "free" and "shared" for the sake of the wealth of Siren Servers—get a huge initial credit based on all the off-the-books value that each might have provided? This intuitively sounds like a bad idea. Big payments at the start of a financial adventure often don't work out well. People who win the lottery don't necessarily have any of the money left after a few years. There needs to be a process in which people get used to earning their way in a new game.

Some sort of rough augmentation of income will probably be due to people who contributed a lot but received little from the Sirenic economy.

If this sounds like an outrageous idea to young cyber-activists now, it will sound awfully nice to them in, say, thirty or forty years. At some point, a transition along these lines will have to take place. It will probably happen after the disaster of the crest of the age wave of baby boomers.

CHAPTER 32

Leadership

Audition for the Lead

If we can overcome Panglossian vanities, and we can also accept the possibility that human actors in our drama can and should take responsibility for events they can knowingly steer—two admittedly hard sells in today's cyber-world—then what actors might step up to take some risks and responsibilities in order to explore the possibility of better information economics?

Here are some of the actors who might show up for an audition:

- A thousand geeks
- Startups
- Traditional governments, central banks, etc.
- Multiplicities of Siren Servers
- Facebook or similar
- Confederacies of Just a few Giant Siren Servers

In the next few sections I'll sketch what scenes these varied players might play. I expect to hear the usual objections that this is a case where thought is moot. Instead, I am often told, we should simply let events play out.

The future always arrives, eventually. Rome fell, and eventually there was a Renaissance.* In order to be concerned with the ques-

---

*If gobs of middle-class jobs go away later in this century, and then there is a socialist backlash that seems pleasant for a moment but then turns morbidly corrupt, and then a backlash against the backlash . . . then in the next century or the one after we will eventually still get to the business of creating a humanistic information economy.

tions asked here, one has to be able to evince at least a meek sense of urgency. If there is to be any difference in time to make a difference to people living, or to their children, then some form of action and actor must appear.

A Thousand Geeks

Since no one else can keep up, highly effective technical people can still make up the future, unfettered to an amazing degree. The society of the brightest computer scientists and engineers is also amazingly small. A thousand top geeks working together could steer the future of the world economy.

That is not to say that even this modest scale of cooperation is likely to appear. It could also be said that a thousand top politicians around the world could work together to steer the political future. That is also a true statement, and yet there is no reason to believe it will happen.

But this is a book of hypotheticals, speculation, advocacy, and the invocation of hope, so why not imagine a thousand top engineers deciding to work together to preserve middle classes and democracy in information economies?

Maybe we'd have one of our typically weird meetings at a quirky, neutral location. There would be popcorn and robots.

We would come up with something along the lines of what was proposed in the "space elevator pitch." We would just do this, without waiting for approval. The management at the various companies would just have to deal with it.

We'd congratulate ourselves for saving the world again, and then order a truckload of espresso and pizza and program something like a tattoo-creating robot overnight. We'd go to bed the next morning, perhaps sore from our fresh robot-applied tattoos, but also ready to sleep very well, knowing that we had not put tattoo artists out of work.

Startups

It happens almost every day. I get a pitch from someone with a startup that hopes to create a humanistic economy out of a little seed. A tiny website with no financing, but just the right design at just the right time, just might grow the way Facebook did, changing the world. It might be something like a social network where people are encouraged to pay each other for contributions from the start.

I don't read these, because I'm not in the startup game these days, and am doing research within the labs of one of the big companies, so it would really not be appropriate. But also, while it's perhaps not an impossible way to make progress, it is probably the hardest way.

A humanistic-economy startup would have to become a Siren Server in order to gain the clout to curb what Siren Servers do. If someone can pull it off, I'll cheer, but it's an intrinsically self-contradictory plan.

That's not to say there's no role for startups that are compatible with humanistic computing ideals. Kickstarter is an example brought up earlier. Maybe a startup can introduce a new template for personal activity that can evolve to have the key benefits of a job even though it isn't called a job. Kickstarter, Etsy, ancient eBay, and similar efforts are legitimate baby steps in that direction. (For that matter, so was Second Life, the now-somewhat-stale virtual world service in which people created, bought, and sold virtual stuff.) Such efforts are in harmony with the principles of humanistic computing.

Even if Kickstarter becomes superhuge, however, even big like an Apple, it probably wouldn't become big enough to compensate for the jobs to be lost to self-driving vehicles and automated manufacturing and resource extraction. It might be one of those paths that could work out well if only we had more time than we do. There has to be a phase change in the whole economy.

The notion that bottom-up change is the only kind of change tends to feed into the problems a humanistic economy would hopefully correct. The reason why is that it's dishonest. It is never true that there is no top-down component to power and influence. Those who cling to the hope that power can be made simple only blind themselves to the latest forms of top-down power.

Every attempt to create a pure bottom-up, emergent network to coordinate human affairs also facilitates some new hub that inevitably becomes a center of power, even if that was not the intent. In the old days, that might have been a communist party. These days, if everything is open, anonymous, and copyable, then a search/analysis company with a bigger computer than normal people have access to will come along to measure and model everything that takes place, and then sell the resulting ability to influence events to third parties. The whole supposedly open system will contort itself to that Siren Server, creating a new form of centralized power. Mere openness doesn't work. A Linux always makes a Google.

The only way to create a distribution of clout on a digital network that isn't overly centralized, so that middle classes and a maximally competitive marketplace can exist, is to be honest about the existence of top-down dynamics from the start. Putting oneself into a childlike position is only an invitation to someone else to play the parent.

That said, a startup-driven scenario is not absolutely impossible. A new startup could conceivably gain more clout than Facebook, and then stay true to its original intent, goading a critical mass of other, older Siren Servers into a new, humanistic phase of activity.

The startup experience is wonderful. I am grateful that I have been able to start companies, and I wish everyone could. If you have a passion to try the startup game, go for it, especially if you don't have children yet. You might get rich, but probably not. You'll learn a great deal, including how hard you can push yourself.

So if you have a startup idea that might help, don't let me discourage you—but also don't send me your business plan.

We should, however, be thinking at least partially in a top-down way about making sure that the information that should be monetized is monetized. This might rub a lot of people the wrong way; bottom-up, self-organizing dynamics are so trendy. But while *accounting* can happen locally between individuals, *finance* relies on some rather boring agreements about conventions on a global, top-down basis. If you repudiate that way of thinking, you make it a lot harder to build up the replacements for the failing levees of the middle class.

Traditional Governments, Central Banks, etc.

It's hard not to be trapped in one's historical moment. The moment during which I'm writing is one in which central banks are not universally trusted, to say the least, and the very idea of government has become a burden to be tolerated but mostly scorned. And yet in my parents' generation, government in the United States created Social Security, went to the moon, and built the Interstate Highway System. It's highly unlikely the unity of systems we call the Internet would have come into existence without government leadership. Governments lately seem timid, beleaguered, and incompetent to keep up with the times. The very thought of regulators keeping up with Silicon Valley or the latest schemes in networked finance! Good luck with that.

Maybe someday government will come back. If and when that happens, then ideas related to those I am sketching here might be expressed in petitions to government, and those petitions might elicit effective action.

Maybe government will never come back. Maybe the power of digital networks is so great that traditional politics can no longer retain its former status. Maybe network tech and finance companies will from here on out be too international, too sophisticated, and too engrained in the affairs of everyone for governments to be able to figure out how to regulate them.

So maybe government gets left behind. Maybe from here on out, the race for Siren Servers might create the new history that matters, and political rights for typical people will only be won by wrestling with whoever gains control of the top servers.

There's a romance in that future, especially for hackers, and it seems to be the future most envisioned in techie culture. It comes up in science fiction constantly: The hacker as hero, outwitting the villain's computer security. But what a crummy world that would be, where screwing up something online is the last chance at being human and free. A good world is one where there's meaning outside of sabotage. Surely it isn't overly utopian to seek that modest virtue in our future.

But then again, maybe government's underdog days are temporary. We live in anomalous times in more than one way. Age waves are overtaking most of the developed world. Good medicine means a lot of old people, who get cranky and control a lot of wealth and votes. Good medicine yields a golden age for the crankiest pundits and politicians.

Not only that, but the immigration waves enabled by modernity have resulted in ethnic shifts in many of the same places with the fastest-growing populations of old people. That's a recipe for universally nutty politics. The window to remake the digital world might only open as the baby boomers, and even me and my dizzy compatriots of "Generation X," die off. Politics and economics might be reborn around the middle of this century once we, and probably also the "Facebook generation," get out of the way.

My primary plea to future technocrats is, please be experimental, patient, nonideological, and slow-moving enough to learn lessons. Find your excitement somewhere other than in manipulating the nature of the economy. The economy is one of those things, like health, that should usually be reliable, constant, and boring.

Multiplicities of Siren Servers

How many Siren Servers are there at present? My sense is that there are many dozens of unavoidable ones, plus thousands of others that will touch your life on occasion. There are perhaps ten that an average person knowingly interacts with directly and frequently, such as Facebook. There are about twice that many in finance, "big data marketing research," and health care that impose a direct influence on most people's lives; many of them are almost unknown to the world at large. There are also the major national intelligence services, illicit efforts, and nonprofit hubs.

Is it possible that this number could increase vastly in the future? If there were many thousands of Siren Servers, it would not create a middle class, but it might at least create an extended persistent upper class that would create enough of a service economy to support a middle class doing things that won't become software-mediated.

But another possibility is that there could be tens of millions of Siren Servers, or maybe even more. A sufficient number of them would create a middle class. At present, this is not how networks seem to be evolving. The big Siren Servers nurture but demonetize niches for small-scale information hubs routinely.

Small policy changes might reverse this trend and create tens of millions of micro spy agencies. For instance, it could become illegal to record information about more than one hundred people on the basis of click-through agreements without direct negotiation for financial compensation to the people whose data is stored. Intermediaries would appear to negotiate data fees.

Suddenly small players, like tiny publishers or record labels, or in the future, esoteric 3D product design houses, would become valuable. That is one imaginable way to get to a humanistic information economy. Perhaps there will be an experiment someday so we can learn whether this path is navigable.

The primary path I promote, however, is to support commercial rights for individuals, not servers. Individuals can always form into groups to create risk and investment pools, but economic designs based primarily on supporting nonpersons will tend to create gaps that people fall through. Making the individual human the bearer of economic rights both preserves the most options and avoids the most pitfalls.

Facebook or Similar

What's Facebook going to do when it grows up? What if it prioritized peer-to-peer commerce? Maybe Facebook could become the seed of a humanistic information economy. That would certainly create the potential for more revenue than advertising by itself.

Is it not pathetic that the big consumer cloud companies have to compete for approximately the same customers with approximately the same product? All the cloud companies are chasing the same batch of potential so-called advertisers.

Facebook and Google have wildly different products and competencies. Why should they have to compete with one another directly?

If advertising is to be the dominant business that earns profits online, then our horizons are limited. As more and more activities become dominated by cloud software, there will be fewer pre-networked products left to advertise. For the moment we advertise physical computers, phones, and tablets, for instance. Someday, however, these items might be spit out of 3D home printers running off of open designs coming from the cloud. Then there would be no company left in the loop to pay for the ads.

Why must Google, Facebook, and the rest face a long-term future of fighting over the same limited—and ultimately diminishing—pie?

Facebook ought to be well motivated to find ways to grow the economy. Only a single person controls the company, so the means is present to overcome resistance from scaredy-cats on the board or among shareholders.

A big enough Siren Server might at least serve as the seed of a humanistic information economy. That's not to say any single big company will be big enough to change the world, but it might lead the way.

Confederacies of Just a Few Giant Siren Servers

The digital world has become remarkably consolidated. While the networking plane is often portrayed as a great wilderness of teeming, mysterious activities, it is actually mostly supervised by a small number of companies. (Even the startups that get anywhere tend to be funded by the same old small club of venture capitalists, and hope to be bought eventually by one of the few big companies.)

These companies are sometimes at each other's throats, though not always. Despite the real tensions, all the companies also maintain friendly relationships and coordinate from time to time. Almost all the Siren Servers are dependent on each other in various ways.

Had this book been written decades ago, when digital networking was still only a theory, then this next fantasy would have called for a smoke-filled room. Today it will instead be set in a clear-aired conference room at a fancy golf resort by the sea. The CEOs of the biggest network companies will sit at the big table, with lawyers and underlings seated along the walls, furiously taking notes. The chiefs of the big Silicon Valley companies will be there, along with the heads of the biggest network-oriented finance ventures.

The CEOs will gather at the golf resort and talk about a core financial problem: In the long term the economy will start to shrink if they keep on making it "efficient" only from the point of view of central servers. At the end of that line there will eventually be too little economy to support even CEOs. How about instead growing the economy?

An agreement would be hatched to make log-ins interoperable. That means someone with an Apple Store account will automatically be logged into Amazon, Windows, etc. The same would go for social networks and other varieties of sites. Each site would initiate a plan to make customers into first-class participants who are earning money as well as spending it, and to make the transition as easy as possible.

Ordinary people will initially start to earn a little when others are interested by their tweets, blogs, social network updates, videos, and the like. This will not in itself generate enough business to transform the economy, but it will serve a crucial transitional, educational function. People will become used to the idea of looking online for opportunities to earn real wealth. Instead of having such lowered expectations as to consider taking on the Mechanical Turk's piecework for a pittance, people will start to compete to sell, say, designs to be wrought by 3D printers. They won't think of earning—and earning well—as an affront to "sharing" but rather as a perfected form of sharing.

Building bridges between the big online services, and turning everyone into a first-class economic participant, might just cause a Nelsonian economy to eventually arise out of the private sector without government intervention.

From a Wall Street perspective, the heretofore unacknowledged but valuable contributions of ordinary individuals will finally be counted in the cloud. That will mean that finance can be built on *all* that people do to create value in the network age. Suddenly investors will be making money from having bet on a confederacy of bloggers (though the bloggers would know about it and risks would not be hidden, as they were when mortgages were leveraged in secret).

The economy will grow spectacularly. A golf resort will be financed on the moon for the next meeting of the CEOs.

I can hear the groans from my lefty friends. Why would we want big players involved? Big-time players aren't aliens. They're just people who are in particular positions. If we were to depose them in a revolution, a new class of big players would appear.

Why would big players cooperate? To kick the economy to the next peak in the energy landscape, great scale is needed, more scale than any one company or financial player can provide. The Apple Store and the Amazon store can't grow as much, and as fast separately as they could together in a universal market.

To understand why, recall some basic algebra. Start with Metcalf's Law, which states that the value of a network is proportional to the square of the number of nodes. The square of the number of Apple users plus the square of the number of Amazon users is far less than the square of the combined user base.

So, the moguls might realize that it makes sense to work together, in a general sort of way that increases competition but increases scale and opportunity even more.

The CEOs would not be colluding in an evil way! Please, antitrust regulators of the future, if a meeting like this seems to be happening, take a moment to think before you barge through the door and arrest everyone. If done right, this baseline of cooperation would make for a more competitive marketplace that would be good for the big businesses represented at the meeting *and* the average person—especially for the average person. This would be an excellent moment for government not to blow it.

You might think this is a mad fantasy. CEOs from all the big network companies in a room, talking to each other rationally, even as they are suing each other over patents or whatever other conflicts hold sway. Sounds unlikely. I can't argue with that assessment, but I can put it in perspective. Is it really any madder than the ways all these companies became powerful in the first place? Is it any madder than the cooperation that made the Internet possible in the first place?

The Fate of Books

BOOKS INSPIRE MANIACAL SCHEMING

If there's one blessed sweet feature of Silicon Valley culture, it's that we don't have many deadly dull mandatory social affairs where you have to sit in an assigned seat at a table and make your choice of beef, fish, or veggies while you pretend to listen to boring toasts and bad jokes until you get to leave. But we do have a few.

I was once seated at a linen-coated affair between Jeff Bezos of Amazon and Eric Schmidt, then the CEO of Google. This was before the Kindle. Two Silicon Alphas eyed each other and suddenly locked into a manic exchange. They started trading figures and anecdotes about the book business. It all happened so fast, a blur.

Someone at the podium was talking about installing a solar-powered computer in Africa. The image came into my mind of an overcaffeinated hyena trying to trump its own reflection. I sat there, mostly staring straight ahead—a patch of background celluloid in a 1920s cartoon, peeking out between frenetic characters mirroring each other, running at double speed.

Eric and Jeff are acquaintances, so I knew they were not actually moving any faster than normal, but on this occasion what counted as normal speed contrasted severely with a lugubrious process I was going through, something called "trying to finish a book." The process of book writing inducts authors into a different kind of time.

AN AUTHOR'S EXPERIENCE OF A BOOK

I had been trying to finish a first book for not just years but decades. The book contract hung over me, a sword of Damocles suspended from a radio-controlled model helicopter, tracking my every move.

You can try to make a joke of endless stress. There was an informal contest among hypertardy deliverers to see who could keep a book contract overdue the longest before having to pay the advance back. Ornette Coleman played for a couple of decades, as did John Perry Barlow.

It wasn't that I was lazy. During the years that I didn't deliver a book I helped found several startups that went on to become parts of big companies. I became a father, led a multiuniversity research program, released a major-label record, had symphonies commissioned and performed, and played music around the world. And I wrote plenty of articles, including a monthly magazine column. But writing a book was different.

A book is not just a read, it is also a summit, a codification of a point of view. My problem with finishing was that, even if I wasn't ready to admit it consciously, my thoughts had not yet matured. It really took all those years for me to be ready to publish *You Are Not a Gadget*. Without the years of trying, I might never have gotten there. When I was finally ready, it came together fairly quickly. To publish before I was ready would have been to lessen the meaning not only of my book but of all books. Meanwhile, these two Silicon titans were in the throes of realizing that the fact that they happened to run some central computers on the Internet put them in a position of potentially taking over the whole book world in just a few years.

IT'S NOT ABOUT PAPER VERSUS EBOOKS

It's not that a book might be read on an electronic tablet instead of paper that bothers me, but the backstage economics and politics—and the sense of time—that that might bring about. What ebooks *might* lose is the pattern of what a book is in the stream of human life and thought. Whether we will destroy culture in order to save/digitize it is still unknown.*

It amazes me that traditional book publishers don't understand the

---

* For those too young to catch the reference, this recalls a comment made by an American military official in a famous documentary about the Vietnam War called *Hearts and Minds* suggesting that a village had to be destroyed in order to be saved.

emotional value of paper, however. They are still trying to sell a one-price-fits-all consumer product in a gilded age, and thus are missing out on the obvious business opportunity under their noses. As long as the Sirenic era lasts, there will be a hollowed-out market with a weakened middle class. To survive, the book business has to define a product for the upper horn, for the rich.

In the music business, that upper tier takes the form of insanely expensive audiophile equipment and super-high-quality limited editions on vinyl. In the book business, there should be hyperlimited editions of books like this one, hand copied by monks onto handmade paper, using organic fair-trade inks, and sold only in VIP rooms at parties where almost no one can get in. Listen up, publisher, you are with these very words publishing the advice that could win you a fortune, but you are choosing to ignore a way to get through these tough times.

THE BOOK AS SILICON VALLEY WOULD HAVE IT

What will books be like once Silicon Valley has had its way with them? The story isn't over, and if I thought any particular outcome was really inevitable, I wouldn't bother trying to influence it. What I can do is capture an impression of what seems to be coming if nothing changes. We've learned a little from watching what has happened with music, video, news, and photography.

Here is a likely, though not inevitable, outcome:

- There will be little barrier to entry for authors, except for writing the damned book. You'd just write a book and upload it. That's already true, but it will become a little truer still. You'll be able to enlist ghost coauthors even more easily than now, and they might be crowdsourced or just plain Artificial Intelligence software. A service will collect splendid blurbs automatically: "The book we have all been waiting for." Self-publishing can yet become a more friction-free experience than it is today. A self-declared author will perhaps pay a fee or just agree to live under a deeper spyglass and be advertised at more intensely.

- The number of published authors will quickly become similar to the number of readers who will pay for a book. This is what happened with music.

- Some good books from otherwise obscure authors will come into being. These will usually come to light as part of the rapid-growth phase, or "free rise" of a new channel or device for delivering the book experience. For instance, if a company introduces a new reading device, there will be heightened visibility for a while for authors who are uniquely available early on on that device. In this way, an interesting author with just the right timing will occasionally get a big boost from a tech transition.

- The total money flowing to authors in the system will decline to a fraction of what it was before digital networks, and that will be paid by a combination of advertising and fees from people who are locked into proprietary devices or delivery channels.

- Most authors will make most of their book-related money in real time, from traveling, live appearances, or consulting instead of from book sales. This will change the demographics of authorship. Authors will tend to be either young and childless, independently wealthy, beneficiaries of an institutional post, or more fundamentally like performers. They will tend not to be independent scholars with families.

- A lot of people will pretend to be commercially successful authors, and will put money into enhancing the illusion. Most of these will rely on family support or inheritance. Gradually an intellectual plutocracy will emerge.

- Readers will be second-class economic citizens. (A recap of why: When you buy a paper book, you own something you can resell. The value of that object might go up or down. When a reader "purchases" an ebook, it is only a contract of access. The reader has no capital, nothing to resell, nothing that might accrue value. This is a fundamental rejection of the very idea of a market economy.* When only certain privileged players can own capital, while everyone else can only buy services, the market will eventually consume itself and evolve into a nonmarket.)

- Books will be merged with apps, video games, virtual worlds, or whatever other digital format becomes prominent. These will make some serious money for authors at first, while they are novel, before the biggest servers commoditize them.

- The distribution of book sales will be even more lopsided than in traditional markets. There will be a small number of super-winners and a huge number of vanity authors, with little in between.

- Many readers will read what is put in front of their eyes by crowdsourcing algorithms, and often will not be aware of the identity of the author or the boundary between one book and another.

- Many books will be available only via a particular device, such as a particular company's tablet.

- Algorithmically generated books and books written in sweat-shops will be plentiful, because they can be made so cheaply in quantity that even tiny streams of revenue can add up to a business proposition.

- There will be much more information available in some semblance of book form than ever before, but overall a lower quality standard.

---

* This inequity disturbs me a great deal. Being a technologist, I have tried to think of solutions. Here is one idea: Suppose you could etch or in some other manner place a permanent author's signature on the back of a reading slate or tablet. Then a reader could accumulate interesting combinations of author's signatures, and the combinations would be intrinsically rare. For instance, one could collect the signatures of all the cyberpunk science fiction authors on one slate.

- A book won't necessarily be the same for each person who reads it or if the same person reads it twice. On the one hand this will mean better updates for some kinds of information and fewer encounters with typos, but on the other will deemphasize the rhythm and poetics of prose, minimize the stakes of declaring a manuscript complete, and expand the "filter bubble" effect.

- The means to find reading material will be where business battles are fought. The fights often will not be pretty. The interface between readers and books will be contested and often corrupted by spam and deception.

- Writing a book won't mean as much. Some will think of this as a democratic, antielitist benefit, and others will think of it as a lowering of standards.

- Readers will spend a lot of time hassling with forgotten passwords, expired credit cards, and being locked into the wrong device or mobile-service contract for years at a time. They'll lose their own libraries, notes, and even their own writing when they switch vendors. Net neutrality will exist in celebrated theory but not in practice.

- Technically adept readers will make fun of other readers who have trouble dealing with the new system. The more hackerlike you are, the more you will feel advantaged.

- Overall, people will pay less to read, which will be lauded as being good for consumers, while people will earn still less from writing. If this pattern held only for music, writing, and other media, it would be just one feature in the transition to an ever-more digital world in which software swallows everything.* However, if it is a precedent to be repeated in transportation, manufacturing, medicine, education, and other major sectors,

* The portrayal of software as an insatiable gourmand is common in Silicon Valley. "Software Will Eat Everything" is the phrasing from a well-known essay by Web pioneer and tycoon Marc Andreessen.

the overall economy will shrink, making capitalism a little less viable in the long term. Well, that's a restatement of a core idea of this book, but at any rate this much can be said:

- By the time books have mostly gone digital, the owners of the top Internet servers that route readers, probably run by Silicon Valley companies, will be more powerful and richer than they were before.

Some of these prospects appeal to me. My favorite is the potential for experiments merging books with apps, games, music, movies, virtual worlds, and all the other forms that can be sent over the 'net. This ought to yield some interesting fruit, though remember culture still takes its time, however fast a technology transition occurs. With time, probably enough time for another generation to come of age, there ought to be some good fun to be had.

The desirability of being more directly connected to readers will vary with each author. I would love it if all I did were write. Since I also make technology and music and parent, I find it's absolutely impossible to find the moments to authentically respond to all the readers who contact me. This is a drag, since there are such lovely notes that come in, but what can one do? I don't want to use lazy social-media interactions to pretend to be more responsive than I really can be, even though that's the fashion. I do know writers, particularly of genre fiction, business books, and self-help books, who adore being tightly connected to their readers and spend hours a day interacting with them.

WHAT IS IT ABOUT A BOOK THAT IS WORTH SAVING?

What's wrong with this bulleted list overall? There are both good and bad things in it, but there's an overall pattern that feels off kilter, a throwing-the-baby-out-with-the-bathwater feeling.

A book isn't an artifact, but a synthesis of fully realized individual personhood with human continuity. The economic model of our networks has to be optimized to preserve that synthesis, or it will not serve mankind.

The Fate of Books

This email is completely typical of what shows up every morning:

I'm a postdoc at [. . .] working on a paper about collaborative creativity and we wanted to see if you can point us to some relevant literature. To be more specific, we are finding empirical evidence [. . .] that collaborative works are more positively received than single-authored works. We are studying this in the context of [. . .] an online community where kids can create their animations, video games, and interactive art.

We read your article on Edge.org on Digital Maoism and we were wondering if you know of anyone else who might be arguing that individual works are of higher quality than collective works.

This came from one of the top computer science labs in the world. Unfortunately, I can become impatient when I attempt to answer questions like this.

No one in the tech world practices what we preach about these ideas. We treat the top entrepreneurs as irreplaceable heroes. I've never, ever seen a serious proposal that a collective or artificial cloud software experiment could replicate the value of a Steve Jobs.

So it's hard to even know where to start to answer email like this. Look at the world, look at history. Rock stars, novels, great physicists. . . . Even the entries in Wikipedia about human achievements are mostly about individuals rather than collectives. How could an old essay of mine from 2006 be the sole reference to the preponderant pattern in the whole of human history?

First, I might point out, the assumption is put forward with no justification that the human role is to produce an output in the same sense that an algorithm or a collective could.* That is wrong. Then, a marketplace method, typically formulated as winner-takes-all, is put forward as the only means of valuing outputs from people and machines.

I do my best to explain this nicely, but end up getting snarky: "Would you want to send a collectively programmed robot to have sex on your

---

*To restate a point made earlier, artificial intelligence programs over networks typically repackage huge amounts of data taken from people, therefore it is ever harder to distinguish a collective output from an "artificially intelligent" algorithmic one.

behalf because it was better at it than you, or would you want to have the sex yourself and get better by doing?"

Human life is its own purpose. What other way of thinking can make sense? But no, that argument fails. This is a response I've heard, paraphrased: "I'd prefer to have the best available robot to please me sexually. Other people should enjoy that benefit too. If I insist on still having real sex once robot partners begin to become available, then I'd be selfishly delaying the improvement of robots by delaying the appearance of data from early robotic sex experiences."

You can try logic: "You can have robotic sex without a robot, but you can't have challenge, weirdness, tenderness, the building of trust, intimacy, or love without a person." No luck, generally.

And then about the criteria for success: "If market pricing is the only legitimate test of quality, why are we still bothering with proving theorems? Why don't we just have a vote on whether a theorem is true? To make it better we'll have everyone vote on it, especially the hundreds of millions of people who don't understand the math. Would that satisfy you?"

If I argue for a half day with people who are imbedded in the new thinking that is amplified by the latest versions of network-based wealth and power, then I can usually get them to think differently for another half day. By the following day, however, the specter of perfect robot-sex partners returns to glory.

Thinking about people in the terms of components on a network is— in intellectual and spiritual terms—a slow suicide for the researchers and slow homicide against everyone else. If the world is to be reconceived and engineered as a place where people are not particularly distinguished from other components, then people will fade.

It's hard to escape the ideas imbedded in the system in which you survive and seek success. If thinking about people as components of network architecture is what creates the greatest economic success, then that thinking is reinforced every moment that you strive to succeed.

We haven't found any more fundamental way to think about a system than as an information system. My argument is *not* against thinking about us in the terms of information. I live that life. Instead, I am arguing that there is more than one way to build an information economy, and we've chosen the self-destructive option.

What Is to Be Remembered?

All This, Just for the Whiff of Possibility

Human beings have been treated with suspicion in these pages. Despite my unapologetic optimism about the big picture, I have at times anticipated that our kind will be gullible and vain, or will attempt to cheat and dominate. I have assumed that we will often choose the lazy answer and suffer indignity happily so long as it is glazed with coolness. And yet at the start, I professed love for people, and said the whole project was about how special people are, and how deserving.

There is no contradiction. To love people is not to be infatuated with them. It's hard to perceive us realistically; it is a leap of faith. What will be left after we acknowledge all our failings?

There are many questions left unanswered, as they should be. My space elevator pitch did not specify the proper limits of government in an advanced information economy. Nor did it consider whether there might be national variations in information economies, or if there must be global coherence.

These and many other huge questions cannot be addressed yet. The purpose for now can only be to demonstrate that there is unexplored legitimate possibility. I hope the pitch persuaded you that we are not bound by the conventions of the current mania for deterministic information technology evolution.

My sketch of a possible future will hopefully prod hotshot young computer scientists and economists to prove they can do better, and to present improved designs.

Please do that, but also please stop once per hour and check yourself: Are you still keeping people in the center? Is it still all about the people? Are you really avoiding the lazy trapdoor of falling back into thinking of people as components and a central server as being the only point of view for defining efficiency or testing efficacy?

The Economics of the Future Is User Interface Design

As technology gets better, economics will have to become less abstract. Economics used to be about the patterns of results that emerged from rules that influenced human social behavior. It focused on the ways that policy engendered outcomes.

But with every passing year economics must become more and more about the design of the machines that mediate human social behavior. A networked information system guides people in a more direct, detailed, and literal way than does policy. Another way to put it is that economics must turn into a large-scale, systemic version of user interface design.*

Some user interfaces are meant to be deliberately challenging, as is the case for games, while others are meant to make complexity easier. The latter variety powers the bigger industries by far, encompassing consumer devices, professional tools, and business productivity. I have engaged for many years in both idioms. They're both hard!

Making a game enticing and addictive is a balancing act. You need to find just the right quivering back and forth between challenge and reward.† The point is not to make the game as hard to use as possible, but to dangle usability just out of reach.

Games are fun and can be wonderful learning tools, but help-

---

*Here I am, a computer scientist, seeing the world my way. Economists are invited to respond that computer science ought to start looking more like economics, and they'll receive a friendly reception from at least this computer scientist.

†If you're curious, you can probably find an old psychedelic game of mine, called Moondust, which I wrote when I was about twenty. It runs on Commodore 64 emulators. It was a commercial success and its proceeds funded the first virtual reality systems in a garage in Palo Alto.

ing people achieve things in the real world on more complex terms than before is the endgame of computer science. There's no greater pleasure for a computer scientist than seeing someone become able to do something that had once been impossible, simply because good data with a good user interface clarified the situation. I have seen surgeons understand how to destroy a tumor because of a better computer simulation and display. I have seen patients with learning disabilities become productive. The everyday sight of people able to use their personal devices is as much a pleasure. This is what we live for.

Making complexity easier is the great craft of our era.

The Tease of the Tease

Thus far, the information economy has resembled gaming more than the practical side of user interface design. That's not to say that online economic activity is being made more difficult than it needs to be, but that it engages the human brain in a teasing way.

The human mind is particularly susceptible to engagement by rapid-fire feedback that taunts on the edge of granting treats. Semi-random feedback is a more intense dominator of attention than consistent feedback.

Before the arrival of digital computation, pastimes that embodied this pattern of seduction were the obsessions of the global human experience. Sports and gambling provide fine examples.

Computation can offer precisely this kind of feedback all too easily. Watch a child playing games on a tablet and then watch someone keeping up with social media, or trading stocks online. We become obsessively engaged in interactions with approximately, but not fully predictable, results.

The intrinsic challenge of computation—and of economics in the information age—is finding a way to not be overly drawn into dazzlingly designed forms of cognitive waste. The naïve experience of simulation is the opposite of delayed gratification. Competence depends on delayed gratification.

This book has proposed an approach to an information economy based more on the craft of usability than on the thrill of gaming, though it doesn't reject that thrill.

Know Your Poison

To paraphrase what Einstein might or might not have said, user interface should be made as easy as possible, but not easier. Dealing with our personal contribution of data to the cloud will sometimes be difficult or annoying in any advanced information economy, but it is the price we will have to pay. We will have to agree to endure challenges if we are to take enough responsibility for ourselves to be free when technology gets really good. There is always a price for every benefit.

When I try to imagine the experience of living in a future humanistic network economy, I imagine frustrations. There will constantly be a little ticker running, and you'll be tempted to maximize the value recorded. For many people, that might become an obsessive game that gets in the way of a more authentic, less prescribed experience of life. It will narrow perspectives and undervalue wisdom. There will be nothing fundamentally new, in that money has always presented exactly that distraction, and yet the temptation could become more comprehensive, thicker in the air.

Information always underrepresents reality. Some of the contributions you make will be unrecognized in economic terms, no matter how sophisticated the technology of economics becomes. This will hurt. And yet by making opportunity more incremental, open, and diverse than it was in the Sirenic era, most people ought to find some way to build up material dignity in the course of their lives.

The spiritual challenge will remain of not losing touch with that core of experience, that little something that doesn't fit into the aspects of reality that can be digitized.

I don't for a moment claim to have proposed a perfect solution. Someone like me, a humanist softie, will complain about the oppressive feeling of having to feed information systems in order to get by.

The only response, which I hope will be remembered should this future come about, is that the complaint is legitimate, and yet the alternative was worse. The alternative would have been feeding data into Siren Servers, which lock people in by goading them into free-will-leeching feedback loops so that they become better represented by algorithms.

We are already experiencing designs related to the kind of ticker I dread, except the present versions are much worse. Your Klout* score, for instance, is worse than the micropayments you'd accumulate in a humanistic economy because it's real-time instead of cumulative. You must constantly suck at the teat of social media or your score plummets. Klout dangles a classical seductive feedback loop, almost making sense, but not quite.

In a humanistic information economy, you'd spend your money in ways you choose; under today's system, you are influenced by phantasms like Klout scores in ways you'll never know.[1] Perversely, such a sense of mystery can make a bad design more alluring, not less.

Is There a Test for Whether an Information Economy Is Humanistic?

One good test of whether an economy is humanistic or not is the plausibility of earning the ability to drop out of it for a while without incident or insult.

Wealth and dignity are different from a Klout score. They are states of being, not instant signals. It is the latitude granted by the hysteresis—the staying power—of wealth that translates into practical freedom.

One should be able to earn the latitude to test oneself, and try out different life rules, especially in youth. Can you drop out of social media for six months, just to feel the world differently, and

---

*Klout is a universal, uninvited ranking service that rates how influential people are, mostly by analyzing social media services like Twitter. Amazingly, Klout scores have influenced hiring. Since I don't use social media, I presumably have a Klout score of zero, which ought to be the superlative status symbol of our times.

test yourself, in a new way? Can you disengage from a Siren Server for a while and handle the punishing network effects? If you feel you can't, you haven't really engaged fully with the possibilities of who you might be, and what you might make of your life in the world.

People still ask me every day if they should quit Facebook. A year ago it was just a personal choice, but now it has become a choice that comes with a price. The option of not using the services of Siren Servers becomes a trial, like living "off the grid."

It's crucial to experience resisting social pressure at least once in your life. When everyone around you insists that you'll be outcast and left behind unless you conform, you have to experience what it's like to ignore them and chart your own course in order to discover yourself as a person.

It can be doubly tricky because the way people talk about conformity is often as though it were a form of resistance to conformity. It is exactly when others insist that it's a sign of being free, fresh, and radical to do what everybody's doing that you might want to take notice and think for yourself. Don't be surprised if this is really hard to do.

My suggestion is, experiment with yourself. Resign from all the free online services you use for six months to see what happens. You don't need to renounce them forever, make value judgments, or be dramatic. Just be experimental. You will probably learn more about yourself, your friends, the world, and the Internet than you would have if you never performed the experiment.

There will be costs, since the way we do things today is vaguely punitive, but the benefits will almost certainly be worth it.

Back to the Beach

I miss the future. We have such low expectations of it these days. When I was a kid, my generation reasonably expected moon colonies and flying cars by now. Instead, we have entered the big data era; progress has become complicated and slow. Genomics is amazing, but the benefits to medicine don't burst forth like a lightning bolt. Instead they grow like a slow crop. The age of silver bullets seems to have retired around the time networking got good and data became big.

And yet, the future hasn't vanished completely. My daughter, who turned six as I finished this book, asks me: "Will I learn to drive, or will cars drive themselves?" In ten years, I imagine, self-driving cars will be familiar, but probably not yet ubiquitous. But it's at least possible that learning to drive will start to feel anachronistic to my daughter and her friends, instead of a beckoning rite of passage. Driving for her might be like writing in longhand.

Will she ever wear the same dress twice as an adult? Will she recycle clothes into new objects, or wash them, as we do today? At some point in her life, I suspect laundry will become obsolete.

These are tame speculations. Will she have to contend with the politics of extreme and selective artificial longevity? Will she have to decide whether to let her children play with brain scanners? Will there be crazed mobs that believe the Singularity has occurred?

Say almost anything bold about the future and you will almost certainly sound ridiculous to someone, probably including most people in the future. That's fine. The future should be our theater. It should be fun and wild, and force us to see everything in our present world anew.

My hope for the future is that it will be more radically wonderful, and unendingly so, than we can now imagine, but also that it will unfold in a lucid enough way that people can learn lessons and be willful. Our story should unfold unbroken by perceived singularities or other breaches of continuity. Whatever it is people will become as technology gets very good, they will still be people if these simple qualities hold.

First Appearances
of Key Terms

Acknowledgments

I gratefully acknowledge *Playboy, The New Statesman, Edge, Communications of the ACM, The New York Times,* and *The Atlantic* for allowing me the space to develop some material that appears in this book, often in significantly different form.

Thanks to Microsoft Research for putting up with a controversial researcher. To say the least, nothing I write was vetted by anyone at Microsoft prior to publication, and this book in no way represents anything related to company thinking or positions. This book is all me, for better or worse.

Thanks to attendees at my talks in 2011 and 2012 for listening to my nascent presentations of these ideas, in which I learned how to express them. Thanks to Lena and Lilibell for putting up with me as I disappear into projects like this book.

Thanks to my early readers: Brian Arthur, Steven Barclay, Roger Brent, John Brockman, Eric Clemons, George Dyson, Doyne Farmer, Gary Flake, Ed Frenkel, Dina Graser, Daniel Kahneman, Lena Lanier, Dennis Overbye, David Rothenberg, Lee Smolin, Jeffrey Soros, Neal Stephenson, Eric Weinstein, and Tim Wu.

Thanks to the musical instrument makers and dealers of Berkeley, Seattle, New York City, and London for providing delightful opportunities for procrastination.

Notes

First Interlude: Ancient Anticipation of the Singularity

1. Aristotle, *Politics,* approx. 350 BC, translated by Benjamin Jowett.

Chapter 3. Money As Seen Through One Computer Scientist's Eyes

1. Matthew Yglesias, "Nobody Knows Where Economic Growth Comes From," *Slate,* posted August 6, 2012.
2. http://www.forbes.com/sites/afontevecchia/2010/11/19/how-many-olympic -sized-swimming-pools-can-we-fill-with-billionaire-gold/.

Chapter 4. The Ad Hoc Construction of Mass Dignity

1. http://www.nytimes.com/2011/07/28/technology/personaltech/spotify -unshackles-online-music-david-pogue.html.

Chapter 6. The Specter of the Perfect Investment

1. http://www.nytimes.com/2012/04/30/business/media/byliner-takes-buzz -bissingers-e-book-off-amazon.html.
2. http://www.nytimes.com/2010/08/08/magazine/08FOB-medium-t.html.
3. http://www.informationweek.com/news/software/bi/240002737.
4. http://flightfox.com/about.
5. http://www.nytimes.com/2012/09/30/technology/flightfox-lets-the-crowd -find-the-best-airfares.html.
6. http://www.firstround.com/our_focus/.

Notes

Chapter 7. Some Pioneering Siren Servers

1. See Charles Fishman, *The Wal-Mart Effect: How the World's Most Powerful Company Really Works—and How It's Transforming the American Economy* (New York: Penguin Press, 2006), or Anthony Bianco, *Wal-Mart: The Bully of Bentonville: How the High Cost of Everyday Low Prices Is Hurting America* (New York: Currency Doubleday, 2007).

Second Interlude: (A Parody): If Life Gives You EULAs, Make Lemonade

1. http://nation.foxnews.com/fox-friends/2012/07/24/lemonade-stand-girls-obama-we-built-our-business.
2. http://en.wikipedia.org/wiki/High_Performance_Computing_Act_of_1991.
3. http://en.wikipedia.org/wiki/End-user_license_agreement.

Chapter 9. From Above: Misusing Big Data to Become Ridiculous

1. http://online.wsj.com/public/page/what-they-know-digital-privacy.html.
2. https://www.eff.org/issues/privacy/.
3. http://purplebox.ghostery.com/?p=1016022352.
4. http://purplebox.ghostery.com/?p=948639073.
5. http://www.cnn.com/2012/02/29/tech/web/protect-privacy-google/index.html.
6. http://bits.blogs.nytimes.com/2009/06/02/google-is-top-tracker-of-surfers-in-study/.
7. www.nytimes.com/2012/02/05/opinion/sunday/facebook-is-using-you.html.
8. www.nytimes.com/2012/06/17/technology/acxiom-the-quiet-giant-of-consumer-database-marketing.html.
9. www.nytimes.com/2012/08/19/business/electronic-scores-rank-consumers-by-potential-value.html.
10. http://www.nytimes.com/2012/05/03/technology/personaltech/how-to-muddy-your-tracks-on-the-internet.html.
11. http://www.makeuseof.com/tag/adblock-noscript-ghostery-trifecta-evil-opinion/.
12. http://www.google.org/flutrends/.
13. http://www.nobelprize.org/nobel_prizes/economics/laureates/2001/akerlof-article.html.
14. http://www.carfax.com/entry.cfx.

Notes

Third Interlude: Modernity Conceives the Future

1. 2012, directed by Mathieu Roy and Harold Crooks.
2. Ronald Wright, *A Short History of Progress* (New York: Carroll & Graf, 2005).
3. http://blogs.smithsonianmag.com/paleofuture/2011/12/boxing-robots-of-the-1930s.
4. http://www.slate.com/articles/technology/robot_invasion/2011/09/will_robots_steal_your_job.html.

Chapter 12. Story Lost

1. Aleksandar Hemon, "Beyond the Matrix," *New Yorker,* September 10, 2012.

Chapter 13. Coercion on Autopilot: Specialized Network Effects

1. Daniel Kahneman has written foundational works on this topic. His book *Thinking, Fast and Slow* (New York: Farrar, Straus & Giroux, 2011) is a primary resource. Another relevant book is Dan Ariely's *Predictably Irrational: The Hidden Forces That Shape Our Decisions* (New York: HarperCollins, 2008).
2. http://bits.blogs.nytimes.com/2010/02/24/yelp-is-sued-after-dispute-over-a-review/ http://www.naturalnews.com/034247_Yelpcom_lawsuit.html; http://www.marketingpilgrim.com/2010/03/yelp-sued-for-extortionagain.html; http://pixsym.com/blog/reputation-management/yelp-extortion-the-lawsuits-dismissed-are-they-back-at-it-in-2012.
3. http://www.pcworld.com/article/255471/want_your_facebook_status_seen_pay_up.html.
4. http://motherboard.vice.com/2011/4/12/on-badoo-the-social-network-for-sex-users-pay-to-get-noticed-and-to-get-other-things-too.

Chapter 14. Obscuring the Human Element

1. http://www.salon.com/2006/07/24/turks_3/.
2. http://news.cnet.com/8301-10784_3-9782813-7.html.
3. http://waxy.org/2008/11/the_faces_of_mechanical_turk/.
4. http://www.readwriteweb.com/archives/study_40_of_new_mechanical_turkers_work_requests_a.php.

Notes

Chapter 15. Story Found

1. http://www.slate.com/articles/technology/technology/2012/09/square_jack_dorsey_s_payments_firm_is_silicon_valley_s_next_great_company_.html.
2. http://techcrunch.com/tag/deadpool/.
3. http://bits.blogs.nytimes.com/2009/09/29/google-wave-becomes-a-bit-more-public/.
4. http://techcrunch.com/2012/02/01/deadpool-alert-google-wave-goes-read-only/.

Fifth Interlude: The Wise Old Man in the Clouds

1. http://www.facebook.com/Jesuits/posts/143094992485238.

Chapter 16. Complaint Is Not Enough

1. http://www.usnews.com/opinion/mzuckerman/articles/2012/04/06/mort-zuckerman-no-easy-solutions-for-big-money-in-politics.
2. http://sloanreview.mit.edu/improvisations/2012/06/20/big-data-and-the-u-s-presidential-campaign/

Sixth Interlude: The Pocket Protector in the Saffron Robe

1. "The Trickster Guru," in *The Essential Alan Watts* (Berkeley, CA: Celestial Arts, 1977).
2. http://cafegratitude.com/menu.
3. http://www.eastbayexpress.com/ebx/i-am-annoyed-and-disappointed/Content?oid=1370662.

Chapter 18. First Thought, Best Thought

1. Kevin Kelly in his Technium blog, January 31, 2008.

Chapter 20. We Need to Do Better than Ad Hoc Levees

1. http://www.facebook.com/notes/facebook-data-team/rethinking-information-diversity-in-networks/10150503499618859.

Chapter 22. Who Will Do What?

1. http://www.slate.com/articles/technology/technology/2012/05/facebook_ipo_has_social_networking_supplanted_real_innovation_in_silicon_valley_.html.

Notes

Chapter 26. Financial Identity

1. See Tim Wu's book *The Master Switch* (New York: Knopf, 2010).

Chapter 28. The Interface to Reality

1. http://www.firstround.com/our_focus/.
2. http://www.naturalnews.com/036476_smart_meters_hacking_privacy.html.

Chapter 29. Creepy

1. See http://www.fellowgeek.com/a-US-security-firm-hacked-by-Anonymous -ix1113.html and http://www.esecurityplanet.com/hackers/panda-security -hacked-lulzsec-is-your-website-safe.html.
2. http://cs-www.cs.yale.edu/homes/freeman/lifestreams.html.
3. See http://totalrecallbook.com/.

Seventh Interlude: Limits Are for Mortals

1. David Brooks, "The Creative Monopoly," *New York Times*, April 23, 2012.
2. http://blakemasters.tumblr.com/post/21169325300/peter-thiels-cs183 -startup-class-4-notes-essay.
3. http://www.dailydot.com/society/facebook-mourning-jenna-ness-death/.
4. http://www.slate.com/articles/health_and_science/human_nature/2009/01/ night_of_the_living_dad.html.
5. http://www.huffingtonpost.com/2012/08/21/tupac-hologram-elvis-presley -marilyn-monroe_n_1818715.html.
6. A Russian political party has been founded to further this goal. See http:// www.gizmag.com/avatar-project-2045/23454/.

Chapter 31. The Transition

1. http://www.npr.org/2012/02/22/147261659/gauging-the-reliability-of-facts -on-wikipedia.

Conclusion. What Is It to Be Remembered?

1. http://www.wired.com/business/2012/04/ff_klout/.

Index

Page numbers in *italics* refer to illustrations.

Index

Index

Index

Index

Index

Index